COLUMBIA UNIVERSITY STUDIES IN ENGLISH
AND COMPARATIVE LITERATURE

THE NEGRO AUTHOR

THE NEGRO AUTHOR

His Development in America to 1900

BY

VERNON LOGGINS

KENNIKAT PRESS, INC./PORT WASHINGTON, N. Y.

TO
MY FATHER
AND
MY MOTHER

PREFACE

If this book were an exhaustive study of the subject to which it is devoted, it would be many times its length. I have attempted to do no more than make of it a general survey of a field of American literature which our literary historians almost without exception have neglected.

Although productive of little that is truly artistic, that field extends far and wide. It embraces in a way the entire struggle for the extinction of slavery, the Civil War, the reconstruction of the South, and the late nineteenth-century problem of racial adjustment. Viewed in the light of its historical associations it is indeed rich. And in the light of the remarkable progress which the Negro has made in letters during the past forty years it is interesting and important.

It is no doubt destined to receive far more study than I have been able to give to it. Negro scholars naturally will come more and more to regard the investigation of it as their own peculiar duty. The greatest service which this book can render is to suggest to them new avenues of approach.

I may appear to have been rather arbitrary in treating the year 1900 as marking the end of the survey. As a matter of fact, I have discussed in detail no works published after that year except certain books by Booker T. Washington, Paul Laurence Dunbar, and Charles W. Chesnutt, the career of each of whom belongs mainly to the nineties and deserves to be regarded as a unit.

The reader might wonder why I have restricted myself to the Negro's consciously produced literature. When I decided four years ago to write this book, my plan was to devote at least one full chapter to the folk song and folk tale. Much of what I intended to say in that chapter was said in Professor Newman I. White's *American Negro Folk-Songs* (1928). Unwilling, however, to publish a book on Negro literature without some discussion of its strongest element, I have appended in the form of a conclusion a brief estimate of the literary significance of that element.

I am happy to express my gratitude to the many who have been of assistance to me in this work. A number of them must be specially named. Professor Dorothy Scarborough convinced me that such a study was needed and that I should attempt it. Mr. Arthur A. Schomburg, who in creating the Schomburg Collection made this and, I hope, many more treatises on Negro literature and history possible, gave hours of his time in helping me clear up obscure matters of all sorts, especially those pertaining to bibliography. Mr. Arthur B. Spingarn allowed me the free use of his excellent library of works relating to the Negro and offered many suggestions which I found most helpful. The officers of the libraries named in the bibliographies extended privileges and rendered services which greatly facilitated the labors of research: to Miss Ernestine Rose and Mrs. Catherine A. Latimer, custodians of the Schomburg Collection, I am especially thankful. Professor Benjamin Brawley, Mr. Bruce Cotten, Professor Charles S. Johnson, Mr. James Weldon Johnson, Miss Mary White Ovington, and Professor Monroe N. Work gave information which was of material assistance in locating and identifying works by Negroes. Professor Ralph L. Rusk, in whose seminar I learned what I know about the methods of research, guided me in this study from the time of its inception; he has helped me in more ways than I can name: his notations on the original manuscript were made liberal use of in the final revision. Professor Robert H. Fife, Professor Dixon Ryan Fox, and

Professor Frederic W. J. Hauser read the manuscript and offered valuable constructive criticism. Miss Bella Gross, of the Columbia University Library, and Mrs. Dorothy Porter, of the Howard University Library, assisted in checking the accuracy of the bibliographies. Mrs. M. M. Hoover, Miss Muriel E. Kern, and Miss Elizabeth J. Sherwood aided in the task of editorial revision and proof reading. Professor Ashley H. Thorndike, always an inspiration to graduate students working in English at Columbia University, generously gave advice out of his sure wisdom from the time he approved the subject as suitable for a doctor's dissertation until he saw the book through the press.

VERNON LOGGINS

COLUMBIA UNIVERSITY
April 16, 1931

CONTENTS

CONTENTS

CHAPTER I

THE BEGINNINGS OF NEGRO AUTHORSHIP, 1760–1790

I know moon-rise, I know star-rise,
     I lay dis body down.
I walk in de moonlight, I walk in de starlight,
     To lay dis body down.
I walk in de graveyard, I walk throo de graveyard,
     To lay dis body down.
I lie in de grave an' stretch out my arms,
     I lay dis body down.
I go to de jedgement in de evenin' of de day,
     When I lay dis body down,
An' my soul an' your soul will meet in de day
     When I lay dis body down.

—From T. W. Higginson's "Negro Spirituals,"
     Atlantic Monthly, June, 1867

I

The Negro, as all the world admits, was received into America for one reason only, and that was for labor. Snatched from Africa and thrust into the most afflicting of manual work, into the degradation of a slavery that was often accompanied by the harshest cruelty and that was at its best attended by a crushing monotony, he was forced to forget his native traditions, or to remember them only in a subconscious way. But there was something within him which determined that he should build all over again. There was a will to survive, to flourish, to find for himself a home in the environment into which he had been dragged. There was a spirit of defiance that made him laugh in the face of oppression, and that turned him to singing songs of confidence and hopefulness.[1] There was a racial optimism which decided that he should play a more important rôle in his American home than that of manual laborer. In spite of the gravest obstructions he insisted upon climbing toward self-assertion. And his evolution was such that by the end of the eighteenth century he had proved not only that he could assume an average civilization, but that he could find his way with a surprising degree of success in the higher refinements. Military tactics, medicine, mathematics, theology, poetry, letter-writing, memoir-making, and oratory were not too elusive for his mentality.

From the year of his advent into American life, 1619, only twelve years after the Anglo-Saxon had established himself in the New World, the Negro became more and more welcome, in the South as a worker on the plantations and in the North as a general servant.[2] It has been estimated that by 1715 there were in all the British colonies in America 58,850 Negroes.[3] According to the first national census, taken in 1790, the number had grown to 757,208, of which 697,897 were slaves. It is safe to assume that during the period when the colonies were struggling for their independence, at least every sixth person making up their population was to be classed as a Negro.[4]

From the beginning of his history in America, the Negro was the source of problems. First, his exact status had to be determined. The earliest blacks brought in were disposed of under the system of indentured servitude, but by the time the Negro was present in considerable numbers perpetual slavery had been established by custom or legalized by statute in each of the colonies.[5] Then, the matter of the salvation of the Negro's soul arose. Since he was a slave, could he be a Christian? This question, although it gave rise to much speculation, was at first answered mainly according to the whim of the individual slave-owner.[6] But toward the end of the seventeenth century, partly by decrees of the Church of England, partly by laws enacted in the colonies, it was universally recognized as answered in the affirmative.[7]

Cotton Mather's brief compilation, "Rules for the Societies of Negroes," written in 1693, typifies the general attitude of the religious leaders interested in the Christianization of the Negro, not only among the Puritans, but also among the adherents of the Church of England. Mather wrote in introducing a copy of the "Rules" into his diary:

> Besides the other praying and pious Meetings, which I have been continually serving, in our neighborhood; a little after this Time, a company of poor *Negroes*, of their own Accord, addressed mee, for my Countenance, to a Design which they had, of erecting such a *Meeting* for the Welfare of their miserable Nation that were Servants among us. I allowed their Design and went one evening and pray'd and preach'd (on Ps. 68. 31) with them; and gave them the following orders, which I insert only for the Curiositie of the Occasion.[8]

The orders referred to contain no evidence that Mather, although he felt a friendliness for the Negro, desired to see him more than a servant strengthened in honesty and in usefulness by religious piety.[9] A similar opinion concerning the education of blacks was held by the Church of England missionaries who were directly sponsored by the Society for the Propagation of the Gospel in Foreign Parts, such as the Reverend Samuel Thomas, who conducted a school for Negroes in Goose Creek Parish, South Carolina, as early as 1695, and Elias Neau, who opened a school for Negroes in New York in 1704.[10]

It is not likely that the early religious training given the Negro was of any considerable value in his intellectual advancement.[11] The austerity of the Puritan teachers, with their doctrine of the elect of God—to which the lowly Negro could scarcely hope to belong—probably made little impression upon his temperament, except perhaps to add something to his discipline as a slave. The formalism of the Anglican ritual must have bewildered him. It is certain that he did not become constructively religious until the great evangelical awakening began to shake the colonies in the second quarter of the eighteenth century. Gustavus Vassa, who had been baptized in the Church of England while still a slave, wrote as follows about hearing George Whitefield preach in Philadelphia in 1766:

When I got into the church I saw this pious man exhorting the people with the greatest fervor and earnestness, and sweating as much as I ever did while in slavery on Montserrat beach. . . . I was very much struck and impressed with this; I thought it strange that I had never seen divines exert themselves in this manner before, and was no longer at a loss to account for the thin congregations they preached to.[12]

Such a reaction was a common one. The Christianity which Whitefield and his emotional predecessors preached in America brought to the Negro a religion which he could understand, and which could stir him to self-expression. He responded to it with enthusiasm, allowed his imagination to run riot with it, loved it with passion. It afforded him a mental escape from the wretchedness of his social position, whether he was a slave or free, and it stimulated him to assert himself as a human being. More than any other force it aided him in adapting himself to the ways of Western civilization. The first Negroes in America who attempted authorship owed their main inspiration for achievement to emotional religion.

But before he could become an author, the Negro of a literary turn needed more than the stimulation of an exciting religious faith. It was not until the beginning of the nineteenth century that he could look to his own race for any support. The years between 1780 and 1810, which saw the emancipation of the slave completed or at least begun in all the North, saw also the first independent Negro churches firmly established in the United States, the earliest self-sustained organizations of any consequence devoted to the general improvement of the people of color.[13] The Negroes in considerable numbers had not until then developed a consciousness of their own possibilities. They had not until then, except in their spasmodic slave insurrections, all of which were on a comparatively small scale, made any organized effort to stand as a social unit. Before this time, the Negro of superior talent was wholly in the keeping of a capricious fate. If a slave, he might be owned by an understanding and considerate master. If a free man, he might through display of unusual merit attract the attention of some humanitarian sympathizer. In either event, he would be given encouragement. If he was not so lucky, he was lost in the welter of slavery, or in the degraded position in society—not much better than a state of slavery—that was the lot of the average free black.

Phillis Wheatley, thinking probably of what she owed to John Wheatley, her Boston owner, and to the Countess of Huntingdon, opened her *Poems on Various Subjects* with verses in praise of Maecenas. In doing so she, perhaps unwittingly, suggested a truth regarding each member of her race who rose to a position of some distinction during the age in which she lived. The great humanitarian wave that swept over Western civilization in the eighteenth century, of which the democratization of the church was a minor eddy, supplied protectors in abundance for the unfortunate blacks. Powerful champions, stirred by the doctrine that "all men are created equal," arose to combat the wrongs which the Negroes were suffering. There had been organized protests against slavery in America since 1688, when Franz Daniel Pastorius and his associates drew up the celebrated memorial against the system for the German-town Quakers. Now these protests took on the significance of a stupendous moral and political issue, engaging the support of such Englishmen as Edmund Burke, John Fox, the younger Pitt, John Wesley, William Cowper, Adam Smith, Thomas Clarkson, and William Wilberforce, and of such Americans as Benjamin Franklin, Patrick Henry, Thomas Jefferson, John Woolman, and Benjamin Rush. But the aspiring Negro of talent was usually not to find his Maecenas among the statesmen and leaders of thought. They were fighting slavery as a social institution; they were building for the future of the expatriated Africans as a whole.[14] The true Maecenas of the Negro of talent was found rather among those humanitarians who sought to prove by actual experiment that the colored man was not of an inferior race, that if treated with justice and allowed a chance he could assimilate the highest education and contribute something of real worth to the world's culture.

Several eighteenth-century Negroes who were thus given free opportunity for cultural development in Europe proved themselves most worthy of the trust placed in them by their sponsors. Ibrahim Petrovich Hannibal, an Abyssinian black who was educated in Russia and in France under the supervision of none other than Peter the Great, rose to the rank of lieutenant-general in the Czar's artillery. A great-grandson of Hannibal and his second wife, a Russian noble-woman, was Alexander Pushkin, usually accorded first place among Russia's poets.[15] Anthony William Amo, a native of Guinea who owed his European education to the

Prince of Brunswick, published at Halle in 1738 a meta-
physical essay written in Latin, *Tractatus de arte sobrie et
accurate philosophandi.*[16] James Eliza John Capitein, kidnapped from Africa when he was seven or eight years of
age and educated in Holland at the expense of a philanthropic Dutch merchant, published at Amsterdam in 1742 a
volume of sermons, *Witgewrogte Predikatien,* and a Latin
treatise, *Dissertatio de servitute,* which, strange as it may
seem, defends slavery as a social institution.[17]   Francis
Williams, born of free black parents in Jamaica about 1700,
"was picked to be the subject of an experiment, which, it is
said, the Duke of Montagu was curious to make, in order to
discover, whether, by proper cultivation and a proper tuition
at school and the university, a Negroe might not be found as
capable of literature as a white person."[18]   Williams, trained
at English grammar schools and at Cambridge, was the
author of a Latin ode, *Integerrimo et fortissimo viro,
Georgio Holdano,* written on Holdane's assuming the gov-
ernorship of Jamaica and printed at least as early as 1774,
when it was included in Edward Long's *History of
Jamaica.*[19]   Williams has also been accredited with the
authorship of a published ballad, apparently no longer extant, *Welcome, Welcome, Brother Debtor!*[20]   The Duke of
Montagu seems to have been instrumental in fostering an
extraordinary love for reading and the stage in another
talented Negro, Ignatius Sancho, who, born in 1729 on
board a slave ship bound for South America, was for more
than twenty years of his life in the service of the Montagu
family as a butler.[21]   His *Letters,* published in London in
1782 in a two-volume edition, form a work not equalled
perhaps in charm and literary merit by any other butler,
white or black, before Sancho's day or since.[22]   Ottabah
Cugoano, liberated from slavery in Grenada and placed as

a servant in homes in England where he had the opportunity for mental growth, was at least partially responsible
for a volume published in London in 1787 as his own,
*Thoughts and Sentiments on the Evil and Wicked Traffic of
Slavery and Commerce of the Human Species.*[23]

It is indeed paradoxical that such a number of these
protectors of members of the most despised race came from
the ranks of the most privileged and autocratic of Europeans. In the provincial and middle-class America of the
eighteenth century there were comparatively few whites who
enjoyed the educational advantages which were afforded
Hannibal, Amo, Capitein, and Francis Williams. However,
the overflowing of humanitarian feeling in America, especially in the immediate pre-Revolution years, was scarcely
paralleled in Europe. Certainly the democratic religious
exuberance of the American was greater than that of the
European. The Negroes were in America in enormous
numbers, in direct and daily contact with the white population. The fates which controlled their destinies placed the
great majority where there was no chance for intellectual
development. A few were fortunate enough to fall into the
hands of men of influence, willing, most frequently because
of a consciousness of religious brotherhood, to give encouragement and aid. These few proved that they were useful
for more than manual labor. They began in a modest and
humble manner to make their contribution to the higher
American achievement. One of them, James Derham, won
distinction as a physician in Philadelphia and New Orleans.[24] Another, Thomas Fuller, a Virginia slave, gained
recognition for his phenomenal gifts as an arithmetician.[25]
Another, Benjamin Banneker, of Maryland—who, as we
shall see later, deserves a place in the history of Negro literature—made marked progress in astronomy and general sci-

ence. A group, Crispus Attucks chief among them, displayed a superior heroism, mainly through their own initiative, in the War of the Revolution.[26] And by the year 1790 the first writers, working separately, in most cases not aware of what other exceptional members of their race were accomplishing, had made the simple and interesting beginnings of American Negro literature.

II

Probably the first poem published by an American Negro is a broadside of eighty-eight lines entitled *An Evening Thought: Salvation by Christ with Penetential Cries: Composed by Jupiter Hammon, a Negro Belonging to Mr. Lloyd, of Queen's Village, on Long Island, the 25th of December, 1760.* Little is known of Jupiter Hammon.[27] Born about 1720, he lived through the years when the church in America was being democratized, through the period when the Revolution was remaking the thought of the country, and on until the definite establishment of the United States as a nation. All of his life he passed in slavery, belonging, as the title-pages of his publications attest, to three different members of the Lloyd family of Long Island. Except for the time during the War of the Revolution when the British were in possession of Long Island and the patriot Lloyds with their slaves were in exile in Hartford, Connecticut, Jupiter Hammon's residence was probably on the Lloyd estate near Queen's Village. Aside from his own statement that he was "able to do almost any kind of business,"[28] there seem to be no records giving information regarding his exact status as a slave; and we do not know whether he was a farm laborer, a household servant, or a workman at some trade.

The Lloyds were evidently humane and considerate masters; for Hammon, addressing his fellow slaves, wrote in 1786:

I have good reason to be thankful that my lot is so much better than most slaves have had. I suppose I have had more advantages than most of you who are slaves have ever known, and I believe more than many white people have enjoyed.[29]

Whatever advantages and privileges the Lloyds might have granted him, there is no indication in his writings that they gave him opportunity for instruction beyond the most elementary training in reading and writing.[30] But they undoubtedly allowed him to go freely to church, where he absorbed the doctrines of the Calvinistic Methodists, of which all of his work is an echo. His masters also, it seems, left him free at times to engage in preaching.[31] Stimulated by religious indulgences, he read with avidity the Bible and hymn books and possibly such pious poems as Michael Wigglesworth's *The Day of Doom.*[32] It was in all probability through this reading that he taught himself what he knew about prose style and the art of versification.

Hammon said in 1786: "When I was at Hartford, in Connecticut, where I lived during the war, I published several pieces which were well received, not only by those of my own colour, but by a number of the white people, who thought they might do good among the servants."[33] *An Address to Miss Phillis Wheatly,* a poem of twenty-one ballad stanzas, appeared as a broadside in 1778. In 1779, came *An Essay on the Ten Virgins,* of which no copy seems to exist. That it was published, however, is scarcely to be doubted, since it was advertised in the *Connecticut Courant* for December 14, 1779.[34] *A Winter Piece,* a sermon in prose with "A Poem for Children with Thoughts on Death" tacked on at the end, appeared in pamphlet form in 1782. Another prose pamphlet, *An Evening's Improvement,* including also a dialogue in verse entitled "The Kind Master and the Dutiful Servant," was published at Hartford without date. These four pieces written during the Revolution, with *An Evening Thought* (1760) and *An Address to the Negroes in the State of New-York* (1787), make up all of the known writings of Jupiter Hammon.[35] That he produced other broadsides and pamphlets of which there is at present no apparent trace is altogether possible.

It is an interesting coincidence that most of Hammon's poetry was published at Hartford at a time when that Connecticut town was the literary capital of America. But if the neoclassical "Hartford Wits" read his poems, they no doubt looked upon them as chaotic effusions of crude thoughts poured out in a verse not inappropriate to the cheapest balladry. To the twentieth-century mind, which places a high value on the artlessness of folk poetry, Jupiter Hammon's work takes on a new meaning. There is a strength of wild and native religious feeling in what he wrote, a strength which he achieved without conscious effort. From hearing evangelical sermons and from reading the Bible according to his own untrained fancy, he picked up strange notions regarding salvation, penitential cries, redeeming love, tribunal day, the Holy Word, bounteous mercies. His mystic Negro mind played with these notions; and, endowed with the instinct for music which is so strong in his race, he sang out his impressions in such meters as he had become familiar with in the hymns of Charles Wesley and Augustus Montague Toplady, and in such rimes as for the moment pleased his ear. Indeed, his method of composition must have been that of the unknown makers of the spirituals.[36]

Like the spirituals, the poems of Jupiter Hammon were composed to be heard. There is evident in his verse that peculiar sense for sound which is the most distinguishing characteristic of Negro folk poetry. A word that appeals to his ear he uses over and over again, in order, it seems, to cast a spell with it. In *An Evening Thought* the word *salvation* occurs in every three or four lines. Any impressionable sinners who might have heard Jupiter Hammon chant the poem when in the ecstasy of religious emotion no doubt went away to be haunted by the sound of the word *salvation* if not by the idea. A few lines will illustrate the effectiveness of the repetition:

> Salvation comes now from the Lord,
> Our victorious King.
> His holy name be well ador'd,
> Salvation surely bring.
> Dear Jesus give thy spirit now,
> Thy grace to every Nation,
> That han't the Lord to whom we bow,
> The author of Salvation.
> Dear Jesus, unto Thee we cry,
> Give us the preparation;
> Turn not away thy tender eye;
> We seek thy true Salvation.

In the original broadside the poem was printed, as here quoted, without a break between stanzas; however, the metrical arrangement is that of the ballad stanza with alternating rimes, a verse form which is often found in the early Methodist hymns, and which is the basis for the stanza in Wigglesworth's *The Day of Doom*. Hammon followed this pattern in all of his poems, though not without marked irregularities. There are numerous cases of wrenched accents demanding an outrageous pronunciation. There are many examples of syncopation, so characteristic of Negro dance rhythms, evident in the omission at times of one syllable and at other times of two, as in the following line, which is supposed to be tetrameter:

> Thou mightst   been left behind.

But the most interesting irregularities are the strange rime combinations—such as, *word* and *God*, *Lord* and *God*, *call* and *soul*, *sound* and *down*. Since we know little about how English was spoken by the Negroes on Long Island in the eighteenth century, we cannot determine how far astray Jupiter Hammon's ear was in hearing exact rimes in such combinations. We can say with definiteness that the riming words which he selected are always sonorous.

While the imagery in Hammon's poems is in general restrained, often taken bodily from the New Testament, there are unexpected turns in the thought which suggest the wild extravagance of the spiritual. The unusual association of ideas in the following stanza from *An Address to Miss Phillis Wheatly* is probably the result of a necessity for rimes:

> God's tender mercy brought thee here;
> Tost o'er the raging main;
> In Christian faith thou hast a share,
> Worth all the gold of Spain.

The last three lines of the following stanza from the same poem might not seem out of place in a spiritual:

> That thou a pattern still might be,
> To youth of Boston town,
> The blessed Jesus set thee free
> From every sinful wound.

In two stanzas of "A Poem for Children with Thoughts on Death" Hammon pictures the dread terror of the day of final judgment. Back of the ominous words of warning to sinful children there is a delightful feeling of playfulness, suggestive of a traditional Southern mammy threatening a wilful infant with the imminent approach of a voodoo man.

> Then shall ye hear the trumpet sound,
> The graves give up their dead,
> Those blessed saints shall quick awake,
> And leave their dusty beds.

> Then shall ye hear the trumpet sound,
> And rend the native sky,
> Those bodies starting from the ground,
> In the twinkling of an eye.

In "The Kind Master and the Dutiful Servant," written in dialogue, a form which indicates that the author might have known something of the English popular ballad, Hammon suddenly leaves the drama six stanzas from the end and naïvely addresses his readers in his own person.

> Believe me now, my Christian friends,
> Believe your friend call'd Hammon:
> You cannot to your God attend,
> And serve the God of Mammon.

It must not be supposed that Jupiter Hammon was only primitive and naïve, merely a folk poet incapable of consistent and orderly reflection. *An Address to Miss Phillis Wheatly,* his second poem, written eighteen years after his first spontaneous and chaotic effort, *An Evening Thought,* shows a balanced structure of ideas, based on the theme that it was a divine providence which brought Phillis Wheatley from heathen Africa to a land where she could know the true religion and teach it to others.[37] Both this poem and "A Poem for Children with Thoughts on Death" are provided with scriptural glosses, and in each the thought association with the Biblical citations is fairly logical and exact. While the two earlier prose pamphlets, *A Winter Piece* and

An Evening's Improvement, intended as sermons, are rhapsodic and incoherent, the *Address to the Negroes in the State of New-York* displays a regular and firm organization. It opens with personal reminiscences, and these are followed by a series of moral precepts. Negroes are admonished to be obedient and faithful to their masters, to be honest and not to steal, to be energetic and not to dally when sent on errands, to be always religious and never profane. In the closing section, which deals with the subject of freedom for the slaves, Hammon praises the blessings of liberty. But concerning his own condition of slavery he mildly concludes:

Now I acknowledge that liberty is a great thing, and worth seeking for, if we can get it honestly; and by our good conduct prevail on our masters to set us free: though for my own part I do not wish to be free; for many of us who are grown up slaves, and have always had masters to take care of us, should hardly know how to take care of themselves; and it may be for our own comfort to remain as we are.

Perhaps because of this conciliatory attitude toward slavery, Jupiter Hammon's work was disregarded by the early Negro leaders, who in most cases kept alive the personalities of their predecessors of any distinction whatsoever. The name of America's first Negro poet dropped into oblivion soon after his death, to remain there for more than a century.[38] His attempts at thoughtful composition, such as *An Address to the Negroes in the State of New-York,* fall low in the class of the subliterary. It is his poetry, with all of its artlessness and crudeness, which makes his name important. As the product of the uncultivated Negro imagination and temperament, his verse, slight as the body of it is, forms a unique contribution to American poetry in the eighteenth century. The reader of today is likely to find a more sincere feeling in it than in most religious verse written in America during Hammon's age. It is a quaint prelude to the rich and varied songs which were to burst spontaneously from the Negro folk a little later, songs which make up the great gift from Africa to the art of America.

While the verse of Jupiter Hammon is remarkable for the touch of originality which it contains, that of America's second Negro poet to appear, Phillis Wheatley, is noteworthy as an accomplishment in imitation. Her work is sophisticated rather than primitive, artificial rather than spontaneous, polished rather than crude. With the exception of certain specific passages in which the author identified herself, it contains nothing which marks it as the work of a member of the African race.[39] It is in spirit and in execution little different from the sentimental poems turned out, both in England and in America, by numerous skillful versifiers of the eighteenth century who knew well the neoclassical rules for writing poetry and who followed them with studied care. Like the rest of neoclassical sentimental verse, her poems offer slight interest to the modern reader. But she is prominent among those minor authors of the past who are most often discussed. The world is still wondering about her as it wondered in 1770, when her first publication, *An Elegiac Poem on the Death of George Whitefield*, appeared in at least six different editions, in Boston, Philadelphia, and New York, within a few months.[40] Although there can at the present day be little emotional response to her poems, there is justly enough the greatest curiosity over the manner in which she composed them. The facility and thoroughness with which she, a slave transported from Africa, imitated the artful idiom of Alexander Pope and his meticulous school while she was still scarcely more than a child present one of those marvels of precocity which baffle psychological explanation.

As a number of passages in Phillis Wheatley's letters and poems attest, she always felt that it was a divine providence which guided her to America and into the ownership of John Wheatley, a wealthy Boston tailor and merchant.[41] The slave ship which brought her from Africa in 1761 might, indeed, have carried her to any one of a hundred other destinations where, with her frail health, she probably would have succumbed to the rigors of slavery within a few months. At any rate, she was placed on sale in the Boston slave market, was bought by John Wheatley to serve as maid for his wife, and was taken into a serious and religious home. There her talents were discovered and encouraged, and books were placed at her disposal as soon as she learned to read. John Wheatley in a letter to her London publisher dated November 14, 1772, wrote:

Phillis was brought from *Africa* to *America,* in the Year 1761, between Seven and Eight Years of Age. Without any Assistance from School Education, and by only what she was taught in the Family, she, in sixteen Months Time from her Arrival, attained the English Language, to which she was an utter Stranger before, to such a Degree, as to read any, the most difficult parts of the Sacred Writings, to the great Astonishment of all who heard her.

As to her Writing, her own Curiosity led her to it; and this she learnt in so short a Time, that in the Year 1765, she wrote a letter to the Rev. Mr. Occom, the *Indian* Minister, while in England.

She has a great Inclination to learn the Latin Tongue, and has made some progress in it. This Relation is given by her Master who bought her, and with whom she now lives.[42]

"To the University of Cambridge, in New-England," which she wrote in 1767, only six years after she had been kidnapped from her native environment and when she was no more than fourteen years of age, contains lines such as the following:

See Him, with hands outstretch'd upon the cross!
Divine compassion in his bosom glows.
He hears revilers with oblique regard.
What Condescension in the Son of God!
When the whole human race, by Sin had fall'n;
He deign'd to die, that they might rise again,
To live with Him beyond the starry sky,
Life without death, and Glory without End.[43]

The graceful regularity of these lines, in both rhythm and thought, explains completely enough the progress of the slave girl's education in America.

Under date of July 19, 1772, she wrote to Obour Tanner, a young woman of her own race, then living in Newport, Rhode Island: "I have been in a very poor state of health all the past winter and spring, and now reside in the country for the benefit of its more wholesome air."[44] She had seen her elegy on Whitefield appear in print on October 11, 1770; her teacher and the person in the world whom she loved most, the daughter in the Wheatley family, had on January 31, 1771, become the wife of the Reverend John Lathrop; and on August 18, 1771, christened simply as "Phillis, servant to Mr. Wheatley," she had been received into the communion of the Old South Church.[45] Although she was still regarded as a slave, John Wheatley arranged for her to accompany his son, Nathaniel Wheatley, on a trip to England, where it was hoped that the change in the climate would cure the indisposition of which she complained to Obour Tanner. She was in England probably during the summer of 1773.[46] The elegy on Whitefield, of which two London editions had appeared, had already made her name known with favor in Calvinistic Methodist circles in England; and she was received during at least part of her sojourn abroad, not as a slave but as an honored guest, in the house of the Countess of Huntingdon, the patroness of Whitefield and of all the Calvinistic Methodist movement.[47] Among other notables whom she probably met was Brook Watson, afterwards Lord Mayor of London, who gave her a copy of *Paradise Lost*.[48] It has been said that she would have been presented at the court of George III if the illness of Mrs. Wheatley had not caused her to hasten her return to Boston.[49] If her *Poems on Various Subjects* had not already appeared in print before her departure from England, the arrangements for the publication had undoubtedly been completed.[50] On October 30, 1773, evidently some time after her return to Boston, she wrote in a letter to Obour Tanner: "I can't say but my voyage to England has conduced to the recovery (in a great measure) of my health. The friends I found there among the nobility and gentry, their benevolent conduct towards me, the unexpected civility and complaisance with which I was treated by all, fills me with astonishment. I can scarcely realize it. This I humbly hope has the happy effect of lessening me in my own estimation."

Mrs. Wheatley died on March 3, 1774,[51] and from this time on Phillis Wheatley's life was a series of misfortunes. The disturbances of the Revolution came on, and we find her, an ardent patriot, in the autumn of 1775 in Providence. It was apparently there that she wrote the often quoted poem, "His Excellency General Washington," which she dispatched to Washington with a letter dated October 26, 1775.[52] Early in March, 1778, John Wheatley died; his son had become a permanent resident of England, and his daughter, as we have noted, had since 1771 been married. Thus, the only home which Phillis Wheatley had known in America was broken up. She had undoubtedly by this time received her manumission; for the official records show that on April 1, 1778, she as a "free negro" obtained a license to marry John Peters, a man of her own race.[53] Her marriage

only increased her misfortunes. Peters was proud and
irresponsible, and not only estranged his wife's white friends
from her, but also forced poverty upon her and upon the
three children whom she bore him.[54] Four months after
her marriage she lost through death any possible assistance
from Mrs. Lathrop, perhaps the last white person in America who might have felt a special responsibility toward her.
In 1779 her fellow communicants in the Old South Church
and the numerous persons to whom she had addressed consolatory verses in time of sorrow might have helped her by
subscribing for a new volume of her poems, proposals for
which were published; but the troubles of the Revolution
had apparently made the Bostonians forget for the time
being their "slave poet," for the necessary number of subscriptions for the book was evidently never secured. In
spite of her misery and wretchedness, she published in the
last year of her life at least three poems. "To Mr. and
Mrs.*******, on the Death of Their Infant Son," appeared
in the *Boston Magazine* for September, 1784.[55] *An Elegy
Sacred to the Memory of That Great Divine, the Reverend
and Learned Dr. Samuel Cooper* and an ode on the termination of the Revolution, called *Liberty and Peace,* were both
issued as pamphlets. Not one of these poems, it is remarkable to note, contains the slightest allusion to her own un-
happiness. We know that until three months of the time
of her death she had not abandoned hope for the publication
of a second volume.[56] The end came for her on December
5, 1784, when she was certainly not more than thirty-one
years of age.[57]

Before Phillis Wheatley's *Poems on Various Subjects,
Religious and Moral* was published, at least four pieces included in the volume had already appeared in print.[58] All
were personal elegies, one being the poem on Whitefield.

In *Poems on Various Subjects* there are thirty-five other pieces. Remaining poems of hers which are known to have been printed before her death number six: two untitled poems "addressed to a gentleman of the navy," published in the *Royal American Magazine* for December, 1774, and January, 1775;[59] "His Excellency General Washington," first published in the *Pennsylvania Magazine* for April, 1776, while Thomas Paine was serving as the editor; and the three poems which have been named as having been published during the last year of her life. Only one other poem has been definitely identified as Phillis Wheatley's, "Thoughts on His Excellency Major General Lee Being Betray'd into the Hands of the Enemy by the Treachery of a Pretended Friend," which seems to have remained in manuscript until it was printed in the *Proceedings of the Massachusetts Historical Society, 1863–64.*[60] That she was the author of a body of poems almost equal to that which has been published cannot be doubted. In the *Evening Post and the General Advertiser* (Boston) for October 30, 1779, and in several subsequent issues of that newspaper, appeared an advertisement headed thus: "Proposals, for printing by subscription a volume of Poems and Letters, dedicated to the Right Honourable Benjamin Franklin, Esq.: One of the Ambassadors of the United States at the Court of France. By Phillis Peters."[61] The titles of the thirty-three poems to be included were given, of which number only the verses addressed to Washington and to General Lee were, so far as we know, ever printed.[62] Thirteen letters were promised, of which three were to the Countess of Huntingdon and one to Dr. Benjamin Rush.[63] The author was characterized as a "Female African, whose lot it was to fall into the hands of a *generous* master and *great* benefactor." The advertisement stated that the volume would run to about three hundred pages. It has been naturally assumed that the book was not printed because a sufficient number of subscribers could not be secured. The only remaining writings of Phillis Wheatley which we can say with definiteness have seen print are the seven letters to Obour Tanner, first published by the Massachusetts Historical Society in 1864, and the letter to Washington, published in 1776 with the poem addressed to him.

The main body of Phillis Wheatley's verse belongs to that class of poetry which we call occasional. Eighteen out of her forty-six poems which are known to have come down to us are elegies. It has been said that she wrote them as consolatory poems at the request of friends.[64] Five are on ministers, two on the wives of a lieutenant-governor and a celebrated physician, and the rest on unknown persons, including a number of children who died in infancy. The material is in each instance conventional, true to the traditions of the elegy in an elegy-making age, especially in Boston, where the writing of poems of condolence and epitaphs had been in great vogue since the days of Anne Bradstreet and Urian Oakes. The treatment is in accord with neoclassical standards. Whatever feeling there is, is impersonal and artificial; the method for achieving effect is mainly that of hyperbole; the ornamentation is elaborate and sumptious, with frequent invocations of the Muses, allusions to pagan gods and Biblical heroes, overuse of personification, and pompousness of diction. "To the Rev. Mr. Pitkin on the Death of His Lady," which suggests the general mood of the elegies, opens in this strain—

> Where Contemplation finds her sacred Spring;
> Where heav'nly Music makes the Centre ring;
> Where Virtue reigns unsullied, and divine,
> Where Wisdom thron'd, and all the Graces shine;

There sits thy Spouse, amid the glitt'ring Throng;
There central Beauty feasts the ravish'd Tongue;
With recent Powers, with recent Glories crown'd,
The choirs angelic shout her welcome round.[65]

Six of the poems were inspired by public events of importance, such as the repeal of the Stamp Act, the appointment
of Washington as commander-in-chief of the Revolutionary
forces, the betrayal of General Lee into the hands of the
British, and the return of peace after the close of the Revolution; and a number are on minor happenings, such as the
voyage of a friend to England, and the providential escape
of an acquaintance from a hurricane at sea. These, like
the elegies, are affected, written with an exaggerated dignity, with a straining attempt to force high eloquence.

But not all of Phillis Wheatley's poems are occasional.
Following the New England custom of versifying selections
from the Bible, begun back in the early days when the
Bay Psalm Book was compiled, she worked out paraphrases
of eight verses from the fifty-third chapter of Isaiah, and of
the passage in the first book of Samuel which describes
David's fight with Goliath. It is unnecessary to say that
her neoclassical couplets deaden entirely the fire of Isaiah's
rhapsody; she was so far away from the true Biblical ardor
that she opened the paraphrase by invoking the "heav'nly
muse." Her "Goliath of Gath" is more successful. In
hearing the following lines one might feel that he is listening to the steady music of the opening of Pope's version of
the *Iliad:*

Ye martial pow'rs, and all ye tuneful nine,
Inspire my song, and aid my high design.
The dreadful scenes and toils of war I write,
The ardent warriors, and the fields of fight:
You best remember, and you best can sing

> The acts of heroes to the vocal string:
> Resume the lays with which your sacred lyre,
> Did then the poet and the sage inspire.[66]

Also among her better achievements is the adaptation of that portion of the sixth book of Ovid's *Metamorphoses* which tells of Niobe's distress for her children.[67] This classical paraphrase belongs to the small group of poems for which Phillis Wheatley did not look to her New England predecessors for models. Her pieces on abstractions, including "Imagination," "Recollection," and "Virtue," probably owe their subject matter to English rather than to American influences. And her companion hymns, "Morning" and "Evening," place her among those eighteenth-century poets, numerous in England, who felt so greatly the splendors of Milton's "L'Allegro" and "Il Penseroso" that they attempted imitations.

What one most wishes Phillis Wheatley had done, she left undone: she wrote too rarely about herself. Her intimate personal interests were ignored . She composed verses on the deaths of those who meant little to her, but, so far as we know, she remained silent after the deaths of Mrs. Wheatley and Mrs. Lathrop and her own children. She dwelt at length on the common notions of her day regarding liberty, but she neglected almost entirely her own state of slavery and the miserable oppression of thousands of her race. In all of her writings she only once referred in strong terms to the wrongs of the Negro in America. The reference is in the poem addressed to the Earl of Dartmouth upon his appointment as George III's secretary for North America:

> Should you, my lord, while you peruse my song,
> Wonder from whence my love of *Freedom* sprung,
> Whence flow these wishes for the common good,

> By feeling hearts alone best understood,
> I, young in life, by seeming cruel fate
> Was snatch'd from *Afric's* fancy'd happy seat:
> What pangs excruciating must molest,
> What sorrows labour in my parent's breast?
> Steel'd was that soul and by no misery mov'd
> That from a father seiz'd his babe belov'd:
> Such, such my case. And can I then but pray
> Others may never feel tyrannic sway?[68]

But with all of·her outward neglect of self, Phillis Wheatley was too honest to veil her true personality in what she wrote. The sincerity of childhood and the delicacy of young womanhood, uniform in both the black race and the white, are constantly reflected, even when she is most artificial. Her gentle character, so often commented upon, lies revealed in every poem and letter.

But the dominant trait in the personality which her writings reveal is a capacity for intense religious faith. Without that faith she probably would never have written a line. She was not devout with the primitive adoration of a Jupiter Hammon, but with a belief balanced and controlled by Puritan training, such a belief as that of any other member of the Old South Church who might have seen worth in the emotionalism of George Whitefield. Every poem which was born in her mind, even the adaptation from Ovid, came forth filled with religious feeling. Her letters to Obour Tanner are to a great extent dissertations on the mercies and goodness of God. The one wholly subjective poem which came from her pen, "On Being Brought from Africa," proves what religion was in her life.

> 'Twas mercy brought me from my *Pagan* land,
> Taught my benighted soul to understand
> That there's a God, that there's a *Saviour* too:
> Once I redemption neither sought nor knew.

Some view our sable race with scornful eye,
"Their colour is a diabolic die."
Remember, *Christians, Negros* black as *Cain,*
May be refin'd, and join th' angelic train.[69]

It is interesting to speculate what her thinking might have been if it had not been nurtured by the Puritanism of eighteenth-century Boston and by the simple doctrines of the Countess of Huntingdon's circle.[70] But speculate as we will, we cannot conceive of a philosophical system, whether based on the assumption that the savage is noble and superior or on any other assumption, which might have replaced her deep trust in the God of the Puritans.

That which is most important in a consideration of her work is her talent—a talent all the more difficult to explain because it is contradictory, in one respect spontaneous and intuitive, and in another respect rational and exceedingly self-conscious. Her success in absorbing the music of Alexander Pope, master of England's neoclassical verse-makers, gives her poems their highest claim to distinction; and it seems that she was not aware of what she was doing when she achieved that success. We are told that there were three books in the Wheatley library for which she had a particularly strong affection—the Bible, a collection of tales from classical mythology, and Pope's Homer.[71] Her first publication, the elegy on Whitefield, shows that she was familiar with Gray.[72] We know that after her visit to England she possessed a Milton, and that after 1774 she owned a collection of Shenstone's poems.[73] There is reason to believe that she read every poem which she could find, whether in book, magazine, newspaper, or broadsheet. But it was Pope's translation of Homer which taught her most. We have already noticed, in the quotation from "Goliath of Gath," how near she could come to her great master's idiom whenever her subject matter gave her the opportunity. In writing the following lines from "Thoughts on His Excellency Major General Lee," she was probably thinking of the first book of *Paradise Lost,* but it is Pope's music which she reproduced:

> While thus he spake, the hero of renown
> Survey'd the boaster with a gloomy frown,
> And stern reply'd: "O arrogance of tongue!
> And wild ambition, ever prone to wrong!
> Believ'st thou chief, that armies such as thine
> Can stretch in dust that heaven-defended line?"[74]

Even in her one poem in blank verse, "To the University of Cambridge, in New-England," a quotation from which has been given, the line, with its strong rise, marked cæsura, and hastened fall, is that of Pope. Indeed, reproduction of Pope's versification characterizes all of her poems with the exception of the few which she wrote in lyrical measures.[75] She lived during the age when the poetical fashion in America was to imitate Pope; and while John Trumbull, Timothy Dwight, Joel Barlow, the Philip Freneau of the political satires, and numerous others among her contemporaries caught more of his general spirit, she perhaps excelled them all in reproducing his rhythms. Her power to attain this place of eminence must be pronounced as due to her instinct for hearing the music of words, an instinct which was possibly racial. As in Jupiter Hammon and many other Negro poets, in her the strange sense for imitating sound exercised itself of its own will. She never mentioned Pope, and only rarely touched upon themes such as he treated; but before she began writing, she had read his Homer with her deep-searching ear open for impressions which were to endure.

Another Negro poet, Albery A. Whitman, was a century later than Phillis Wheatley to come perhaps as near reproducing the sonorousness of Byron's *Childe Harold* as any one else has ever come.[76] But a more exact parallel to her genius for imitating sound is to be found in the extraordinary musicianship of Thomas Greene Bethune, the Negro pianist, commonly known as "Blind Tom." For a period of over forty years, down to the time of his death in 1908, his unique concerts were exploited on vaudeville and music-hall stages both in Europe and in America. Although blind and mentally unbalanced, he possessed the power of imitating the playing of the most skilled pianists. All that he needed in order to interpret a movement from a Beethoven sonata was to hear it played. While the nuances which make the virtuoso escaped him, his reproduction of rhythm, tempo, melody, and harmony was exact.[77]

But Phillis Wheatley was reproducing the more subtle sounds of words, and those words were carrying ideas. She possessed not only a musical precocity comparable to Bethune's, but a clear, logical mentality that created images which in most instances are true and precise. In her ability to write with all the practical common-sense control demanded by the neoclassicists is exhibited a still greater psychological puzzle than in her talent for music. Like all neoclassical poets, she borrowed images freely. One finds in her poems the favorite eighteenth-century *clichés,* such as *vaulted skies, roving fancy, crystal shower, feathered warbler, smiling fields, graceful tresses,* and *pensive bosoms.* One also finds an imagination imitating with a remarkable accuracy. The images indicated by italics in the following lines are the invention of a mind working with precision and with a clean recognition of nice artistic adjustment:

All-conquering Death! by thy resistless pow'r,
Hope's tow'ring plumage falls to rise no more![78]

We trace the pow'r of Death from tomb to tomb,
And his are all the ages yet to come.[79]

The frozen deeps may break their iron bands,
And bid their waters murmur o'er the sands.[80]

Aeolus in his rapid chariot drove
In gloomy grandeur from the vault above:
Furious he comes. His winged sons obey
Their frantic sire, *and madden all the sea.*[81]

He drops the bridle on his courser's mane,
Before his eyes in shadows swims the plain.[82]

Swift thro' his throat the feather'd mischief flies,
Bereft of sense, he drops his head, and dies.[83]

Images of like character abound in Phillis Wheatley's poems.
They are not direct copies, and they cannot be created by a
mind that is not a master of itself. They prove as well as
the smooth music in Phillis Wheatley's verse her genius at
imitation. And it is not too much to presume that if she
had been taught by a Wordsworth, who would have convinced her of the value of turning to her sincere religious
self for her subjects and of using an idiom drawn out of
her own personality, her work would stand on its own merits rather than on the fact that she, a Negro and a slave,
produced it. If she had not fallen under the sway of the
New England elegists and of Pope and his school, she might
today be considered one of the ornaments in American literature as well as one of the most interesting curiosities.

According to Henri Grégoire, the earliest historian of
Negro literature, there was another eighteenth-century
American Negro, Caesar, a native of North Carolina, who

attained a reputation as a poet.[84] None of his verses seem to have been preserved. However, since Grégoire compared him with Robert Bloomfield, the English peasant poet, there is a possibility that he is to be identified with the author of a "Negro's Prayer," claimed to have been written in 1790 by a "slave in the lower part of Virginia" and appended by A. Mott to his abridged edition of *The Life and Adventures of Olaudah Equiano, or Gustavus Vassa* (1829). Such lines as the following might easily admit of comparison with certain passages in Bloomfield's *The Farmer's Boy:*

> Stolen or sold in Africa,
> Imported to America,
> Like hogs and sheep in market sold,
> To stem the heat and brook the cold,
> To work all day and half the night,
> And rise before the morning light;
> Sustain the lash, endure the pain,
> Expos'd to storms of snow and rain.

III

It is a strange coincidence that the earliest known American Negro poet and the earliest known American Negro prose writer should have had the same surname and should have emerged with publications in the same year. About the prose writer, Briton Hammon, we know nothing except what we are told in the fourteen-page pamphlet ascribed to his authorship, *A Narrative of the Uncommon Sufferings and Surprising Deliverance of Briton Hammon, a Negro Man,* published in Boston in 1760. It purports to be the account of the experiences of a Negro who for an unexplained reason left Plymouth, Massachusetts, at the end of the year 1747 with his master's permission to go to Jamaica. Shipwreck, captivity among Florida Indians, imprisonment by his Spanish rescuers, escape to England, and in 1760 the accidental meeting with his master on the ship on which he was returning to Massachusetts make up his story of "uncommon sufferings and surprising deliverance." Hammon begins with an apology—

As my Capacities and Conditions of Life are very low, it cannot be expected that I should make these Remarks on the Sufferings I have met with, or the kind Providence of a good God for my preservation, as one in a higher Station; but shall leave that to the Reader as he goes along, and so I shall relate matters of fact as they occur to my mind.

The "matters of fact" are so bluntly expressed that it is not difficult to accept Hammon as the author. The generosity which he attributes to his master, "General Winslow, of Marshfield, in New England," could not have allowed him to go without any education whatsoever in his boyhood.[85] And certainly no high degree of training in letters was necessary for the composition of such a colorless recital of events as the pamphlet proves to be. Its one distinction in Negro literature is probable priority.

Briton Hammon was apparently as firm a believer in "blessed providences" as were Jupiter Hammon and Phillis Wheatley; but perhaps the most picturesque religious devotee among the early Negro writers was John Marrant. His publications include *A Narrative of the Lord's Wonderful Dealings with J. Marrant, a Black . . . Taken Down from His Own Relation* (London, 1785), the *Journal of John Marrant* (London, 1789), and a *Sermon* (Boston, 1789). Marrant was obviously so absorbed in religion that he did not go to the trouble to identify himself as a Negro in any of his writings. However, he is designated as "a black" on the title-pages of several editions of the *Narrative*, and the title-page of the *Sermon* attests that he was the chaplain of the African Lodge of Masons in Boston in 1789. He was born, according to his own statement, in New York in 1755. He tells us in both the *Narrative* and the *Journal* of his boyhood in the South, of his conversion under the preaching of Whitefield, of his captivity among the Cherokees, of his services with the British Navy in the Revolutionary War, and of his going to England, where he undoubtedly came under the protection of the Calvinistic Methodists.[86] It was possibly at the instigation of the Countess of Huntingdon herself that his *Narrative* was prepared for the press; and he claimed that it was she who in 1785 persuaded him to go to Nova Scotia as a missionary. The last that we hear of him is on the occasion of his preaching his *Sermon* in Boston on June 24, 1789.

Marrant's *Narrative* is not only one of the earliest of the Negro autobiographies written in English; it is also one of the most interesting. Its popularity, indicated by the number of editions which were issued, was deserved. Although we cannot determine to what degree Marrant was aided in the composition by his amanuensis, "the Rev. Mr. Aldridge," there is in the account a childlike instinct for sensing the marvelous and the wonderful which suggests strongly the primitive Negro imagination. Most of the *Narrative,* indeed, is written with the simple ecstasy of a folk tale. We are told after a rather flat opening how Marrant, led to one of Whitefield's meetings in Charleston through curiosity, turns cold and feels an overwhelming force grasp him as he hears the words, "Prepare to meet thy God, O Israel!" His "conviction" is so strong that he is thrown into a trance; and he is finally driven to wandering in the forests, given up as insane by his mother and sisters. He does not realize how far he has gone until he falls upon an Indian hunter, who after days of journeying leads him to a village of the Cherokees, where he is immediately taken prisoner and condemned to die. His blissful resignation in approaching what he calls martyrdom for Christ mysteriously frightens his captors, and they decide to take him to the king of the tribe for a trial. The king, described as haughty and stern, demands his death; but a young princess, another Pocahontas, is touched by the mild manner of the captive, and through her entreaties he is allowed to speak in his own defense. Although he has been with the Indians for only a few days, he begins to pray in their language. They become more and more alarmed, and cry out repeatedly, "Where is the Lord Jesus Christ to whom you speak? We want to see him!" There is a miracle. The Indians are converted, and what has been planned as his execution by sticking burning wooden pegs into his body is turned into a Methodist "love feast." Another delightful section of the little book describes his experiences in a storm at sea. He is twice hurled into the raging waters and back to the deck again. After the second escape from being drowned, he ties himself to a mast; but the rope is snapped in two, and when he is washed into the sea again he is attacked by sharks. Finally thrown back on deck a third time, he realizes that God has been simply testing his faith. Thus "embellished with a good deal of adventure, enlivened by the marvellous, and a little touch of the miraculous,"[87] Marrant's *Narrative* is most unbelievable and most readable.

The *Journal*, supposedly written by Marrant without aid, is scarcely more than an adaptation of the *Narrative*. The *Sermon* is a panoramic survey of the history of the world since the Creation, a type of Negro sermon which has been often parodied. Since it is addressed to a body of Masons, much is made of the building of Solomon's temple. The

Biblical details are expanded, and a naïve picture of color
and splendor is presented. Even though Marrant had evidently by 1789 become something of a racial leader, neither
the *Journal* nor the *Sermon* contains the slightest allusion
to the pitiable condition of his people in American life.[88]

IV

Little of any literary value has been produced by the
American Negro, even in the folk songs, which is not related
to racial wretchedness. Yet the writers who have been
treated so far either ignored the subject of slavery entirely,
or else touched upon it in a conciliatory manner. They
were fortunate in gaining the support of kind masters and
powerful protectors, and became so absorbed in religion
that they could not see beyond it into the sufferings of the
thousands of enslaved Africans who were more unfortunate
than themselves. But there were Negroes of exceptional
ability in America in the eighteenth century who were not
mystic and otherworldly and indifferent. There were Negroes too practical in their attitude toward life to be swayed
by the notion that servitude so long as it provided the privilege of Christianity was a blessing for the African race.
Out of the ranks of these more independent thinkers arose
a number who wrote their conclusions for publication.

In February, 1782, there was presented to the Senate
and House of Representatives of Massachusetts the "Petition of an African." Five years later the brief appeal was
published in Matthew Carey's *American Museum*.[89] The
author signed herself simply Belinda. She was reported as
seventy years of age at the time the "Petition" was written,
the most interesting part of which is a picture of her childhood in Africa. The purpose of Belinda in presenting the

"Petition" was not to attack slavery directly, but to demand protection for herself and her daughter from her owner, Colonel Isaac Royall, a Loyalist, then in exile. But the tragic picture ·which she paints of herself as one who has "not yet enjoyed the benefits of creation" forms a protest against slavery of no slight strength. It is not surprising that the appeal was selected for publication in the *American Museum*, scarcely an issue of which did not contain articles condemning slavery. The piece is too well written for us to attribute more of it to Belinda than the mere facts cited. However, it bears her signature, and is therefore important as probably the first recorded indictment of slavery for which an American Negro was supposed to be directly responsible.

In the November and December numbers of the *American Museum* for 1788 appeared "An Essay on Slavery,"[90] the two parts of which are dated respectively May 10 and May 23, 1788. Of the author we know nothing except that he used the pen name "Othello," that he represented himself as a native of Maryland, and that he was a writer who, either independently or with the aid of a trained editor such as Matthew Carey, could think clearly and logically and express himself in a florid oratorical style. The essay, orderly in arrangement, is finished according to the rules of old-fashioned, pompous eloquence. It begins with a consideration of the lethargic attitude of Americans toward slavery:

To what cause are we to impute this frigid silence—this torpid indifference—this cold inanimated conduct of the otherwise generous Americans? Why do they remain inactive amidst the groans of injured humanity, the shrill and distressing complaints of expiring justice and the keen remorses of polluted integrity? Why do they not rise up to assert the cause of God and the world, to drive the fiend injustice into remote and distant regions, and to exterminate oppression from the fair fields of America?

It is claimed that already in 1788 the causes for which the
Revolution was fought have been forgotten; the example of
antislavery activity in monarchic France and England is
pointed out to democratic America not without the expected
sarcasm. The first section ends with a picture of the horrors of snatching Africans from their native homes. Other
sections deal with the evil influences of slavery on the slave
owners themselves, the vanity which is making weaklings
of the children of Maryland planters, the sordidness under
which slaves live on plantations, the brutalities practiced in
beating slaves, and the question, then newly raised, of
colonizing the Negroes in the West. Regarding this scheme
of colonization, "Othello" concludes that anything is acceptable that will abolish slavery. The mood of the whole
essay is that of the following sentences:

No longer shall the United States of America be famed for
liberty. Oppression pervades their bowels; and while they
exhibit a fair exterior to other parts of the world, they are
nothing more than painted sepulchres, containing nought within
them but rottenness and corruption.

It is to be regretted that we cannot definitely place
the man who could write with such sophistication. With the
present available evidence, any conclusion regarding his
identity must be conjecture. There is reason to believe that
he was not a Negro at all, but a white antislavery propagandist who sought for many possible causes to veil his
identity in the pseudonym "Othello." The "Essay" contains
no internal evidence which points positively to the author as
a member of the African race. However, since he did sign
himself "Othello," there is basis for the belief that he really
was a Negro.[91] The fact that he might have desired anonymity is understood when one considers the precarious social
position of the cultivated free Negro in America in the

eighteenth century and the severe nature of the attack made
on slave owners in the "Essay."[92]

There is no doubt that there were Negroes in America
in 1788 with the intellectual capacity to produce the essay
signed by "Othello." One of them was Benjamin Banneker, astronomer, almanac-maker, mechanician, surveyor,
botanist, zoölogist, philosopher, wit, letter-writer, versifier,
and above all a man of such admirable character that he
is counted among the best loved of American Negroes. Most
of his varied activities, such as making a clock when he had
never seen one, helping survey the city of Washington,
experimenting with the velocity of sound waves, computing
almanacs, playing the flute and violin, lie outside the realm
of literature. But we have the famous letter which he wrote
to Thomas Jefferson, at least one of his quaint rimes, and
possibly one of his political essays; and we know that he
was the author of other things which have apparently not
been preserved.

He is one of the few American Negroes of distinction
whose ancestry has been traced, with authority it seems,
back to the seventeenth century. According to the account
handed down from George Ellicott, the man mainly responsible for his education, Banneker's paternal grandmother
was Molly Welsh, an English servant girl, who about 1665
was deported from England on the charge that she had
stolen a pail of milk. She was bound, we are told, as an
indentured servant in Maryland, and by 1692 was not only
a free woman but an owner of land and of two Negro slaves,
one of whom insisted upon keeping his African name,
Banneker, and upon worshipping his African gods. The
account states further that Molly Welsh in time not only
liberated Banneker but married him, and that from this
union there was descended Benjamin Banneker, born in

1731 on the farm near Baltimore which his grandmother had developed.[93] We know positively that little of extra-ordinary nature happened to Banneker until about 1772, when Ellicott, a Maryland planter of broad education and liberal views, began encouraging him in scientific and astro-nomical studies. In the month of August, 1791, appeared the first of his almanacs, that for the year 1792. From this, time until his death, in 1804, he was something of a celebrity in Maryland, known for his likable disposition as well as for his successes in the numerous achievements mentioned above.[94]

When Banneker finished his first almanac, he dispatched a manuscript copy of it to Thomas Jefferson, then Secretary of State, along with a rather lengthy letter pleading for Jefferson's influence in bringing about a rightful recognition of the true worth of the Negro. The letter, dated August 19, 1791, begins as follows:

I am fully sensible of the greatness of that freedom, which I take with you on the present occasion; a liberty which seemed to me scarcely allowable, when I reflected on the distinguished and dignified position in which you stand, and that almost general prejudice and prepossession, which is so prevalent in the world against those of my complexion.[95]

Banneker then appeals to Jefferson's sense of liberalism, reminding him of the doctrines expounded in the *Declaration of Independence.* He speaks boldly of the wrongs of slavery, and comments on his own providential escape from it. Referring to his work on the almanac, he writes:

This calculation is the production of my arduous study, in this my advanced stage of life; for having long had unbounded de-sires to become acquainted with the secrets of nature, I have had to gratify my curiosity herein, through my own assiduous application to astronomical study, in which I need not recount to you the many difficulties and disadvantages, which I had to encounter.[96]

His reason, he asserts, for sending the almanac in manuscript form is that Jefferson might see it sooner and in the compiler's own handwriting. Jefferson's reply is adequately summed up in the statement: "Nobody wishes more than I do, to see such proofs as you exhibit, that nature has given to our black brethren talents equal to those of other colours of men; and that the appearance of the want of them, is owing merely to the degraded condition of their own existence, both in Africa and America."[97] The letter to Jefferson was published in Philadelphia in 1792, and was afterwards frequently reprinted. Perhaps no other protest against slavery written by an early Negro was so often used as antislavery propaganda down to the time of the Civil War.

Banneker wrote nothing else, so far as we know, on slavery. It has been claimed, but without satisfying evidence, that several of the anonymous sketches included in his almanacs are the work of his pen. It seems impossible to say definitely that he contributed more than the astronomical calculations. Unlike Franklin and Ames, his chief American predecessors in almanac-making, he was not his own printer. The almanacs, issued for at least each year from 1792 to 1797, were brought out either in Baltimore, Philadelphia, Wilmington, Trenton, or Richmond; and it is likely that the printers were responsible for whatever literary bits were included. A brief essay, "A Plán for a Peace Office," placed prominently in the 1793 *Almanac*, has been attributed to Banneker. While there seems to be no positive proof that he wrote it, it proposes such a scheme, the establishment of a Department of Peace in the national administration to offset the existing Department of War, as his ingenious mind might have evolved.[98] It has been said that he wrote dissertations on the habits of bees and locusts, which were among the papers left by will to George Ellicott and later destroyed by fire.[99] It is also supposed that these papers contained copies of the rimed problems which Banneker was accustomed to make up for the amusement of his friends.[100] One of these problems, addressed to George Ellicott and handed down through his family, is fortunately not too long to quote:

> A cooper and a vintner sat down for a talk,
> Both being so groggy that neither could walk;
> Says cooper to vintner, "I'm the first of my trade,
> There's no kind of vessel but what I have made,
> And of any shape, sir, just what you will,
> And any size, sir, from a tun to a gill."
> "Then," says the vintner, "you're the man for me.
> Make me a vessel, if we can agree.
> The top and the bottom diameter define,
> To bear the proportion of fifteen to nine;
> Thirty-five inches are just what I crave,
> No more and no less in the depth will I have;
> Just thirty-nine gallons this vessel must hold,
> Then I'll reward you with silver and gold,—
> Give me your promise, my honest old friend."
> "I'll make it tomorrow, that you may depend."
> So, the next day, the cooper, his work to discharge,
> Soon made the new vessel, but made it too large;
> He took out some staves, which made it too small,
> Then cursed the vessel, the vintner, and all.
> He beat on his heart, "By the powers," he swore
> He never would work at his trade any more.
> Now, my worthy friend, find out if you can,
> The vessel's dimensions, and comfort the man![101]

Banneker's character was in itself an argument against slavery. But perhaps the most powerful direct protest against the system for which an eighteenth-century Negro was in any way responsible came in one of the most important books attributed to American Negro authorship. That book is the autobiography, *The Interesting Narrative of the Life of Olaudah Equiano, or Gustavus Vassa, the African.* With the exception of his folk songs, the Negro's most valuable contributions to American literature have been in the form of personal memoirs. The social history of the African in America has been such that until the race produces a Pushkin or a Dumas, a creator whose work is of such excellence that his own personality is entirely overshadowed by it, there is going to be more interest in how a Negro has achieved a certain accomplishment than in the accomplishment itself. The life of practically every American Negro who has attained distinction in any field of activity has been an evolution filled with drama. He has in most cases sprung from slavery, or the most humble social position. His climb has demanded a struggle of adventure, involving often the strange, exciting, and thrilling. It is not surprising that Booker T. Washington's *Up from Slavery* is counted among the more widely read American books, and that Frederick Douglass was called upon to revise his memoirs until they grew from a thin booklet to a massive volume. From the point of view of American literary history, Gustavus Vassa's *Life* is of greater significance than either of these. At the time it was published, in 1789, few books had been produced in America which afford such vivid, concrete, and picturesque narrative.

Because of the fullness of his autobiography, we have perhaps a more complete picture of Gustavus Vassa than of any other eighteenth-century Negro. The book, elaborately detailed throughout, tells of his childhood in Benin, where, according to his own statement, he was born in 1745; of his seizure by Negro hunters when he was eleven years of age; of his experiences as a slave, first for a short period on a

Virginia plantation, then in the illegal service of a British
naval officer, who saw that he was given a fair education,
and finally on plantations and in small trading vessels in
the West Indies as the property of a Philadelphia merchant;
of his saving enough money to buy his freedom from his
American owner, who became his adviser and protector; of
his extensive travels and adventures as a ship's steward; of
his conversion to Methodism; and of his settling down in
England to engage in antislavery work. His one big contribution to the cause of abolition was his autobiography, completed in 1788 and already in the eighth edition by 1794.
According to the dedicatory remarks in a 1790 issue of the
Life, he in that year presented to Parliament a petition for
the suppression of the slave trade. The anonymous author
of an 1815 edition of the *Life,* who stated that he had been
unable to determine where Vassa died, suggested 1801 as
the probable date of his death.

Since Vassa lived so little of his life in the United States,
any place accorded him in American Negro literature might
be questioned. However, England, where he spent most of
his years when he was not on the sea, has not claimed him.
The custom, at least with book cataloguers, has been to
group him with the American writers; and, after all, America was as much his home as any other country except
Africa. While he was in slavery, one of his masters, according to his *Narrative,* was a Virginia planter and another
was a Pennsylvania Quaker. During his many years on
the sea, he seems to have passed much time in the American
Atlantic coast towns, from New York to Savannah. Besides, his book, although originally published in England
and popular there in antislavery circles during the first ten
years of its life, has been many times reprinted in America.
In the stressful abolition period, it shared a place of promi-

nence with Phillis Wheatley's poems and Benjamin Banneker's almanacs among the works most often pointed to as
examples of what the Negro mind could accomplish.

It is the naturalness of the style which gives the book
its strength. Unlike Williams, Sancho, Phillis Wheatley,
and "Othello," Vassa did not imitate. His details are, as
Henri Grégoire claimed, the impressions of a child of nature, and he recorded them without art.[102] There is almost
continuous narrative in the book, of the spontaneous variety
which one associates with Bunyan or Defoe. Whenever
there is explanation, as in the chapters on his religious experiences and conversion, it is enlivened by concrete pictures.
Vassa remained the African, gifted with an imagination
which foreign environment could not destroy. His temperament was not made over again by the civilization with which
he came in contact, and which he seems always to have
evaluated according to his native African standards. One
feels in his pages the Negro's mysticism, his unquestioning
acceptance of the strange, his genius for adapting himself,
his almost uncanny common-sense insight into the characters of those around him, his spirit of laughing resignation
when in adversity, and his fully awake sensitiveness to the
concreteness of life.

The idealized pictures of Africa, especially in the chapters in which Vassa recounts his memories of his childhood,
make up perhaps the most valuable section of the book. Of
all the Negro slaves who wrote of their lives, Cugoano and
Vassa are unique in having distinct recollections of their
childhood days in Africa.[103] Cugoano's style is chaotic, and
his brief description of his early life is vague. Vassa, on
the contrary, retained clearly in his mind the little things;
his pictures of his life in the "kingdom of Benin" are
definite and realistic and full of a simple charm. He tells

about how the gods are worshipped, how justice is admin-
istered, how marriages are celebrated, how wars are planned
and fought, and how crops are grown and harvested and
bartered. And there is never a note of condemnation for
the customs of his native country. One statement shows his
general attitude when comparing life in Africa with that in
Europe: "Our manner of living is entirely plain; for as yet
the natives are unaccustomed with those refinements in
cookery which debauch the taste."[104] Although his recollections of his childhood impressions are too sentimentalized to
be of value to the sociologist devoted to a study of African
habits, they are indeed an interesting unconscious contribution to the literature of the simple life, the literature of the
"noble savage," already popular in Europe at the time Vassa
wrote.

He also fits interestingly into the program of the rising
romanticists of his day in stressing with a calm *naïveté* the
unusual, the marvelous, the supernatural. In relating the
experiences of his kidnapping, he does not emphasize so
much his misfortunes as his wonder in seeing new places
and new people. When after months of travelling with
different African masters he finds himself in chains on a
ship, he casually concludes that the white men whom he
views for the first time are spirits. When he is settled on
a plantation in Virginia, he is sent one day to fan his master,
who is sleeping.

The first object which engaged my attention was a watch
which hung on the chimney, and was going. I was quite sur-
prised at the noise it made, and was afraid it would tell the
gentleman anything I might do amiss: and when I immediately
after observed a picture hanging in the room, which appeared
constantly to look at me, I was still more frightened, having
never seen such things before.

When he witnesses a snowfall for the first time, he is convinced that the heavens are raining down salt. He never gave up his African superstitions. The following was written long after he had become Christianized, after he had planned to go back to Africa as a missionary to his people:

We have serpents of different kinds, some of which are esteemed ominous when they appear in homes, and these we never molest. I remember two of these ominous snakes, each of which was as thick as the calf of a man's leg, and in color resembling a dolphin in water, crept at different times into my mother's night-house, where I always lay with her, and coiled themselves into folds, and each time they crowed like a cock.

His temperament responded with enthusiasm to the Christian belief in divine providences. The phenomenon of an earthquake in Montserrat is explained as the destructive visitation of a God wrathful over the evils of slavery. Profanity is one of the sins which he has difficulty in renouncing when he is undergoing his conversion to Methodism. With a crushing fear in his heart, he observes a curse of God on one of his fellow sailors:

One morning a young man was looking up to the foretop and in a wicked tone, common on shipboard, d—d his eye about something. Just at that moment some small particle of dust fell into his left eye, and by the evening it was much inflamed. The next day it grew worse, and within six or seven days he lost it.

On a trading voyage from Montserrat, the cargo is composed of bullocks and turkeys, the latter of which belong to Vassa. The bullocks all die before an American port is reached, but the turkeys live and are sold at a good profit. In this fateful kindness Vassa sees the hand of a democratic God favoring the lowly. His spirit of credulity, perhaps the main source of his charm, is not confined to religious marvels. Off the coast of Greenland he sees one morning "vast quantities of sea-horses, which neighed exactly like any other horses." A comment on social conditions in New York in 1784 is given with absolute belief:

While we lay here, a circumstance happened which I thought extremely irregular. One day a malefactor was to be executed on the gallows; but with a condition that if any woman, having nothing on but her shift, married the man under the gallows, his life was to be saved. This extraordinary privilege was claimed; a woman presented herself; and the marriage ceremony was performed.

In writing his book Vassa certainly did not know that he was following any new fashions in literature. But he did know that he was fighting slavery. Several chapters are devoted exclusively to arguments for abolition; and whether he is dealing with African customs, his superstitions, his conversion, or his experiences as a sailor, the subject of slavery is likely to be dragged in. That his dominating aim in writing was to attack slavery is constantly before the reader. And he put his protest into such a readable narrative that it is perhaps not an exaggeration to say that he did more than any other Negro before Frederick Douglass to stir up antislavery feeling.

It is certain that the *Life* underwent editing before it was submitted to the public. The opening pages, in which there is the conventional apology for writing an autobiography, do not exhibit that simplicity and artlessness which characterize the style after Vassa gets into the story of his life. The very first sentence manifests an eighteenth-century formality which is totally different from the Bunyan-like simplicity found in the narrative which follows: "I believe it is difficult for those who publish their own memoirs to escape the imputation of vanity; nor is this the only disadvantage under which I labor: it is also their misfortune, that what is uncommon is rarely, if ever, believed, and what is obvious we are apt to turn from with disgust, and to charge the writer with impertinence." The formal arguments against slavery in the concluding chapters contain similar evidences of an affected style. Fortunately, these evident emendations are few. The book as a whole is written with the ingenuousness of a naïve and candid soul. And it is that ingenuousness which makes *The Interesting Narrative of the Life of Olaudah Equiano, or Gustavus Vassa* a memorable book, a work which is one of the chief adornments of American Negro literature. The estimate of a 1789 commentator still holds as valuable:

We entertain no doubt of the general authenticity of this very intelligent African's interesting story. . . . The narrative wears an honest face: and we have conceived a good opinion of the man from the artless manner in which he has detailed the variety of adventures and vicissitudes which have fallen to his lot.[105]

CHAPTER II

WRITINGS OF THE PIONEER RACIAL LEADERS, 1790–1840

I build my house upon a rock, O yes, Lord!
No wind nor storm shall blow dem down, O yes, Lord!
March on, member,
Bound to go!
March on, member,
Bound to go!
March on, member,
Bound to go!
Bid 'em fare you well.

—From *Slave Songs of the United States,* compiled
by William Francis Allen, Charles Pickard Ware,
and Lucy McKim Garrison, 1867

I

For a biographical pamphlet on Paul Cuffe, originally published as an article in 1811 in the *Liverpool Mercury,* the anonymous author used as a motto the following excerpt quoted from the *Edinburgh Review:*

On the first of the present month of August, 1811, a vessel arrived at Liverpool, with a cargo from Sierra Leone, the owner, master, mate, and whole crew of which are free Negroes. The master, who is also owner, is the son of an American slave, and is said to be very well skilled both in trade and navigation, as well as to be of a very pious and moral character. It must have been a strange and animating spectacle to see this free and enlightened African entering as an independent trader, with his black crew, into that port which was so lately the *nidus* of the Slave Trade.

Paul Cuffe, the "master and owner," the "free and enlightened African," thus referred to was one of the first of

American Negroes to rise to a position of economic independence and leadership among his people, a position attained not through the support of any humanitarian sympathizer, but through self-reliant enterprise. Born free, near New Bedford, Massachusetts, in 1759, the son of an Indian mother and a native African father, he was self-taught and self-made.[1] While still very young he went to sea, learned navigation, and by the time he reached middle age he was the owner of several vessels and was a trader of importance. Filled with the moral earnestness of the religious sect to which he belonged, that of the Quakers, he devoted his mature years to what he believed was the one means of saving the American Negroes from the abuses of slavery and social discrimination. That was the return to Africa as colonists. His work in the cause of colonization amounted to little.[2] But the fact that he contributed his wealth and his energy toward the dream of bringing about the rehabilitation of his unfortunate race during the dark period when the free Negro in the United States was groping his way independently and the slave was becoming more and more brutalized is most significant in the social history of the expatriated African. Paul Cuffe stands as an appropriate symbol of what the American Negro of intelligence and courage was attempting at the beginning of the nineteenth century.

The fifty years extending from 1790 to 1840 form a period of hard pioneering for blacks of the type of Paul Cuffe. The eighteenth-century humanitarian wave that had stirred up sponsors interested in testing the intelligence of individual members of the colored race had by 1790 spent its force. It was not until after 1840 that the American antislavery agitators came fully to recognize the worth of the Negro writer and orator in the fight for abolition. Although experimental and therefore most difficult and trying, the period from 1790 to 1840 determined once and for all that the Negro was in America to stay, that he was to work out his destiny side by side with the white man, and that a definite place had to be made for him in the American social organization.[3] In the South, where the Negroes outnumbered those in the North by approximately eight to one, the bonds of slavery were being constantly tightened, and the privileges extended the free blacks were each year being lessened by more stringent local police regulations and by legislative statute. The few Negroes there who were allowed in a measure to assert themselves as human beings owed their better situation to chance. But by 1830 the long process of freeing the slaves in the North, begun as early as 1777 when the constitution of the state of Vermont was adopted, was completed.[4] In 1790, there were in all the United States 59,466 free persons of color; in 1830 the number was 319,599, and in 1840 it had grown to 386,303.[5] In certain centers, such as Philadelphia, New York, Boston, New Bedford, and Albany, the Negroes were present in sufficient numbers to form distinct social units, self-conscious as groups; and out of these centers arose the original organizers of Negro society as it has survived in the United States. Most of the writing and publishing done by Negroes during the half century ending in 1840 came from these early organizers.

The majority of them, like Paul Cuffe, were self-taught. One of the last of American Negroes to become the subject of a social experiment and to receive at the expense of sympathetic whites an intensive education was Robert Chavis, who studied at Princeton at the end of the eighteenth century, distinguished himself as a Latin and Greek scholar, and later had charge of a very successful academy for whites in his native state, North Carolina.[6] Schools for the blacks steadily grew in number in all of the important Northern cities·with each decade of the nineteenth century.[7] But whatever instruction was offered in these schools was most elementary, affording scarcely more than such a training as would improve the efficiency of the blacks as manual laborers. Still, the writings of the Negroes of the period reveal often a fairly extensive knowledge, concise thinking, and an adequate command of the English language. Lemuel B. Haynes, a colored Congregationalist minister who devoted his time to white churches, received what he called a "chimney-corner education"; yet he was considered important enough in his church by 1805 to be honored with the degree of Master of Arts by Middlebury College. It seems that there was only one of the negro writers of the period who finished a college course; that was John B. Russwurm, one of the founders of Negro journalism in America, who was graduated from Bowdoin in 1826, probably the first American Negro to receive a regular academic degree. Theodore S. Wright, a New York Negro preacher of the Presbyterian denomination, completed a theological course at Princeton, where he was a student between 1825 and 1828.[8] But the number who profited by higher instruction was indeed limited.

Of more importance than schools and colleges in the education of the Negro of the period was the establishment of independent churches for the people of color. The religion which had been the main force in stirring up the Negroes of the eighteenth century to self-expression was not only transmitted by the whites but controlled by them. It is true that Negroes were admitted to the churches as members, but they were made to feel that they were receiving only the crumbs of a religion, the real feast of which was enjoyed by their masters and social superiors. As early as 1776, there was founded in Petersburg, Virginia, a Baptist church intended exclusively for the colored. Other Negro churches representing the same denomination were in 1785 in Williamsburg, Virginia, and Savannah, Georgia, and in 1790 in Lexington, Kentucky.[9] Lack of sympathy from the slaveholders in the South, and finally the enactment of laws in a number of the southern states against public meetings of any sort held by Negroes in isolated groups, prevented the progress of such churches as were organized. With the free Negroes of the North conditions were more encouraging. In 1787, the African Free Society of Philadelphia was founded as a semireligious organization under the leadership of Richard Allen and Absalom Jones. Out of the African Free Society developed the Bethel Church, Methodist, of which Richard Allen was the organizer, and St. Thomas' Church, Episcopal, with Absalom Jones the first rector.[10] By 1816 there was a sufficient number of exclusively Negro churches in Pennsylvania, Maryland, and New York to call for the establishment of the African Methodist Episcopal Church, a national organization. The Negro Baptist Church had its definite beginnings in the North with the organization of congregations in Boston, Philadelphia, and New York in 1809. The popularity which these two churches have had with the Negro can be attributed no doubt to the emphasis which each has placed upon emotional appeal. However, the other sects did not neglect the Negro in his desire to have his own church. In addition to the church of St. Thomas in Philadelphia, there were in 1840 Negro Episcopalian churches in New York and Baltimore; and by the same time there were Negro Congregational and Presbyterian churches in New York.[11] There had to be officers for these church organizations. Ministers and teachers were needed, and from the Negro ranks they came, depending usually on strength of character and innate ability rather than on formal training.

The churches were not the only organizations demanding leaders which became firmly established during this period. Negro freemasonry, a great influence in the improvement of the race, was begun through the efforts of Prince Hall, who in 1797 secured a charter for the first Negro Masonic Lodge in America. By 1840 freemasonry was represented in all of the important Negro centers.[12] In 1830, three years before the founding of the American Antislavery Society, there was held in Philadelphia a national convention of the American people of color, a general organization of Negro antislavery agitators, representing seven of the northern states.[13] Libraries, reading rooms, and debating societies, intended primarily for Negroes, were reported in Philadelphia as early as 1833.[14] Because Negroes were not given free privileges in the libraries of New York, David Ruggles, secretary of the Committee of Vigilance of New York, opened in 1838 a reading room for the exclusive use of blacks.[15]

Nothing shows more convincingly the progress which the Negro was making through self-initiative than the establishment of Negro journalism. In March, 1827, there appeared in New York the first number of *Freedom's Journal*, a weekly, edited by Samuel E. Cornish, a minister, and John B. Russwurm, who has been referred to as a graduate of Bowdoin College. With the issue of September 14, 1827, Cornish withdrew from the paper, leaving Russwurm in sole control. The publication continued as *Freedom's Journal* until at least February 14, 1829, when Russwurm gave up the editorship and Cornish took it over independently. Under the name of *Rights for All* the paper was issued until as late as October 9, 1829.[16] In the *Liberator* for March 12, 1831, appeared proposals for the establishment at Albany of a newspaper to be called the *African Sentinel and Journal of Liberty*, with John G. Stewart, a man of color, as the editor. At least two issues of this paper were published.[17] It was not until 1837 that a third Negro newspaper appeared, the *Colored American*, called originally the *Weekly Advocate*. "Established for and devoted to the moral, mental, and political improvement of the people of color," it endured until 1841, edited at first by Samuel E. Cornish, then by C. P. Bell and James McCune Smith, and finally by Charles B. Ray. In 1838 came the first attempts at magazines, the *Mirror of Liberty*, edited and published in New York by David Ruggles, and the *National Reformer*, edited by William Whipper and published in Philadelphia by the American Moral Reform Society.

More and more as the Negro progressed in building up a civilization of his own in the United States he became awake to the fact that he had had a past, a culture of his own, a tradition in which he could feel pride. Benjamin Lundy's admonition uttered in 1831 did not fall upon deaf ears:

Rouse ye! and shew to your traducers, beyond the power of contradiction, that the African bosom yet glows with the generous emulation that erst nourished the arts and sciences to maturity in Ethiopia and Egypt,—while Asia made less pretensions to knowledge and moral grandeur, Europe was involved in Barbarism, and America was unknown to the civilized world.[18]

Negro personalities in other lands who had arisen above slavery and degrading social barriers became the subjects of orations and published articles. Henri Grégoire's defense of the Negro, *De la littérature des nègres*, published

in an English version in Brooklyn in 1810, was a source of
frequent quotation. A similar work, also popular among
the Negroes, was A. Mott's *Biographical Sketches and Interesting Anecdotes of Persons of Color,* published in New
York in 1826. Stories of the lives of such eighteenth-century
Negro personalities as Benjamin Banneker, Phillis Wheatley, and Gustavus Vassa were told and retold. But the
Negro hero making the greatest appeal was Toussaint
L'Ouverture, the "Haitian Washington," who in 1794
formed the first independent Negro government outside of
Africa. From the time of his tragic death, due to the treachery of Napoleon, the account of Toussaint L'Ouverture's
exploits was again and again brought before the readers of
whatever Negro authors in America produced, whether
pamphlets, sermons, or articles in newspapers. The white
antislavery publications, particularly Lundy's *Genius of
Universal Emancipation* and Garrison's *Liberator,* did
much toward awakening a racial pride in the Negro. In
the course of 1831 a large number of Phillis Wheatley's
poems were reprinted in the *Liberator.* In the same publication appeared several poems by John Boyd, a self-taught
Bahaman Negro, whose imitations of Milton rival in skill
Phillis Wheatley's imitations of Pope. Yet, in spite of all
that was being done to bring about a consciousness of cultural potentiality in the Negro, the two great modern figures
who might have inspired pride were entirely neglected.
Alexandre Dumas, the father, whose drama, *Henri III et
sa cour,* brought the author immediate fame when it was
produced in Paris in 1829, was comparatively unknown in
America before 1840. Likewise unrecognized was Alexander Pushkin, who lived his life between 1799 and 1837,
and who published his *Boris Godunov* in 1825 and his *Eu-
gene Onyegin* in 1832. If Dumas and Pushkin had lived in

America, they would have been classed with the free Negroes. Neither was much less African in ancestry than Paul
Cuffe, and both were certainly more African in ancestry
than several among those who kept alive the American
Negro literature which had been so interestingly begun in
the eighteenth century.

In taking up the Negro writings of the period for discussion, it is necessary to consider first the work of those
who might be called the pioneer racial leaders. These fall
conveniently into three groups, belonging respectively to
Pennsylvania and Maryland, the state of New York, and
New England.

II

It was reported of the funeral of Bishop Richard Allen,
who died in 1831:

The immense concourse of coloured people, who attended the
funeral of this pious patriarch, exceeded perhaps anything of
the kind ever witnessed in this country. No other African
corpse, it is presumed, was ever attended to the place of interment, in America, by as great a number, or more sincere
mourners.[19]

Bishop Allen deserved such an honor. He was the first
American Negro to plan and build up an extensive national
organization which has proved practical and enduring in the
uplift of the colored race. If the title of "Father of the
American Negro" belongs to any one, it belongs probably to
Richard Allen. His place in a general history of the American Negro, or in a history of the Negro church, is of more
importance than his place in a history of Negro literature.
However, his position in his church demanded that he write
some things for publication; and, because of the rugged
pioneer honesty of the style in which they are produced,

they are things in themselves of such a character as to merit attention.

The main facts in the life of Richard Allen he gave us himself in a brief autobiography, written a few years before his death, but apparently not published until 1880, when it appeared with the title, *The Life, Experience, and Gospel Labors of the Rt. Rev. Richard Allen.* According to this account, he was born on February 4, 1760, the slave of a Philadelphian. When four years old, he was sold to a Delaware planter, a master so generous after his conversion to Methodism that he allowed his slaves the privilege of "working out" in order to accumulate enough money to pay for their freedom. By "cutting cord wood," laboring in a brickyard, and serving the American army as a wagoner for a while during the Revolution, Allen was on September 3, 1783, able to pay for his liberty. He had a few years before, when he was "upwards of twenty," become a Methodist. Describing his "conversion," he wrote:

One night, I thought hell would be my portion. I cried unto Him who delighteth in the prayers of a poor sinner, and all of a sudden my dungeon shook, my chains flew off, and, Glory to God! I cried.

The three years following his liberation he was a strolling preacher, conducting services for whites, it seems, as well as for blacks in New Jersey, Pennsylvania, and Maryland.

In 1786, he settled definitely in Philadelphia, and in that year he took a leading part in the events which led to the organization of the first independent Negro church in the North. A number of the blacks in Philadelphia, including Absalom Jones, Allen's friend, also a preacher, had for years been regular communicants at St. George's Church. At first the rear of the main floor was reserved for them, and later the gallery. Privilege to worship even there having been finally denied them, there was nothing for them to do except to leave St. George's entirely. That they did; and, led by Allen and Jones, and encouraged by prominent Philadelphia whites, among whom was Dr. Benjamin Rush, they established a church of their own, which Allen claimed to be "the first African church or meeting house that was erected in the United States." A majority of the members of the new congregation voted to remain Episcopalian. Therefore, Allen, always faithful to his Methodist affiliations, left the body, drew around him a number of sympathizers, and began holding services for his own congregation in a blacksmith shop. Although discouraged, unable at first to have his work recognized by the general Methodist Church of America, he remained undaunted. Determined, persevering, and patient, he fought for Negro Methodism until he saw it a success. In 1816, when the African Methodist Episcopal Church was established as a national organization, he was consecrated as the first bishop. From this time until his death, he enjoyed an esteem amounting almost to a veneration not only from Negro Methodists but from Negroes of all sects.

Allen was the earliest of many American Negro leaders whose careers prove as false the generally accepted theory that a spirit of submission is a racial characteristic found in all blacks. Unlike his contemporary Paul Cuffe, who showed himself a dreamer in his quixotic scheme for colonization, Allen was always practical. Moreover, he was a fighter. He struggled against economic barriers when he was a slave, and won out in saving enough money to pay for his freedom. He kept on struggling, and taught his race the good lesson of financial independence by leaving at his death a fortune of between thirty and forty thousand dollars. His method of fighting and teaching at the same time was not always direct; for example, to make his parishioners in Philadelphia feel everlastingly the sting of their delinquency in paying his salary, he formally bequeathed to them in his will the arrearages due him.[20] His opinions on all sorts of Negro problems were frequently asked; and he gave advice in courageous and unequivocal terms. The idea of African colonization he dismissed as visionary and impossible; Canadian colonization he favored, because he saw it as workable.[21]

But that which best shows Richard Allen as a practical man of courage is his first publication, part of the title being *A Narrative of the Proceedings of the Black People during the Late Awful Calamity in Philadelphia; and a Refutation of Some Censures Thrown upon Them in Some Late Publications.* The pamphlet, written in collaboration with Absalom Jones, was first printed in 1794.[22] The "late awful calamity" referred to in the title was the yellow-fever epidemic in Philadelphia in 1792 and 1793, and the "censures thrown upon" the blacks formed an important section of Matthew Carey's *Short Account of the Malignant Fever,* published in Philadelphia in 1793. Allen and Jones sought to make of their pamphlet a direct answer to Carey's charges that the blacks, since they were not so subject to the infection as the whites, should have done more in nursing the sick and burying the dead, that they should not have demanded such high wages for the services which they did render, and that, above all things, they should not have plundered and pilfered in the stricken homes where they acted as nurses and undertakers. Statistics are offered to prove that the proportion of blacks who suffered from the disease was as great as that of the whites. As to the charge that the Negroes took advantage of the opportunity to profiteer and steal and rob, Allen and Jones point out that Carey fled Philadelphia in terror when the plague came on, that he was too far away to know what was really taking place in the city, and that he had become the victim of malicious rumors. Dismissing the accusation as absurd, they ingenuously ask, "Is it a greater crime for a black to pilfer than for a white to privateer?" With the following stroke of irony, no doubt unconsciously executed, the answer to Carey is ended:

We shall now conclude with the following old proverb, which we think applicable to those of our colour who exposed their lives in the late afflicting dispensation—

"God and a soldier, all men do adore,
In time of war, and none before;
When the war is over, and all things righted,
God is forgotten, and the soldier slighted."

Among the miscellaneous bits printed in the pamphlet are "An Address to Those Who Keep Slaves and Approve the Practice" and "To the People of Color," in the latter of which are introduced some rough verses which Allen himself might have composed. *A Narrative of the Proceedings of the Black People* is as crude as a piece of printed writing might well be; but it is honest and courageous.

With the exception of this little work, in the composition of which Allen's part cannot be determined, and the autobiography, summarized above in the sketch of Allen's life, his published writings are few. *The Doctrine and Discipline of the African Methodist Episcopal Church* (1817), the joint work of Allen and Jacob Tapisco, is no more than a formulation of a ritual copying closely that used in the general Methodist Episcopal Church. A "Letter on Colonization," originally published in *Freedom's Journal* for November 2, 1827, quoted almost entirely in David Walker's *Appeal* (1829), and reprinted in full in the *Genius of Universal Emancipation* for April, 1831, is a brief and forceful exposition of Allen's opposition to African colonization. A few personal letters, of no value except as a reflection of Allen's direct manner of expression, have been recently printed.[23]

Such homespun sentences as the following abound in Allen's writings:

A great part of this work having been written many years after events actually took place, and as my memory could not point out the exact time of many occurences, they are, however (as many as I can recollect), pointed out; some without day or date.[24]

His education seems never to have advanced far beyond the elementary knowledge in reading and writing which he acquired, as he tells us, at the time of his conversion to Methodism. However, his writings are entitled to a place of distinction in Negro literature. The sense of absolute honesty which made him a success in practical living, which directed him in his labors as an organizer and executive, was the guiding force in whatever he wrote. It can be accepted with safety that the publications to which he gave his name are undoubtedly the product of an American Negro mind during the period when the free blacks in the United States were emerging as a self-sustaining social unit. His temperament, even though undeniably African, did not admit of that skillful imitation of the whites which has characterized the work of so many American Negro writers.

Because of his one important independent publication, Absalom Jones, whose name has so often been combined with Allen's, must be classed with the group of imitators. Like Allen, he was born a slave.[25] Reference has been made to the part which he played in the formation of the African Free Society, of his appointment as rector of the church of St. Thomas in Philadelphia, and of his collaboration with

Allen in writing *A Narrative of the Proceedings of the Black People*.[26] If the publication to which Jones's name alone is attached was written by him without aid, the progress which he made between 1794 and 1808 in building up a vocabulary in English and in mastering the requirements of standard usage in the language was a marvelous achievement. In the latter year there was printed in Philadelphia his *A Thanksgiving Sermon, Preached January 1, 1808, in St. Thomas's, or the African Episcopal Church, Philadelphia: on Account of the Abolition of the African Slave Trade*. As in the case of so many publications ascribed to the authorship of Negroes, there is no way of determining whether this work is of Jones's sole composition. The style bears no similarity to that of any passage of *A Narrative of the Proceedings of the Black People*. The simple directness, the concrete and vivid pictures, and the constant evidences of illiteracy found in the *Narrative* are replaced in the *Sermon* by an oratory, dignified and painfully pompous, not unlike that of many other uninteresting sermons which were delivered on the same occasion and afterwards printed and circulated as antislavery propaganda.[27]

The Reverend Daniel Coker, Richard Allen's chief rival for the bishopric at the time of the establishment of the African Methodist Episcopal Church, is remembered more for his work as a promoter of colonization of blacks to Africa than for his prominence as a pioneer preacher. His two publications, *A Dialogue between a Virginian and an African Minister* (1810) and the *Journal of Daniel Coker* (1820), indicate that his education was far superior to that of Allen. According to a tradition, he was unpopular with the early Negro Methodists as a national group because he was a mulatto, his mother being an English woman and his father a pure African.[28] However, he was not unpopular in his native city, Baltimore, where his advancement of Negro Methodism probably surpassed that of Allen in Philadelphia.[29] His *Dialogue* is an ingeniously arranged and well written antislavery tract. The *Journal*, a record of a voyage to Africa, where Coker went in 1820 under the sponsorship of the Maryland Colonization Society,[30] shows no attempt at finish. But it has interest; and it is the work by which Coker's name was kept alive, obviously with slight favor by the later Abolitionists who saw in the Maryland Colonization Society a strong proslavery organization.[31]

A Philadelphia Negro leader who was to be regarded as a hero by the Abolitionists was James Forten, as staunch a fighter for the civil rights of the Negro as Richard Allen was for the religious rights.[32] Of free parentage, Forten was born in Philadelphia on September 2, 1766, when, according to one of his funeral eulogists, "there were not ten free colored families in the city."[33] Whatever schooling he had was received at the institution founded in Philadelphia by Anthony Benezet for the training of colored children. Service as a "powder boy" with the Patriot Navy and an apprenticeship at sail-making in Philadelphia during the years immediately following the Revolution prepared him for his life's occupation, the manufacture of sails. We are told that in 1798, when he was thirty-two, he had saved a sufficient amount of money to buy out his employer's business and that within a few years he was a man of considerable wealth, employing in his factory "twenty-five apprentices and a large number of hands." Economically independent, he was in a position to be of great service to his race; and in whatever promised the welfare of the Negro, Forten was actively interested down to the time of his death in 1842.[34]

As important a figure as Forten was in the affairs of his

people for almost half a century, the place which he has been accorded in Negro literature might be one which he does not really deserve. There is at least one brief publication which we can identify as exclusively his, a smoothly worded "Letter," written in his old age and published in the *Liberator* for September 17, 1841. "An Address to the Humane and Benevolent Inhabitants of the City and County of Philadelphia," published in the *Minutes of the Proceedings of a Special Meeting of the Fifteenth American Convention Held in Philadelphia, December 10, 1818,* was the joint work of Forten and Russell Parrott, a young colored man of Philadelphia, who was in 1818 a student of theology.[35] The *Address,* a plea for the general rights of the Negro, is fervid and vigorous. It is impossible to decide how much of it can be attributed to Forten. However, the style has a simple strength which is wholly lacking in an independent publication by Parrott, *An Address on the Abolition of the Slave-Trade* (1816). Tradition has named Forten the author of a work really significant in Negro literature, *Letters from a Man of Colour,* published anonymously in Philadelphia in 1813. Forten was undoubtedly the logical colored man in Philadelphia at the time to produce the *Letters.* His possible desire for anonymity is understood when one bears in mind the fact that the sails which he manufactured were sold to white clients and that the content of the *Letters* is of a dangerous controversial character. Several recent commentators have unquestionably accepted him as the author of the work.[36] But if it was really written by him, he maintained anonymity so successfully that today there seems to be no absolute evidence to prove his authorship.

The *Letters from a Man of Colour* was published as a protest against a bill introduced into the legislature of

Pennsylvania early in 1813, according to the provisions of which further immigration of free persons of color was to be prohibited. The sponsors of the bill feared what they called a "black invasion." Each year an increasing number of free Negroes from the South and other sections were coming to settle permanently in Pennsylvania, believing that in that state the Negro enjoyed greatest liberty.[37] The bill was left unconsidered at the close of the 1813 session of the legislature, but there was possibility that it would be taken up for consideration at the succeeding session. While discussion of it was at an agitated stage, the *Letters from a Man of Colour* appeared. It was planned in general after the numerous epistolary controversial works popular in America from the pre-Revolutionary days of John Dickinson's *Letters from a Farmer in Pennsylvania*. Explaining his position in publishing the *Letters*, the author said:

They are the simple dictates of nature and need no apology. They are not written in the gorgeous style of a scholar, nor dressed in the garments of literary perfection. They are the impulse of a mind formed, I trust, for feeling, and smarting under all the rigours which the bill is calculated to produce.

The "rigours" are gone into with elaborated detail; the attempt is apparently made to arouse the reader to a conviction that the future complete annihilation or secure sustenance of the Negro race depends upon the passage of this particular bill. But behind all of the exaggerated oratory there rings a tone of sincere indignation such as no American Negro had before put into writing. The black man is crying out for what he calls a natural place in the society into which he has been dragged. This natural place is defined as a position in which a man is made safe against legalized discrimination because of his color. Regarding the framers of the Constitution who worked on the principle that "all men are created equal" it is said,

They knew we were deeper skinned than they were, but they acknowledged us as men, and found that many an honest heart beat beneath a dusky bosom.

Arguing for a continued and everlasting recognition of the principle of civil equality, the author asks,

Are we not sustained by the same power, supported by the same food, hurt by the same wounds, wounded by the same wrongs, pleased with the same delights, and propagated by the same means? And should we not then enjoy the same liberty, and be protected by the same laws?

The protest might have had some influence on the Pennsylvania legislature; for the bill which it attacked so warmly was never taken up for consideration.

The author of the *Letters* estimated the style rightly when he said that the booklet was "not dressed in the garments of literary perfection." There are frequent inaccuracies of expression. The diction is homely, and the phrasing unimaginative. A quotation from Addison used as a motto for "Letter I" seems indeed out of place in a work which is so decidedly unliterary. But there is a sincerity in the mood which gives genuine strength. If Forten did not write the booklet, the author must have been a colored man of stable character.

Another Negro to be placed with the Philadelphia group of progressive fighters was a son-in-law of James Forten, Robert Purvis, who was born free in Charleston, South Carolina, in 1810. At an early age he was sent by his white father, a wealthy merchant, to Philadelphia, where he was given a sound private education. His father willed to him an easy competence, and he lived his life as a man of means. Attacked in 1853 by Frederick Douglass on account of his riches, called "blood-stained" because they had been inherited from a Southerner, Purvis replied in a public letter:

As touching the matter of the *'blood-stained riches'* to which this shameless ingrate and base slanderer alludes, I have but to say, that my father (from whom I inherited my property) was never a slave-holder—that he made his money as a merchant, by honest mercantile pursuits—and was known while living as a friend and benefactor of the free and enslaved colored man, (as there are now living witnesses to testify). My own early detestation of slavery was owing, doubtless, to the seeds implanted in my bosom by my revered parent, by furnishing me with Dr. Torrey's Portraiture of Slavery and the work entitled 'Sanford and Merton.' But why pursue this matter? A life's consistent hatred of slavery in every form, a willingness, to the best of my ability, to do and suffer with my oppressed brethren, to maintain a reputation unspotted before the world, and thereby live down the calumnies of the enemies of our race, is, in the fury and violence of this meanly ambitious man and foulmouthed slanderer, of no account.[38]

Purvis lived up to what he claimed for himself in this letter. Even though he was of so fair a complexion that he was mistaken by many (among whom was Daniel O'Connell, the Irish patriot) as a white man,[39] he proudly identified himself with the colored race, and throughout his long life was active in whatever pointed to the uplift of his people. He lived until 1898, and much of his activity in behalf of the Negro belongs to the period after the Civil War. However, he began his work at such an early age that he is properly grouped with the pioneer racial leaders.

He might have been considered compromising and conciliatory by the radical Frederick Douglass in 1853, but a work of his published in 1838 is of an outspoken directness which Douglass might have envied. This work was entitled *Appeal of Forty Thousand Citizens Threatened with Disfranchisement to the People of Pennsylvania.* Legislative action to deprive the Negroes of Pennsylvania of the vote was proposed, a convention of the people of color to voice a protest was called, and the *Appeal* was drawn up by Purvis as chairman of a committee selected for the purpose. Originally published as a pamphlet, it was reprinted in the antislavery journals and freely circulated.[40]

The argument, like that of *Letters from a Man of Colour,* is a reminder of Revolutionary principles. While in the earlier work the declaration that "all men are created equal" is made a sort of text, in the *Appeal* the main theme is the "taxation without representation" idea. Maintaining that it is only for "the industrious, peaceable, and useful part of the colored race that we plead," Purvis offers the following as proof of what members of this constructive class are accomplishing:

That we are not neglectful of our religious interests, nor of the education of our children, is shown by the fact that there are among us in Philadelphia, Pittsburg, York, Westchester, and Columbia, 22 churches, 48 clergymen, 26 day schools, 20 Sabbath schools, 125 Sabbath school teachers, 4 literary societies, 2 public libraries, consisting of about 800 volumes, besides 8,333 volumes in private libraries, 2 tract societies, 2 Bible societies, and 7 temperance societies.

Of the part played by the Negroes of the past in building up the state of Pennsylvania it is said:

Our fathers shared with yours the trials and perils of the wilderness. Among the facts which illustrate this, it is well known that the founder of your capital, from whom it bears the name of Harrisburg, was rescued by a *colored man,* from a party of Indians, who had captured and bound him to the stake for execution.

The *Appeal,* only eighteen pages in length, is too brief to furnish convincing support of all the points offered in the argument for the rights of free suffrage of the Negro property holders in Pennsylvania. But the firmness of the style makes the pamphlet a valuable contribution to the great mass of Negro controversial writing.

Purvis' publications began as early as 1834, when probably the first of his open letters appeared in the *Liberator*.[41] In 1836 his *A Tribute to the Memory of Thomas Shipley, the Philanthropist*, a memorial discourse of the conventional uninteresting type, was published in Philadelphia. His *Letters and Speeches*, an incomplete collection published without date, contains an interesting reply to a claim made by Bayard Taylor that the Egyptians were not Negroid. But none of his writings equal in strength the brief *Appeal*, produced when he was twenty-eight years of age.

By the time that Robert Purvis began his long career as a fighter for his race, another Pennsylvania Negro of considerable wealth, William Whipper, emerged as a leader of a different type. Nurtured evidently in Garrisonian doctrines, he was certainly interested in the emancipation of his enslaved compatriots, but perhaps equally interested in fantastic notions about world peace and general moral reform. In attacking the abuses of drunkenness and slavery, he chose indirect weapons, such as the encouragement of the patronage of free-labor and temperance stores.[42] He came into public notice as early as 1833, when he published in Philadelphia *Eulogy on William Wilberforce*, a trying example of bombastic oratory. In 1835, he was active in the organization of the American Moral Reform Society, made up exclusively, it seems, of persons of color.[43] When this society began the publication of an organ, the *National Reformer*, Whipper was named as the editor. The first number appeared in September, 1838, and monthly issues came regularly through at least December, 1839.[44] The little magazine is of interest only as one of the pioneer efforts at Negro journalism. Its reform policies were, however, so general that it can hardly be identified as a Negro publication. This is also true of Whipper's most ambitious attempt at writing, a rather elaborate essay entitled "An Address on Non-Resistance to Offensive Aggression," which was published serially in the *Colored American* in 1837.[45] The thesis is stated thus: *"Resolved,* That the practice of non-resistance to physical aggression is not only consistent with reason, but the surest method of obtaining a speedy triumph of the principles of universal peace." The resolution is defended with a strong sense of logic. The argument is firm and concise. The style is simple, not marked with the bombastic wordiness of the *Eulogy on William Wilberforce.* The essay measures up well with the articles on the same subject which abound in the *Liberator* and other reform journals of the time. It is interesting to note that the editor of the *Colored American,* Samuel E. Cornish, did not fail to recognize the sentimentality of the thesis. He wrote in introducing the essay to his readers:

We publish this address with pleasure, hoping our readers will make the most of all the principles and arguments presented in favor of universal "Peace." But we honestly confess that we have yet to learn what virtue there would be in using moral weapons, in defense against kidnappers or a midnight incendiary with a torch in his hand.

There remains one other name, that of Prince Saunders, to be considered with the Pennsylvania group. Since his death in 1839, most of the commentators who have referred to Saunders have accepted him as Haytian and have not made any investigation of his remarkable knowledge of the English language. As a matter of fact, he was American, born and reared in Vermont.[46] About 1806, he was the teacher of a free colored school in Colchester, Connecticut. Later he emigrated to Hayti, and in time became a minister of education in Henri Christophe's government. In 1816, he was in England, a sort of plenipotentiary of Christophe; and in that year he brought out in London his *Haytian Papers,* a sizable volume made up of translated extracts from the *Code Henri* and other Haytian laws, with generous notes and comments apparently of Saunders' own composition. On his return to Hayti, he was dismissed by the capricious Christophe; and in June, 1818, we find him in Boston, ready for the publication of the American edition of the *Haytian Papers.* By September of that year he had taken up his residence in Philadelphia, where he engaged in lecturing and preaching until the new government set up in Hayti after the fall and dramatic suicide of Christophe in 1820 made it advantageous for him to go back to his adopted country.[47] He once more arose to power in Hayti, and at the time of his death he was the Attorney General.

Saunders' first publication in Philadelphia, *An Address Delivered at Bethel Church . . . Before the Pennsylvania Augustine Society, for the Education of People of Colour,* appeared in print in 1818. It is a piece of platitudinous generalization, written in a pompous and highly affected style, with no practicable suggestions for the improvement of education among the American Negroes. *A Memoir Presented to the American Convention for Promoting the Abolition of Slavery,* published in Philadelphia later in the same year, is similar in spirit and in style. It is more interesting, however, because it is more revelatory of the author's character. It is filled with flattery for all Philadelphians, white and black; and no opportunity is missed by Saunders to draw attention to his own importance, his close personal intimacy with the great English Abolitionists, including Clarkson and Wilberforce, and his services for the kingdom of Hayti, for the official American recognition of which he introduces an exaggerated plea. Saunders was an opportunist, and his experiences at Christophe's court had made him a sycophant. He was far remote in character from men of the sincerity of Allen and Forten and Purvis.[48] The editor of the *Emancipator* in announcing his death referred to him as a "humbug, fathered and flattered by none in America except the Colonizationists."[49] But the obstacles which he overcame in following up his career, however unworthy it might have been, prove that he was a man of extraordinary ability.

III

Although the state of New York, in which the slaves were not entirely freed by law until 1827, had never been known for such liberalism toward the colored race as Pennsylvania was reputed to show, the advance of the Negro in the city of New York between 1790 and 1840 was perhaps more pronounced than in Philadelphia. In the separate church movement, in education, and in the promotion of antislavery and Negro welfare organizations, the colored people of New York were most active. Indeed, it may be said that with the establishment of Negro journalism in New York in 1827 that city became what it has remained, the great center of American Negro cultural progress.

Among the early leaders who developed there, Peter Williams, Jr., stands easily as the most interesting and perhaps the most important. He was born in New Brunswick, New Jersey, during the Revolution. His father, Peter Williams, Sr., a slave, was purchased in 1783 by the John Street Methodist Church of New York. He was straightway liberated; but he preferred to look upon this church always as his "master," and remained in its employ as sexton until his death in 1823.[50] Although he could neither read nor write, Peter Williams, Sr., was an important figure in the establishment of Negro Methodism in New York.[51] His son, precocious as a child, was in some way trained for the Episcopal priesthood, and was in 1820 ordained a clergyman and appointed rector of St. Philip's Church in New York, which he served until the year of his death, 1840. During the decade between 1820 and 1830 no other New York Negro was held in such high respect and esteem as Peter Williams. However, because of his reluctance in taking a firm stand in the arguments over African colonization, his reputation as a defender of his race went into decline during the last ten years of his life.[52]

Williams' three extant publications embrace a sufficient lapse of years in his life for us to form some opinion of his mental growth and changes. The first, *An Oration on the Abolition of the Slave Trade,* was printed as a pamphlet in 1808. On the last page are given testimonials to prove that the work, with the exception of a "few immaterial verbal alterations," was entirely of Williams' composition. The piece throughout is written in an unrestrained oratorical style, of which the following quotation is suggestive:

> Rejoice, Oh! Africans! No longer shall tyranny, war and injustice, with irresistible sway, desolate your native country: no longer shall torrents of human blood deluge its delightful plains: no longer shall it witness your countrymen, wielding among each other the instruments of death; nor the insidious kidnapper, darting from his midnight haunt on the feeble and unprotected: no longer shall its shores resound with the awful howlings of infatuated warriors, the death-like groans of vanquished innocents, nor the clanking fetters of wo-domed captives. Rejoice, Oh, ye descendants of Africa!

The next publication, *A Discourse, Delivered on the Death of Capt. Paul Cuffe,* which was printed late in 1817, opens with a dread apostrophe to death, which hints that Williams

might have been reading Bryant's *Thanatopsis,* published a
month earlier than the date of delivery of the *Discourse.*
He soon passes from empty sentimentalizing over mortality,
and presents a simple and neat sketch of Cuffe's life. And
in the conclusion of the piece, in which he attempts to point
the morals to be derived from Cuffe's career, he surprises
the reader by remaining specific and failing to drop into
such verbosity as tempts most orators who are called upon
to moralize. His third publication, *Discourse Delivered
. . . for the Benefit of the Coloured Community of Wilberforce, in Upper Canada,* printed in 1830, is his best piece of
writing. It shows that the young dreamer who had seen
in the suppression of the Slave Trade a millennium for the
Negro has turned into a man fatigued with the hard reali-
ties which the blacks in the United States in 1830 were
forced to face. Even though it has the offending purple
patches of popular oratory, it is an eloquent protest against
the abuses to which race prejudice in New York had sub-
jected the Negro. In the end, there is a clear presentation
of the working plans for the Negro colony in Canada, which
is given Williams' enthusiastic endorsement. However, in
his mild allusions to the African Colonizationists, whom he
does not denounce as a pack of rascals in league with the
slaveholders of the South, but whom he sees as a group of
well-meaning but ill-advised men, Williams began to dis-
please his race. In spite of the spirit in which it was received, the last *Discourse* is a work of mature thinking,
which entitles Williams to an important place among
American Negro orators.

He was not the only author of occasional orations to be
counted among the New York Negroes of the period. When
he delivered his *Oration on the Abolition of the Slave
Trade,* he was introduced to his audience by Henry Sipkins,

who at the time of his death, in 1838, was characterized as the "Jefferson of the Negroes."[53]   On January 1, 1809, when he was no more than nineteen years of age,[54] Sipkins delivered his own *Oration on the Abolition of the Slave Trade,* simpler and perhaps better than Williams' speech on the same subject given in the same church a year earlier.[55]   But apparently nothing from Sipkins' pen got into print after he grew into maturity, and we do not know why he was called the "Jefferson" of his people.   His name appears as a member of a committee appointed at a meeting held in New York in September, 1833, to arrange for a memorial service for William Wilberforce, who had died on the previous July 29. The orator chosen for the occasion was Benjamin F. Hughes, principal of a free colored school in New York. Hughes's oration was subsequently published under the title of *Eulogium on the Life and Character of William Wilberforce, Esq.*   The word *eulogium* used in the title and the opening sentence, "The praises of departed greatness have ever been said or sung, in the lofty tones of the orator, or in the enchanting strains of the poet," suggest the mood of the speech.   The freeing of the slaves in New York stirred Nathaniel Paul, the Negro minister of a colored Baptist church in Albany, to produce *An Address Delivered on the Celebration of the Abolition of Slavery in the State of New York,* published as a pamphlet in 1827.[56] It is fortunately not the only work by which we can judge Paul's talents as a writer.   His letters to the *Liberator*— written mostly from England, where he went late in 1831 in the interests of the Negro colony in Wilberforce, Canada, with which he was afterwards directly connected—prove that he could control the emotions which he poured unstintingly into the 1827 *Address.*[57]

It was not until Peter Williams' 1830 speech, delivered

in support of the Negro colony in Canada, that we have from a New York Negro a direct protest against the abuses which the blacks in America, slave and free, were suffering. With the rapid growth of antislavery activities between 1830 and 1840 such protests came frequently. Nothing apparently provoked more the opposition of New York colored men of independent mind than the idea of African colonization. James Forten's declaration in Philadelphia in 1817 that the Negroes "would never leave the land" became a rousing slogan for those fighting against the colonization movement.[58] All of the New York leaders, with the exception of the compromising Peter Williams and the outspoken protagonist for colonization, John B. Russwurm, were to be classed among the anti-Colonizationists. No one of them wrote more strongly on the question than Theodore S. Wright, a Presbyterian minister in charge of a colored congregation in New York. His "Address," delivered at a meeting of the New York State Anti-Slavery Society held at Utica on September 20, 1837, is a clear and vigorous arraignment of the whole colonization plan. In a work published three years later, *The Colonization Scheme,* written jointly by Wright and Samuel E. Cornish, the main argument attempts to answer completely the contention often made by the Colonizationists that the Negro could never "rise" in a land where he was greatly in the minority. The ironic mood of the style is suggested by the following "Prayer of a Colonizationist," ingeniously introduced:

We thank thee, O God, for the success which has thus far attended the efforts which have been made to raise up and increase prejudice against the work of thy hand in the person of our colored brethren; carry it on to a full consumation; but if this cannot be granted, change, thou, then their color, and in all things pertaining to their form and visage let the work of thy Infinite Wisdom be so modified as to adapt itself to the prejudices of us, a happier and more favored portion of the race—that we may, thus, be persuaded to love them as brethren belonging to the great family thou hast made.

Equally satiric is the absurd picture of Christianity among the American slaves, an answer to the claim made by the Colonizationists that if the Negroes were returned to Africa the entire population there would be converted to Christianity. It is unfortunate that we cannot determine what the contribution of each collaborator was in this admirably written little treatise.

Wright was not so old or so reactionary as to be lost in the radicalism of the Negro leaders after 1840. A third publication, *An Address to 3,000 Colored Citizens of New York*, which appeared in 1846, the year before the author's death, is a spirited plea to the blacks who had settled on lands donated to them by Gerrit Smith to prove themselves worthy of their benefactor.

But among Wright's publications nothing has such interest as his earliest bit of printed writing, an open letter addressed to Dr. Alexander, of the Princeton Theological Seminary, where Wright received his training for the ministry. At the ceremonies of the Princeton commencement in 1836 he was present as an alumnus. According to one report of the occasion, he was "brutally attacked and actually kicked out of the chapel, by the son of a southern slaveholder, a member of the junior class." The letter which Wright wrote to the head of the seminary regarding the matter was published in the *Emancipator* for October 27, 1836. It should be considered a little classic among Negro writings. In every respect a gentleman's comment on a personal insult and injury, it is the reflection of a clean and well-disciplined mind.[59]

Samuel E. Cornish, Wright's collaborator in writing *The Colonization Scheme,* was another New York Negro of the period who acted with no compromise in defending the rights of his race. In 1837, he spoke of having been for seventeen years a resident of the city of New York, and of having been a minister of the Presbyterian Church for twenty-five years.[60] In 1840, he was in charge of a colored congregation in Newark, New Jersey.[61] In 1831, he had acted as agent in a movement, which proved unsuccessful, for the establishment of a "collegiate school on the manual labor system," probably the Negro's first attempt at industrial education.[62] But his important work in the interests of his race was in the field of journalism. He has with justice been called the father of the American Negro newspaper. Reference has been made to his connection with *Freedom's Journal, Rights for All,* and the *Colored American.* With the exception of occasional signed editorial comment, it is impossible to decide what his contributions to his papers were. But it is probably due mainly to his merit that *Freedom's Journal* was made a fairly complete organ of the colored people of the United States in 1827 and that the *Colored American* met surprisingly well the standards which had been set by the average antislavery newspapers by 1837.

John B. Russwurm, Cornish's colleague in his first journalistic venture, was in the eyes of many of his contemporaries, a man of an exactly opposite character. There was apparently nothing for Cornish but praise; Russwurm, however, was considered a traitor. Even before the first issue of *Freedom's Journal,* an offer had been made for his services in the work of the American Colonization Society.[63] At first he refused; but in the issue of *Freedom's Journal* for September 5, 1827, one week before Cornish's resignation from the paper was announced, there is comment on colonization which indicates that Russwurm was yielding. By 1831, after he had been in Africa long enough to establish the *Liberia Herald,* he was being generally denounced in the American antislavery press as one who had "sold his birthright for a mess of pottage";[64] and thereafter most of the Negro leaders looked upon his name as one of opprobrium.[65] Russwurm's positively identified writings published in America are too slight to entitle him to a place of importance in Negro literature. He should be remembered as one of the founders of American Negro journalism. But his real work in behalf of his race was done in Liberia, where he was for many years a leader of distinction.[66]

The most fearless and the most radical of the New York Negro leaders of the period was David Ruggles, who, according to all reports, was of pure African ancestry. His writings show that he was a man of considerable education. He at least once referred to himself as a minister.[67] But regarding the means by which he obtained his training and the extent of his work in the church apparently nothing is known. We hear of him as early as 1833, when he was on a lecture tour of western New York and Pennsylvania.[68] In the following year he appeared on the scene of Negro action in the city of New York, publishing *The "Extinguisher" Extinguished.* By 1838 he was being freely commented on in the New York newspapers for his work as secretary of the Committee of Vigilance.[69] The aims of this body, made up of about one hundred persons, were "to protect unoffending, defenceless, and endangered persons of color, by securing their rights as far as possible, by obtaining for them when arrested, under the pretext of being *fugitive slaves,* such protection as the law will afford." The work which Ruggles was called upon to perform as secretary of the

committee was of a kind to merit the title later accorded
him, "the first promoter of the Underground Railroad."
Among the fugitive slaves passing through New York who
were given assistance by him was Frederick Douglass.[70]

Ruggles' writings, whether in his two small books or in
the magazine which he founded or in the occasional letters
which he contributed to the antislavery newspapers, are
always controversial. In 1834, two publications appeared
in New York for which he provided an answer. One of
them was Dr. David M. Reese's *A Brief Review of the First
Annual Report of the American Anti-Slavery Society*, and
the other was Herman Howlett's *An Address on Slavery
and against Immediate Emancipation*. The fighting mood
of Ruggles' answer, which was published in the same year,
is suggested by the title, *The "Extinguisher" Extinguished,
or, David M. Reese, M. D., Used Up*. Ruggles' "big-stick"
method of dealing with the mild and loosely defended argument against the American Anti-Slavery Society set forth
by Dr. Reese justifies the term "used up." Characteristic
of Ruggles' manner of attack is his reply to Reese's claims
that the Abolitionists approve intermarriage between whites
and blacks. "What of it?" retorts Ruggles. "It is certainly
not repugnant to nature." Less brusque in replying to
Howlett's defense of colonization, he argues:

History cannot point us to a colony so well calculated to chris-
tianize the heathen as the colony of Puritans which landed upon
the rock of Plymouth in 1620. And where are the pious Indians that can refer to the Puritans as their spiritual fathers in
Christ Jesus? The soil that was once peacably pressed with
their footsteps, has been drenched with their blood; they are
hunted down and driven from mount to mount like the wild
beasts of the forest.

Four years after *The "Extinguisher" Extinguished* was
published, an anonymous attack on the American Anti-

Slavery Society appeared in New York, entitled *An Appeal to the Reason and Religion of American Christians,* of which Ruggles suspected Reese as the author. Therefore, he forthwith published a reply, *An Antidote for a Poisonous Combination Recently Prepared by a "Citizen of New York," alias Dr. Reese.* Applying the process of elimination in arriving at the conclusion that Reese wrote *An Appeal,* Ruggles reasons—

This pamphlet—charged with scurrility, abuse, and falsehood, is, I suspect, an emanation from my old friend, Dr. Reese. I may be pardoned this surmise when I declare that the thing is so like him, that it is either his own or a counterfeit—and who would counterfeit Dr. Reese?

Having finished the claim that Reese had used anonymity because he had feared such a cudgeling as he had received in *The "Extinguisher" Extinguished,* Ruggles proceeds to the attack more vigorously than ever. He uses all of his old weapons, his thrusts being premised by the following, which refers to Reese's pamphlet:

It is extremely shallow, unspeakably low, and abusive, and so illogical and absurd in its pretended arguments as to remind the reader forcibly, that the author was exemplifying the words of the poet which he quotes, "Whom God wishes to destroy he first makes insane!"

No American Negro before Ruggles, with the exception of David Walker, whose work will be discussed below, was so vituperative in his protests for the rights of his race. But there is such a straining after an effect of wit in his writings that the outraged anger which he no doubt sought to express is submerged. His magazine, *Mirror of Liberty,* of which it is doubtful that more than two numbers, those for August, 1838, and January, 1839, ever appeared,[71] is almost entirely made up of contributions from Ruggles' own pen. These

are mainly notices and comment regarding his work as secretary of the Committee of Vigilance, done in the antagonistic
style which marks the attacks on Dr. Reese. The distinction of the publication in Negro literature is that it was in
all probability the American Negro's first attempt at a magazine, having preceded by one month Whipper's *National
Reformer*. In 1842, Ruggles' health became so impaired
that he was obliged to give up his work in New York. He
went to Northampton, Massachusetts, where he first became
a member of the abolition community, the Northampton
Association of Education and Industry, and then the pro-
prietor of a successful water-cure establishment.[72] Until
the year of his death, 1849, occasional letters from him
appeared in the antislavery papers, showing that he was by
no means in the rear guard of fighters in this fighting decade, that his message to his race still was—

> Know ye not who would be free,
> Themselves must strike the first blow![73]

IV

From the days of Phillis Wheatley there has not been
a decade when there was not some New England Negro who
aspired to authorship. During the period from 1790 to 1840,
the Negroes of New England, possibly because they were
less numerous, developed no such centralization of activities
as marked the progress of the colored race in Pennsylvania
and New York. However, some of the best known and
most able Negroes of the period came out of New England.
Paul Cuffe, a native of southeastern Massachusetts, has
been taken as a suitable symbol for the Negro leader of the
period. Reference has been made to the Haytian career of
Prince Saunders, who was born in Vermont. Charles B.

Ray, who controlled the destinies of the *Colored American* during its last years, was reared in Falmouth, Massachusetts. Mention has been made of the work of Prince Hall, for many years a citizen of Boston, in the founding of Negro freemasonry. Although they lived in a comparatively isolated environment, the New England Negroes had by 1840 contributed in a great measure toward the advancement of the American Negro culture which was slowly and humbly being formed.

Paul Cuffe wrote nothing intended for publication. However, one of the communications which he sent back from Africa to his friends in New York was printed in 1812 as *A Brief Account of the Settlement and Present Situation of the Colony of Sierra Leone.* Moreover, the journal which he kept on his voyage to Africa and a number of his letters have been preserved in manuscript.[74] *A Brief Account* tells us of the geography of Sierra Leone, of the schools maintained for the inhabitants, and of the courts of justice. It is a singular little document, written in a compact style. There is about it the mood of stern sincerity. The manuscript letters, more than fifty in number, including one to President Madison, dated May 23, 1812, and one to James Forten, dated "8 mo. 14. 1815," were mostly written in the interests of colonization. The first entry in the journal, which embraces forty-three closely written foolscap pages, is for December 4, 1810, when Cuffe was in Philadelphia making the final arrangements for his first tour of inspection to Sierra Leone. The last entry is for May 22, 1813, shortly after Cuffe had landed at Westport, Connecticut, on his return from the voyages abroad, which included the trip direct to Sierra Leone, then a trip to Liverpool, a return to Sierra Leone, and the voyage back to the United States. The entries are scattered and brief. The following, recording incidents of the year 1811, are typical:

1 mo. 20th. 19 days out from Philadelphia to Sierra Leone. Our minds were collected together to wait on the Lord notwithstanding we were on the great deep.

2 mo. 2. At three A. M. wind and sea struck us down on our beam ends, washed John Masters overboard, but by the help of some loose rigging he regained the ship again.

2 mo. 21st. The dust of Africa lodged on our rigging. We judged that land to be about twenty-five leagues off.

Throughout the letters and the journal the English is faulty. But there is a charm in the quaint Quaker phrasing. And the simplicity and directness reveal the staunch seaman and ardent servant of his race that Paul Cuffe was.

Cuffe was half Indian. A contemporary of his, Prince Hall, a Negro leader whose service for his race was to be more effective and enduring, was of a mixed French, English, and Negro ancestry. Born in the Barbadoes, in 1748, Hall migrated to America in his youth, was converted to Methodism, became the minister of a church in Cambridge, Massachusetts, and in 1787, after years of interesting effort, received a charter from the Grand Lodge of England for the first Negro Masonic Lodge organized in the United States.[75] "Our Patron and Our Founder" the Negro Masons call him today. One of his Masonic sermons, *A Charge Delivered to the African Lodge, June 24, 1797, at Metonony, Mass.*, has come down to us. Although Hall was probably more English or French than he was Negro, his utterances in *A Charge* are what is conventionally accepted as African in mood. There is such a lugubrious undertone in the pictures of the monotony of slavery as one finds in the spirituals; and there is also the *jubilee* theme so prominent in the folk songs of the Negro. After mournfully reviewing the blighting ignorance of the colored population of the United States, Hall appeals to the Negro's native adaptability for patient endurance. He picturesquely says, referring to the neglected blacks:

So in the observation of the heavenly bodies, this same class without a telescope or other apparatus have through a smoak'd glass observed the eclipse of the sun: One being asked what he saw through his smoak'd glass? said, Saw, saw, de clipsy, or de clipseys:—and what do you think of it?—stop, dere be two;—right, and what do they look like—Look like, why if I tell you, they look like two ships sailing, one bigger than tother; so they sail by one another and make no noise. As simple as the answers are they have a meaning and shew, that God can out of the mouth of babes and Africans shew forth his glory; let us then love and adore him as the God who defends us and supports us and will support us under our pressures, let them be ever so heavy and pressing. Let us by the blessings of God, in whatsoever state we are, or may be in, to be content; for clouds and darkness are about him; but justice and truth in his habitation; who hath said, Vengeance is mine and I will repay it, therefore let us kiss the rod and be still, and see the works of the Lord.

The admonition "let us kiss the rod and be still" was by no means to be heeded by the progressive Negroes who were soon to arise in New England.

Chief among these was David Walker, who in 1829 published in Boston his famous *Appeal*, the most widely circulated work that came from the pen of an American Negro before 1840. Walker was born on September 28, 1785, in Wilmington, North Carolina. His father, who was a slave, died before his birth; and he was brought up, without learning to read and write, by his mother, a free woman. His own words regarding the place where he passed his childhood were:

If I remain in this bloody land, I will not live long. As true as God reigns, I will be avenged for the sorrow which my people have suffered. This is not the place for me—no, no. I must leave this part of the country. It will be a great trial for me to live on the same soil where so many men are in slavery; certainly I cannot remain where I must hear their chains con-

tinually, and where I must encounter the insults of their hypo-
critical enslavers. Go, I must.[76]

The time when he left the South seems to be unknown.
According to his own statement, it was in Boston that he
learned to read and write.[77] By 1827 he was a small clothing merchant there, and in 1828 was prosperous enough to
marry. The publication of the *Appeal* in 1829 brought him
an immediate notoriety. Even some of the most advanced
Abolitionists turned against him. Benjamin Lundy said of
the *Appeal:*

A more bold, daring, inflammatory publication, perhaps, never
issued from the press of any country. I can do no less than
set the broadest seal of condemnation on it. Such things can
have no earthly effect than to injure our cause.[78]

Within a year the *Appeal* went through three editions, the
last containing supplements still more radical and revolutionary in spirit than the original. Shortly after his work
on the third edition was finished, Walker suddenly died.
The rumor that he was poisoned by some one who sought
to receive a reward supposedly offered for his head by
southern slaveholders has never been proved nor disproved.[79]

From the time the *Appeal* was published until after the
turmoil created by Nat Turner's insurrection had settled
down, Walker's name was prominent in the public eye. His
book was broadly circulated, especially in the South. Its
reception in one southern state, North Carolina, was described as follows:

If Perkins' steam-gun had been charged with rattle-snakes, and
shot into the midst of a flock of wild pigeons, the fluttering could
not have been greater than has recently been felt in the eastern
part of this state by a few copies of this perishable production. . . . When an old negro from Boston writes a book and
sends it among us, the whole country is thrown into commo-
tion.[80]

Governor Owen of North Carolina and Governor Giles of Virginia, spurred on by the dangerous tone of the *Appeal*, sent special messages to their legislatures regarding it.[81] The governor of Georgia wrote to the mayor of Boston requesting firmly that the book be suppressed.[82] Naturally, with such attention drawn to it, the Negro authorship of the book was questioned. William Lloyd Garrison, who, like Lundy, disapproved of Walker's radicalism, made the following statement about the authorship, a conclusion which still seems tenable :

Mr. Walker was personally unknown to us; but we are assured, by those who intimately knew him, that his Appeal was an exact transcript of his daily conversations; that, within the last four years, he was hurtfully indefatigable in his studies; that he was not "vulgar," either in manners or language; and that he was a blameless professor of religion. The historical facts which he has collected were too familiar to have required extraordinary research. Besides, the internal evidence of the pamphlet clearly substantiates its authorship.[83]

The structure of the work is planned roughly after that of the Constitution of the United States, the complete title being *Walker's Appeal, in Four Articles; together with a Preamble, to the Coloured Citizens of the World, but in Particular and Very Expressly to Those of the United States of America, Written in Boston, State of Massachusetts, Sept. 28, 1829.* The "Preamble" begins thus :

Having travelled over a considerable portion of these United States, and having, in the course of my travels, taken the most accurate observations of things as they exist—the result of my observations has warranted the full and unshaken conviction, that we, (coloured people of these United States), are the most degraded, wretched, and abject set of beings that ever lived since the world began; and I pray God that none like us ever may live again until time shall be no more.

After describing with vivid details this most unhappy lot of the American Negro, and after laying the responsibility for such wretchedness upon those whom he ironically styles "Christian Americans," Walker ends the "Preamble" with a statement of his purpose in writing, publishing, and circulating the book:

But against all accusations which may or can be preferred against me, I appeal to Heaven for my motive in writing— who knows that my object is, if possible, to awaken in the hearts of my afflicted, degraded, and slumbering brethren, a spirit of inquiry and investigation respecting our miseries and wretchedness in this *Republican Land of Liberty!*

"Article I," in which Walker continues the description of the sufferings of the Negro begun in the "Preamble," contains an interesting digression on the subject of intermarriage between whites and blacks. He says, in the homely style which is repeatedly mixed in with attempts at high oratorical effect:

I would wish, candidly, before the Lord, to be understood, that I would not give a *pinch of snuff* to be married to any white woman I ever saw in all the days of my life. And I do say it, that the black man, or man of colour, who will leave his own colour (provided he can get one, who is good for anything) and marry a white woman, to be a double slave to her, just because she is *white,* ought to be treated by her, as he surely will be, viz: as a NIGER ! ! !

"Article II," devoted to the subject of education for the Negro, is firmer as argument. After describing, at times with humor, the ignorance of members of his race, Walker admonishes them:

Be looking forward with thankful hearts to higher attainments than *wielding the razor and cleaning boots and shoes.*

"Article III" is a satiric indictment of American Christianity, which, Walker says, passes over slavery with only the Biblical reminder, "Servants, obey your masters!" and fails to recognize that in slavery rests "the fountain head of all evils in America." In "Article IV" he discusses what he considers the baneful effect which African colonization would have on the American Negro. In support of his argument, he quotes from Richard Allen's "Letter on Colonization," which had been originally published in *Freedom's Journal*. It is interesting to observe that throughout the *Appeal* Walker pays tribute to only two American members of his race, Richard Allen, for whom he expresses great admiration, and Samuel E. Cornish, whose newspaper, *Rights for All*, he highly recommends. The *Appeal* ends with a crude prayer in verse, possibly of Walker's own composition; and tacked on as a sort of postscript are one of Wesley's hymns and a quotation from the *Book of Common Prayer*.

The third edition of the *Appeal*, dated 1830, the last brought out by Walker himself, contains frequent "Additions," notes bearing little logical relation to the passages to which they are supposed to refer. It is the lack of logical arrangement throughout the book that marks it as the work of a rhapsodic and untrained imagination rather than that of a schooled thinker. The allusions to characters and events out of the Bible and ancient history are, as Garrison claimed, "too familiar to have required extraordinary research." The style, as the quotations given above indicate, often lapses into the colloquialism of a man who has lived his life among the lowly. Since no external evidence to the contrary exists, there is little reason to doubt that Walker, ingenious enough to break away from the environment in which he had been brought up, intelligent enough to find his way into a successful business in the locality which he selected for his residence, and serious enough to apply himself to a study of the history of his race, was the independent author of the *Appeal*. It was the emotionalism with which he put his very soul into his style that made his work so provocative. Other Negro writers before him had been as extreme in crying out against what they felt as white oppression, and many after him have been much bolder in urging the defense of what they consider their rights. Walker's *Appeal* came at a dramatic moment in the history of the American Negro. It breathed the very life of an unhappy and outraged black at a time when the general public could only with difficulty comprehend that a Negro might express himself. Therefore, it created a sensation. That it was Walker's one great gesture of service for his race, that it came just at the end of his life, and that there is still felt the vague possibility that it occasioned his death, have made him in the eyes of American Negroes perhaps their most favored martyr.

Eight years later than Walker's *Appeal*, there was published in Boston a Negro work equally radical in thought. However, it seems to have been ignored by the public. The full title is *A Treatise on the Intellectual Character and Civil and Political Condition of the Coloured People of the United States, and the Prejudice Exercised towards Them.* The author, Hosea Easton, a minister, residing in Hartford at the time he wrote the preface, said of himself—

I wonder that I am a man; for although the third generation from slave parents, yet in body and mind nature has never been permitted to half finish her work. Let all judge who is in the fault, God, or slavery, or its sustainers.[84]

His decision to go into a special study of the American prejudice against people of color was made, as he said, during a trip of investigation through Massachusetts, Connecticut, and New York to find out why Negroes did not attend the churches. His conclusion was that in the white churches they "were made to feel different."[85] Study of the psychological aspects of this condition led him in time to write *A Treatise,* an example of reasoning which proves that, contrary to his own opinion, nature really had in producing him more than half finished her work. In the essay, about sixty pages in length, he exhibits a clear logical sense. His method of treating his subject is suggested by the following, written in reference to nature:

All must confess she possesses a mysterious power to produce variety. We need only visit the potato or corn patch, (not a costly school), and we shall be perfectly satisfied; for there in the same hill, on one stalk, sprung from one potato, you may find several of different colours; and upon the same stalk you may find two ears, one white or yellow, and the other deep red; and sometimes you may find an astonishing variety of colours displayed on one ear among the kernels; and what makes the observation more delightful, they are never found quarreling about their colour, though some have shades of extreme beauty. If you go to the field of grass, you will find that all grass is the same grass in variety; go to the herds and flocks, or among the feathered tribes, or view nature where you will, she tells us all that we can know, why it is that one man's head bears wooly, and another flaxen hair.

Following this, he says:

Mind can act on matter, but matter cannot act upon mind; hence it fills an entirely different sphere; therefore, we must look for a cause of difference of intellect elsewhere, for it cannot be found in nature.

In such a manner he reasons, arriving finally at the conclusion that it is public sentiment fostered by an undemocratic education that scorns the black, not because of his color but because of his condition of servitude.

Having thus established his thesis, he proceeds to a

defense of the intellectual capacities of the Negro, pointing, it must be confessed with less historical accuracy than enthusiasm, to the black man's cultural past in Egypt and Ethiopia and to the part he played in the dissemination of ancient civilization. It is in this section of *A Treatise* that one finds even a bolder radicalism than Walker had uttered in the *Appeal*. For example, Easton declares that

the European branch of Japhet's family have but very little claim to the rank of civilized nations. From the fourth up to the sixteenth century, they were in the deepest state of heathenish barbarity. Their spread over different countries caused almost an entire extinction of all civil and religious governments, and of the liberal arts and sciences. And ever since that period, all Europe and America have been little else than one great universal battlefield. . . . It is true that there is a great advance in the arts and sciences from where they once were; but whether they are anywhere near its standard, as they once existed in Africa, is a matter of doubt. . . . The Egyptians have done more to cultivate such improvements as comport to the happiness of mankind than all the descendants of Japhet put together.

Easton was a Negro standing firmly and proudly on his own feet. That his *Treatise* did not attract the attention created by Walker's *Appeal* was probably due to its limited circulation. It contains enough of the insurrectionary to stir up excitement.

In a note at the end of *A Treatise* Easton announced the future publication of a second book, to be called *Lectures on Civil, Social, and Moral Economy*. If this book was ever printed, no copy seems to be extant. *His Treatise* remains what he claimed for it, his "mite, contributed for his afflicted brethren."

In 1836, one year before the publication of Easton's *A Treatise*, R. B. Lewis, a Bostonian of mixed Negro and

Indian ancestry,[86] copyrighted his *Light and Truth, Collected from the Bible and Ancient and Modern History, Containing the Universal History of the Colored and the Indian Races, from the Creation of the World to the Present Time.* The book was not published until 1844, when it was issued in Boston by a "Committee of Coloured Gentlemen." It is a volume of more than four hundred pages, made up of a chaotic mass of pseudo-historical facts. The author accepts as positive truth the legend that the American Indians are descendants of the lost tribes of Israel, and in some way reasons that they are therefore the only true American Christians. Among the celebrated Negroes of antiquity he places Hannibal, Pompey, Plato, Epictetus, and Boethius. After he has devoted three chapters to biographical sketches of "modern eminent colored men," among whom he includes Gustavus Vassa, Ignatius Sancho, Phillis Wheatley, Hosea Easton, and David Walker, he brings in two chapters in which he attempts to trace the history of the ancient Arabians and Hebrew prophets. The phrasing is as wild as the arrangement of the contents. The most homely idiom is placed by the side of a Latin quotation from Seneca, or a French quotation from Voltaire. Throughout is that strained sonorousness characteristic of a primitive Negro sermon. If any unified impression is produced by the book, it is that the author was seeking to display with true fireworks effect his mad erudition. *Light and Truth* has, however, some claim to distinction in Negro literature. It is the first of the long line of books produced by Negroes which seek to give information about their prominent leaders, works which we shall have occasion to consider in succeeding chapters. Moreover, it is the first extensive effort of an American Negro to dig into the story of his past.

Chapter III

BIOGRAPHY, POETRY, AND MISCELLANEOUS
WRITINGS, 1790–1840

In eighteen hundred and twenty three
They said their people should be free!
It is wrote in Jeremiah,
Come go along with me!
It is wrote in Jeremiah,
Go sound the jubilee!

—Quoted in Martin R. Delany's *Blake,*
or, The Huts of America, 1859

I

The organizers of the Negro society that was being developed in the United States between 1790 and 1840 were not the only members of the race who during the period wrote things for publication. There was another group of writers made up of individuals representing various sections of the country. These became authors by chance. Like their predecessors in the eighteenth century, they worked usually without knowing what other promising Negroes were doing. Among their publications are books, pamphlets, and newspaper articles, forming a greater volume of writing than that produced by the better known racial leaders. There is interest in the work of these obscure authors. For if an American Negro of the early nineteenth century wrote at all, he was an unusual person with something out of the ordinary to say.

That unique and problematical type of Negro writing, the slave narrative, so well represented in the eighteenth century by *The Interesting Narrative of the Life of Olaudah*

Equiano, or Gustavus Vassa, has in no generation been absolutely dead in America since the accounts of the adventures of Briton Hammon and John Marrant were published respectively in 1760 and 1785.[1] However, the type did not become progressively alive until about 1835, when white fiction writers recognized its possibilities.

With the exception of Richard Allen, no one of the racial leaders whose work has been surveyed recorded the story of his life. As we have observed, Allen's autobiography lay in manuscript until probably 1880. Three other narratives written between 1790 and 1830 came from the most unexpected sources. Abraham Johnstone, who was born a slave in Delaware and who later became a free laborer in New Jersey, was on July 8, 1797, hanged at Woodbury, New Jersey, having been convicted of the murder of a man of his own race. It was claimed that on the morning of his execution he handed out from his dungeon a crude narrative of his life. The account, containing much incidental protest against slavery and injustice for the blacks, was before the end of the year 1797 published in Philadelphia as *The Address of Abraham Johnstone.* It is impossible to trust the narrative as more than one of those sensational pre-execution confessions of which there is a great abundance in American pamphlet literature. The real author, whoever he was, was even thoughtless enough to put into the mouth of Johnstone, who is continually bewailing his illiteracy, such sentences as, "I fear that I become too speculatively refined in my sentiments." In 1798, a more trustworthy Negro autobiography, *A Narrative of the Life and Adventures of Venture, a Native of Africa,* was published at New London, Connecticut.[2] Venture is represented as relating the story when he was sixty-five years of age, and the homeliness of the idiom indicates that he might have had a faithful amanuensis.[3] He tells us that he was something of a giant, "weighing three hundred pounds and measuring six feet around the waist." According to tradition, popular tales about Venture's great size and strength were current in certain communities of Long Island and Connecticut as late as 1896.[4] The little autobiography which he is supposed to have dictated might have, therefore, a folkloristic value. Less readable is the *Narrative of the Most Remarkable Particulars in the Life of James Albert Ukawsaw Gronniosaw, an African Prince, as Related by Himself,* published in Leeds, England, in 1814. According to the account, Gronniosaw, living in England under the guardianship of the Countess of Huntingdon's Calvinistic Methodist circle at the time of the composition of the *Narrative*,[5] had been a slave in New York. In relating the story of his experiences he was too preoccupied in describing what he owed to Bunyan and Baxter's *Call to the Unconverted* to give us many of the "remarkable particulars" promised in his title.

With the rapid development of the abolition movement at the time of the founding of the *Liberator* and the formation of the American Anti-Slavery Society, slave narratives, recognized as excellent propaganda for the cause of abolition, were published more and more frequently. A number of them are merely biographical sketches written by whites about Negroes. A volume of fair size, *The Missionary Pioneer; or, A Brief Memoir of the Life, Labours, and Death of John Stewart, (Man of Colour,) Founder under God of the Mission among the Wyandotts at Upper Sandusky, Ohio,* was published in New York in 1827. The author was not named.[6] The book contains a letter, dated May 25, 1817, attributed to Stewart, and his "Address" to the Indians whom he has converted from Catholicism, in which appears the characteristic passage:

If you persevere in the way of well doing, you will find in your path clusters of sweet fruits, that will satisfy your hungering souls, and being faithful to your Lord's commands, when you have made your way through much tribulation, and lie down on your dying bed, you will be filled with the glorious prospects of the reward that awaits you; guardian angels wait around your bed, to bear your soul away to those bright worlds of everlasting day, where the friend of poor sinners reigns.

In 1832, a "Lady of Boston" published her *Memoir of Mrs. Chloe Spear, a Native of Africa, Who Was Enslaved in Childhood, and Died in Boston, January 3, 1815.* Memoirs of Phillis Wheatley by Margaretta Matilda Odell and B. B. Thatcher appeared in 1834.[7] The anonymous *Incidents in the Life of Solomon Bayley,* an account of a slave who bought himself, turned Quaker, and went as a colonist first to Hayti and then to Liberia, was published in Philadelphia some time between 1836 and 1839.[8] The *Memoir of James Jackson* (1833), written by Susan Paul, is the story of a child who died at the age of seven, "a very interesting colored Sabbath school scholar."

Narratives published as "dictated" were the most popular, and some of them we can probably trust as being authentic relations of fact. The *Anecdotes and Memoirs of William Boen* (1834) is the account of a colored New Jersey Quaker, published at the instigation of a "monthly meeting of Friends."[9] Boen counted John Woolman as one of his best friends, and was so true to the strict teachings of the Quakers that he "thought it right to have all his clothing of the natural colours, and made very plain and simple." His piety was a handicap when he related the story of his life; for the account is on little besides his rather flat religious experiences. *Memoirs of Eleanor Eldridge* (1838), written in the third person by an unnamed biographer, is the complaint of a New England colored woman who had never been a slave but-who claimed that she had been "cheated out of her fortune because of prejudice against her color."[10] Eleanor Eldridge seems to have found indirect authorship profitable: she was in Philadelphia early in 1839 selling her book,[11] and in the preface used for the 1846 and 1847 editions it is said: "Ellen will go forth with her little book in her hand; and will any one who can afford himself the luxury of kindness refuse to purchase it?" Her sentimental tale of woe inspired at least one poem, "The Hard Fate of Poor Ellen."[12] It is a relief to turn from Eleanor Eldridge's wail to the vigorous *Recollections of Slavery*, attributed to a "Runaway Slave" when it was published as a serial in 1838 in the *Advocate for Freedom*.[13] It presents pictures of plantation life in South Carolina along with a fugitive's adventures in escaping to freedom. While there is no doubt exaggeration in the description of the hardships of slavery, the narrative as a whole seems honest. The style has every mark of illiteracy, and the editor of the *Advocate for Freedom* in concluding the *Recollections* published an attestation affirming that the story was really dictated by the man whose experiences it recounts and that it was committed to writing in approximately his own words.

But such attestations cannot, of course, be trusted too far. Two years before the publication of *Recollections of Slavery* was begun, *The Slave; or, Memoirs of Archy Moore*, was published anonymously in Boston. It was at first received by the antislavery public as a true relation of facts; but it was later identified by Richard Hildreth, the historian, as his own story of a purely fictional hero.[14] An equally well written and in many respects a more exciting romance, *Slavery in the United States: a Narrative of the Life and Adventures of Charles Ball, a Black Man* (1836), was never claimed as his own by the undoubtedly skilled writer who produced it. Lydia Maria Child wrote of the two books in a letter to Garrison:

It is said in your paper that some think Charles Ball equal to Archy Moore. The extracts I have seen from Charles Ball are certainly highly interesting; and they have a *peculiar* interest, because an actual living man tells us what he has seen and experienced; while Archy Moore is a skillful grouping of incidents which we all know are constantly happening in the lives of slaves. But it *cannot* be equal to Archy Moore! Why, it does not belong to the same year, scarcely to the same age, to produce two such books. If I were a man, I would rather be the author of that work than of anything ever published in America.[15]

As a matter of fact, *Archy Moore* was probably as much an actual history as *Charles Ball*. In the introduction to the latter, the recorder of the story claimed to be related by Ball is called "Mr. Fisher." But that person never made his real identity clear. Indeed, the book has a notorious reputation as a work of deception. It was reprinted in its original version as late as 1853; but in 1858 it appeared in a new form with the title *Fifty Years in Chains; or, The Life of an American Slave,* sufficient changes having been made to bring Ball's story up to date and the following prefatory remarks having been provided:

The story which follows is true in every particular. Responsible citizens of a neighboring State can vouch for the reality of the narrative. The language of the slave has not at all times been strictly adhered to, as a half century of bondage unfitted him for literary work. The subject of the story is *still a slave* by the laws of this country, and it would not be wise to reveal his name.[16]

A third obviously deceptive narrative published before 1840 is Charles E. Lester's *Chains and Freedom; or, The Life and Adventures of Peter Wheeler, a Colored Man Yet*

Living (1839). Although it pictures Peter Wheeler in slavery, "on the deep sea," in love, and "at the cross," it has none of the exciting interest of *Archy Moore* and *Charles Ball*. These three books show the slave narrative merging into the type of fiction which was to reach its highest a little more than a decade later in Harriet Beecher Stowe's *Uncle Tom's Cabin*.[17]

But the most interesting deceptive narrative of the period was a forgery of a singular type. It is the *Narrative of James Williams*, undoubtedly dictated by a Negro known as James Williams and committed to writing by none other than John Greenleaf Whittier. But the story which Whittier unwittingly recorded as true was later found out to be a work out of Williams' own imagination.

Early in 1838, Whittier was in New York, often in the home of John W. Hill, "whose house was the resort of the slave and the slave's friend."[18] Among the Negroes who came under Hill's protection at this time was James Williams, a supposed fugitive, who claimed that he had been a slave in Virginia and Alabama, and that he had with great difficulty escaped from the latter state. His story was considered so valuable as propaganda for the emancipation cause that it was committed to writing by Whittier and published by the American Anti-Slavery Society as the dictated *Narrative of James Williams*, the amanuensis not being named.[19] The little book was freely circulated throughout the country;[20] a copy was sent to each member of Congress,[21] and very soon it attracted attention in the counties in Virginia and Alabama where Williams claimed he had been held in slavery. Residents of these counties challenged the story as untrue, and the executive committee of the American Anti-Slavery Society began an investigation.[22] Having defended the work as a true and honest

recital of actual experiences until the evidence from the
South proved without a doubt that it was false, the committee was forced to yield; and in October, 1838, the circulation of the *Narrative* was ordered suppressed.[23]

The controversy over Williams was the sensation of the
year in the antislavery press. In a letter published in the
Emancipator for September 20, 1838, Whittier wrote:

We have examined the southern testimony; and, while we
candidly admit that it has created a doubt in our mind of the
accuracy in some minute particulars of the statement made by
the fugitive to several gentlemen in this state and in New York,
(and which was written down from his lips by ourself), we
are still disposed to give credit in the main to his narrative.
We perceive by the last Emancipator, that some additional
testimony in favor of the veracity of the fugitive is to be
expected. We shall wait for it with anxiety; and, in the
meantime, shall be glad to hear further from Alabama. Our
cause needs no support of a doubtful character; and if the
narrative in any essential particular is untrue, the slaveholders
of Virginia and Alabama would confer a favor upon us by
immediately producing testimony to that effect.

He seems to have published no statement after the *Narrative* was suppressed. Indeed, he seems to have made no
written allusion to his connection with it until late in life,
when, in a letter dated March 6, 1886, he said:

I think the story of my writing the life of an escaped
slave—James Williams at Friend Hill's in Water St., N. Y. is
correct. Prof. Follen of Harvard University and a friend of
his an Italian patriot refugee were with me. I remember the
latter drew the slave's portrait. I think this was in the summer
of 1837.[24]

Long before the controversy over his *Narrative* came
on, James Williams had been sent to England, to be insured
against capture as a fugitive slave.[25] What his real life

was before he first told his story in Pennsylvania late in 1837 is not known,[26] and his experiences after he arrived in England are a like mystery.[27]   That he was gifted with a remarkable imagination no one who reads his *Narrative* can deny. With vivid and strikingly realistic detail he pictures his supposed early life as a favorite servant in the home of a wealthy and aristocratic Virginian. But the fate which he has always dreaded befalls him: he is sep- arated from his wife and children and carried away with two hundred and thirteen other slaves to a plantation in the "desolate Alabama country." Here, as a confidential "driver" for his master, he observes atrocities. A Negro is torn to pieces by bloodhounds; another is allowed to die in stocks after he has been tortured by having the claws of a maddened cat drawn up and down his back; one who refuses to be whipped is murdered outright by an infuriated overseer who then morbidly indulges himself in an orgy of beating, one slave after another being brutally attacked. Spurred on by a letter from his wife, Williams makes a dash for freedom; and, "guided by the north star," he winds his hazardous way through Alabama, Georgia, the Carolinas, Virginia, and Maryland. The story which he told had already been told in *Archy Moore* and *Charles Ball*, and it was to be related hundreds of times again. But it is perhaps nowhere else made so simple and credible. Wil- liams was a rare person. He not only had the wit to dupe his protectors; he had also the ingenuity to make up a highly interesting and impressive tale of adventures. Of his deceived amanuensis it is only necessary to say that, except in the brief preface, there is little hint of Whittier's hand in the style of the *Narrative*.

The reception given the *Narrative of James Williams* upon its appearance was most enthusiastic.[28]   Before it was ordered suppressed, three editions had been printed. It is doubtful whether its circulation was ever actually stopped. After the controversy over it had died down, it was again listed for sale among the books sponsored by the American Anti-Slavery Society.[29]   Yet book collectors today find it an exceedingly rare item.

There remains for discussion one more important Negro autobiography published between 1790 and 1840, the *Narrative of the Adventures and Escape of Moses Roper, from American Slavery* (London, 1837).[30]   It is scarcely less interesting than James Williams' story, and it has the great added merit of most probable authenticity.   Roper had been in England for almost three years when his *Narrative* was published.[31]   And practically all of that time he had been in school.[32]   William Lloyd Garrison said of him: "With Moses Roper we are somewhat acquainted, and can testify to the uprightness of his character and the intelligence of his mind."[33]   Dr. T. Price, the English clergyman who provided a preface for the *Narrative,* said of the composition: "It is his own production, and carries with it internal evidence of truth."[34]   The homely English in which the book is written might certainly have been that of the man whose story is told.

According to the account, Roper was born in Caswell County, North Carolina.   His mother, he claimed, was a mulatto slave, and his father her master.[35]   The most interesting passage in the book is perhaps the description of a drama supposed to have been enacted in his master's house soon after Roper's birth.   His mistress, jealous of his mother, attempts to stab him in order to get revenge. His master, overcome with dread as to what might be the outcome, sells the mother and child into a distant part of the state.   Situations of this sort were to be made the very

essence of antislavery fiction. The account continues with
the separation of Roper and his mother. He is sold to
first one master and then another, and is thus able to observe slavery in North Carolina in all its forms, which he
describes as at times almost pleasant and at other times
most brutal. Always rebellious, sensitive over the taunts
which he receives because of his fair skin, he makes many
attempts to escape. Finally, he gets to Savannah, thence
to New York by boat, and to Boston; and in the fall of
1835, after what he describes as a flight extending over
sixteen months, he arrives in Liverpool. His serious religious character and quick intelligence win friends for him
in England, and he is sent to school to be trained to go as
a missionary among the Negroes of the West Indies.[36] But
probably his most enduring service to his race was what is
to all appearances the sincere telling of the story of his
life in slavery.

II

Negro poetry between 1790 and 1840 is represented
mainly by the work of a North Carolina slave, George
Moses Horton. There are few other names to consider.
Two of the prose writers who have been discussed, Richard
Allen and David Walker, were the possible authors of
doggerel hymns.[37] In *Freedom's Journal* for June 8, 1827,
appeared a little poem, called "The Black Beauty," copied
from the *New Haven Chronicle*. It was claimed that the
anonymous author was a "son of Africa." Not only is the
poem a confessed imitation of *Solomon's Song*, but also an
interesting reminder of William Blake's "The Little Black
Boy," which the author in all probability did not know. The
poem expresses so simply the romance of religion for the
Negro mind that it deserves to be quoted entire.

Black I am, oh! daughters fair!
But my beauty is most rare.
Black, indeed, appears my skin,
Beauteous, comely, all within:
Black when by affliction press'd,
Beauteous, when in Christ I rest;
Black, by sin's defiling blood,
Beauteous, wash'd in Jesus' blood;
Black I am in my own eyes,
Beauteous in my Lord's I rise:
Black I am to men, 't is true,
Beauteous in the angel's view:
Black, if Jesus frowns a while,
Beauteous, when I see him smile;
Black, while in the tomb I lie,
Beauteous, when I mount the sky.

One characterized as a "young lady of color," who wrote under the name "Ada" and who dispatched her contributions from Philadelphia, had a number of poems published in the *Liberator* during its early years. Her pieces, thin imitations of the popular sentimental antislavery verse of the period, add little to Negro poetry.[38] Other verse by Negroes published in the antislavery newspapers of the time is by Phillis Wheatley, George Moses Horton, John Boyd of the Bahamas, and a "Colored Female of the Barbadoes."[39]

Possibly as strange a book as was ever printed in America, *The Rock of Wisdom . . . to Which Are Attached Several Interesting Hymns,* was published in 1833, the place of publication not being indicated.[40] The author, the Reverend N. C. Cannon, a "man of color," refers vaguely in the book to his boyhood spent with his father in Sussex County, Delaware, to a year passed "on the water" following the death of his father in 1813, and to a sojourn in Philadelphia, where the "vision" which was ever afterwards to attend him first came to him and commanded him to go forth and preach. He became a Methodist exhorter, and in turn a licensed preacher. His missionary strollings led him, it seems, as far as Zanesville, Ohio.[41] Cannon is not grouped with the poets of the period merely because of the fifteen hymns included in his book. He might easily have written them, among which there is one on slavery, called "Of the Christian's Barbarity," and another with this sounding climax:

> For this love let rocks and mountains,
> Purling streams, and crystal fountains,
> Roaring thunders, lightning blazes,
> Shout the great Messiah's praises!

Cannon's place among the Negro poets is fully justified by the section of his book printed as prose, the part to which the title, *The Rock of Wisdom,* belongs. More than a hundred pages in length, it is in the form of a letter to the African Methodist Episcopal Church, in which the author proposes to discuss prayer, to interpret parts of the Old Testament, to give a résumé of world history, and to devise a new and proper ritual for the Methodist marriage ceremony. If the scheme seems mad, the treatment is found to be still more mad. Cannon follows no line of thought; he is too occupied in sporting with distorted Biblical images and with swinging rhythms. Such an irregularly rimed passage as the following is suggestive:

And now, pious friends, when you have read these lines which have been penned by me, think of me in solemn prayer; let me be on land or sea, I intend to stand for liberty, for Christ has set me free.

Cannon was probably a faithful Methodist, unconscious of the true character of his guiding "vision"; it is not difficult for us to identify that "vision" today as the African muse of rhythm and song.[42]

George Moses Horton was guided by the same muse. But he was a more fleshly man than Cannon; indeed, if the comparison may be dared, he belongs as a poet to that psychological *genre* so well illustrated by the singing, life-drunk and wine-drunk François Villon and Robert Burns. Much gossip has been written about Horton, and in the maze of it all it is difficult to see just what was the true man. Likewise, it is difficult to determine just what were the main events in his strangely romantic life.

According to a brief biographical sketch accompanying the first volume of his poems, *Hope of Liberty*, published in Raleigh, North Carolina, in 1829, he had by that year reached the age of thirty-two. Thus, the date of his birth has been usually given as 1797. The place has been determined as a plantation in Northampton County, North Carolina.[43]   Of pure African descent, but, according to the description of some who knew him personally, of a brown rather than a black type, he was born a slave and remained one until the extinction of slavery in the United States, belonging to three different members of the family from which he received the name Horton.[44]   When he was six years of age, James Horton, his master at the time, moved to Chatham County, not far distant from Chapel Hill, the seat of the University of North Carolina. It was on a plantation in Chatham County that George Moses Horton grew up, in what was probably a mild form of slavery. Certainly he was allowed to attend "camp meetings," where Methodist hymns were stored in his memory word for word.

At what time and under what circumstances he was first permitted to stay in Chapel Hill to "hire out his time," paying his master, as tradition records, fifty cents a day for

the privilege, we do not know. All that we can accept as
a certainty is that for many years he was a familiar figure
to the students and faculty of the University of North
Carolina.[45] His first volume of poems had probably already
appeared in print before he went to Chapel Hill, and when
he became known there as the author of a published volume
he must have been regarded as something of a celebrated
curiosity. If reports to the effect may be accepted as true,
he gained some of the money to pay to his master for
his time in Chapel Hill by composing poems to order for
the students of the University. It has been said, "When
his employer was willing to pay fifty cents, his poem was
generously gushing; twenty-five cents procured one more
lukewarm in passion."[46] He no doubt earned much more
by working as a servant in the home of Dr. Caldwell, the
President of the University, with whose encouragement and
aid, we are told, he was taught to read and to commit to
writing the verses which he composed.[47] It seems that
Horton's extraordinary talent, perhaps because he was a
slave, perhaps also because he was often drunk, was not
taken seriously by any one in Chapel Hill after the death of
Dr. Caldwell in 1838. Tradition claims that he was paid
to compose verses by the young men of the University just
as another slave in Chapel Hill at the time was paid to allow
planks to be broken over his head.[48]

In the North, there was very early a strong sympathy
expressed for Horton, of which he perhaps knew nothing.
Some of his verses were possibly published in Boston newspapers before his 1829 volume appeared.[49] In introducing
his work to the readers of the *Liberator* in 1834, the editor
wrote:

The following lines, from the *Lancaster Gazette,* were written
by a Carolinian slave, named George Horton, whose education

was attained in hours stolen from sleep. The talents of the degraded race of black people appear better of late as they have been exhibited by the revolution in Hayti, than we have been accustomed to consider them; and from the power with which a few individuals have sprung up amid darkness and misfortunes, it seems probable that good opportunities for education, would in a few generations, give them a high standing among the nations of the earth. Look to it, statesmen![50]

Horton's case was looked into, but nothing was done except to print and reprint his verses, and to refer to his talent as stifled by slavery. In the first northern edition of *Hope of Liberty*, published in Philadelphia in 1837 as *Poems by a Slave*, the editor in a brief prefatory note hinted that the money realized from the sale of the original edition was kept by the North Carolina publisher, Weston R. Gales, for his own use. Gales ignored the hint in his reply, and merely stated that the amount obtained from the sale of the book was not sufficient for the purpose for which it was intended, namely, to secure enough money to pay for Horton's liberation and to satisfy his desire to go to Liberia as a colonist. Later, Horace Greeley was made interested in Horton, and published in the New York *Tribune* a versified plea for liberty which the slave poet had addressed directly to him. The mood of the plea is suggested by the two stanzas which follow:

> Bewailing 'mid the ruthless wave,
>   I lift my feeble hand to thee;
> Let me no longer be a slave,
>   But drop the fetters and be free.
>
>   .   .   .   .   .
>
> Then listen all who never felt
>   For fettered genius heretofore,
> Let hearts of petrification melt,
>   And bid the gifted negro soar.[51]

The editor of Horton's *Naked Genius* (1865), Will H. S.
Banks, a captain in the Federal Army, wrote of the conditions under which Horton finally obtained liberty:

Having no other hopes of freedom, our author was doomed to
remain in slavery, to toil without rest, under the unrelenting eye
of his master, till the occupation of Raleigh by our troops, when
he escaped to our lines for protection, and is now with the
writer hard at work both day and night composing poems for
his book, and writing acrostics for the boys on their sweet-
hearts' names, in which he takes great delight.[52]

At last a free man, Horton settled in Philadelphia. On August 31, 1866, a special meeting of the Banneker Institute of
Pennsylvania was held, "the object being to receive Mr.
George Horton, of North Carolina, a poet of considerable
genius."[53] Regarding his remaining years little is known.
The date of his death has been given as 1880, and also as
1883.[54]

Nothing speaks more convincingly of the advantages of
the poetic temperament for human happiness than the
strange career of this African slave. There was everything
in the world to crush him. But his verse shows that he
was care-free, filled with the irrepressible feelings of the
moment, that he was intoxicated with his own cleverness,
as Jupiter Hammon and Phillis Wheatley before him were
intoxicated with religion. A nice irony lies in all the talk
which his northern sympathizers stirred up about him. A
close examination of his writings is likely to lead one to the
conclusion arrived at by a southern commentator:

George never really cared for more liberty than he had, but he
was fond of playing to the grandstand. It was a common saying in Chapel Hill that Poet Horton owned Mr. Horton and
all but owned the president of the University.[55]

Horton's first volume, *Hope of Liberty* (Raleigh, 1829),
reissued as *Poems by a Slave* (Philadelphia, 1837), and

reprinted entire a third time in the *Memoir and Poems of Phillis Wheatley, a Native African and a Slave: Also, Poems by a Slave* (Boston, 1838), is made up of twenty-one pieces. It has been claimed that a volume of Horton's "miscellaneous poems was published at Hillsboro, North Carolina, in 1845 by Dennis Heartt, editor of the *Hillsboro Recorder*";[56] that "a volume of his verses along with his autobiography was published in Boston in 1852";[57] and that there were also volumes issued in 1850 and 1854.[58] If any of these were actually printed, they are apparently no longer extant.[59] So far as we know today Horton's poems which appeared in book form are contained in only two volumes, the second being *Naked Genius* (Raleigh, 1865), in which there are one hundred and thirty-two pieces. Among the published poems included in neither of these volumes are the plea for liberty referred to above as published by Horace Greeley in the New York *Tribune* and "The Pleasures of a Bachelor's Life," apparently printed for the first time in Kemp P. Battle's *History of the University of North Carolina* (1907).[60] There seems to be no foundation for the statement which has been made that Horton after he settled in Philadelphia syndicated for various newspapers prose versions of Biblical stories.[61] He undoubtedly contemplated publishing in 1865 an autobiography, to be called *The Black Poet*.[62] But there seems to be no evidence that the book was ever printed.[63]

Hope of Liberty contains pieces on religion, love, death, nature, and the author's own experiences as a slave and maker of verses. The volume opens with a hymn, "Praise of Creation," all of which is as imitative and affected as the first stanza:

> Creation fires my tongue!
>   Nature, thy anthems raise;
> And spread the universal song
>   Of thy Creator's praise!

"On the Truth of the Savior," an ingenuous attempt to
prove the reality of Christ's miracles, has such imagery as—

> At his command the water blushed,
> And all was turned to wine,
> And in redundance flowed afresh,
> And owned its God divine.

"Heavenly Love," on the powers of God's goodness, has the
following traditional Methodist conception:

> Love which can ransom every slave,
> And set the pris'ner free;
> Gild the dark horrors of the grave,
> And still the raging sea.

The one religious poem in the book based on an original
idea is "To the Gad-fly"—in which a gad-fly constantly
guarding a plow horse against the attacks of other insects
is likened to God watching over the soul of the poet! The
love poems are on such subjects as the "silence" of a young
lady who has been jilted, the despair of the bride who must
leave her parents, the "consequences of a happy marriage,"
and the farewell of a philandering lover. The three pieces
on death are poems of condolence, probably addressed to real
persons. The nature pieces are "Spring," "Summer,"
"Winter," and "On the Evening and Morning," in the last
of which appear the lines:

> When Evening bids the Sun to rest retire,
> Unwearied Ether sets her lamps on fire;
> Lit by one torch, each is supplied in turn,
> Till all the candles in the concave burn.
>
> . . . . .
>
> At length the silver queen begins to rise,
> And spread her glowing mantle in the skies,
> And from the swirling chambers of the east,
> Invites the eye to her resplendent feast.
>
> . . . . .

> Aurora's smiles adorn the mountain's brow,
> The peasant hums delighted at his plough,
> And lo, the dairy maid salutes her bounteous cow.

The three poems on slavery are less naïve, and therefore less interesting. Each develops the lament:

> Alas! and am I born for this,
>   To wear this slavish chain,
> Deprived of all created bliss
>   Through hardship, toil, and pain?

"On the Poetic Muse" is possibly more subjective.

> My towering thoughts with pinions rise,
>   Upon the gales of song,
> Which waft me through the mental skies,
>   With music on my tongue.

> And when the vain tumultuous crowd
>   Shakes comfort from my mind,
> My muse ascends above the crowd
>   And leaves the noise behind.

Naked Genius is a much more extensive, and at the same time a much more intimate, volume. Religion, love, death, nature, and slavery are again treated. And there is a most important addition, a true Negro conception of the fun in life. The crudities of *Hope of Liberty* might make us smile at Horton's posing as a poet; the bluntness of *Naked Genius* shows that he is laughing at himself with us. The book no doubt brings us close to what must have been the real character of the slave poet. The title suggests how delightfully conceited he was. In the second piece in the volume, "George Moses Horton, Myself," we are told, and not plaintively,

I feel myself in need
Of the inspiring strains of ancient lore,
My heart to lift, my empty mind to feed,
And all the world explore.
I know that I am old
And never can recover what is past,
But for the future may some light unfold
And soar from age's blast.

"The Art of the Poet" explains some of the problems which evidently did not puzzle Horton too much:

True nature first inspires the man,
But he must after learn to scan,
And mark well every rule;
Gradual the climax then ascend,
And prove the contrast to the end
Betwixt the wit and fool.

In the enormous and dreary mass of antislavery verse it is refreshing to come across such a metaphor as the following, which appears in Horton's "The Slave":

Because the brood-sow's left side pigs were black,
Whose sable tincture was by nature struck,
Were you by justice bound to pull them back,
And leave the sandy colored pigs to suck?

"The Woodman and the Money Hunter" was probably intended to be a contrast between the care-free lover of nature and the wealth-seeking man of the world, but it is interesting as a picture of an experience in which Horton doubtless many times in his life took part.

Then let us roam the woods along,
And drive the coon and coney;
Our lead is good, our powder strong,
To shoot the pigeons as they throng,—
But sing no more the idle song,
Nor prowl the chase for money.

The spirit of merriment which permeates the volume is perhaps strongest in such a poem as "The Creditor to His Proud Debtor," which contains the stanza:

> My duck bill boots would look as bright,
> Had you in justice served me right;
> Like you, I then could step as light,
>   Before a flaunting maid.
> As nicely could I clear my throat,
> And to my tights my eyes devote;
> But I'd leave you bare, without the coat
>   For which you have not paid.
>   Then boast and bear the crack,
>   With the sheriff at your back,
>   Huzzah for dandy Jack,
>   My jolly fop, my Jo!

A number of the poems are on Civil War figures, Confederate as well as Union.   Of Stonewall Jackson it is said,

> Hark! from the mighty hero's tomb,
>   I hear a voice proclaim
> A sound which fills the world with gloom,
>   But magnifies his name.

However, the tribute to Jackson is closely followed by "Jefferson in a Tight Place," in which Jefferson Davis is compared to a fox caught in a hunt.   One of the most often recurring themes in the book is, strange to say, the fickleness of woman.   And it is usually brought out with such humor as we find in the following lines:

> Woman, thou bloom of every danger,
>   From whose charms my sorrows rise,
> To thee I'd live and die a stranger;
>   He who shuns thee must be wise.

Horton's verse occupies a middle ground between the naturalness of Jupiter Hammon's pieces and such sophisti-

cated imitation as distinguishes the poems of Phillis Wheatley. Echoes of familiar Methodist hymns are heard throughout *Hope of Liberty* and *Naked Genius.* There are also
echoes of Pope, Byron, Tom Moore, Burns, and even Milton, all of whom Horton undoubtedly read or heard read.
But he did not have Phillis Wheatley's talent for absorbing
the music of great poets. He got it all mixed up, and
brought in much of his own invention. Therefore, one is
likely to hear in his verse a curious mingling of the rhythms
of "Come, Thou Fount of Every Blessing," *Paradise Lost,*
and the Negro folk song.

His imagery is a similar hodgepodge, made up of free
borrowings from the masters and homely conceits of his own
coinage. In "Gen. Grant, the Hero of the War," we have:

> To hold position in the field is thine,
> To sink in darkness, or to rise and shine.

In another poem, prosperity is personified and thus addressed:

> Meet me 'mid the wreathing bowers,
> Greet me in the citron grove,
> Where I saw the belle of flowers,
> Dealing with the bloom of love.

In "Lines, On Hearing of the Intention of a Gentleman to
Purchase the Poet's Freedom," Horton expresses his feelings over the possibilities of liberty as follows:

> 'Twas like the evening of a nuptial pair,
> When love pervades the hour of despair—
> 'Twas like fair Helen's sweet return to Troy,
> When every Grecian bosom swelled with joy.

In "The Loss of Female Character," he sees the prostitute
first like Jersualem fallen, then like a star wandered away
from "its cluster," and finally—

She looks like some Queen who has boasted in vain,
    Whose diamond refuses to glitter.

She looks like the twilight, her sun sunk away—
    He sets; but to rise again never!
Like the Eve, with a blush bids farewell to the day,
    And darkness conceals her forever.

In 1843, an unsuccessful attempt was made to have some of Horton's poems published in the *Southern Literary Messenger*.[64]   They are certainly not of a merit to be considered suitable for publication in a magazine of artistic standards. But because they are so pronouncedly inartistic, they are possibly today of greater interest than much of the verse which was printed in the *Southern Literary Messenger*.   In Horton's grotesque music and bizarre imagination something which is foreign to the Caucasian mind is delightfully revealed.   As veiled as it appears in his conventional hymn-like meters, it is easily recognizable.   For the Negro folk song has made it familiar.   Moreover, Horton's poems expose the author as a most interesting person.   They make us realize that a certain poetic temperament, that manifesting itself in an exuberance which no human force can crush, is as likely to appear in an African slave as in a roving French thief or a tippling Scotch peasant.

III

George Moses Horton, a slave in North Carolina, was no more remote from the movement for the advancement of the Negro in the United States between 1790 and 1840 than was the man who in many respects showed himself the most able colored American of the period, Lemuel B. Haynes, a minister of the Congregational Church.   Although he was born of a pure African father, Haynes never identified himself with the black race. He died in 1833, at the age of eighty. Evidence of the high esteem in which he was held by his denomination is the full-length biography, published in 1839, *Sketches of the Life and Character of the Rev. Lemuel Haynes, A. M.,* the work of Dr. Timothy Mather Cooley, one of the eminent Congregational ministers of the time. Lemuel Haynes's mother was white, a servant on a Connecticut farm. Abandoned by her when he was only a few days old, he was cared for in his earliest infancy by her employer, from whom he received the name Haynes.[65] One of those kind providences in which he put such great faith was apparently visited upon him when he was very young; for, as he afterward said,

When I was five months old I was carried to Granville, Massachusetts, and bound out as a servant to Deacon Daniel Rose till I was twenty-one. He was a man of singular piety. I was taught the principles of religion. His wife, my mistress, had peculiar attachment to me: she treated me as though I were her own child. I remember it was a saying among the neighbors that she loved Lemuel more than her own children.[66]

According to his biographer, Haynes "got his education in the chimney corner" of the Rose farmhouse. The deciding point in his life came with his "conversion," which he described in a letter to a friend:

I remember I often had serious impressions, or fearful apprehensions, of going to hell. I spent much time in what I called secret prayer. I was one evening greatly alarmed by the *Aurora Borealis,* or Northern Lights. It was in that day esteemed a presage of the day of judgment. For many days and nights I was greatly alarmed, through fear of appearing before the bar of God, knowing that I was a sinner; I cannot express the terrors of mind I felt. One evening, being under an apple tree, mourning my wretched state, I hope I found the Saviour. I always visit the place when I come to Granville, and, when I

can, I pluck some fruit from the tree and carry it home: it
is sweet to my taste. I have fear at times that I am deceived,
but still I *hope*. Reading a verse in Mr. Erskine's sonnets a
little strengthened me. In describing marks of grace, he asks,

> Dost ask the place, the spot of land,
> Where Jesus did thee meet?
> And how he got thy heart and hand?
> Thy husband then was sweet.

Soon after I united with the church in East Granville, and was
baptized by the Rev. Jonathan Huntington, minister or pastor
of the church in Worthington.[67]

Jonathan Edwards, of whose *Personal Narrative* this letter
is a near echo, was to remain for Haynes the rest of his life
the chief spiritual support and inspiration. Mysticism and
Puritan logic were to absorb him so completely that there
was to be nothing of him left to fight against the degradation
of the race to which his father belonged.

Although his term as an indentured servant ended in
1774, he apparently remained with the Rose family until
1776, when he joined the Patriot Army. He had already
for two years done service as a "minute man." And as an
active soldier he took part in the Ticonderoga campaign.
After his discharge from the army, he set about preparing
himself to become a minister. He succeeded in being admitted into the home of a pastor, on whose farm he labored
in order to pay for his board and for tuition in Latin and
Greek. In this way, says his biographer, he not only mastered the Latin and Greek languages, but read extensively in
belles lettres and composed sermons and verses.[68] Of a
prodigious memory, he had been able as a boy to repeat to
his playmates "with wonderful accuracy the morning sermon."[69] It was said of him that—

At the age of fifty he could repeat nearly the whole of Young's *Night Thoughts*, Milton's *Paradise Lost*, Watts' *Psalms and Hymns* and large unbroken passages from different authors, and more of the Sacred Scriptures than any man I ever knew. When he had listened to a sermon or a conversation of great length, he could report the whole, and much of it in the very terms in which it was given. His memory was a safe depository for everything he thought worth retaining.[70]

Since he possessed in his middle age a memory which with all due allowance for possible exaggeration must have been extraordinary, it is no wonder that the tutelage for the ministry undertaken in his youth was soon completed. In 1785, he was ordained, and became pastor of a church in Torrington, Connecticut. Three years later, he was called to a parish in Rutland, Vermont, where he remained until 1818. Other charges were at Manchester, Vermont, and Granville, New York, at the latter of which places he lived during the last eleven years of his life. After the publication of his most famous sermon, *Universal Salvation*, preached in Rutland, Vermont, in June, 1805, regarding which his biographer said in 1839, "This discourse has been printed and reprinted, both in America and Great Britain, till no one pretends to give any account of the number of editions,"[71] Haynes was considered an important figure in the Congregational Church, enjoying the friendship and esteem of such leaders in the denomination as President Dwight of Yale and President Humphrey of Amherst.[72] Among his celebrated friends outside of the church was Royall Tyler, author of *The Contrast*, usually considered the first American comedy, who, as Chief Justice of Vermont, was often in Rutland and "frequently spent an evening with Mr. Haynes, of whose talents and principles he ever expressed himself in terms of the highest admiration."[73]

Haynes's portrait reveals that, had he ever so much desired, he could not have denied his partial Negro ancestry; for his face is stamped with the undoubted African features which he inherited from his father. Yet he lived his life among the whites, acting as a white man. He married a white woman, and reared his seven children as whites, one of whom was reported in 1837 as a respected lawyer, and another as a successful physician.[74] In all of his extant writings there seems to be not the slightest allusion to his connection with the Negro race. In his biography, Timothy Dwight Cooley treats him as a churchman, at no time offering his case as an argument against slavery or race prejudice. Such references as are made to his color are illustrated by the following, an excerpt from a letter written by the Reverend Milton Huxley:

There is a man of my acquaintance who feels that he owes much, under God, to the preaching of Mr. Haynes, while at Torrington. He was disaffected that the church should employ him, and neglected meeting for a time. At length, curiosity conquered prejudice so far that he went to the house of God. He took his seat in the crowded assembly, and, from designed disrespect, *sat with his hat on.* Mr. Haynes gave out his text, and began with his usual impassioned earnestness, as if unconscious of anything amiss in the congregation. "The preacher had not proceeded far in his sermon," said the man, "before I thought him the *whitest* man I ever saw. My hat was thrown under the seat, and I found myself listening with the most profound attention."[75]

The following, according to his biographer, shows how his color was regarded in Rutland, where he remained with one church for thirty years:

The young men, by way of pleasantry, would often remind the youth in the West Parish of their *coloured minister!* The latter would strenuously reply, "His soul is pure! All white! Snow white!"[76]

The singular career of Lemuel B. Haynes is most important in a study of the psychological reasons underlying race prejudice in America. It was said of him in 1837:

He is the only man of *known* African descent who has ever succeeded in overpowering the system of American *caste*. And this he did by wisdom and piety, aided also by the more favorable state of the times in which he lived.[77]

However, there was later at least one other Negro, Samuel Ringgold Ward, who served as the pastor of a white church in the United States.[78]

The earliest of Haynes's writings which got into print is a brief sermon made up by his biographer from notes dated 1776.[79] On the idea of spiritual rebirth, it is developed with the type of scholastic reasoning which Haynes learned from his great master, Edwards, and which he was to use so extensively in his later sermons. The English is careful and exact, remarkable as the production of one who at the time of the composition of the notes had received little formal instruction. However, like Patrick Henry's celebrated speech on liberty, it is really a compilation by another hand, and cannot therefore be given serious consideration in an estimate of Haynes's work as a writer. Probably the first sermon of his that was printed during his lifetime is *The Character and Work of a Spiritual Watchman Described: a Sermon Delivered at Hinesburgh, February 23, 1791.* It was published at Litchfield, Connecticut. The title indicates what it really is, an ordination sermon. The framework of the thought, as in so many discourses composed by Haynes's Puritan predecessors, is made so obvious that the reader follows the whole as he might reason out the proof of a geometrical proposition. Also firm, but not so syllogistic in development, is *The Important Concerns of Ministers, and the People of Their Charge, at the Day of Judgment,* published at Rutland in 1798. A discourse delivered at the funeral of a minister, it is Puritan enough in its allusions to death and in its warnings to those still alive; but it is more remarkable for the steady roll of its rhythms. The phrases move with the heavy precision of a funeral march, not unlike the beat of the melancholic iambics of Young's *Night Thoughts*. Other examples of sonorous oratory are *The Nature and Importance of True Republicanism* (1801), a sermon attacking Jefferson's political principles, and a memorial sermon printed in the Reverend Job Swift's *Discourses on Religious Subjects* (1805).

Probably the first of the many editions of Haynes's most famous sermon, usually called *Universal Salvation,* the preface of which is dated December 30, 1805, appeared at Rutland in 1806. The descriptive title of the pamphlet in which it was originally printed is:

An Interesting Controversy, between Rev. Lemuel Haynes, Minister of a Congregational Church in Rutland, Vt., and Rev. Hosea Ballou, Preacher of the Doctrine of Universal Salvation, consisting, *First,* of a sermon by Mr. Haynes, delivered at West Rutland, in the year 1805, entitled "Universal Salvation, a Very Ancient Doctrine: with Some Account of the Life and Character of Its Author," immediately after hearing Mr. Ballou zealously exhibit his sentiments in support of that Doctrine. *Second,* an Epistle from Mr. Ballou to Mr. Haynes, being a reply to his Sermon delivered at West Rutland. *Third,* a Letter of Mr. Haynes to Mr. Ballou in reply to the Epistle.

The sermon opens calmly, with a picture of Adam and Eve in the Garden of Eden.

Happy were the human pair, amidst this delightful Paradise, until a certain preacher, in his journey, came that way, and disturbed their peace and tranquillity, by endeavoring to reverse the prohibition of the Almighty, as in our text—"Ye shall not surely die!"

Continuing, Haynes quotes from Milton:

> She pluck'd, she ate:
> Earth felt the wound; nature from her seat,
> Sighing through all her works, gave signs of wo,
> That all was lost.

Thence, he proceeds to build up a biography of Satan, the preacher, who is pictured as spending much of his time in expounding the doctrine of universal salvation. Lightly and deftly Haynes draws Satan's character, sustaining at all times a mood of mock seriousness. His irony accumulates until he reaches the peroration, in which he puts forward with true Puritan earnestness the thesis of his text, "And ye *shall* surely die!" Ballou's "Epistle," often published with the sermon, is resentful, almost insulting; and Haynes's reply to him shows that he was a fighter as well as a logician and satirist. Timothy Dwight Cooley's estimate of *Universal Salvation* as "one of the finest pieces of satire to be found in all the annals of pulpit eloquence" is perhaps over-enthusiastic. However, not because of the forgotten doctrinal controversy which it treats, nor because of the fact that it was produced by a man of the colored race, but because it is a subtle and clever example of irony, *Universal Salvation* is still most readable. It belongs to that choice and rare and exceedingly small group of Puritan sermons which even today provide entertainment.

But Haynes's most readable work is not to be found in his sermons. Mysticism was as evident a quality of his mentality as was a logical sense. His numerous letters printed in Cooley's biography are crowded with observations of "special providences." It was said of him that one of his favorite quotations was John Newton's statement, "Did I not believe in the particular providences of God, I should not dare to step my foot out of doors."[80] While he was living in Manchester, Vermont, it fell to his lot to study carefully what he came to recognize as a chain of events in which the hand of God from the beginning to the end was made especially manifest. Russell Colvin, a harmless, feeble-minded person, disappeared mysteriously from a village near Manchester. Suspicions that he had been murdered were aroused, and in time two brothers, Stephen and Jesse Boorn, were arrested as his slayers. The circumstantial evidence brought against them at their trial was so strong that they were convicted of having murdered Colvin and of having burned his body to hide their guilt. One was sentenced to be hanged, and the other to be imprisoned for life. Shortly before the date set for the execution of the more severely judged brother, Russell Colvin turned up in Manchester, declaring mildly that he did not know where he had been. Suspicion that he might be a ghost was set aside when it was found that he had suffered a lapse of memory and had been away, as far as New Jersey, visiting among relations who had heard nothing about the conviction of his supposed murderers. Haynes studied the whole affair with a realist's eye for detail. As he turned the matter over in his mind, it took on romantic proportions; and he saw in it a visitation of God, giving warnings and teaching manifold lessons. While the affair was still a public sensation, he published his conclusions regarding it in a small volume, entitled *Mystery Developed; or, Russell Colvin . . . in Full Life . . . and . . . His Convicted Murderers Rescued from Ignominious Death by Wonderful Discoveries.* The book appeared at Hartford in 1820, and before the end of the year had gone through a second edition. The first part presents a "narrative of the whole transaction"; the second part is a sermon which Haynes preached on the affair; and the third and last part is a detailed report of the trial. The concreteness with which the story is related and the ingenuity with which the notion of "special providences" is worked in show that if Haynes had lived in a later time he might have been the author of successful mystery tales. The moral and religious lessons which he draws are forgotten in the vividness with which he relates the narrative and in the imagination with which he shows his reaction towards it. Although written in a loose style, with no particular effort made to create suspense, it stirs the reader to go on to the end, even through the sermon, without laying the book aside.

The other writings of Haynes which have been preserved are apparently all included in Cooley's biography, and were, it seems, first printed in that volume. Among them are many letters, dated from 1795 to 1818; brief moral anecdotes, compiled from notes for sermons; "ingenious remarks on passages of Scripture," also taken from manuscript notes; a short journal of a trip from Massachusetts to Vermont; and extracts from many sermons, including "God's Decrees," pronounced by many of Haynes's contemporaries his strongest specimen of pulpit oratory.

This sermon lacks the subtlety and irony which make *Universal Salvation* so readable. But in one respect it is more interesting than its celebrated predecessor. In the conclusion, which is a plea for the sending of missionaries to foreign lands, a Hottentot is represented as complaining—

What a pity, what a sin it is, that you Europeans, who have for so many years enjoyed in great abundance the heavenly bread, should keep it all to yourselves and not spare one little crumb to the millions of poor heathen!

Such a plea is a sad commentary on the character of Lemuel B. Haynes. Since he begged for succor for the Hottentots of Africa and turned his back on the sufferings of the blacks in America, his career must be looked upon as a sort of tragedy. If he had felt the scourge of slavery as strongly as he felt the scourge of a Puritan God, he might, with all his talents, have been an earlier Frederick Douglass for the race with which the America of today identifies him.

Chapter IV

WRITINGS OF THE LEADING NEGRO ANTISLAVERY
AGENTS, 1840–1865

Die on the field of battle,
Die on the field of battle,
Glory to my soul!
Oh, I'm going to glory,—won't you come along with me?
Don't you see the angels beck'ning, and calling me away?
Don't you see the golden city and the everlasting day?
O, Canaan, bright Canaan,
I'm bound for the land of Canaan!

—Quoted in Harriet Beecher Stowe's
Uncle Tom's Cabin, 1852

I

By 1840, the movement for the abolition of slavery was
being felt in every section of the United States. The might-
iest struggle in American history was definitely begun, not
to end until the slave was completely emancipated. The
main thought of the age, becoming more and more fermented
as the crisis of the Civil War was approached, centered
about one subject—the destiny of the Negro. Under whatever disguises the great controversial issues of the day appeared before the public, whether they were social, political,
economic, or religious, the place of the blacks in American
life was usually the real theme of dissension.

The Negro was by no means passive in the stormy conflict which was waged about him. A chief among the Abolitionists, John G. Whittier, wrote in 1847:

With such examples of the intellectual capacity of the colored
man as are afforded by L'Ouverture and Petion of Hayti;
Dumas, of France; Pushkin of Russia; and Placido, the slave

poet and martyr of Cuba, to say nothing of such men as James McCune Smith, Frederick Douglass, Henry H. Garnet, and Henry Bibb, in our own country, it is scarcely in good taste for white mediocrity to taunt the colored man with natural inferiority. Do not Toussaint's deeds for freedom, and Pushkin's songs of a great nation, waken within all hearts the sympathies of a common nature?

"There spoke our brother! Then our father's grave
    Did utter such a voice!"

In the colored man's follies and crimes, his loves and hatreds, his virtues and weaknesses, we but recognize our common humanity, and realize the truth of the inspired apostle's language—"God hath made of one blood all the generations of men."[1]

Working for the widespread recognition of the principle so voiced by Whittier formed one of the most important divisions of antislavery agitation. The Abolitionists were ever on the alert for the discovery of the Negro of extraordinary promise; and when he was found, he came under their encouragement and tutelage. Thus championed, the African race in the United States during the twenty years prior to the Civil War progressed with gigantic strides.

The attempt to provide the higher education necessary for the Negro leader occasioned one of the most extended and dramatic fights which the Abolitionists had to engage in, a fight marked with strange paradoxes. In 1833, Prudence Crandall was arrested for conducting an academy for colored girls in Canterbury, Connecticut; in the same year, Oberlin College was founded in Ohio as an institution admitting students of all colors on equal terms. In 1839, the Noyes Academy, at Canaan, New Hampshire, at which a number of colored boys were in attendance, was broken up by mob violence. The main building was wheeled away and dumped into a swamp, and the Negro students were given a limited time in which to get out of the town.[2] A number of them immediately repaired to the Oneida Institute, at Whitesboro, New York, a newly founded college under the control of Beriah Green, a celebrated Abolitionist who tolerated no distinctions because of color. Central College, located at McGrawville, New York, an institution of like character, employed during the late forties and early fifties at least three Negro professors—Charles L. Reason, George B. Vashon, and William G. Allen.[3] In 1841, Thomas Paul, a Negro, was graduated from Dartmouth.[4] Martin R. Delany, also colored, was accepted as a medical student at Harvard in 1851, after having been refused admission at the University of Pennsylvania, Jefferson College, and the medical schools at Albany and Geneva, New York.[5] Negroes in some way succeeded in being admitted into other leading colleges.[6] Yet Edward W. Blyden, perhaps the most distinguished of the Negroes who emigrated to Liberia, could not find a creditable college which would receive him as a student when, in 1850, he came to this country from his native home in St. Thomas, West Indies, in order to procure an education. Nineteen years later the honorary degree of Master of Arts was conferred on him by Lafayette College in recognition of his missionary and educational work in Africa.[7] According to a tradition, James W. C. Pennington, one of the most noted of the colored preachers of the day, honored with the degree of Doctor of Divinity by the University of Heidelberg while he was still legally a slave, was refused admission as a regular student at Yale but was not interfered with when he stood outside the doors of class rooms in order to hear professors' lectures.[8]

Few of the prominent Negroes of the period were college-trained. The antislavery conflict, stirring up in its intensity the greatest extremes of sympathy and hatred for the colored race, provided in itself an education for the

Negro. That he was insulted and buffeted by one element of the white public meant that there was another into whose companionship he was all the more freely and readily admitted. Frederick Douglass was extremely illiterate when he began his work for the abolition cause; but after a few years of close association with such Americans as William Lloyd Garrison, Wendell Phillips, and Theodore Parker, and with such Englishmen as George Thompson and Douglas Jerrold, he was developed into an exceptional orator, writer, and editor. When he took up his residence in Rochester late in 1847, he was held as a pariah by his fellow townsmen; but it has been said that such an American as James Russell Lowell never passed through the city without staying long enough to pay him a visit.[9] Because he was a Negro, Samuel Ringgold Ward was not permitted to take his meals in the public dining saloon of the Cunard vessel on which he crossed to England in 1853; but, as he tells us in his autobiography, the most distinguished passenger on board the ship, William Makepeace Thackeray, called on him each day for a conversation.[10] The Reverend James W. C. Pennington, although the holder of an honorary degree from one of the oldest and strongest of German universities, was forced to discharge his pastoral duties by walking over the great distances of New York City because colored people were not allowed to ride in public conveyances.[11]

The Negro was contending with such abuses as had never before been measured out to him, and at the same time he was receiving such support as he had never been privileged to enjoy. He fought the abuses, and he thrived on the support. In 1860, the colored population of the entire country was 4,441,830, of which the small minority of 438,970 was counted as free. The Negroes of the North, the only ones for whom abolition intervention could be of direct cultural benefit, were estimated at 225,274.[12] Included in this number were lawyers, physicians, politicians, officeholders, preachers, inventors, educators, manufacturers, and men holding responsible positions in business.[13] Few activities, not excepting the arts of music, sculpture, painting, engraving, and acting, were unengaged in by the Negro during the stirring years when his presence in the United States was considered the gravest of the country's problems.[14] He left few fields of literature unattempted. Among his publications we find newspapers and magazines conducted under his own editorship, letters and articles contributed to periodicals controlled by whites, speeches printed as pamphlets and reported phonographically for the antislavery and general press, sociological treatises, histories, books of travel and exploration, biography, literary criticism, the informal essay, poetry, the novel, the short story, and the drama.

Of the Negroes who tried authorship, none had such excellent opportunities as those employed as antislavery agents. The plan of operations decided upon by the American Anti-Slavery Society at its first convention, held in 1833, called for the engagement of agents to be sent far and wide for the purpose of lecturing, scattering tracts and pamphlets, receiving subscriptions for the antislavery newspapers, and spreading abolition propaganda in every way possible.[15] Such a plan was adopted later by other abolition organizations. The psychological effect upon the public of the Negro as an antislavery agent was soon recognized. By 1838, Charles Lenox Remond, a Massachusetts Negro, had begun his long career as an abolition agent for various New England societies.[16] In 1839, Samuel Ringgold Ward, born a slave in Maryland, became an agent for the American Anti-Slavery Society.[17] The number of Negroes so employed after 1840 grew in leaps and bounds. Fugitives from the South were especially in demand. Some when inducted into the abolition service could do no more than stand before an audience and relate the story of their experiences in slavery. Others, including both fugitives and northern Negroes born free, came to be classed with the foremost Abolitionists. The most distinguished, and the most valuable in their services to Negro literature, were Charles Lenox Remond, Frederick Douglass, William Wells Brown, and Samuel Ringgold Ward. In the battle for abolition all four stood as worthy and willing lieutenants for such generals with opposing views as William Lloyd Garrison and Gerrit Smith. All four began their work as lecturers. But, encouraged in every possible way by their sponsors, they soon learned to write their messages, to bring them before the public often in a most interesting and entertaining form.

II

By 1840 Charles Lenox Remond's work as an abolition agent had so impressed the American Anti-Slavery Society that he was chosen by that body to go as a delegate to a world abolition convention held in London the following year.[18] From the time of his visit abroad he was internationally known as a lecturer and as a contributor of letters to the antislavery newspapers, especially the *Liberator*. While in England in 1841, he inspired an English versifier, I. G. Blanchard, to compose a poem, the full title of which is "On Hearing Mr. C. L. Remond, a Young Colored Man of Talent but Slight Education, Lecture on Prejudice against Color in the United States."[19] Yet regarding his worth as an orator, William Wells Brown wrote in 1874:

Mr. Remond's abilities have been much overrated. His speeches, when in print, attracted little or no attention, and he was never able to speak upon any subject except slavery, upon which he was never very deep.[20]

His printed letters and speeches prove that he was of slight education, that he was not profound, and that he was probably overrated by the Garrisonian wing of the abolition public.[21] Whatever influence his oratory exerted was doubtless due to his color and his personality. For there was no originality in what he said.

He was never more than a faithful, plodding imitator of the conservative antislavery lecturers who seem to have arisen by the hundreds in New England. The following passage from a speech which he delivered in Ireland before the Hibernian Anti-Slavery Society might have come from any one of a dozen defenders of Garrison's principles:

My bosom swells with pride and pleasure when I reflect that I am standing before Irishmen—men who in the year 1841 have the name of philanthropists. Be it yours, my friends, to retain the lofty title, conditioned as you are as to your political influences, rather than having the name of republicans and democrats, to nurture slavery and to countenance oppression. Give me a monarchy—give me an oligarchy—give me an autocracy—yea, or even give me a despotic and tyrannical government, if, despite the pride of place and the "proud man's contumely," I see the living spirit of liberty glowing bright and imperishable in the people's breast, rather than a republicanism whose watchwords are, "Equality to all, and mastery to none," but whose deeds belie their splendid promises, and whose actions are those of oppression and persecution. "Despotism" is a fearful scourge, but there is no delusion in the word. "Despotism" is not a sound which wins softly and deceptively on the ear, lulling it to ruin: it closes no man's mouth—it steals not away the sense—it blinds not the victim: stern and detestable in itself, it falls strongly and detestably on the ear; but give it to me, with all its horrors, rather than that which is in itself a lie—professing, indeed, to be all that is sweet and goodly, but doing such deeds as, to think of, makes men's blood to freeze.[22]

Although the unwieldy sentence structure is typical, the passage is perhaps too purple to be taken as representative of Remond's style. He was usually commonplace as well as trite and heavy. As a Negro orator who flourished between 1840 and 1865, he had the misfortune to have been born of free parents and to have been reared in the comparatively remote town of Salem, Massachusetts. He never saw slavery, which, as William Wells Brown declared, was his one topic, except through abolition literature.

III

When he was on a lecture tour in the state of New York in 1843, Remond was accompanied by the Hutchinsons, the celebrated abolition singers, and by Frederick Douglass, who five years before had been a slave on a Maryland plantation.[23] The Hutchinsons were along to arouse audiences to tears by singing sentimental abolition verses, and Douglass was there for no other purpose than to relate the story of his experiences as a bondman. At that time his friends and promoters were not willing to allow him to attempt more on the abolition platform.[24] But within a few years the whole world knew that in Frederick Douglass the abolition cause had found the ideal orator, a fugitive able to describe with the most realistic detail the life of the Negro in slavery, and at the same time a speaker who could demand respect from any audience, not by the display of himself on the platform as a runaway black, but by the clean logic and intellectual vigor of his message. Remond's greatest service for abolition was in preparing the American and English public for Douglass.

Frederick Douglass was much more than an antislavery orator. He has been frequently called, no doubt with justice, the greatest of American Negroes. Certainly, no other American Negro has achieved such a high degree of success in so many fields of endeavor. And few Americans, white or colored, have exhibited such courage and common sense in living a life marked with the most phenomenal evolution. William Lloyd Garrison wrote as follows of his discovery of Douglass at a general antislavery meeting held at Nantucket in 1841:

I shall never forget his speech at the convention—the extraordinary emotion it excited in my own mind—the powerful emotion it created upon a crowded auditory, completely taken by surprise. . . . There stood one in physical proportion and stature commanding and exact—in intellect richly endowed—in natural eloquence a prodigy—in soul manifestly "created but a little lower than the angels"—yet a slave, ay, a fugitive slave, trembling for his safety, hardly daring to believe that on American soil, a single white person could be found who would befriend him at all hazards, for the love of God and humanity.[25]

Before this time, Frederick Douglass had been for twenty-one years a slave in Maryland and then for three years a laborer in New Bedford, Massachusetts. During most of his time in bondage he had experienced the severest hardships; but he had been fortunate enough to serve for short periods in Baltimore, where he had at least learned to read and to write. As a fugitive living in New Bedford, he became acquainted with the significance of the abolition movement. But it was not until he met Garrison, who immediately employed him as an antislavery agent, that his serious training in the abolition school began. His rapid progress proved his genius, a sureness and quickness of mentality, which he was always gallant enough to regard as an inheritance from his African mother instead of from his never identified white father.[26]

For four years, from 1841 to 1845, Douglass was directly under Garrison's guidance, travelling extensively as an anti-slavery agent, repeating the story of his bondage before hundreds of audiences. From 1845 until 1847, he lectured in Great Britain; and, inspired by the broader and more practical views of the English Abolitionists, he grew in self-reliant thinking. Shortly after his return to the United States came the establishment of his newspaper, the *North Star*, which marked the beginning of the break with Garrison.[27] His tutelage was ended, and he was launched into his career as an independent advocate of the rights of his race. In 1851, he formally renounced the Garrisonian doctrines of disunion and aloofness from politics, and joined the Liberty Party, which was later to merge into the Republican.[28] He was now to remain what he was until he saw the extermination of slavery—editor and politician as well as orator. After 1865, editing, except for the brief period when he published the *New National Era* in Washington, was given up; but until the year of his death, 1895, he was strenuously engaged in lecturing, in contributing to newspapers and magazines, and in practical politics. Throughout his long public life, extending well beyond half a century, his was the Negro voice in America most respected by the whites and most venerated by his own race.

If all the writings of Frederick Douglass which were printed could be collected, they would fill a considerable number of lengthy volumes. But such a collection will in all probability never be possible. A great mass of his writings, including the only complete files known to have been preserved of his *North Star, Frederick Douglass' Paper*, and *Douglass' Monthly*, was lost when his house in Rochester was destroyed by fire in 1872.[29] Many other productions from his pen have no doubt perished with the loss of other

antislavery newspapers. However, the published writings
which are extant are enormous in quantity.
The earliest are open letters, printed usually in the abolition journals. In the issue of the *Liberator* for November
18, 1842, appeared the first, an overstrained and crudely
written expression of Douglass' feelings in regard to the
case of George Latimer, whose imprisonment in Boston as a
fugitive slave claimed in Norfolk, Virginia, was then stirring the abolition North. The letter is concluded with an
appropriate apology:

> I can't write to much advantage, having never had a day's
> schooling in my life, nor have I ever ventured to give publicity
> to any of my scribbling before; nor would I now, but for my
> peculiar circumstances.

Although this originial effort shows little promise, three
years later Douglass' letters became what might be called
a regular feature of the antislavery press. They were
usually printed first in the *Liberator* or the *National Anti-
Slavery Standard,* and then were copied extensively in the
lesser abolition journals. The majority of these communications, the style of which shows a constant improvement,
are on his experiences as an antislavery lecturer, especially
in Great Britain.[30] Characteristic of the letters at their
best is one to Horace Greeley, written at Glasgow, April 15,
1846, and published originally in the New York *Tribune* for
May 14, 1846. It begins:

> I never wrote nor attempted to write for any other than a
> strictly anti-slavery press; but being encouraged by your mag-
> nanimity, as shown in copying my letter written from Belfast,
> Ireland, to the *Liberator* at Boston, I venture to send you a few
> lines direct from my pen.

Then follows, in the tone of restrained invective of which
Douglass was becoming a master, an answer to a charge

made against him in the *New York Express* as a "glib-
tongued scoundrel, running a muck in greedy-eared Britain
against America, its people, its institutions, and even its
peace." He says in beginning his defense:

> Of the low and vulgar epithets, coupled with the false and
> somewhat malicious charges, very little need be said. I am
> used to them. Their force is lost upon me in the frequency of
> their application. I was reared where they were in the most
> common use. They form a large and very important portion of
> the vocabulary of characters known in the South as plantation
> 'negro drivers.' A slave-holding gentleman would scorn to use
> them. He leaves them to find their way into the world of
> sound, through the polluted lips of the hired 'negro driver'—
> a being for whom the haughty slave-holder feels incomparably
> more contempt than he feels towards his slave. And for the
> best of all reasons—he knows the slave to be degraded because
> he cannot help himself; but a white 'negro driver' is degraded
> because of original, ingrained meanness. If I agree with the
> slave-holders in nothing else, I can say that I agree with them
> in all their burning contempt for a 'negro driver,' whether born
> North or South. Such epithets will have no prejudicial effect
> against me on the mind of the class of American people whose
> good opinion I sincerely desire to cultivate and deserve. And
> it is to these I would address this brief word of explanation.

His assailant thus dismissed, Douglass clearly shows his position as that of an enemy of no American institutions except
slavery and discrimination against blacks.

Equally strong is the letter in which he replies to an
attack made by the Reverend Samuel H. Cox. In a com-
munication published in the *Evangelist* (New York), Cox
claimed that at a world's temperance convention at Covent
Garden Theatre, London, in August, 1845, Douglass "lugged
in Anti-slavery or abolition, no doubt prompted to it by
some of the politic ones, who can use him to do what they
themselves would not adventure to do in person." The

insult was made all the deeper by the insinuation that Douglass was probably "well paid for the abomination." In his answer Douglass takes up each item of the charge and tears it to pieces. In the end he has shown that his irony was daring enough to meet the invective of a celebrated minister. The letter was so prized by the American Anti-Slavery Society that it was in 1846 printed as a pamphlet, entitled *Correspondence between the Rev. Samuel H. Cox, D. D., of Brooklyn, L. I., and Frederick Douglass, a Fugitive Slave,* probably the first of Douglass' long line of pamphlet publications.[31]

Douglass' last term of employment as an antislavery agent ended in 1847. In December of that year he began, in spite of the protests of Garrison and others, the publication of the *North Star,* for the founding of which funds had been subscribed by friends in England.[32] In setting out upon his career as an independent journalist he ended what might be conveniently called his apprenticeship as author. It was the time when he was perfecting himself in public speech as well as in learning to write. In addition to the open letters, a number of his orations were printed in the antislavery press.[33] But the most important production of his period of apprenticeship was the *Narrative of the Life of Frederick Douglass,* the first edition of which appeared at Boston in 1845.

Among the American makers of autobiography, Frederick Douglass is unique. Probably no other American, not excepting Benjamin Franklin, lived a life marked with such contrasts. George L. Ruffin said in his introduction to Douglass' *Life and Times,* originally published in 1881:

Up to this time the most remarkable contribution this country has given to the world is the author and subject of this book, now being introduced to the public, Frederick Douglass. . . .

For every other great character we can bring forward, Europe can produce one equally as great; when we bring forward Douglass, he cannot be matched.

Such praise might on the surface be regarded as no more than the bombastic advertisement of a book. But if it is considered as Ruffin no doubt intended, we must agree that there is an element of truth in it. The intellectual and moral growth which Douglass attained, in spite of the long years which he spent as a slave and in spite of the lifetime of struggle which he experienced because of prejudice against his color, makes him a most remarkable figure among the celebrated Americans. And modern Europe has no match for him, simply because modern Europe has never known such violent racial discrimination as was practiced against the blacks in America throughout the period when Douglass lived. He recognized the drama in his career, and recorded it at appropriate times in four autobiographical works.

The first, *Narrative of the Life of Frederick Douglass*, follows in general the plan of the conventional slave autobiography, which had by 1845 become something of a distinct literary type. Its main difference is that it is immeasurably better than any previous narrative which we can without doubt ascribe wholly to Negro authorship. The book was hailed by the abolition public with enthusiasm. It was pronounced by the *Lynn Pioneer* "the most thrilling work which the American press has ever issued, *and the most important.*"[34] An anonymous writer in the New York *Tribune*, who saw in Douglass' style what he felt was the African rhythm and spontaneity responsible for the literary success of Dumas and Soulié, declared:

Considered merely as a narrative, we have never read one more simple, true, coherent, and warm with genuine feeling. It is an excellent piece of writing, and on that score can be prized as a specimen of the powers of the black race, which prejudice persists in disputing.[35]

Within a little more than two years after the appearance of the book, a translation into French was in the hands of the printers.[36]

There is still interest in Douglass' *Narrative,* even considered apart from the fact that he, a fugitive, only seven years out of the degradation of slavery, produced it. His experiences as an abolition lecturer had taught him valuable lessons about holding and pleasing and convincing an audience. By nature strongly emotional, he had learned how to stir emotions in others. From the store of his memories of his intimate contact with slavery he selected details for his *Narrative* which at one moment provoke laughter and at the next, pity. They are always clear and concrete, and from them we build up a unified picture of Douglass' life from his infancy to the year in which he became an antislavery agent. Nothing argues more strongly for the precociousness of his mind than the detached perspective with which he looks back upon his wretched past even though removed from it by a very brief lapse of time.

The style of the *Narrative* is childlike in its simplicity. But it is marked with two effects, no doubt brought about unconsciously, which many writers labor vainly to obtain. One is evident in the following passage, illustrative of the manner in which a weight of feeling is compressed into very few sentences:

I never saw my mother, to know her as such, more than four or five times in my life and each of these times was very short in duration, and at night. She was hired by a Mr. Stewart, who lived about twelve miles from my home. She made her journeys to see me in the night, travelling the whole distance on foot, after the performance of her day's work. She was a field hand, and a whipping is the penalty of not being in the field at sunrise, unless a slave has special permission from his or her master to the contrary.

An equally difficult stylistic accomplishment is seen in the gracefulness with which Douglass mingles argument with incident. His sole purpose in writing his autobiography was to produce antislavery propaganda. Unlike the great majority of abolition writers, however, he possessed the ability to bring out his sermon without destroying his story. The following passage, which happens to be probably the first printed commentary made by a Negro on the folk songs of his race, preaches while it tells:

The slaves selected to go to the Great House Farm, for the monthly allowance for themselves and their fellow slaves, were peculiarly enthusiastic. While on their way they would make the dense old woods, for miles around, reverberate with their wild songs, revealing at once the highest joy and the deepest sadness. They would compose and sing as they went along, consulting neither time nor tune. The thought that came up, came out—if not in the word, in the sound;—and as frequently in the one as in the other. They would sometimes sing the most pathetic sentiment in the most rapturous tone, and the most rapturous sentiment in the most pathetic tone. Into all of their songs they would manage to weave something of the Great House Farm. Especially would they do this, when leaving home. They would sing most exultingly the following words:—

"I am going away to the Great House Farm!
O, yea! O, yea! O!"

This they would sing as a chorus to words which to many would seem unmeaning jargon, but which, nevertheless, were full of meaning to themselves. I have sometimes thought that the mere hearing of those songs would do more to impress some minds with the horrible character of slavery, than the reading of whole volumes of philosophy on the subject could do.

I did not, when a slave, understand the deep meaning of those rude and apparently incoherent songs. I was myself

within the circle; so that I neither saw nor heard as those without might see and hear. They told a tale of woe which was
then altogether beyond my feeble comprehension; they were
tones loud, long, and deep; they breathed the prayer and complaint of souls boiling over with the bitterest anguish. Every
tone was a testimony against slavery, and a prayer to God for
deliverance from chains. The hearing of those wild notes
always depressed my spirit, and filled me with ineffable sadness.
I have frequently found myself in tears while hearing them.
The mere recurrence to those songs, even now, afflicts me; and
while I am writing these lines, an expression of feeling has
already found its way down my cheek. To those songs I trace
my first glimmering conception of the dehumanizing character
of slavery. I can never get rid of that conception. Those
songs still follow me, to deepen my hatred of slavery, and
quicken my sympathies for my brethren in bonds. If any one
wishes to be impressed with the soul-killing effects of slavery,
let him go to Colonel Lloyd's plantation, and, on allowance
day, place himself in the deep woods, and there let him, in
silence, analyze the sounds that shall pass through the chambers
of his soul,—and if he is not thus impressed, it will be only
because "there is no flesh in his obdurate heart."

Douglass' second autobiographical work, *My Bondage
and My Freedom,* appeared in 1855, near the middle of the
period of his maturity as an author, which we might say
extended from 1848 to the close of the Civil War. Almost
four times the length of the *Narrative,* it reveals in more
respects than in size that it is the work of the mature
Douglass. The introductions by Garrison and Phillips which
served the *Narrative* give way to an introduction by a
member of Douglass' own race, James McCune Smith.
The dedication is to Gerrit Smith, who on account of his
leadership in the Liberty Party had replaced Garrison as
Douglass' idol among the Abolitionists. One of the earliest
attacks which the Garrisonians made upon Douglass was
that, by the act of permitting English friends to pay the

price, seven hundred and fifty dollars, set upon him by his
Maryland owner, he had recognized the legality of slavery
as an American institution.[37]   That his position as a free
man could not be disputed when he wrote *My Bondage and
My Freedom* was of great advantage to him.   The book
brings out in elaborate detail the story of his life as a slave,
including minute descriptions of customs on a great Maryland plantation.   What he did not dare say in the *Narrative*
he now says with boldness.   The book is in every sense a
surer and bigger work than the earlier autobiography.
While the style shows the same simplicity and compression,
it is more accurate.   If there is more argument, there is
also more human interest, especially humor.   The following description of a Christmas celebration among slaves is
suggestive of the pictures with which the book abounds:

Not to be drunk during the holidays, was disgraceful; and he
was esteemed a lazy and improvident man, who could not afford
to drink whiskey during Christmas.

The fiddling, dancing and *"jubilee beating,"* was going on in
all directions.   This latter performance is strictly southern.
It supplies the place of a violin, or of other musical instruments,
and is played so easily, that almost every farm has its "Juba"
beater.   The performer improvises as he beats, and sings his
merry songs, so ordering the words as to have them fall pat
with the movement of his hands.   Among a mass of nonsense
and wild frolic, once in a while a sharp hit is given to the
meanness of slaveholders.   Take the following for an example.

> "We raise de wheat,
> Dey gib us de corn;
> We bake de bread,
> Dey gib us de cruss;
> We sif de meal,
> Dey gib us de huss;
> We peal de meat,
> Dey gib us de skin.

An' dat's de way
Dey takes us in.
We skim de pot,
Dey gib us the liquor,
And say dat's good enough for nigger.

Walk over! walk over!
Tom butter and de fat;
Poor nigger you can't get over dat;
                    Walk over!"[38]

In his autobiographical accounts as in everything else
he wrote, Douglass seems to be speaking from the platform.
His genius lay in his passion for meeting an antagonistic
public with the spoken word.   All of his writing is in the
spirit of spontaneous and racy and stirring oratory.   Reference has been made to the effect which his first convention
speech made upon Garrison.   Before he had ever written a
line for publication, the newspapers were praising his power
as an orator.[39] In 1843, he was named along with such
abolition notables as Garrison and Phillips for a course of
lectures in Boston.[40] In the same year an attempt was made
by the Abolitionists of Ohio to secure his services as an
antislavery agent exclusively in that state for a period of
twelve months.[41] One who had heard him speak in Concord,
New Hampshire, in 1844 wrote:

The close of his address Sunday evening was unrivalled. I can
give no adequate description of it. I have heard the leading
anti-slavery speakers, as well as the pro-slavery orators, and the
great advocates at the bar; and I have never seen a man leave
the platform, or close a speech, with more real dignity and
eloquent majesty.[42]

Even the enemies of the abolition principles which Douglass
expounded in his early speeches did not hesitate to praise
him.   One wrote in 1845:

Pity so noble a specimen of man should have been spoiled by the miserable fallacies of the Garrisonian philosophy![43]

The poems which were written in tribute to Douglass as an orator, especially by his English admirers, would make up a volume of fair size.[44]

Douglass' supremacy as a platform speaker was established by the time he returned from his first trip to Great Britain.   There were few questions that arose in regard to his race during the succeeding eighteen years upon which we do not have a printed speech from him. A typical Garrisonian polemic against slavery is an address given at an anniversary of the American Anti-Slavery Society held in New York on May 11, 1847. Defenders of slavery in Baltimore saw in the impracticable program which it advocated what they thought was a suitable boomerang, and published it as a pamphlet, entitled *Abolition Fanaticism in New York: Speech of a Runaway Slave from Baltimore.* It was apparently the first of Douglass' many orations circulated as pamphlets.   A less visionary work, such as his opponents could in no way exploit, was a diatribe against Henry Clay and the American Colonization Society, spoken at Faneuil Hall, Boston, in 1849 and reported phonographically for the press.[45] Perhaps the best known of the orations devoted to the general subject of abolition are two addresses published at Rochester in 1851 as *Lectures on American Slavery.*   Interesting for its irony is a Fourth of July speech published in 1852 as *Oration, Delivered in Corinthian Hall, Rochester,* the mood of which is suggested by the quotation—

What, to the American slave, is your Fourth of July? I answer: a day more than all other days in the year, the gross injustice and cruelty to which he is the constant victim.

At the commencement exercises of Western Reserve College in 1854 Douglass was a guest, and delivered before the literary societies of that institution his *Claims of the Negro Ethnologically Considered,* a soundly reasoned protest against the popular notion of African inferiority. The address was in the same year published at Rochester. A lucid defense of Douglass' desertion of Garrisonianism is *The Anti-Slavery Movement,* a lecture given before the Rochester Ladies' Anti-Slavery Society and printed in 1855. The same topic is discussed in a speech delivered at Canandaigua, New York, on August 4, 1857, in celebration of the anniversary of the emancipation of the slaves in the British West Indies. This address was published, probably in 1857, along with another, on the Dred Scott Decision, in a pamphlet entitled *Two Speeches of Frederick Douglass.*[46] One of the earliest of Douglass' many obituary orations on antislavery workers was the *Eulogy of the Late Hon. Wm. Jay,* delivered before a colored audience in New York and published in 1859. While in Great Britain in 1860, where Douglass took up temporary refuge after accusations had been made against him as an accomplice in John Brown's raid,[47] he gave a lecture at Glasgow, later printed at Halifax as *The Constitution of the United States: Is It Pro-Slavery, or Anti-Slavery?* It is a vigorous reply to an attack on his activity in American politics made by George Thompson, his chief supporter on his first visit to England.[48] Typical of the Civil War speeches is a rousing appeal for Negro enlistments delivered in Philadelphia in 1863 and published in *Speeches by the Hon. W. D. Kelly, Miss Anna E. Dickinson, and Mr. Frederick Douglass.*[49] Similar in mood is *What the Black Man Wants,* a plea for the full enfranchisement of the Negro delivered at Boston in 1865, and published the same year with speeches by William D. Kelly and Wendell

Phillips in a pamphlet called *The Equality of All Men before the Law.*

The publication of Douglass' orations was continued throughout his third and final period of authorship, extending from 1865 to the year of his death. As representative as any speech which we have from him is *John Brown,* delivered a number of times before it was finally given at Harper's Ferry in 1881 in the form in which it was printed as a pamphlet. The occasion of its delivery at Harper's Ferry was dramatic. Andrew Hunter, who as a district attorney had prosecuted John Brown, was on the platform. The proceeds from the sale of the printed speech were to be devoted to the founding of a John Brown Professorship in Storer College, established at Harper's Ferry in 1867 mainly for the instruction of the colored.

Avoiding the apology with which he was wont to begin so many of his early speeches, Douglass gets into his subject with a sustained periodic sentence, such as the fashions of nineteenth-century oratory freely permitted:

Not to fan the flame of sectional animosity now happily in the process of rapid and I hope permanent extinction; not to revive and keep alive a sense of shame and remorse for a great national crime, which has brought its own punishment in the loss of treasure, tears, and blood; not to recount the long list of wrongs inflicted on my race during more than two hundred years of merciless bondage; nor yet to draw, from the labyrinth of far-off centuries, incidents and achievements wherewith to arouse your passions, and enkindle your enthusiasm, but to pay a just debt long due, to vindicate in some degree a great historical character, of your own time and country, one with whom I was myself well acquainted, and whose friendship and confidence it was my good fortune to share, and to give you such recollections, impressions, and facts, as I can, of a grand, brave, and good old man, and especially to promote a better understanding of the raid on Harper's Ferry, of which he was the chief, is the object of this address.

Then follows a skillfully constructed summary, scarcely more than a page in length, of the events leading up to Brown's execution. The main theme is brought out in a few flash-like sentences.

There is, in the world's government, a force which has in all ages been recognized, sometimes as Nemesis, sometimes as the judgment of God, and sometimes as retributive justice; but under whatever name, all history asserts the wisdom and beneficence of its chastisements, and men become reconciled to the agents through whom it operates, and have extolled them as heroes, benefactors, and demi-gods. . . . That startling cry of alarm on the banks of the Potomac was but the answering back of the avenging angel to the midnight invasions of Christian slave-traders on the sleeping hamlets of Africa. The history of the African slave-trade furnishes many illustrations far more cruel and bloody.

The body of the speech, in which the central idea is frequently repeated, is devoted to an account of Douglass' various meetings with Brown. There is a picturesque recital of the last conference between the two, held in a deserted stone quarry near Chambersburgh, Pennsylvania, just twelve days before the raid. There are occasional touches of humor, such as the reference to those who accused Douglass of being an accomplice of Brown—

Governor Henry A. Wise was manifestly of that opinion. He was at the pains of having Mr. Buchanan send his Marshals to Rochester to invite me to accompany them to Virginia. Fortunately I left town several hours before their arrival.

After a tribute to Shields Green, the loyal fugitive slave executed with Brown, Douglass begins the peroration. He makes of it a restatement of his main theme. The Civil War, of which John Brown is named the first great hero, is proclaimed as the retributive justice which divine right had visited upon the slaveholder.

In spite of the flimsiness of the philosophy on which Douglass based the idea of the speech, and in spite of his faithfulness in following the standards of old-fashioned oratory, held in debasement by the taste of today, he produced in *John Brown* an oration that still stirs. Even in print, it seems warm and passionate. Fired by emotion, the message moves in a rhythm in which there is no hint of halt or hesitation. But Douglass in his maturity never allowed feeling to run away with him. The admirable structure of *John Brown* is an evidence of the exactness of his sense of logical symmetry. Each phrase, however sonorous it may be, has a definite and practical meaning. And *John Brown* is only one of a great number of orations of excellence which Douglass delivered and printed after 1847. Suggestive of the tributes paid to his genius as an orator when he was in his prime by many respected critics, including his enemies as well as his friends, is a statement made by Thomas Wentworth Higginson:

I have hardly heard his equal, in grasp upon an audience, in dramatic presentation, in striking at the pith of an ethical question, and in single illustrations and images, as 'For the negro the Republican party is the deck; all else is the sea.'[50]

In the oratory of Frederick Douglass, American Negro literature aside from its folk song has reached perhaps its highest plane. And the significance of his speeches lies in their intrinsic merit, not in the fact that they were created by a Negro who for the first twenty-one years of his life was a slave.

Douglass made the following statement in 1883:

If I have at any time said or written that which is worth remembering, I must have said such things between 1848 and 1860, and my paper was the chronicle of most of what I said during that time.[51]

When he returned to the United States from England in April, 1847, he came with the determination to fight slavery through the press as well as from the lecture platform. After wavering for a few months, considering whether he was to become associated with the *Ram's Horn,* a Negro newspaper then being published in New York, or whether he was to confine his journalistic work to contributions to such broadly circulated publications as the *Liberator* and the *National Anti-Slavery Standard,* he at length decided to devote the gift of money tendered him by Abolitionists in England to the use intended by them, namely, the establishment of a newspaper of which he was to be the owner and the editor.[52] The name selected was the *North Star,* symbolical of the slave's guide to a land of freedom; and Rochester, New York, because of its remoteness from the fields of other strong abolition journals, was definitely chosen as the place of publication, after Cleveland, Ohio, had been considered.[53] One number appeared before the year 1847 was ended; and the journal lived as a weekly (known after 1850 as *Frederick Douglass' Paper*) until August, 1860. It was then merged with *Douglass' Monthly,* which had been begun in June, 1858, as a small magazine planned for circulation in England. A monthly in its last years, Douglass' paper continued until he was able to announce in its columns Lincoln's Emancipation Proclamation.[54]

Douglass began his journalistic venture conservatively. The obvious models for the *North Star* were the *Liberator,* the *National Anti-Slavery Standard,* and the *Pennsylvania Freeman,* all much alike in matter and makeup, even though differing in policy. The motto chosen for the *North Star* was "Right is of no sex—Truth is of no color—God is Father of us all, and all we are brethren." The object as

stated in each number was "to attack slavery in all its forms
and aspects; advocate universal emancipation; exalt the
standard of public morality; promote the moral and intellectual improvement of the Colored People; and hasten the day
of Freedom to the Three Millions of our enslaved Fellow
Countrymen." The issue, like that of most newspapers of
the day, consisted of four pages. Editorials, letters, brief
notes, and copious extracts from the general and antislavery
press brought to the readers of the *North Star* news of
current abolition activities, as well as information on allied
reform movements, such as women's rights, temperance,
and better living conditions for laborers.[55] There was a
poetry column, in which, as in the *Liberator*, verses on general as well as on antislavery themes were published. The
North Star, except for contributions concerning Douglass
himself, such as his manumission papers and the series of
letters to Thomas Auld, his master when he was in slavery,
was a general abolition paper. It contained little to identify
it as a publication controlled and edited by a Negro, who at
first had as his chief asociates two other Negroes, Martin R.
Delany and William C. Nell.

It was perhaps less a Negro journal when the name was
changed to *Frederick Douglass' Paper*. The new title was
adopted at the time Douglass became a publicly confessed
convert to the abolition theories of Gerrit Smith. The
Liberty Party Paper, which had been published at Syracuse
under the editorship of John Thomas, was merged with the
North Star;[56] and, since the policies as well as the organization of the paper were revolutionized, and also since, as
Douglass afterwards declared, he felt that there were too
many "*stars* in the newspaper firmament," the new name
was decided upon.[57] What had been begun as just another
antislavery paper was thus turned into a political organ,

without the financial support of the party which it sponsored. Although it bore Douglass' name, and although he was the chief contributor as well as the editor, the discussion of Negro affairs found place only when not crowded out by Presidential messages, speeches in Congress, reports of party caucuses and conventions, Douglass' answers to the political enemies who were attacking him right and left, and his apparently endless defenses of the Constitution as an antislavery document. But however embroiled in politics it became, Douglass' paper remained the champion of the people of color. He went into politics as a Negro fighting sincerely for the welfare of his race; and the turn of events in the Civil War proved that in renouncing Garrison's radical doctrine of disunion he showed himself a more practical, farsighted, and useful fighter.

Maintaining a newspaper for such an extended period of time meant for Douglass a trying struggle. Financing the enterprise was at first exceedingly difficult. The money subscribed by English Abolitionists, amounting to a little more than two thousand dollars,[58] was sufficient to begin the paper; but to keep it going he had to depend mainly on his own resources, especially on raising money by lecturing.[59] At the end of 1848, when one volume of the *North Star* had been completed, he issued a statement to the effect that the publication could not be continued without more subscriptions or donations.[60] Although articles were contributed gratuitously,[61] and the privilege of using extracts from other publications was almost unrestricted, the expenses were estimated at eighty dollars for the week.[62] When conditions were at their worst, Julia Griffiths, an Englishwoman, who in 1853 and 1854 edited and published in this country an antislavery annual, *Autographs for Freedom*, came to the rescue;[63] and through her aid the circulation of Douglass' paper was increased until an average of three thousand subscribers could be depended upon.[64]   With such a subscription list, and with a fair income from advertising, the paper was financially stable until the John Brown troubles forced Douglass to seek a temporary refuge abroad, during which time the weekly publication of his paper was permanently discontinued.[65]

But financing was not the only stumblingblock which Douglass encountered.   The more he became involved in politics, the more enemies he found.   Those who had been his best friends became often his most scathing critics, members of his own race as well as whites.[66]   In spite of all, Douglass fought and won.   With the exception of the *Genius of Universal Emancipation* and the *Liberator,* his was the one abolition paper not sponsored and supported by an antislavery organization which survived for a considerable length of time and which exerted a broad influence towards the emancipation of the slave.[67]   Since Douglass never attempted to make of it an exclusive organ of his people, it can scarcely be considered as belonging to the field of the Negro journalism of the time.   But he, a Negro, was the very heart of its existence, and it was not inappropriate that during most of its life it was called *Frederick Douglass' Paper.*

After the Civil War, Douglass had no paper of his own in which to record his numerous speeches and communications to the public, except for the years from 1869 to 1872, when he conducted and edited at Washington the *New National Era,* a Negro weekly.   But his final period of authorship was none the less productive.   In a letter to Whittier, dated March 18, 1873,[68] he spoke of having lectured during the preceding winter "from Bangor to Omaha, and from St. Louis to St. Paul."   There were few winters from 1865 to 1894 when he was less active on the lecture platform. Many of his later orations, like *John Brown,* were printed as pamphlets.   In 1881 appeared his third autobiographical work, the *Life and Times of Frederick Douglass.*   The fourth and final autobiographical account came in 1892, the *Life and Times* enlarged by more than a hundred pages. In either edition, the story related is a strange one, peculiarly American.   A man who has been a United States Marshal, a Recorder of Deeds, a Minister to Hayti, looks over his dramatic past, back into the desperate years which he spent in servitude in Maryland.   Occasional passages reveal the oratorical Douglass still brimming with emotion.   An example is the tribute to Theodore Parker, introduced into a brief description of a visit to the graves of Parker and Elizabeth Barrett Browning in Florence.

The preacher and the poet lie near each other. The soul of each was devoted to liberty. The brave stand taken by Theodore Parker during the anti-slavery conflict endeared him to my heart, and naturally enough the spot made sacred by his ashes was the first to draw me to its side. He had a voice for the slave when nearly all the pulpits of the land were dumb. Looking upon the little mound of earth that covered his dust, I felt the pathos of his simple grave. It did not seem well that the great American preacher should rest thus in a foreign soil, far away from the hearts and hands which would gladly linger about it and keep it well adorned with flowers. Than Theodore Parker no man was more intensely American. Broad as the land in his sympathy with mankind, he was yet a loving son of New England and thoroughly Bostonian in his thoughts, feelings and activities. The liberal thought which he taught had in its native land its natural home and largest welcome, and I therefore felt that his dust should have been brought here. It was in his pulpit in Roxbury that I made my first anti-slavery speech.

But the *Life and Times* is the work of an aging man. One finds in it verbosity and tediousness, not the compression which makes the earlier autobiographies very readable. Also in his last period came a number of contributions from Douglass to leading periodical publications.[69] He was the first of American Negroes to get into the company of the prominent magazine writers.

It is a relief to find his writings in the careful print of such a periodical as the *North American Review*. Most of the work which he produced in his prime, including his autobiographies, was evidently rushed through the press. There is at least one notable exception, "The Heroic Slave," an account of Madison Washington's mutiny, which appeared in 1853 in *Autographs for Freedom*, an annual remarkable for its artistic typography. To see Douglass' writing in such decent dress, when the great mass of it is in timeworn newspapers or cheaply printed pamphlets, makes one feel that justice has not been done to the greatest of American Negroes, the most important figure in American Negro literature before 1900. Douglass' extant writings are worth preservation in a complete and scholarly edition.

IV

As extensive as Douglass' experience with slavery was, it was probably not so varied as that of William Wells Brown. When Brown became a lecturer for the Western New York Anti-Slavery Society in 1843, he had a stirring story to relate. According to his numerous autobiographical accounts, he was born in Lexington, Kentucky, but grew up in Missouri, where he was engaged in such occupations as laboring on plantations, working as an office boy, serving a slave trader who travelled up and down the Mississippi, and assisting in a newspaper office in St. Louis, which he claimed to be that of Elijah P. Lovejoy.[70]   He was almost white. Rumor, he tells us, declared that his mulatto mother was a daughter of Daniel Boone, and that his white father was a man "connected with some of the first families of Kentucky." After serving two owners, he was fortunate enough to be taken by a third, Enoch Price, a river boat captain, to Cincinnati. He broke away without difficulty, and "followed the north star" until he reached the Great Lakes. This was in 1834, when he was probably not more than twenty years of age.[71] The one helper whom he found during his flight was a Quaker, Wells Brown, from whom he received a surname and to whom he later dedicated his *Narrative:*

Thirteen years ago, I came to your door, a weary fugitive from chains and stripes.   I was a stranger, and you took me in. I was hungry, and you fed me.   Naked was I, and you clothed me.   Even a name by which to be known among men, slavery denied me.   You bestowed upon me your own.   Base, indeed, should I be, if ever I forget what I owe to you, or do anything to disgrace that honored name!

Living as a free man, he worked at various jobs in Cleveland, on a Lake Erie boat, and in Buffalo.   During his spare time, he studied spelling books, grammars, and histories;[72] and, as he tells us in his *Narrative*, he read the *Genius of Universal Emancipation* and the *Liberator*.   Participation in the open discussions of a colored temperance society in Buffalo accustomed him to speaking in public; and when he became an antislavery agent, he was ready to relate the story of slavery as he had experienced and observed it.

After serving less important abolition organizations, he was in 1847 called by the Massachusetts Anti-Slavery Society, possibly to replace Douglass, who was beginning his

independent work as a journalist. Brown remained a devoted Garrisonian, lecturing almost without interruption
either in this country or in Europe until he saw the complete
eradication of slavery. Without extraordinary talent for
public speech, he was never recognized as a rival of Douglass
in the field of oratory.[73] Nothing from his pen attains the
literary merit of even some of Douglass' less pretentious
speeches. But in the development of Negro literature he
is in one sense of more historic significance than any of his
contemporaries. For he was the first American Negro to
attempt seriously the novel, the drama, and travel literature.
And at the time he ceased writing he was the best historian
that the colored race had produced in America.

From 1844 until the outbreak of the Civil War Brown
was a frequent contributor to the abolition journals. Most
of his contributions were in the form of open letters, hastily
written communications regarding his work as an anti-
slavery agent.[74] A few offer special interest. Following
the precedent set by Douglass in writing the series of letters
to Thomas Auld, Brown in 1849 addressed an appeal to
Enoch Price, his last master in slavery, and at the time of
the composition of the letter still his legal owner.[75] Brown
states his point of view as follows:

Connected as I am with the slaveholders of America by the
blood that courses through my veins, if I could I would throw
the mantle of charity over the disgusting institution and everything connected with it.

He then makes of the letter as ingenious a bit of defiant
irony as one might easily find in antislavery literature.
Interesting for an altogether different reason is "To the
Public," a lengthy reply to a scandalous attack made on
Brown by the New York *Tribune* because of his separation

from his wife, an attack which led to an investigation by
the executive committee of the Massachusetts Anti-Slavery
Society, resulting in Brown's complete exoneration.[76] Perhaps the most finished writing which Brown showed in his
contributions to the abolition press is in his "Visit of a
Fugitive Slave to the Grave of Wilberforce," published in
Autographs for Freedom for 1854. It is a brief descriptive
essay, suggesting that the author was not unfamiliar with
Washington Irving's *Westminster Abbey*.

It was estimated that Brown delivered more than a
thousand addresses while he was in Great Britain, from
July, 1849, to September, 1854.[77] He was equally active in
this country during the more than twelve years which he
passed as an antislavery agent. Many of his speeches are
represented by excerpts in the abolition newspapers; but apparently only two were printed as pamphlets—*A Lecture
Delivered before the Female Anti-Slavery Society of Salem*,
published in 1847, and *St. Domingo: Its Revolutions and Its
Patriots*, printed in 1855 as it had been given before audiences in London and Philadelphia. The first contains too
many press clippings to be effective as popular oratory; but
it has for a conclusion one of those sounding outbursts by
which, unfortunately, the worth of an antislavery orator
was to a great extent measured:

If you have not liked my grammar, recollect that I was born
and brought up under an institution, where, if an individual was
found teaching me, he would have been sent to the State's prison.
Recollect that I was brought up where I had not the privilege
of education. Recollect that you have come here tonight to
hear a Slave, and not a man, according to the laws of the land;
and if the Slave has failed to interest you, charge it not to
the race, charge it not to the colored people, but charge it to
the blighting influences of Slavery,—that institution that has
made me property, and that is making property of three millions

of my countrymen at the present day. Charge it upon that institution that is annihilating the minds of three millions of my countrymen. Charge it upon that institution, whether found in the political arena or in the American churches. Charge it upon that Institution, cherished by the American people, and looked upon as the essence of Democracy,—AMERICAN SLAVERY.

St. Domingo, produced when Brown was at his maturity, shows a marked improvement. It is in the main a vivid and interesting narrative of the rise and fall of Toussaint L'Ouverture, with few words wasted in the attempt to be florid. Moreover, it is important in Brown's career as an author in that it is one of his earliest efforts in the field in which he was to be most industrious, that of Negro history. That Brown did not print more of his orations as pamphlets can possibly best be explained by the fact that when he became known at all he was known as a writer rather than as a speaker. After the appearance of his *Narrative,* his work demanded that he continue lecturing; but much of his time was occupied in publishing new books and in bringing out fresh editions of old ones.

The first edition of the *Narrative of William W. Brown* was issued by the Massachusetts Anti-Slavery Society in the early summer of 1847, and by February of the following year there was a demand for an enlarged edition.[78] A third edition was published in the fall of 1848, and a fourth in the late spring of 1849.[79] A London edition, prefaced with a poem by Brown, "Fling Out the Anti-Slavery Flag," and with a note stating that the first three American editions, amounting to eight thousand copies, had been sold within less than eighteen months, was published soon after Brown's arrival in England, in July, 1849. The original book had by this time been almost doubled. There are good reasons for its popularity. It is one of the most readable of the slave autobiographies, mainly because it is developed with incident rather than with comment. One story after another, such as the following, is introduced:

During our stay in New Orleans I met with a young white man with whom I was acquainted in St. Louis. He had been sold into slavery under the following circumstances. His father was a drunkard, and very poor, with a family of five or six children. The father died, and left the mother to take care of and provide for the children as best she might. The oldest was a boy, named Burrill, about thirteen years of age, who did chores in the store kept by Mr. Riley, to assist his mother in procuring a living for the family. After working with him for two years, Mr. Riley took him to New Orleans to wait on him while in that city on a visit, and when he returned to St. Louis, he told the mother of the boy that he had died with the yellow fever. Nothing more was heard from him, no one supposing him to be alive. I was much astonished when Burrill told me his story. Though I sympathized with him I could not assist him. We were both slaves. He was poor, uneducated and without friends; and, if living, is, I presume, still held as a slave.

However much the sensationalism in the book might tax the credulity of the reader, there is interest in it. The character most completely presented, Walker, the slave trader, far more diabolic than the terrible Covey of Douglass' autobiographies, is perhaps as near an approach to the melodramatic villain as antislavery literature had to offer before Simon Legree appeared in *Uncle Tom's Cabin*. The style of the *Narrative* is all the more telling because of its simplicity. The idiom throughout is almost monosyllabic, such as one might expect from a runaway slave who had never been to school. Brown drew freely from the *Narrative*, copying passages word for word, for the autobiographical sketches with which he prefaced a number of his later books; and it formed the basis of the *Biography of an*

American Bondman, published in 1856, the work of his daughter, Josephine Brown.[80]

In 1848, while he was enlarging and bringing out new editions of his *Narrative,* Brown published *The Anti-Slavery Harp,* a compilation of songs to be used at abolition meetings. The pieces included are by many hands, and considered as verse are perhaps as mean as any that ever got into print. Yet one reviewer referred to the collection as containing "the best songs of previous publications, with many that have not before been published";[81] and there was a demand for a second edition in 1849.

In the summer of that year Brown went to Europe with the intention of returning to the United States after he had given a few lectures in Great Britain and had represented the American Peace Society at the international convention of pacifists held in Paris at the end of the year. Before his mission as originally planned had been completed, the Fugitive Slave Law had been passed. This meant that he must stay away from the United States, or face the imminent probability of being sent back to slavery. Unemployed by any antislavery organization, he decided to remain abroad and support himself and his family by free-lance lecturing and by writing. Thus, until 1854, when he came back to his native country, the price set upon him by his owner in Missouri having been paid, Brown was a professional literary man.[82] And the venture proved to be surprisingly lucrative.

During the spring and summer of 1852, Brown got ready for the press a travel book, which was published in the autumn as *Three Years in Europe: or, Places I Have Seen and People I Have Met.* A volume written by an American Negro could not have been issued in England at a more propitious time. The excitement over *Uncle Tom's*

Cabin was at its highest. However, readers who bought *Three Years in Europe* because the author was styled on the title-page "A Fugitive Slave" must have been disappointed in the book. There is constant allusion to slavery in it, but little realistic picturing of slavery in the United States. Presented as a series of letters, it is Brown's own story of his experiences and impressions from the day he sailed from Boston, July 18, 1849, until the late spring of 1852. Europe is a wonderful land to him, because there he feels for the first time in his life no prejudice against his color. He is interested in all of the historic monuments, which he sees very much as the guidebooks prescribe. But he is most interested in great men, especially literary celebrities. In Paris, he meets Victor Hugo, who presides over the Peace Congress to which Brown has been sent as a delegate. At the *Opéra* he naturally finds the presence of Alexandre Dumas, as much African as Brown himself, more beguiling than the music of *Norma*. When he sees Ira Aldridge, an America Negro, play Othello in London, he watches the effect of the performance upon Bulwer-Lytton. As naïve as his comment frequently is, it often contains a sound native wit. The following passage about Carlyle, whom he sees by chance in an omnibus, is typical:

He was a tall man, with strongly marked features, hair dark and coarse. There was a slight stoop of the shoulder,—that bend which is always characteristic of studious men. But he wore on his countenance a forbidding and disdainful frown, that seemed to tell one that he thought himself better than those about him. His dress did not indicate a man of high rank, and had we been in America, I should have taken him for an Ohio farmer. . . . I had read his 'Hero Worship' and 'Past and Present,' and had formed a high opinion of his literary abilities. But his recent attack upon the emancipated people of the West Indies, and his laborious article in favor of the reëstablishment

of the lash and slavery, had created in my mind a dislike for
the man, and I almost regretted that we were in the same
omnibus. . . . As a writer, Mr. Carlyle is often monotonous and
extravagant. He does not exhibit a new view of nature, or
raise insignificant objects into importance; but generally takes
commonplace thoughts and events, and tries to express them
in stronger and statelier language than others. . . . He cares little
what he says, so that he can say it differently from others. To
read his works is one thing; to understand them is another. If
any one thinks that I exaggerate, let him sit for an hour over
'Sartor Resartus,' and if he does not rise from its pages, place
his three or four dictionaries on the shelf, and say that I am
right, I promise never again to say a word against Thomas
Carlyle.

Whoever and whatever he sees are vitally real to Brown.
Being in Europe is to him a rebirth. Whether he approves
or disapproves of what he runs upon, he is in high spirits.
Because of the enthusiasm which he poured into it, and because of the rough naturalness of the style, *Three Years in
Europe* is what a critic in the *Literary Gazette* of London
called it at the time it was published—"a pleasing and
amusing volume."[83]

In whatever he wrote Brown depended mainly for effect
on the sensational. He was tireless in picturing atrocities
on southern plantations and in discussing the social compli-
cations arising from the mixture of races in the South.
While in London he sponsored an exhibition of waxworks
depicting the horrors of slavery, for which the undated
catalogue was entitled *A Description of William Wells
Brown's Original Panoramic Views of the Scenes in the
Life of an American Slave, from His Birth in Slavery to
His Death, or His Escape to His First Home of Freedom on
British Soil.* In his *Anti-Slavery Harp*, he included a song,
"Jefferson's Daughter," to which the following note, ascribed
to *Tait's Edinburgh Magazine,* was appended:

It is asserted, on the authority of an American newspaper, that the daughter of Thomas Jefferson, late president of the United States, was sold at New Orleans for $1,000.[84]

Like the gossip regarding Zachary Taylor, who, according to antislavery rumor, owned four hundred slaves, seventy of whom were his concubines, the scandal touching Jefferson was bandied about by the more sensational Abolitionists.[85] Encouraged by the public reception of *Three Years in Europe,* Brown published in 1853 a novel based on this story about Jefferson and developed with such pictures as he had displayed in his exhibition of waxworks. The book, so far as we know the first novel attempted by an American Negro, was called *Clotel; or, The President's Daughter: a Narrative of Slave Life in the United States.*

English readers might have been disappointed in *Three Years in Europe* because of the limited space given to pictures of Negro life in the American South. But they no doubt found the sordidness and tragedy of slavery portrayed with far more daring and range in *Clotel* than in *Uncle Tom's Cabin.* The time of the opening of the story is the beginning of the nineteenth century, and the place is Richmond. A Negro woman, Currer, who for a time in her youth had been the housekeeper and mistress of Thomas Jefferson, is living peacefully with the two daughters whom she has borne him, Clotel and Althesa. He has long been out of their lives. They are all three slaves, the property of a wealthy Virginian; but they are enjoying a sort of liberty. Currer is known as the most skillful laundress in Richmond, and by her earnings pays her master for the time which he has the right to demand from her and her two daughters. The girls, provided with a tutor, a free Negro, grow up as ladies. All runs smoothly until the master dies and his seventy-nine slaves are put up for sale. Thus begun, the action moves rapidly, developed along two main plot lines—the adventures and tragic fate of each of the two daughters. The shifting scenes bring the reader in contact with slavery in Virginia, in Washington, on a plantation near Natchez, in New Orleans, and on the Ohio and Mississippi River steamboats. There are slave pens, auction blocks, bloodhounds, monstrous "nigger drivers," whites pressed into servitude, seductions, suicides, murders, and a burning. The yellow fever epidemic in New Orleans in 1831 and Nat Turner's insurrection in Virginia in 1832, both described with the harrowing horrors that accompanied them, are brought in as motivating situations. Jefferson never enters the story, but his utterances on liberty and slavery are skillfully woven into the frequently recurring essay· comment. And an effect of irony worthy of a trained novelist is gained by having the main catastrophe acted out in an environment associated with Jefferson's name : the fleeing Clotel, hemmed in by slave trappers on the "Long Bridge" at Washington, drowns herself in the Potomac, "within plain sight of the President's house and the Capitol of the Union."

The great weakness of *Clotel* is that enough material for a dozen novels‚ is crowded into its two hundred and forty-five pages. Excellent stories have been written after much worse plans. But Brown did not realize the drama of his plot. He was too eager, it seems, to get to the end of the tale. The movement is so fast that we never see any one person in the story at any time long enough to get a clear impression of his character. A scene which might stir the emotions is sketched in a few sentences and passed by as completed. The humor is often close to the heart of the Negro. For example, there is a minor character, Sam, who, although he is a submissive slave, is in the habit of saying things with a double meaning and of making up half defiant rimes, such as :

> The big bee flies high,
> The little bee makes the honey;
> The black folks makes the cotton,
> And the white folks gets the money.

However, what humor there is is introduced in digressive episodes, the main characters being at all times deadly serious. *Clotel* was by no means what Brown probably intended to make it, a successor to *Uncle Tom's Cabin*. But it was a promising beginning for American Negro fiction.

In July, 1854, the formalities of Brown's manumission were completed,[86] and in September he was back in the United States.[87]   Before the end of the year, the American edition of *Three Years in Europe* appeared as *Sketches of Places and People Abroad*.   It is a considerable and judicious enlargement of the original, and was commented on most favorably by the antislavery reviewers, a number of whom hailed Brown as "the Fugitive Slave turned Author."[88]   Although an immediate American edition of *Clotel* was urged,[89] it did not come until 1864.   The novel, possibly because it was based on a scandalous rumor which the author had evidently made no attempt to prove as true, had not won the approval in England which had been accorded *Three Years in Europe*.   Brown must have recognized his mistake in making Jefferson the focus of the story; for when the American edition did finally appear, Jefferson was replaced by an "unnamed Senator," and the new title adopted was *Clotelle: a Tale of the Southern States*.   Numerous changes were made, all, with the exception of dropping Jefferson, for the worse.   Certain passages were so mutilated that they are not intelligible.   Since the copyright was secured by the publisher, one might reasonably accept the edition as brought out without Brown's knowledge if he himself had not in 1867 copyrighted an almost perfect facsimile of it, which was published as *Clotelle; or, The Colored Heroine.*

From 1854 to 1863 Brown is regularly referred to in the antislavery papers as engaged for lectures. During this most active period of his career as an abolition agent, he possibly took the time to make a trip to the West Indies,[90] and he is credited with having written during this period a second novel, *Miralda, or, The Beautiful Quadroon.* But if such a work was ever printed, it seems to be no longer in existence.[91] This is likewise true of *Doughface,* a drama, which has been attributed to Brown and which might possibly have been written before 1858.[92] But since we cannot prove that *Doughface* ever existed, we must take Brown's *The Escape; or, A Leap for Freedom,* published in 1858, as the American Negro's first definitely known attempt to write a play.

Brown claimed that he wrote *The Escape* for his "own amusement." He said:

I read it privately, however, to a circle of friends, and through them was invited to read it before a Literary Society. Since then the Drama has been given in various parts of the country.[93]

He meant, of course, that he had given it as a reading; and it seems that the public for a time preferred it to his lectures.[94] The play is made up of five acts, each divided into many scenes. Some of the farcical episodes are diverting, but the attempts at seriousness are unpardonably forced. The slave heroine, Melinda, pours out freely such sentiments as the following, which she speaks to her amorous master after he has lured her to a hut on one of his remote plantations:

Sir, I am your slave; you can do as you please with the avails of my labor, but you shall never tempt me to swerve from the path of virtue.

Her husband, Glen, also a slave, indulges in endless anti-slavery heroics. One does not wonder that it is good luck rather than the initiative of the two which in the end lands them safe in Canada. *The Escape* as a play is far more feeble than *Clotel* is as a novel. However, since *The Escape* is a pioneer venture of the American Negro into the field of the drama, it is a landmark in his literature.

In 1863, Brown published his first extensive attempt at history, *The Black Man: His Antecedents, His Genius, and His Achievements*. Following the plan for historical accounts of the Negro made popular by Henri Grégoire in his *De la littérature des nègres* (1808), Brown opened the work with a discussion of ancient civilization in Egypt and Ethiopia, and then followed it with biographical essays of more than fifty Negroes who had gained distinction of some sort in Western civilization. The publication came at a most convenient time for attracting sales, just after Lincoln issued the Emancipation Proclamation. Many of the essays, such as the one on Nat Turner, were provided with the sensationalism which Brown always depended upon for gaining a hearing. Before the end of a year the book had been enlarged, and was in a third edition. It continued to be reprinted after the publication of Brown's second historical work, *The Negro in the American Rebellion: His Heroism and His Fidelity*, issued in Boston in 1867. While the rôle played by the Negro in the Civil War is the subject of the major portion of the book, there is also a discussion of the activities of the colored people in the Revolution and War of 1812. For the part dealing with the Civil War Brown drew his material from newspapers, from which he culled the most exciting and picturesque reports regarding the Negro soldiers in battle, "contrabands" picked up by the Union armies, contacts with slaves serving in the Con-

federate lines, "thrilling meetings" between long-lost fugitives and their families, Negro boys entertaining regiments
with their strange songs and dances, and the effect on the
Negro of the South brought about by the breaking down of
slavery. He had no true historical perspective on his material; but he treated it in an informal and gossipy style, and
thus made of *The Negro in the American Rebellion* a readable book.

In his most pretentious and most important historical
work, *The Rising Son*, published in 1874, Brown reprinted
much of the serious matter which he had included in *The
Black Man* and in *The Negro in the American Rebellion*.
He had by 1874 in some way learned medicine, and was
settled in Cambridgeport, Massachusetts, as a practicing
physician. What cessation from the nerve-straining work
of public life meant to him is manifest in *The Rising Son*.
Collecting and arranging the material required time and
repose. For the book is an effort to treat in a methodic and
orderly manner the history of the Negro in ancient Africa,
modern Europe, South America, the West Indies, and the
United States. At the time it was published it was the most
complete and thorough general history of the Negro which
had been produced in America, and such it remained until it
was superseded in 1883 by the more scholarly *History of the
Negro Race in America from 1619 to 1880*, the work of
another colored man, George W. Williams.[95] Brown had
one great advantage over Williams: he was older, and had
lived close to much which he wrote about. But he lacked
Williams' sense of accuracy in recording facts. It is
scarcely to be expected that Brown the propagandist should
after the age of sixty turn into Brown the historian. While
the style of *The Rising Son* is far less exciting than that of
the earlier histories, the work is in the main propaganda

brought out through entertaining episodes. The public accepted the book as readable—to the extent of buying ten thousand copies within less than a year from the time of its publication.

In his last book, *My Southern Home: or, The South and Its People,* published in 1880, Brown reverted to fiction. But fortunately, this work, his nearest approach to real literature, is neither a novel nor a play. It is a series of narrative essays, made up, as Brown tells us in the preface, dated May, 1880, of memories of his childhood and impressions gathered on trips to the South after the Civil War. The stories told in many of the essays, a number of which are presented in dramatized form, had been used in his earlier books. But given as the reminiscences of an old man, they gain in effect. Humor and picturesqueness are the characteristics which dominate. One essay tells of how Cato and Hannah, both slaves, get married according to the ceremony, described in detail, of "jumping the broom-stick." Hannah's present from her mistress is "some whiskey"; and Cato, who is something of a rimester, composes his own wedding hymn, of which one stanza is:

> Father Gabriel, blow your horn!
> I'll take my wings and fly away,
> Take Hannah up in the early morn,
> An' be in hebben by the break o' day.

Another essay describes Aunt Nancy's experiences in trying to make cheese. "Runnet" is required; and at her order a sheep is slaughtered to provide the "runnet." When the substance is not found in the animal's stomach, she recalls that it is obtainable only from a calf. To avoid being whipped she pleads:

Missis, when de moon is cold an' de water runs high in it, den I have to put calf's runnet in de milk instead of sheep's. So las' night I see de moon is cold an' de water is runnin' high.

Other essays describe a slave auction at Congo Square in New Orleans and the announcement of the Emancipation Proclamation in a slave cabin in South Carolina. The Negro's songs, many of them undoubtedly of folk origin, are freely introduced, among which is the following street cry, recorded, Brown tells us, as it was sung in a town in South Carolina shortly after the Civil War:

> Here's yer chitlins, fresh an' sweet,
>   *Who'll jine de Union?*
> Young hog's chitlins hard to beat,
>   *Who'll jine de Union?*
> Methodist chitlins, jest been biled,
>   *Who'll jine de Union?*
> Right fresh chitlins, dey ain't spiled,
>   *Who'll jine de Union?*
> Baptist chitlins, by de pound,
>   *Who'll jine de Union?*

Unfortunate for the general artistic effect of *My Southern Home* is the fact that in each story, in each anecdote, and in each song Brown is present as the propagandist. But the message which the book brings to his people is perhaps the most important he ever preached. He summarized it in the concluding sentence, "Black men, don't be ashamed to show your colors, and to own them!"

Four editions of *My Southern Home* had been published by 1884, the year of Brown's death. Weighed down by sermon and produced in a crude and often ungrammatical English, the book had little chance to live on as story. For the year of its original publication, 1880, was the year of the appearance of Joel Chandler Harris' *Uncle Remus, His Songs and His Sayings.* As a message for the Negro, *My Southern Home* was at the same time too old-fashioned and too far ahead of its day. Neither it nor any one of Brown's earlier books was strong enough to keep his name alive. Yet in the development of American Negro literature he deserves a place of high importance.

V

Proslavery sympathizers were always ready to attribute the success of Douglass and Brown to their white blood. The Abolitionists had an answer for such detraction of the Negro in the person of Samuel Ringgold Ward, who, according to Wendell Phillips, was so black that "when he closed his eyes you could not see him."[96] Ward everywhere passed as pure African in ancestry, but he himself declared that there was a strain of Caucasian blood in his mother.[97] Although born a slave, and after the passage of the Fugitive Slave Law forced to go to Canada for safety,[98] he never experienced bondage except in his infancy. In 1820, when he was three years old, his parents fled with him from the plantation in Maryland where they were bound and brought him to New York.[99] He grew up in what he called "this city of evercrushing Negro hate," received an education sufficient to fit him for teaching, and after a few years as a schoolmaster became in 1839 a minister of the Congregational Church and an agent of the American Anti-Slavery Society. In December of that year he met Gerrit Smith, who "adopted" him much as Garrison was two years later to "adopt" Douglass.[100] Under Smith's direction he went over to the New York Anti-Slavery Society; and from this time until 1851, when he left the United States never to return as a permanent resident, he was regarded as a leading lecturer for the Liberty Party. But his work during this period was not confined exclusively to lecturing. He served two churches as pastor, one of them being a congregation at

South Butler, New York, made up entirely of whites, of whom he wrote:

The manly courage they showed in calling and sustaining, and honouring as their pastor a black man, in that day, in spite of the too general Negro-hate everywhere rife (and as professedly pious as rife) around them, exposing them as it did to the taunts, jeers, and abuse of too many who wore the cloak of Christianity—entitle them to what they will ever receive, my warmest thanks and kindest love.[101]

And he also during these years dabbled in medicine, read law, and engaged in two newspaper ventures, "both of which," he said in 1855, "I survive, and in which I sunk every shred of my property."[102]

The first of these newspapers was the *Impartial Citizen,* published for a brief period at Syracuse in 1848.[103] The second, also published at Syracuse, was the *Northern Star and Colored Farmer,* of which Ward became an assistant editor after the failure of the *Impartial Citizen.*[104] While both of these newspapers in all probability represented Liberty Party policies,[105] they seem to have been designed for colored readers. But what type of journalism they represented and what Ward's contributions to them were cannot be determined. For, as in the case of most early Negro newspapers, there is apparently not a single surviving number of either paper today.

In order to judge Ward's oratory, we have to turn to his one book, *The Autobiography of a Fugitive Negro: His Anti-Slavery Labours in the United States, Canada, and England,* published in London in April, 1855.[106] It was written in England, where Ward went in 1853 to lecture under the auspices of the Anti-Slavery Society of Canada.[107] Of the many orations which he delivered both in this country and abroad,[108] not one seems to have been printed in complete form.[109]   But his book is to a great extent argument expressed as though it were spoken from the platform. His life is sketched in less than forty pages, and the rest of the volume, containing altogether more than four hundred pages, is given over to diversified discussions of slavery. The style is vigorous.   There is an abundance of anecdotes, intimate personal references, and humorous asides.   The man revealed is self-confident, appealing for justice for the Negro and not pity.   The argument is practical and firmly logical.   There is little indicating that the author was a minister.   The book has been frequently classified among the slave narratives; but, like Douglass' *My Bondage and My Freedom*, it belongs to a different and more important category.   As a sociological study of the Negro of the period it has value.   An examination of the book convinces one that Ward was in all probability what his contemporaries declared him, a formidable rival of Douglass as a platform speaker.   Douglass himself said of Ward—

No colored man who has yet attracted public attention in this country, was ever capable of rendering his people greater service than he.[110]

But Ward is a lesser figure in Negro history and literature.   He lacked the perseverance to put to use the talents which might have made him a great public servant of his people.   The publication of *The Autobiography of a Fugitive Negro* was his last work in the interest of abolition. Before the book was out of the hands of the printers,[111] he was on his way to Jamaica, where he lived, rarely heard from in the United States, until his death, probably in 1864 or 1865.[112]

CHAPTER V

WRITINGS OF THE RACIAL LEADERS, 1840–1865

So now, I tell ye, Sambo,
  Ye're born a man to-day;
Nobody gwine for contradic'
  What Massa Linkum say.

Him gwine for free de nigger:
  De Lord him gib de word;
And Massa Linkum's writ 'em down,—
  O Sambo, praise de Lord!

> —From "A Contraband's Poetical Version
> of the President's Emancipation Proclamation,"
> quoted in William Wells Brown's *The Negro in
> the American Rebellion,* 1867.

I

The idea expressed in a statement made by Samuel Ringgold Ward, "Any Negro living well is an anti-slavery fighter,"[1] is a constantly recurring theme in antislavery literature. The Abolitionists understood fully the importance to the struggle against slavery of the advancement of the Negro church, Negro schools, Negro industries, and such varied society as the Negro was developing for himself. They were always ready to point to prosperous communities of free blacks as a living refutation of the argument, insisted upon by proslavery defenders, that the Negro was incapable of energy and thrift and initiative. Spurred on by the abolition movement, such independent Negro society as had been established in the United States by 1840 made the most pronounced progress during the succeeding twenty-five years. By 1850, there was a distinct Negro colony, with its churches, schools, lodges, and possibly its shopping district, physicians, lawyers, and newspaper, in every city of the North where there was any considerable Negro population.[2] The leaders who were carrying on the work of advancing this separate Negro society were not content merely to "live well." It was impossible for them to refrain from active participation in the fight for abolition. Few of them were ever employed as antislavery agents. But they printed lectures and sermons, and published books and pamphlets and newspapers, all of which furnished antislavery propaganda. Moreover, the writings of these leaders are a clearer reflection of what was being done towards the development of the colored people as a social unit than are the better known works of Remond, Douglass, Brown, and Ward.

A healthful sign of progress was the interest which the Negro came to manifest in his past. And along with this there was an evident desire to study scientifically the contemporary sociological status of the race.

The first Negro to make a serious attempt at an extensive historical record of the activities of the colored people in the United States was William C. Nell, who for a great part of his life was associated with the editorial and printing offices of the *Liberator*. He was born in Boston, where his father had settled in 1812.[3] His schooling, it seems, was no more than elementary. We hear of him as early as 1846 in advertisements in the *Liberator,* in which his services as "copyist, accountant, and collector" are offered to the public, and in which he is spoken of as "one of the most deserving and exemplary of our colored citizens, amiable and modest in his deportment and intelligent in mind."[4] Except for a few years which he spent in Rochester, where he was for a time associated with Douglass in the publication of the *North Star,* Nell seems to have lived his life in Boston.

Among the valedictory communications which appeared in the last number of the *Liberator,* that for December 29, 1865, there was perhaps none more sincere than Nell's "Farewell to the Liberator." His frequent public utterances prove that his devotion to Garrison and Garrisonian principles was always steadfast.

When Douglass adopted the policies of the Liberty Party for his paper, Nell's connection with it was no longer possible.[5] However, it was while he was in Rochester, under Douglass' influence, that he took up seriously his researches in Negro history. The idea of the work, as he tells us, was suggested to him by Whittier, who in a statement published in 1847 lamented the fact that no attempt had been made to preserve a record of "the services and sufferings of the colored soldiers of the Revolution."[6] Nell undertook to prepare such a record; and in 1851 his first efforts were published in Boston as a pamphlet of twenty-four pages, called *Services of Colored Americans in the Wars of 1776 and 1812.* In 1852, a second edition of the pamphlet, enlarged to forty pages and provided with an introduction by Wendell Phillips, was published. Encouraged by the reception of these little works, Nell began intensive investigation for more material in the field, and in 1855 brought out *The Colored Patriots of the American Revolution, with Sketches of Several Distinguished Colored Persons: to Which is Added a Brief Survey of the Condition and Prospects of Colored Americans.* A full volume, containing almost four hundred pages, it appeared in an attractive binding. Phillips' introduction to the 1852 pamphlet was reprinted, and a second introduction, by Harriet Beecher Stowe, was added.

The book came in an important year in American Negro literature, the year of Douglass' *My Bondage and My Freedom,* Brown's *Sketches of Places and People Abroad,* and

Ward's *The Autobiography of a Fugitive Negro*. *The Colored Patriots* is not the least meritorious of these works. Unlike his only Negro predecessor in the field of secular history, R. B. Lewis, whose *Light and Truth* (1844) is little more than an emotional outpouring,[7] Nell followed in his humble way the methods of the true historian. He devoted himself to facts and to what he saw as a faithful presentation of them. In order to dig up historical data, he examined national and state papers, military records, and an extensive range of antislavery writings. He was far more serious in his research than William Wells Brown was to be when he turned to Negro history eight years later. As the full title of *The Colored Patriots* discloses, it is more than an account of the Negro's services in the Revolution and War of 1812. It is in reality a survey of the Negro's participation in American affairs from the last quarter of the eighteenth century until Nell's own day. There are lengthy portraits of such outstanding figures as Phillis Wheatley, Crispus Attucks, Benjamin Banneker, Paul Cuffe, and James Forten. The style is brusque, not so finished as Nell often showed in his newspaper contributions.[8] Only in the brief conclusion is there an apparent attempt to write well; and the effect here is oratorical and unhappy. The book contains an abundance of facts which speak for themselves. While it is not so extensive and readable as Brown's works on Negro history, it is probably more trustworthy.

The social status of the free Negro in the United States was the theme on which James McCune Smith, probably the most prominent New York Negro of the period, produced a number of speeches, pamphlets, and articles. Smith was frequently held up by the Abolitionists as an example of what cultural training could do for the ambitious black. In 1837, he returned to this country from Scotland, where he had spent a number of years at the University of Glasgow, from which he received the degree of Doctor of Medicine. His reception by the colored population of his native New York was in the nature of a triumph.[9] From this time until at least as late as 1874,[10] he resided in New York, respected alike by whites and blacks as a successful physician and as a man of steady character and unusual cultural attainments.[11]

No other American Negro leader before Smith had profited from an intensive education in a country where prejudice against color was comparatively unknown. Not only his successes in his profession, but his writings, published occasionally over a period of more than twenty years, stand as evidence that he responded to university training in a stable manner. Probably his first completely reported speech was delivered at the annual meeting of the American Anti-Slavery Society in 1838.[12] It is a brief summary of abolition activities in England and France, produced in a simple, expository style. Alike in clarity are the occasional signed contributions from Smith to the *Colored American,* of which he was an assistant editor from January until May, 1839.[13] His first attempt to show in fairly extensive manner what the Negro might accomplish in Western civilization was in his *Lecture on the Haytien Revolutions, with a Sketch of . . . Toussaint L'Ouverture,* published as a pamphlet in 1841. Although necessarily compressed, it surveys with surprising adequacy the broad field which the title suggests. But it is especially interesting as argument brought out by narrative detail. All the stronger because of the restrained style in which it is written is "Freedom and Slavery for Africans," a controversial essay in the form of two connected letters, published originally in the New York *Tribune* in 1844.[14] Smith's aim in writing the essay was to refute a claim made with considerable elaboration by the Reverend O. Dewey that the slaves of the South were happier than the free Negroes of the North. Smith states his position as that of "the son of a slave, owing his liberty to the Emancipation Act of the State of New York, and having kindred in a Southern state, some of them slave-holders, and others slaves," and then furnishes statistical facts to prove the fallacy of Dewey's hypothesis. Such a scientific method of defending the intellectual capacity of the Negro is employed in an essay, "Civilization: Its Dependence on Physical Circumstances," published in the *Anglo-African* in 1859.[15] Smith's admission into the New York Geographical Society came as the result of an essay, apparently never printed, on a similar topic, namely, the effect of physical environment on the character of the islanders of the South Seas.[16]

Certain pieces which Smith published were obviously intended to be literary as well as controversial. In the 1854 volume of *Autographs for Freedom* there is a brief essay from his pen, "Freedom—Liberty," developed with abstract ideas and produced in the rhythm of a prose poem. Also marked with a verse-like rhythm is "John Murray (of Glasgow)," a tribute to a Scotch Abolitionist, printed in the *Autographs* for 1853. The introduction which Smith provided for Frederick Douglass' *My Bondage and My Freedom* (1855) offers another example of smooth and graceful phrasing. The concluding paragraph is typical of the movement of the piece as a whole:

It is not without a feeling of pride, dear reader, that I present you with this book. The son of a self-emancipated bondwoman, I feel joy in introducing you to my brother, who has rent his own bonds, and who, in his every relation—as a public man, as a husband, and as a father—is such as does honor to the land which gave him birth. I shall place this book in the hands of the only child who is spared me, bidding him to strive and emulate its noble example. You may do likewise. It is an American book, for Americans, in the fullest sense of the idea. It shows that the worst of our institutions, in its worst aspect, cannot keep down energy, truthfulness, and earnest struggle for the right. It proves the justice and practicability of Immediate Emancipation. It shows that any man in our land, "no matter in what battle his liberty may have been cloven down, . . . no matter what complexion an Indian or an African sun may have burned him," not only may "stand forth redeemed and disenthralled," but also may stand up a candidate for the highest suffrage of a great people—the tribute of their honest, hearty admiration. Reader, *Vale!*

Pleasing in style and at the same time informing is Smith's introduction, comprising more than sixty pages, to Henry Highland Garnet's *A Memorial Discourse; Delivered in the House of Representatives* (1865).

The most carefully educated American Negro among Smith's contemporaries, the Reverend Alexander Crummell, a graduate of Queen's College, Cambridge, once referred to him as the most learned Negro of his day.[17] Although Smith's publications are so limited in quantity that they form a slight basis for judgment, they are on the whole produced in a style which makes Crummell's estimate seem justifiable.

Less learned than Smith and inferior as a stylist, but with many more attempts at literature to his credit, was Martin Robison Delany, another Negro physician of the period who was interested in a study of the sociological status of his race. According to his biographer, Delany was born free at Charlestown, Virginia, in 1812. He had no schooling until he was ten years of age, when his parents moved to Chambersburgh, Pennsylvania. Later they settled in Pittsburgh; and there Delany grew to maturity, obtaining, as he afterwards declared, invaluable training for his future career as a worker for his race from an organization of which he was a leading member, the Theban Literary Society, composed of young colored men.[18] In 1839, he made, it seems, an extended trip into the Southwest, going into Louisiana and Texas and gathering impressions which he was to use much later in his novel, *Blake, or, The Huts of America*. In 1843, he began the publication of a Negro newspaper in Pittsburgh, the *Mystery*, which he seems to have issued regularly until 1847, when he became associated with Douglass in the founding of the *North Star*.[19] From this time on he was a national figure in Negro affairs, dwelling on no one activity long enough to achieve genuine success. He studied at the Harvard Medical School,[20] became a physician, and practiced medicine in Pittsburgh and in Canada. He tried his hand at inventions; he became interested in a scheme for colonizing Negroes in Central America; he lived for a time in a Negro colony in Canada; he led a party of Negro explorers, prospective colonizers, into the Niger Valley region of Africa; and as an officer in the United States Army during the years immediately following the Civil War he rose to the rank of major. In 1883, two years before his death, he was considered important enough to be made the subject of a carefully constructed biography of more than three hundred pages, the work of a member of his race who wrote under the name of Frank A. Rollin.[21] An interesting comment on Delany is that of William Lloyd Garrison, who referred to him as "black as jet, and a fine fellow of great energy and spirit."[22]

Delany's first published writings appeared, no doubt, in his newspaper, the *Mystery*, the files of which, like those of most Negro newspapers which existed before 1865, have apparently not been preserved. If his early literary efforts are to be judged by the crudity of an 1847 publication, *Eulogy on the Life and Character of the Rev. Fayette Davis,* printed at Pittsburgh, his association with Douglass' *North Star* meant for him an education. With the exception of occasional letters, and brief notes signed "M. D.," it is impossible to determine what his written contributions to the *North Star* were. But in 1852, the year following his withdrawal from Douglass' paper, he published a work which shows him at his best, *The Condition, Elevation, Emigration, and Destiny of the Colored People of the United States, Politically Considered.* Delany's main purpose in writing the book, as the concluding chapters show, was to encourage the emigration of free blacks to Central America. Because of his interest in such a plan, he was severely attacked by Abolitionists in Pennsylvania as a man ready to compromise with the still hated idea of colonization, and therefore as a deserter from the cause of immediate emancipation. Instead of trying to defend his stand, Delany confessed his mistake in publishing the book and ordered its circulation stopped.[23] Whatever its original reception might have been, the work is still a valuable source for a study of the social position of the free Negro in the United States during the period preceding the Civil War. According to a statement made in the preface, the book, well over two hundred pages in length, was written in New York within one month's time, while the author "was engaged in business during the day and in lecturing on physiology during the evening." It has, to be sure, all the marks of a too hasty preparation. But the trustworthy facts given regarding Negro life are probably more extensive than in any other one book, by either a white or a black, produced during the period. A much briefer and more carefully executed work on the same subject was a speech delivered at Cleveland in 1854 and printed as a pamphlet with the title, *Political Destiny of the Colored Race on the American Continent*, a copy of which was sent by Delany to each member of Congress.[24]

At a national emigration convention of colored men held in Cleveland in 1858, Delany was appointed leader of an exploring party to be sent to Africa for the purpose of studying the Niger Valley as a possible place for the settlement of colored emigrants from the United States. The expedition, carried on entirely by Negroes, was made during 1859 and 1860; and in 1861 Delany published an account of it in the *Official Report of the Niger Valley Exploring Party*. It is of book size, and is fairly readable as a recital of African travels and adventures; but Delany evidently attempted to make of it no more than an official report. The task of providing a more literary record of the expedition was left to a lesser member of the party, Robert Campbell, whose account, *A Pilgrimage to My Motherland*, was published also in 1861. While his book has interest, Campbell wrote in the labored style which Delany had long before outgrown.[25]

The serial publication of Delany's novel, *Blake, or, The Huts of America*, was begun in the *Anglo-African* in 1859, shortly before his departure for the Niger Valley. Three chapters selected from the middle of the book appeared in the January number of the *Anglo-African*, with a statement from the editor that the story was later to be published as a volume. Plans for the publication in this form evidently failed. In the February number of the magazine the first five chapters of the story were printed, and it was continued through July, when the twenty-fourth chapter was reached. Apparently, no more of the story ever saw print. Enough of it exists to enable us to place it in the expected category, among the numerous analogues of *Uncle Tom's Cabin*. The hero is drawn after George Harris; and what we see of the heroine, who is sold very early in the story and sent away to Cuba, strongly suggests Eliza. There is all over again the Negro life in the "quarters," "huts" in Delany's novel replacing the "cabins" in Harriet Beecher Stowe's. Pictures of supposed atrocities on southern plantations make up much of the development, perhaps the most extreme being a description of a slave auction held in a church. An abundance of conventional adventure is provided for the hero, who as a runaway from slavery has been through Texas and Louisiana before the fragment breaks off. William Wells Brown had a gift for story-telling which Delany entirely lacked. Perhaps the one merit of *Blake* is that the rambling style permitted the introduction of several folk songs which are in all probability genuine.

Delany's experiences with medicine naturally led him into scientific speculation. In addition to an installment of his novel he contributed to the *Anglo-African* for January, 1859, an essay, "The Attraction of Plants." It is much better written than his attempt at fiction, and forms an interesting preparatory study for his most ambitious work, a volume of considerable size, the complete title of which is *Principia of Ethnology: The Origin of Races and Color, with an Archaeological Compendium of Ethiopian and Egyptian Civilization, from Years of Comparative Examination and Enquiry.* It was published in Philadelphia in 1879, and in the following year a second edition was issued. The book is an attempt to prove that "the two extremes of color, from the most negative white . . . up to the blackest, are produced by the same material and essential properties of color." As a contribution to anthropological knowledge the tedious treatise is no doubt of negligible value. But as an example of an attempt to reason from scientific principles it is a creditable performance for an American Negro whose development belongs to the period preceding the Civil War.

Another interesting contribution to the sociological studies of the Negro came from William G. Allen, who first received public notice because of his association with the *National Watchman,* a newspaper begun at Troy, New York, possibly as early as 1842.[26] Apparently not a single number has been preserved. At the time it was discontinued, in 1847, Allen, referred to as a "young man of color," was named as the publisher.[27] According to his own statement, he was a quadroon, a graduate of the Oneida Institute with the class of 1844, and later a student of law in Boston.[28] Soon after the failure of the *National Watchman* he was engaged by Central College, an abolition institution situated at McGrawville, New York, as "professor of the Greek and German languages and of Rhetoric and Belles Lettres." Following his marriage to one of his white students, he went to England.[29] Shortly after his arrival in that country, in 1853, he published his *American Prejudice against Color: an Authentic Narrative, Showing How Easily the Nation Got into an Uproar.* It is a lively account of an event which led to mob violence in Phillipsville, New York, and which received notorious comment in the press of every section of the United States, namely, Allen's marriage. Addressed to a British public, it is exceedingly anti-American in tone ; but woven in with the humorously expressed contempt of American institutions is a thoughtful recognition of the problem of the color line. The book is well written. Also carefully done are several letters which Allen contributed to the *Liberator.*[30] But his place in Negro literature should be determined by a brief essay, "Placido," published in *Autographs for Freedom* for 1853. After a verbose introduction, he goes into such a treatment of the Cuban poet as makes of the essay an admirable bit of literary appreciation.

Several other writers belong to the group whose main interests were in the sociological status of the Negro. One who called himself "A Southerner" published in Philadelphia in 1841 *Sketches of the Higher Classes of the Colored Society in Philadelphia.* Internal evidence, especially the intimate knowledge of Negro life displayed, convinces the reader that the author was in all probability colored. As a source of information on American Negro life during the twenty years preceding the Civil War the little work is an interesting supplement to Delany's *Condition, Elevation, Emigration, and Destiny of the Colored People.* Mainly sociological is Jesse Ewing Glasgow's *The Harper's Ferry Insurrection,* a pamphlet published in Edinburgh in 1860. The author was a young American Negro studying at the University of Edinburgh and, according to what he himself said, partially supporting himself by writing for newspapers.[31] On a trip back to his native country, probably early in 1860, he gathered the material for his very readable account of John Brown's raid and execution. The style is roughly journalistic; but there is strength in the manner in which the reader is made to feel that he is seeing the whole disturbing situation from the point of view of the free Negro.[32] The problem of the color line is the subject treated in *A Review of the Cause and Tendency of the Issues Between the Two Sections of the Country* (1859), the work of Lewis H. Putnam, who at the time of the composition of the essay was living at Bedford, Long Island.[33] The one solution seen is the emigration of the blacks to Liberia. However, his expression is so wordy that one can only with patience understand his message. To read John B. Meachum's plea for education, *An Address* to *All the Colored Citizens of the United States* (1846), is also a trying experience. But *The Late Contemplated Insurrection in Charleston, S. C.* (1850), by one who called himself a "Colored American," is, like Glasgow's *The Harper's Ferry Insurrection,* a readable short narrative and at the same time an interesting expression of the free Negro's attitude towards an alarming social condition.

II

A type of history in which the Negro has been most productive, that treating the Negro church, had its beginnings before 1865. Probably the earliest venture into the field was the generalized and comparatively unimportant *Short Account of the Rise and Progress of the African Methodist Episcopal Church in America* (1843), written by Christopher Rush with "the aid of George Collins." It is gossipy and controversial. But the work of two other early church historians, William T. Catto and William Douglass, is of a commendable type. Each was far better equipped for historical research than either William Wells Brown or William C. Nell. And each was concerned with relating actual facts rather than with producing antislavery propaganda.

In 1857, Catto's *A Semi-Centenary Discourse, Delivered in the First African Presbyterian Church, Philadelphia, . . . with a History of the Church from Its First Organization* was published in Philadelphia. Catto, previously a Methodist,[34] had been pastor of the church about which he wrote since 1855.[35] The discourse occupies comparatively little space in the more than one hundred pages which make up the book. The major portion treats in detail the history of the Presbyterian movement among the Negroes of Philadelphia from the organization of the first separate congregation in 1807 until Catto's own day. The facts, we are told, were drawn mainly from minutes and church records and verbal testimony. Much information on other Negro churches in Philadelphia besides the Presbyterian is introduced. Catto evidently made no effort to produce a readable account. The prefatory discourse shows that he was not weak as an orator. But when he turned to the history of his church, he was content to put down facts in the most direct and abrupt manner. Not the least valuable part of the book is an appendix, in which are listed and briefly described the eighteen Negro churches which existed in Philadelphia in 1857, serving, according to Catto, a colored population of thirty thousand. *A Semi-Centenary Discourse* is a precious source book for the student of the religious and social history of the American Negro.

Even more valuable as a source of reliable information is William Douglass' *Annals of the First African Church, in the United States of America, Now Styled the African Episcopal Church of St. Thomas, Philadelphia,* published in 1862. Douglass, a native of Maryland, had served St. Thomas' church as rector since 1834.[36] As Catto had done, Douglass traced the history of his church from its origins to his own day. The greater and more interesting part of the book is that which treats the founding of the first separate Negro churches in America. The main sources, named on the title-page, were "the minutes of a beneficial society, established by Absalom Jones, Richard Allen, and others in 1787 . . . and the minutes of St. Thomas' Church." Passages from these documents are freely introduced. A number of early letters, dealing with the development of the separate church movement in such centers as Newport and Boston, are quoted in full.

Douglass' book is almost twice the length of Catto's, and
there is probably more compactness in Douglass' style.

As a Negro leader of the fifties, William Douglass was
a unique figure. In 1854 he published a volume entitled
*Sermons Preached in the African Protestant Episcopal
Church of St. Thomas.* The sermons are on such topics
as "The God of Hope," "Peace in Christ," "Mutual For-
bearance and Forgiveness," "The Sin of Grieving the Holy
Spirit," and "The Shortness and Uncertainty of Time."
Slavery, prejudice against color, the racial misery of the
Negro, and the thousand and one controversial topics which
were engaging the minds of the Negro leaders of the day
were left untouched. In the funeral discourse on Peter
Williams, Douglass does refer to the Negroes as "our
people." But one might read most of the book without
ever suspecting that the author was a colored man, occupied
in working directly with colored people. The style of both
the *Annals* and the *Sermons* is clear and pleasing and
careful. William Douglass was one of the best educated of
the Negro writers of the period.

III

A neglect of slavery and racial problems cannot be attributed to James W. C. Pennington and Henry Highland
Garnet, the most prominent New York Negro preachers of
the period. However, both were more noted as Abolitionists
than as ministers. They came before the public as fugitives; and, while neither seems to have been employed at
any time as an antislavery agent, both lectured extensively.
According to all reports, each was of unadulterated African
blood.

Next to David Walker, Henry Highland Garnet was the
most radical of all the active Negro antislavery agitators.

He first attracted attention in 1840 by an address given before an anniversary meeting of the American Anti-Slavery Society, in which he tried to defend the resolution, "That all the rights and immunities of American citizens are justly due to the people of color, who have ever been, and still are willing to contribute their full share to enrich and defend our common country."[37] In all his public utterances he never compromised with the principle so stated. At the time of the delivery of this speech Garnet was in his twenty-fifth year, a student of the Oneida Institute, from which he was graduated a few months later.[38] According to two of his school fellows and lifelong friends, James McCune Smith and Alexander Crummell, he had been born a slave in Maryland; had been brought by his fugitive parents to New York when he was ten years old; had served on the sea for two years as a cabin boy; had been driven out of a school at Canaan, New Hampshire, because of his color; and, like most students at the Oneida Institute, had done farm labor while pursuing his studies, in spite of the fact that he was an invalid, suffering from a disease which ultimately necessitated the amputation of a leg.[39]

In 1843, Garnet delivered an address before a Negro antislavery convention in Buffalo which was considered so revolutionary and dangerous that its adoption was voted down. The objections stated were "that it was war-like and encouraged insurrection, and that if the convention should adopt it the delegates who lived near the borders of the slave states would not dare to return to their homes." It was finally printed in 1848, at the instigation and expense, it has been said, of John Brown, in a volume including a reprint of Walker's *Appeal* and Garnet's biographical sketch on Walker.[40] Entitled *An Address—to the Slaves of the United States of America,* it begins:

Your brethren of the north, east, and west have been accustomed to meet together in national conventions, to sympathize with each other and to weep over your unhappy condition. In these meetings we have addressed all classes of the free, but we have never until this time, sent a word of consolation and advice to you. We have been contented in sitting still and mourning over your sorrows, earnestly hoping that before this day, your sacred liberties would have been restored. But, we have hoped in vain. Years have rolled on, and tens of thousands have been borne on streams of blood, and tears, to the shores of eternity. While you have been oppressed, we have also been partakers with you; nor can we be free while you are enslaved. We therefore write to you as being bound with you.

A type of insurrection unheard of before is urged, a general strike. Death is pictured to the Negroes of the South as better for them than slavery. Therefore, they are begged to lay down their tools and to be assured that even though their annihilation might result they cannot be unhappier. They are urged to:

cease to labor for tyrants who will not remunerate you. Let every slave throughout the land do this, and the days of slavery are numbered. You cannot be more oppressed than you have been—you cannot suffer greater cruelties than you have already. Rather die Freemen, than live to be Slaves. Remember that you are Three Millions.

Garnet might have derived the main idea embodied in the *Address* from the popular discussions on nonresistance, frequently found in the abolition journals of the day, especially in the *Liberator*. The piece has all the emotion of Walker's *Appeal* without Walker's crudities. In the preface to the volume in which the *Address* was printed Garnet said, "May this little book be borne on the winds of heaven, until the principles it contains shall be understood and adopted by every slave in the Union." But, unlike

Walker's *Appeal* when originally published, Garnet's *Address* apparently went unheeded in the South.

From the time of the delivery of the *Address* Garnet was considered in the North as a sort of political Thomas Paine for the Negroes. His public life was varied. He was a Presbyterian pastor, a teacher, an operator of the Underground Railroad, an agent of Gerrit Smith in disposing of land grants to colored families, a traveller in Europe, a missionary to Jamaica, at one time a promoter of African colonization, a college president, and in his old age a United States Minister and Consul General to Liberia.[41] While he was living at Troy, New York, between 1839 and 1848, he undoubtedly published for a time a newspaper, the *Clarion,* no issue of which seems to have been preserved.[42] And it has been said that he was associated with two other papers, the *National Watchman* and the weekly *Anglo-African.*[43] But he was above all things an antislavery orator, lecturing throughout the North and in England. However, besides the 1843 *Address* only two other speeches which he delivered in his maturity seem to have come down to us. In 1848 he gave a lecture at Troy before a women's benevolent society which was published as *The Past and the Present Condition, and the Destiny of the Colored Race.* The rebellious mood of the piece is suggested by such statements as:

By an almost common consent, the modern world seems determined to pilfer Africa of all her glory. It were not enough that her children have been scattered over the globe, clothed in garments of shame—humiliated and oppressed—but her merciless foes weary themselves in plundering the tombs of our renowned sires, and in obliterating their worthy deeds, which were inscribed by fame on the pages of ancient history. . . . The silence that reigns in the region where the pale nations of the earth slumber, is solemn, and awful. But what think ye, when you are told that every rood of land in this Union is the grave of a murdered man, and that their epitaphs are written upon the monuments of the nation's wealth. Ye destroyers of my people, draw near, and read the mournful inscription; aye, read it until it is daguerrotyped on your souls. "You have slain us all the day long—you have no mercy." Legions of haggard ghosts stalk through the land. Behold! see, they come: Oh, what myriads! Hark! hear their broken tones as they clatter together! With deep unearthly voices they cry, "We come, we come! For vengeance we come! Tremble, guilty nation, for the God of justice lives and reigns." The screaming of the eagle as he darts through the lightning and the storm is unheard because of these voices. The tocsin of the sabbath, and the solemn organ are mocked by them. They drown the preacher's voice, and produce discord in the sacred choirs. Sworn senators and perjured demagogues, as they officiate around the altar of Moloch in the national capitol, hear the wailings of the base born democracy, and they are ill at ease in their unexampled hypocrisy. The Father of Waters may roar in his progress to the ocean—the Niagara may thunder, but these voices from the living and the dead, rise above them all.

When slavery was doomed and Garnet had not so much to urge, he was less glowing as an orator. *A Memorial Discourse; Delivered in the Hall of the House of Representatives, Washington, D. C., on Sabbath, February 12, 1865,* published in Philadelphia the same year with a lengthy introduction by James McCune Smith, is sonorously phrased, but not excitedly emotional. With such speeches as those given in 1843 and 1848 to measure Garnet by, we do not wonder that he won the confidence and friendship of the visionary John Brown.

In 1849, James W. C. Pennington, then in England, published his autobiography, *The Fugitive Blacksmith; or, Events in the Life of James W. C. Pennington.* It tells of twenty-one years of his life spent as a slave on a plantation in Maryland, where he was considered especially skilled as a blacksmith; of his perilous escape to New York; of his studying "logic, rhetoric, and the Greek Testament without a master"; and of his beginnings as a Presbyterian minister in Connecticut. The book brought surprising news to the antislavery public, to which Pennington was well known by 1849; for prior to his departure for England he had told few that he was a fugitive.[44]   Before his manumission was finally secured, in 1851,[45] he had received the degree of Doctor of Divinity from the University of Heidelberg, at the conferring of which it was reported as said, "You are the first African who has received this dignity from an European university, and it is the University of Heidelberg that thus pronounces the universal brotherhood of humanity."[46]   A black man whose liberty could not be contested by the Fugitive Slave Law, Pennington came back to the United States; and, in addition to serving a church in New York as pastor, he was an antislavery orator until the termination of the Civil War.

A number of Pennington's speeches have been preserved. *Covenants Involving Moral Wrong Are Not Obligatory upon Man* (Hartford, 1842) is a theological dissertation, with few marks to show that the author was a Negro. *An Address Delivered at Hartford, Aug. 1, 1856,* is on abolition. The argument is presented from the point of view of practicability, the advantage to both whites and blacks of the liberation of the slaves in the British West Indies being presented as justifiable reason for immediate emancipation in the United States. Historical facts and statistical estimates are freely cited to support the thesis. A similar method of persuasion is employed in "A Review of Slavery and the Slave Trade," "The Self-Redeeming Power of the Colored Races of the World," and "The Great Conflict

Requires Great Faith," all published in the *Anglo-African* during the year 1859 after they had probably been delivered as sermons or addresses. Pennington's study of logic and his training in orthodox Puritan theology distinguish his speeches as the most exact and perhaps the most dull to be found in the Negro oratory of the period.

His earliest publication, *A Text Book of the Origin and History . . . of the Colored People,* which was printed at Hartford in 1841, reveals the manner in which he was to preach to his race for the rest of his life. It is, as the title indicates, a textbook, catechetical in arrangement, such questions as the following being presented and answered: "Who are the colored people and whence do they come?"; "What can be said of the degradation of a people once so highly favored?"; "Are colored Americans, in point of intellect, inferior to white people?"; and "Is there any difficulty in accounting for our complexion?" What the answers are might easily be inferred. In this little book, intended for Negro children, Pennington established himself as a school-master for his race, and such he remained in his other extant writings, even in *The Fugitive Blacksmith,* which has too many absolute pronouncements on the wrongs of slavery to afford the readability found in many other slave auto-biographies. It was made up, as we are told in the preface, from lecture notes. But the style is that of pedagogic discussion rather than that of fluent speech. Notwithstanding its comparative lack of interest, the narrative was in its third edition within a year after its first publication.

IV

The passage of the Fugitive Slave Law in 1850 meant a severe trial for certain Negroes who were before the public as antislavery fighters. Brown and Pennington, both abroad when the law went into effect, did not dare return to the United States until their manumission had been assured. America having become a seemingly hopeless home for the blacks, many saw the idea of colonization in a new light. Reference has been made to Delany's interest in plans for the colonization of Negroes, first in Central America, and later in the Niger Valley section of Africa. The latter movement received the approbation and support of Garnet. Ward emigrated to Jamaica. Two other churchmen important in Negro literature before 1865, James Theodore Holly and Alexander Crummell, gave up the United States and became citizens of foreign countries.

Holly is generally known as a Haytian; but he was a native American, born of free parents in Washington in 1829. He came to New York in his youth, studied for the Protestant Episcopal priesthood, and was ordained in 1850.[47] In the autumn of 1853 he returned from his first trip to Hayti.[48] In 1857 came the one publication which entitles him to a place in American Negro literature before 1865, the full title being *A Vindication of the Capacity of the Negro Race for Self-Government, and Civilized Progress, as Demonstrated by Historical Events of the Haitian Revolution, and the Subsequent Acts of That People since Their National Independence*. It is a lecture, which, according to statements made in the preface, had been delivered many times before it was published. The controlling aim is stated in the sentence, "I wish to do all in my power to inflame the latent embers of self-respect, that the cruelty and injustice of our oppressors, have nearly extinguished in our bosoms, during the midnight chill of centuries, that we have clanked the galling chains of slavery." The speech is well written. It is significant in the social history of the American Negro because of its expression of a straightforward

and uncompromising challenge to Anglo-Saxon domination
—the challenge of a colored man who was planning to live
his life in a country where there was no strong white
element to inspire inferiority. And it is of special interest
in Negro literature because of the conditions under which
it was published. It was sponsored by a publishing company
in Hartford organized under the auspices of a national
Negro emigration convention for the purpose of printing
"the literary productions of colored authors, and incidentally
to publish the writings of any other class of authors when
the same shall be deemed serviceable to the great cause of
humanity."[49] Of the works proposed for publication,
Holly's *A Vindication* seems to be the only one which was
actually printed. But that such a company existed at all is
a revelation of the spirit of independence which the free
Negroes were developing towards the end of the period of
slavery. Whether Holly had an active part in the work of
the company we do not know. He later settled in Hayti,
became a bishop, braved attacks from church enemies,[50]
while on a visit to England preached a sermon in Westminster Abbey,[51] and lived an active life until his death at
Port-au-Prince in 1911.

Frederick Douglass, William Wells Brown, and Alexander Crummell form the group of three which did most for
American Negro literature between 1840 and 1865. Douglass and Brown were to a great extent white; but Crummell
was of pure African ancestry. Douglass and Brown owed
whatever education they had to direct participation in the
antislavery conflict; Crummell, never a slave, was a graduate
of the Oneida Institute in the United States and a bachelor
of arts from the University of Cambridge in England.
Douglass and Brown lived their lives where there was the
eternal depressing influence of racial strife; Crummell

spent the years of his strongest productivity in Liberia, where he was accorded the respect of a state's oracle and dictator. His writings have perhaps less general interest than those of Douglass and Brown. He lacked Douglass' genius for oratory, and Brown's skill in story-telling. But his style is immeasurably purer than that of any of his Negro contemporaries. Indeed, Crummell was the most literary of all the American Negroes who wrote before 1900. That a chain of chance circumstances led him to England and then to Africa was fortunate for American Negro literature. For without his training in England and his experiences in Africa the best of his writings would have been impossible.

Crummell was born in the city of New York in 1819. Among his boyhood school fellows were Ira Aldridge, the actor, James McCune Smith, Samuel Ringgold Ward, and Henry Highland Garnet.[52] Inspired and encouraged by Peter Williams, he early made up his mind to take orders in the Episcopal church. He completed his preliminary studies at the Oneida Institute, and then sought admission into the General Theological Seminary in New York. But he was refused because of his color.[53] He was accorded more considerate treatment by a seminary in Boston, and in 1844 he was ordained.[54] However, unsponsored by the proslavery sympathizers who were in control of the work of the Episcopal church in New York, he made slow progress in advancing Negro Episcopal activities in his home city. Finally, at the suggestion of a few influential friends— John Jay, whom he always referred to as "my great patron," among them—he went to England to solicit funds for the building of a church in New York. The trip was the turning point in his life. Sympathizers for the Negro among the English clergy saw in him a man of promise, and through their aid he was enabled to study at Queen's College, Cambridge, from which he was graduated in 1853. Instead of returning to the United States as he had planned, he went to Liberia, because of ill health and the necessity of a warm climate.[55]   He was in Africa from 1853 until 1873. In the latter year he came back to the United States, and took up his work as rector of St. Luke's Church in Washington, where he remained until 1894.   He retired from the regular duties of a clergyman in that year, but continued to write and to lecture until his death in 1898, his last great service for his race being the establishment in 1897 of the American Negro Academy.[56]

Crummell's first publication, *The Man: the Hero: the Christian! A Eulogy on the Life and Character of Thomas Clarkson: Delivered in the City of New York, December, 1846,* was published soon after his departure for England, where he arrived on January 26, 1847.[57]   It is the one work of Crummell's which represents his style before his period of study at Cambridge and association abroad with such families as the Froudes, the Thackerays, the Patmores, and the Caswells.[58]   The speech is in the main a survey of Clarkson's antislavery labors, developed with interesting objective details neatly put together.   The one obvious effort at oratory, the peroration, is forced—puffed with high-sounding scholarly allusions. The roughly printed pamphlet is a crude dress for some of Crummell's polished phrasing. The eulogy is perhaps as able a piece of writing as any American Negro of the time had produced.

Crummell's next important publication, *The Duty of a Rising Christian State to Contribute to the World's Well-Being and Civilization,* came almost ten years later.   It was delivered as the annual oration at the national independence celebration at Monrovia, Liberia, on July 26, 1855, and was published in London the following year.[59]   The speech is a truly eloquent plea—showing a world of improvement over the eulogy on Clarkson—for the Negro in Liberia to shake off any sense of inferiority which his past in the United States might have developed in him.

For the truth must needs be confessed by us all, that our natures have been dwarfed and our souls shriveled by the dread ordeal of caste and oppression through which our fathers, and some of ourselves, have passed.   Why, do not *you*, and *you*, and *you*, fellow-citizens, feel the want, the lack, the incompleteness of being?—the idea that something is gone?—that you need something that has been taken away, and you cannot seize upon it?—so that, at times, the heart swells, and the tears come unbidden, and the mind itself becomes bewildered?   It is the fruit of that old system, which tracks even freemen to freedom's own domain.   It is the remembrance of that old death, which retains vitality and generates agony even in the region of life and blessedness.

The mood, like that of all of Crummell's messages to his race, is optimistic.   The Liberians, he says, will forget their past, will cultivate men, and then—

The results that will proceed from such high endeavors are clear and certain.   We shall raise up on these shores a race of men, a stock of manhood, and a growth of manners, which shall confuse and mystify all the past chronicles of time pertaining to our race.   We shall falsify all the lying utterances of the speculative ethnographies and the pseudo-philosophies which have spawned from the press of modern days against us.   And we shall bring about such an expansion of mind and such a development of character, that the report thereof shall bring to our shores curious travellers to behold here the mature outgrowth and the grateful vision of a manly, noble, and complete African nationality.

Throughout the speech there are echoes of the doctrines of Carlyle and Dr. Thomas Arnold.   The idealism preached to the Negroes of Liberia suggests that Crummell was probably familiar with Emerson's *The American Scholar*. And the style of the speech is not unworthy of the masters who might have helped to inspire the thought. It is an intellectual appeal, firmly organized, and expressed in a varied and tastefully chosen diction.

For the Liberian national independence celebration at Cape Palmas in 1860, Crummell delivered an oration called *The English Language in Liberia*, which was published in New York in 1861. It is on a topic which was of absorbing interest to Crummell. He says, "Our very speech is indication of our sorrowful history; the language we use tells of subjection and conquest." But he adds that for the Liberians the English speech is like the heritage of Christianity, and therefore he exhorts his compatriots to "make indigenous in this infant country the spirit and genius of the English language." While the oration is perhaps not so strong as *The Duty of a Rising Christian State*, it is written in the same admirably careful style.

The two Liberian Independence Day addresses were reprinted in a volume entitled *The Future of Africa*, published in New York in 1862. In the preceding year Crummell came back to the United States on a visit, the ostensible purpose of which was to encourage the emigration of Negroes to Liberia.[60] The mission led him into an indirect association with the American Colonization Society, with the work of which he was to be in sympathy so long as he remained in Africa.[61] His aim in publishing *The Future of Africa* is made clear in the third and fourth orations included in the book, "The Progress of Civilization along the West Coast of Africa" and "The Progress and the Prospects of the Republic of Liberia," both delivered on various occasions in the United States in 1861. The economic and social attractiveness of Liberia as a home for the American blacks is the theme of each. But neither shows Crummell at his best. He was too bookish and too idealistic to be efficient as a practical promoter of an emigration movement. That which makes the volume a distinguished contribution to Negro literature is the inclusion of the Independence Day orations and such articles and sermons as "God and the Nation," a sermon preached at Monrovia in 1854, "The Future of the Gospel," a Christmas sermon preached at Cape Palmas in 1859, "Hope for Africa," announced as previously printed as a pamphlet,[62] and "The Negro Not under a Curse," reprinted from the London *Christian Observer* for September, 1850. Even in the last named piece, probably Crummell's second attempt to write for publication, there is that sensitiveness to purity of style which makes the author an important figure in Negro literature. The titles given suggest the varied nature of the contents of *The Future of Africa.* If there is one theme which dominates the book entire, it is Liberian patriotism. But the work is too fine to be of value in stirring up popular feeling. Certainly, no previous book published by an American Negro exhibits such painstaking finish.

Later African addresses similar in tone to the Independence Day orations are "The Responsibility of the First Fathers of a Country for Its Future Life and Character," delivered at Monrovia in 1863, and "God's Dealing with Nations and Peoples, and the Lessons It Teaches," a sermon preached at Monrovia in 1867. Both were published in the *African Repository.*[63] "Obligation of the American Black Men for the Redemption of Africa," an extended plea for emigration in the form of a series of articles addressed to Negro undergraduates in American colleges, was published in the *African Repository* in 1872.[64] Perhaps the strongest of all the appeals which Crummell made to American blacks in behalf of Africa is an open letter, *The Relations and Duties of Free Colored Men in America to Africa,* published at Hartford in 1861 as a pamphlet. While it is not a plea for colonization, it brings out the advantages to the blacks of life in Liberia. It urges the formation of trade associations to encourage commerce with Africa, but it also has such passages as:

> Alas for us as a race! So deeply harmed we have been by oppression, that we have lost the force of strong, native principles, and prime natural affections. Because exaggerated contempt has been poured upon us, we too become apt pupils in the school of scorn and contumely. Because repudiation of the black man has been for centuries the wont of civilized nations, black men themselves get shame at their origin and shrink from the terms which indicate it.
>
> Sad as this is, it is not to be wondered at. "Oppression" not only "makes a wise man mad," it robs him also of his self-respect. And this is our loss; but having emerged from slavery, it is our duty to cast off its grave-clothes and resist its deadly influences.

One other admirably written African oration should be at least named, *An Address Delivered at the Laying of the Corner Stone of St. Andrew's Church, Buchanan, Bassa County, Liberia, West Africa, on the 24th February, 1870.* It was printed in Preston, England, at Crummell's instigation and expense.[65]

Crummell was really never definitely settled in Liberia. He was there as a missionary for his church, as a professor in Liberia College, and as a promoter of the interests of the American Colonization Society. When his daughters were ready for college, they were sent to Oberlin.[66] When he was in this country in 1862, an effort was made to secure his permanent services as rector of St. Philip's Church in

New York.[67]   Possibly because of the encouragement which
he was receiving from the Colonization Society, he refused
this offer.   Ten years more of adverse struggle in Liberia
threatened his health.   However, when, in 1872, he came
back to the United States to stay, he did not come as a man
who had failed.   His later writings show that he never gave
up his youthful hopes for Liberia as a thriving republic of
Christian black men.

A considerable number of articles and speeches printed
as pamphlets belong to the final period of Crummell's
authorship.   Besides, he published in 1882 a volume of
twenty sermons, entitled *The Greatness of Christ,* and in
1891 a volume of addresses and discourses, *Africa and
America,* included in which are his earliest publication, the
eulogy on Clarkson, and several other orations which had
been previously printed.   The majority of the sermons are
charmingly written religious talks, with only a hint now and
then that they are the work of a Negro.   But after his
return to America Crummell by no means remained aloof
from the agitation over race problems.   Answering the
question "Can a Negro in America forget that he is
colored?" he says in *The Social Principle among a People,*
the preface of which is dated January 14, 1876:

Forget it forsooth when you enter a saloon and are repulsed
on account of your color! Forget it when you enter a car,
South or West, and are denied a decent seat! Forget it when
you enter the church of God and are driven to a hole in the
gallery! Forget it when every child of yours would be driven
ignominiously from four-fifths of the common schools of the
country! Forget it, when thousands of mechanics, in the large
cities, would make a "strike," rather than work at the same
bench, with a black carpenter or brickmaker! Forget it when
the boyhood of our race is almost universally deprived of the
opportunity of learning trades, through prejudice! Forget it,

when in one single state, 20,000 men dare not go to the polls on election day, through the tyranny of caste! Forget it, when one great commonwealth offers a new constitution for adoption; by which a man like Dumas, the younger, if he were a North Carolinian, could be indicted for marrying the foulest white woman in the State; and merely because she was white. Forget that you are colored in these United States! Turn, mad man, and go into a lunatic asylum; and then, perchance, you may forget it! But, if you have any sense or sensibility, how is it possible for you, or me, or any other colored man to live oblivious of a fact of so much significance in a land like this? The only place I know of in this land where you can "forget that you are colored" is in the grave!

Even though some of the strongest pages of his later writings are pictures of abuses which the Negro suffers in the United States, Crummell declared in one of his last messages, *The Shades and the Lights of a Fifty Years' Ministry,* an anniversary sermon preached in Washington on December 9, 1894:

One other large truth I wish to put before you, namely, that standing now more than three score years and ten, in age; the scars of bitter caste still abiding, I am, nevertheless, a most positive Optimist.

Filled with the "jubilee" spirit so characteristic of his race, he saw for the American Negro a future as bright as that which he saw earlier in his life for the Liberian. Discussing the matter of social equality in *The Race Problem in America* (1889), he said:

The question of equality pertains entirely to the two domains of civil and political life and prerogative. . . . There is something ignoble in any man, any class, any race of men whining and crying because they cannot move in spheres where they are not wanted. . . . Let me say that the social idea is entirely excluded from this consideration. It is absolutely a personal matter, regulated by taste, condition, or either by racial or family affinities, and there it must remain undisturbed forever.

That the blacks in America are so situated, he argues in "The Destined Superiority of the Negro," the last sermon in *The Greatness of Christ,* is of no disadvantage to them. Their genius for imitation will save them.

A people devoid of imitation are incapable of improvement, and must go down; for stagnation of necessity brings with it decay and ruin.

Thus, making over for themselves the best qualities of other races, the Negroes in America are seen by Crummell as a race whom God has preserved "to do something with."

Alexander Crummell's sure self-confidence and bounding hopefulness made him one of the strongest defenders of the doctrine of challenge which the Negro race in America has produced. His education in England and his long sojourn in Africa gave him an outlook on racial problems in the United States which he would never have developed if he had remained in this country during the decade preceding the Civil War. It is no wonder that apostles of the doctrine of challenge among the Negroes of our own day see in Alexander Crummell a hero.[68]

As significant as Crummell's message was, his distinction in Negro literature rests more on how he wrote than on what he wrote. The charge, frequently and unjustly made, that Negro writings are corrected and made over before they get into print can easily be proved false in the case of Crummell. Manuscript copies of a great mass of his publications are in existence.[69] They are mainly in his own handwriting; and, marked by numerous changes and erasures, they reveal the stylist working with patience and painstaking care. Crummell's interest in the English language was one of the great interests of his life. It is his extraordinary feeling for the precise word that makes even his dissertations on economic problems readable matter.

And when he was writing on a subject with which he was sincerely sympathetic, he often created a prose that is soundly artistic.

V

There remains for discussion the work of one other racial leader, Thomas Hamilton, who seems to have lived all of his life in New York.[70] His place in Negro literature rests upon his establishing the *Anglo-African,* one of the most important of the Negro magazines which have been published in the United States. Negro newspapers issued between 1840 and 1865 were fairly numerous, representing as diverse sections of the country as New York, Pennsylvania, Ohio, and California.[71] Most of them were short-lived; and apparently no one took them seriously enough to see that they were preserved for posterity. Reference has been made to the journalistic ventures of Samuel Ringgold Ward, Martin R. Delany, William G. Allen, and Henry Highland Garnet. It seems that the *North Star* and *Frederick Douglass' Paper* are the only Negro newspapers of the period which exist with sufficient completeness to allow critical examination. The three Negro magazines undoubtedly published between 1840 and 1865 are the *African Methodist Episcopal Magazine, Douglass' Monthly,* and the *Anglo-African.* The first named, begun in 1841 and probably discontinued the following year not to be revived until 1884, was exclusively a church organ, and is of negligible value in the development of Negro literature. *Douglass' Monthly* has been referred to as an abolition organ, intended mainly for circulation in England. Hamilton's purpose in founding the *Anglo-African* was evidently to make of it a literary periodical, a sort of Negro *Atlantic Monthly.*

The magazine was begun in January, 1859, and appeared regularly thereafter for each month through at least March, 1860.[72] Each number consisted of thirty-two double-column pages, with no advertising except on the back cover. According to the prospectus published late in 1858, one of the aims of the magazine was "to afford scope for the rapidly rising talent of colored men in their special and general literature."[73] Following this policy, Hamilton claimed that he published only the work of colored contributors.

If he was the author of "An Apology," an editorial printed in the first number of the *Anglo-African*, he was by no means a feeble writer. If the editing was entirely in his own hands, he was a sound judge of the best which the Negroes of his day could produce. For some of the strongest writing done by Negroes of the time is found in the pages of the *Anglo-African*. In spite of the fact that all the compensation which Hamilton could offer his contributors at the end of the first year of the magazine was a word of thanks,[74] he was ingenious enough to procure articles, essays, poems, and stories from the most talented of the English-speaking members of his race, including the Liberians, Alexander Crummell and Edward W. Blyden.[75]

The magazine was, as one might expect, antislavery in general policy; but it was in no sense a direct abolition organ. It was rather an expression of the challenge of the Negro to white cultural domination. One finds such titles as "Myself at the Breakfast: by Neither the Autocrat nor the Professor"; "What Shall We Do with the White People?"; and "The Anglo-African Empire." In the issue for March, 1860, there is an anonymous essay on Darwin's theory of the origin of the species, entitled "A Word for the Smith Family." The number for January, 1860, contains an article on Ira Aldridge, who is compared with the greatest actors of the day and is proclaimed superior to all of them.[76]   A frequent contributor, William J. Wilson, who wrote under the pen name "Ethiop," was undoubtedly clever, if not profound, in his bumptious denunciation of European civilization.[77]   Verse from many hands was printed, most of it showing a great advance in thought over the writings of earlier Negro poets.   Perhaps the most often recurring theme in it is Negro independence of mind. Especially remarkable as a reflection of the Negro's determination to stand on his own feet is a satirical poem in blank verse published in the number for February, 1860, called "Lines, Inspired by a Cold Interview with an Abolitionist," the work of a woman poet, A. E. Chancellor.[78] The attempts at fiction, represented by such efforts as Delany's *Blake* and Frances Ellen Watkins' short story, "The Two Offers,"[79] are puerile.   But they are offset by such contributions as the scientifically reasoned and carefully written essays of James McCune Smith.

The *Anglo-African* offers an interesting summary of the intellectual strivings of the Negroes in the United States during the period which saw the downfall of slavery.   It is adequate evidence that by 1859 the free blacks were looking at themselves as a self-conscious unit in the artistic and cultural life of America.   As negligible as that unit might be when compared with the great company of American artists and writers and thinkers of the time, it is most interesting that it existed at all.   It must be admitted that the *Anglo-African* was premature.   The American Negro was not ready in 1859 for a literary magazine exclusively his own.   But in the attempt to establish it and maintain it at all hazards, Thomas Hamilton proved himself one of the most farseeing Negroes of his day.   Not until after the end of the nineteenth century was there to be another periodical published by the American Negro with a program similar to that of the *Anglo-African*.[80]

CHAPTER VI

BIOGRAPHY, POETRY, AND MISCELLANEOUS
WRITINGS, 1840–1865

Cheer up, cheer up, we're gaining ground
Down by the river.
Old Satan's kingdom we'll pull down,
Down by the river side.

Shout, dear children, for you are free,
Down by the river,
Christ has brought to you, liberty,
Down by the river side.

—Quoted in *An Autobiography of Josiah Henson,*
Mrs. Harriet Beecher Stowe's "Uncle Tom," 1878

I

The period of intense abolition agitation saw the full
flowering of Negro biography. As we have observed, the
form had by 1840 become something of a distinct, if humble,
type in American literature.[1] After that year it was extrav-
agantly cultivated. Not only the antislavery public, but the
whole world, it seems, was eager to hear the life story of
any Negro who had escaped from slavery or who had done
anything else extraordinary. Genuine autobiographical accounts, such as those of Douglass, Brown, Ward, and
Pennington,[2] appeared as pamphlets, as serials in newspapers, and as full volumes. Other narratives were represented as dictated, and still others were written by able
hands as pure biographies. In the mass of such writing truth
was undoubtedly of secondary importance. There came a
number of purely fictitious biographies, which, like the
Memoirs of Archy Moore,[3] were originally thrust upon the

public as genuine. Without a single exception, the Negro biographies written before 1865 have been long out of print, and are today comparatively unknown. But they are in themselves of interest, and in Negro literature of the greatest importance. And as an influence over the kind of American fiction which was in the middle of the nineteenth century perhaps the most widely read, that represented by such a work as Harriet Beecher Stowe's *Uncle Tom's Cabin,* they have been too much disregarded by critics.

Among the lesser Negro leaders of the period who published narratives of their lives no one was more outstanding in his experiences and in his achievements than Henry Bibb. He was one whom Whittier referred to as an example of what the more intelligent blacks in America could accomplish.[4] When Harriet Beecher Stowe was preparing to write *Uncle Tom's Cabin* as a serial for the *National Era,* she thought of him as one who might give her information regarding the intimate customs of slaves on cotton plantations.[5] After he had settled permanently in Canada, he was an acknowledged leader among his people, editing for a time a newspaper called the *Voice of Freedom.*[6] His autobiography, published in 1849, was made up of details which he as an antislavery agent had recounted on lecture tours in the East and in the West, where he spoke mainly to farmers at meetings held in "log cabins and schoolhouses."[7]

The book appeared as *Narrative of the Life and Adventures of Henry Bibb, Written by Himself.* The author of the introduction, Lucius C. Matlock, to whom the task of editing the manuscript was entrusted, claimed that "the work of preparation for the press was that of orthography and punctuation merely, an arrangement of the chapters and a table of contents—little more than falls to the lot of publishers generally." That which distinguishes the *Narrative,* that which no doubt aroused Mrs. Stowe's interest in Bibb, is the elaborate portrayal of the actual life of slaves in the South. Bibb's experiences as a bondman carried him from Kentucky to New Orleans, thence to the borders of the Red River country, and finally to Missouri. Conscious that he was more white than black, possessed of a belligerent disposition, and awake to the abuses of slavery, he related his impressions with vividness and allowed them to argue for themselves. Suggestive of the material which makes up the body of his *Narrative* are the descriptions of the superstitions among the Negroes of the South. He speaks of receiving from a "conjurer" an antidote against "being struck by any one."

After I had paid him his charge, he told me to go to the cow-pen after night, and get some fresh cow manure, and mix it with red pepper and white people's hair, all to be put into a pot over the fire, and scorched until it could be ground into a snuff.

Another "conjurer" seeks to aid him in winning the affections of any girl whom he might desire.

After I had paid him, he told me to get a bull frog, and take a certain bone out of the frog, dry it, and when I got a chance I must step up to any girl whom I wished to make love me, and scratch her somewhere on her naked skin with this bone, and she would be certain to love me, and would follow me in spite of herself; no matter who she might be engaged to, nor who she might be walking with.

He tries the scheme on a girl with whom he is in love, but wins nothing but the fire of her anger. He meets with a similar distressing experience when he pulls a lock of hair from his sweetheart's head, intending to gain her everlasting devotion by wearing the lock in his shoe. Built up with such details, Bibb's *Narrative* has interest. The style might easily have been his own. The passages quoted illustrate the consistent homeliness of the idiom and the faultiness of the grammar.

Mrs. Stowe probably never met Henry Bibb, for he was already definitely settled in Canada when she made her inquiries regarding him. But while she was engaged in the composition of *Uncle Tom's Cabin*, she did very likely interview Josiah Henson, another lesser Negro leader of the period.[8] And she undoubtedly built up in a measure her portrait of Uncle Tom from impressions which she received from reading Henson's first autobiography, which was published in 1849 as *The Life of Josiah Henson, Formerly a Slave, Now an Inhabitant of Canada, as Narrated by Himself*.[9] It is a pamphlet of seventy-six pages, the anonymous editor of which asserted that it was composed from Henson's dictation, that it was read to him for verification, and that "the substance of it, therefore, the facts, the reflections, and very often the words, are his; and little more than the structure of the sentences belongs to another." At the time of the publication of the *Life* Henson was, according to his own statement, sixty years of age. He blunderingly tells the story of his forty years of slavery, during which time he served as a farm laborer in Maryland and as a superintendent of a plantation in Kentucky. There is considerable comment on his piety, on his success as a Methodist preacher, and on his view, long maintained, that it was a sin to get out of slavery by deception. He becomes more interesting when he tells of his conversion from this view, after, as he claimed, he had been cheated by his unscrupulous master out of the sum of money which he had accumulated to pay for his manumission and had escaped being sold in the New Orleans slave market by the merest chance. His easy flight to Canada, where he states that he arrived in October, 1830, is described in detail; and the account ends with a brief sum-

mary of his experiences as a Canadian agent of the Underground Railroad.

Although the *Life* seems to have attracted little attention
in antislavery circles,[10] it at least led to Mrs. Stowe's interest
in Henson.[11]   Shortly before the publication of *Uncle Tom's
Cabin* was begun, when Henson was in England acting as the
self-appointed representative of a Negro colony in Dawn,
Canada, he was publicly accused of being an impostor.[12]
But after he was popularly identified with Mrs. Stowe's
hero, his honesty was apparently never questioned.   Since
he was everywhere known as the real Uncle Tom, the publication of his autobiography became a profitable pursuit for
him.   In 1858 came *Truth Stranger than Fiction: Father
Henson's Story of His Own Life,* a volume of more than
two hundred pages, supposedly written by Henson himself.
It was provided with an introduction by Mrs. Stowe, in
which she declared, "Among all the singular and interesting
records to which the institution of American slavery has
given rise, we know of none more striking, more characteristic and instructive, than that of Josiah Henson."   The book
shows too much that Henson was trying to live up to the
ideal of the fictional hero whose creation he had helped to
inspire.   If the Uncle Tom of Mrs. Stowe's novel had ever
gone to England as a free man and had visited the Archbishop of Canterbury, he might have spoken of the occasion
as Henson claimed he experienced it in 1851.

The Archbishop expressed the strongest interest in me, and
after about an hour's conversation he inquired, "At what university, sir, did you graduate?"   "I graduated, your grace,"
said I in reply, "at the university of adversity."   "The university
of adversity," said he, looking up in astonishment; "where is
that?"   "It is my lot, your grace," said I, "to be born a slave,
and to pass my boyhood and all the former part of my life as
a slave.   I never entered a school, never read the Bible in my

youth, and received all my training under the most adverse circumstances. This is what I mean by graduating in the university of adversity." "I understand you, sir," said he. "But is it possible that you are not a scholar?" "I am not," said I. "But I should never have suspected that you were not a liberally educated man. I have heard many negroes talk, but never have seen one that could use such language as you."

In 1876 Henson paid a final visit to England, and another version of his life was published in London in that year as *An Autobiography of Josiah Henson (Mrs. Harriet Beecher Stowe's "Uncle Tom"), from 1789–1876.* An enlarged edition, in which it was claimed that one hundred thousand copies of the book had been sold, was issued in 1878.[13] No one of the versions of Henson's life supports Mrs. Stowe's declaration regarding his interest and singularity. If there is anything which makes him unique in Negro literature, it is the success with which he exploited his identification with her hero.

Josiah Henson said of two other characters in *Uncle Tom's Cabin,* "The white slaves, George Harris, and his wife, Eliza, were my particular friends."[14] About Eliza there might be some doubt, but Henson could easily have known the man who was the chief model for George Harris. He was Lewis Clarke, whom Mrs. Stowe knew personally, and with whose autobiography, *Narrative of the Sufferings of Lewis Clarke, during a Captivity of More than Twenty-Five Years among the Algerines of Kentucky* (Boston, 1845), she was familiar.[15] However, the Clarke revealed in the *Narrative* is too bitter and ungoverned a hater to have found a true portrayal from the Christian and womanly pen of Mrs. Stowe. His calling the slaveholders of Kentucky by the name of Algerines suggests the mood of his book. One of the early sentences is, "The night in which I was

born, I have been told, was dark and terrible, black as the
night for which Job prayed, when he besought the clouds to
pitch their tent round about the place of his birth; and my
life of slavery was but too exactly prefigured by the stormy
elements that hovered over the first hour of my being."
From the beginning to the end of the book he is tempestuous,
unrelenting in his turbulent abuse of slaveholders, especially
those among them who happened to be of the female sex.

Of all the animals on this earth, I am most afraid of a real
mad, passionate, raving, slave-holding woman!

When Clarke escaped from slavery in 1841, he, according to
his *Narrative,* did so by passing as a white man. He claimed
that his father was a native of Scotland, and his temperament certainly seems to be more Celtic than Negro. Of all
the biographical accounts attributed to fugitives his is probably the strongest in revengeful hatred. He is far removed
in character from Mrs. Stowe's gentlemanly George Harris.
It is easily believable that the blunt style of Clarke's *Narrative* is what it was represented as being, a faithful record
of his own dictation.

The year following his flight to freedom Lewis Clarke
began his long career as an antislavery agent, during which
he seems to have done little more than relate his story to
audiences and sell his book.[16] Two of his brothers, Milton
and Cyrus, also succeeded in breaking away from slavery
and also engaged in abolition work.[17] In 1846, Lewis'
Narrative was reprinted along with a parallel account of
Milton's life, the joint autobiography being entitled *Narratives of the Sufferings of Lewis and Milton Clarke, Sons of
a Soldier of the Revolution, during a Captivity of More than
Twenty Years among the Slave-Holders of Kentucky, One
of the So Called Christian States of North America; Dic-*

tated by Themselves. Milton's story is similar to Lewis', but he seems not to have been such a bellicose hater.[18]

If one acquainted with the history of the Negro's past in America were called upon to name the most spectacular and picturesque person whom the race has produced, one would probably think first of Sojourner Truth. She could neither read nor write; but the *Narrative of Sojourner Truth, Northern Slave,* published in 1850 as the work of an anonymous biographer, contains so many quotations attributed to her that she is entitled to a place among the makers of slave narratives. A reprint of the work, issued five years later, was provided with one of Mrs. Stowe's brief prefaces, mainly a plea to the public to buy the little volume and thus aid an African woman confronting old age. Even though this was in 1855, Sojourner Truth characteristically lived on until 1883, long enough for the 1850 *Narrative* to be enlarged into another anonymous biography, *Narrative of Sojourner Truth, a Bondswoman of Olden Time,* published in 1875 and reissued in augmented editions in 1883 and 1884. As early as 1835, when the only name Sojourner Truth had was Isabella, she had been made much of in W. L. Stone's *Matthias and His Impostures* and in G. Vale's reply to that work, *Fanaticism; Its Sources and Influence, Illustrated by the Simple Narrative of Isabella.* Stone, apparently because of his deep hatred of the Matthias cult, considered her the most wicked of the wicked, and accused her of having murdered one man by serving him poisoned blackberries and of having attempted to get rid of an entire family in the same fashion. Vale cleared her of these charges, and pictured her as ignorant, illiterate, and superstitious, possessed with a type of mind that became an easy prey to the extravagant delusions of Matthias. In all of her antislavery and reform work she was to remain a religious fanatic; it was her wild African mysticism that made her such an interesting and bizarre figure.

As we are told in each version of her *Narrative*, she was born a slave in the state of New York near the end of the eighteenth century. Her original master was a Dutch farmer. Through some sort of legal complication which she herself could not exactly explain, she, according to her own statement, did not become free until 1828, one year after all the slaves in the state of New York were supposed to be emancipated. Her main troubles in slavery, including frequent beatings, were due, she said, to the fact that she got into the hands of an English-speaking master and had great difficulty in learning to make herself understood in his language. After her liberation, she came to New York, joined the Methodists and then the followers of Matthias, left the city "because of its wickedness" after she awoke to the realization "that Matthias was mad," and, under the picturesque name of Sojourner Truth, began the series of ramblings which were to last the rest of her life and which were to carry her over the entire North before the end of the Civil War and into the South after the abolition of slavery. She lectured in her homely manner for immediate emancipation and for woman suffrage,[19] and worked at manual labor when she needed what she called "the wherewithal to pay tribute to Caesar." Her association with Matthias' group possibly inculcated in her the desire to join some sort of social and religious community. At one time she considered Amos Bronson Alcott's colony at Fruitlands;[20] and when her *Narrative* was originally published, she was living as a member of the Northampton Association.[21]

Sojourner Truth is best explained by her own sayings. Her 1850 *Narrative* is one of the most interesting of all the

Negro biographies published before 1865 because the unparalleled creature whom it treats is given free rein to show up her true mettle. No passage is more indicative of her character than that dealing with the supposed kidnapping of her son by an Alabama slaveholder. She makes the Southerner a monster, the murderer of his wife.

He knocked her down with his fist, jumped on her with his knees, broke her collar-bone, and tore out her wind-pipe!

To get her child from the clutches of such a man, she turns to God.

Oh, God, you know how much I am distressed, for I have told you again and again. Now, God, help me to get my son. If you were in trouble, as I am, and I could help you, as you can me, think I wouldn't do it? . . . Oh, God, you know I have no money, but you can make the people do for me. I will never give you peace till you do, God.

When she did get her son returned to her, God was given all the credit for her success.

Oh, my God! I know'd I'd have him again. I was sure God would help me to get him. Why, I felt *so tall within*—I felt as if *the power of a nation* was with me.

"The power of a nation" was with her again when she felt it her duty to quiet a crowd of boisterous young men who were trying to break up a "camp meeting" which she was attending.

Shall I run away and hide from the Devil? Me, a servant of the living God? Have I not faith enough to go out and quell that mob, when it is written, "One shall chase a thousand and put ten thousand to flight?" I know there are not one thousand here; and I know I am a servant of the living God. I'll go to the rescue, and the Lord shall go with me and protect me. . . . Oh, I felt as if I had three hearts! and that they were so large my body could hardly hold them!

She approaches the mob with a song, apparently of her own composition, beginning:

> It was early in the morning—it was early in the morning,
>   Just at the break of day—
> When he rose—when he rose—when he rose,
>   And went to heaven on a cloud.

She sings and harangues, and finally the young men promise to go away after she has given them one more hymn. "Amen! it is sealed!" she says, and begins another song:

> I bless the Lord I've got my seal—to-day and to-day—
> To slay Goliath in the field—to-day and to-day;
> The good old way is a righteous way,
> I mean to take the kingdom in the good old way.[22]

Made up of such pictures, the *Narrative of Sojourner Truth, Northern Slave,* was an extraordinary contribution to anti-slavery literature.

Different from most American Negroes who have in any measure served as leaders for their race, Sojourner Truth was no imitator of Anglo-Saxon character and ways. Like the remote southern plantation Negro, she was her true self, an African child of nature living on American soil. The *Narrative* shows her healthy, strong as a man, unafraid, optimistic, singing and preaching with bounding joy, profoundly emotional, and infinitely religious. It has been said that Mrs. Stowe called the attention of William Wetmore Story to her singularity, and that the sculptor was so impressed by her unusualness that he tried to incorporate her spirit into his statue of the Libyan Sybil.[23] It is not unfitting that she should have such a glorification in American art.

A fugitive slave from Tennessee, Jermain Wesley Loguen, became the subject of an anonymous biography of more than four hundred pages published in 1859 with the

title, *The Rev. J. W. Loguen, as a Slave and as a Freeman.*
Although classed as a lesser leader before 1865, Loguen
afterwards became a bishop in the African Methodist Episcopal Church and stood out as a prominent representative of
his race until his death in 1871.[24] Open letters from his
pen, printed as early as 1854,[25] prove that he might have
written the story of his life more effectively than did the
unnamed person to whom the work was entrusted. Few
writings of Negroes show such ironic interest as Loguen's
reply to the illiterate Tennessee mistress, Mrs. Manasseth
Logue, who tried to intimidate him into paying for his freedom after she had heard of his rise in the North. She said
to him in a letter, dated February 20, 1860:

I write you these lines to let you know the situation we are in,—
partly in consequence of your running away and stealing Old
Rock, our fine mare. Though we got the mare back, she never
was worth much after you took her;—and, as I now stand in
need of some funds, I have determined to sell you, and I have
had an offer for you, but did not see fit to take it. If you will
send me one thousand dollars, and pay for the old mare, I will
give up all claim I have to you.

Loguen wrote in his reply, dated March 28, 1860:

You say that you have offers to buy me, and that you shall
sell me if I do not send you $1,000, and in the same breath and
in almost the same sentence you say, 'You know we raised you
as we did our own children.' Woman, did you raise your *own*
children for the market? Did you raise them for the whipping-
post? Did you raise them to be driven off, bound to a coffle in
chains? . . . But you say I am a thief, because I took the old
mare along with me. Have you got to learn that I had better
right to the old mare, as you call her, than Manasseth Logue
had to me? Was it a greater sin for me to steal *his* horse, than
it was for him to rob my mother's cradle, and steal me? If he
and you infer that I forfeit all my rights to you, shall I not
infer that you forfeit all your rights to me? Have you got to

learn that human rights are mutual and reciprocal, and if you
take my liberty and life, you forfeit your own liberty and life?
Before God and high reason, is there a law for one man which
is not a law for every other man?[26]

The dull, tedious, and over-long biography of Loguen contains no passage so biting in its argument as this appeal to
his old mistress, on whom his individualistic logic was no
doubt lost. The biography surveys Loguen's life in slavery;
recounts vaguely the experiences of his flight to freedom,
and discusses his work as a minister and as an agent of the
Underground Railroad at Syracuse. But the main body of
it is obvious and stilted antislavery argument.

A few other Negroes of the period who are accredited
with having written accounts of their lives or who became
the subjects of biographies belong to the class of minor
leaders. Austin Steward, at one time "president" of Wilberforce Colony in Canada, published in 1857 what on the surface seems to be an authentic autobiography, *Twenty-Two
Years a Slave, and Forty Years a Freeman.*[27] Daniel H.
Peterson, who claimed that he was owned in his childhood
by a Maryland relative of President Tyler, became a preacher of some prominence and published in 1854 *The Looking-
Glass,* probably his own work. Although it is characterized
as a "narrative," it is less an account of Peterson's life than
an alluring description of Liberia as the proper home for
unhappy American blacks. Peterson had spent some time
in Africa, and gives his impressions as a "true report." Perhaps no Negro biography offers more interesting pictures
of southern plantation life than Peter Randolph's *Sketches
of Slave Life; or, Illustrations of the Peculiar Institution,*
a second edition of which was published at Boston in 1855.[28]
Randolph had been emancipated by his Virginia master, had
settled in Boston, and, if he produced the *Sketches of Slave*

Life without too much aid from an editor, had learned how to write lively and concrete description. Lunsford Lane, whom a writer in the *Liberator*, possibly William Lloyd Garrison himself, characterized as a "modest, intelligent man, and very prepossessing in his appearance,"[29] evoked considerable sympathy from abolition circles in the early forties.[30] His peculiar situation was described in *The Narrative of Lunsford Lane, Formerly of Raleigh, N. C.*, published in Boston in 1842. He had spent thirty-two years of his life in slavery, serving as "waiter and messenger" two governors of the state of North Carolina. In 1835, he bought himself out of bondage, but was not allowed to remain in his native city. He appealed to northern Abolitionists, and sufficient funds, including a contribution of thirty dollars from Gerrit Smith,[31] were raised to enable him to purchase his wife and children. He came with his family to Boston, told his story on the abolition platform, saw his *Narrative* through a number of editions, and in 1863 was made the subject of a full-length and pleasingly written biography, *Lunsford Lane: or, Another Helper from North Carolina*, the work of William G. Hawkins. No claim was made that Lane was himself the author of the original *Narrative;* but he was named as the publisher and as the holder of the copyright, and the simple style might, it seems, have been his own. The straightforwardness of the pamphlet is very different from the dull tediousness of Israel Campbell's *Bond and Free*, the one other autobiography supposedly by a Negro leader which should be mentioned. The book, a long and incoherent survey of the life of a preacher so pious that he thought it a sin for a Negro to run away from slavery, was published in Philadelphia in 1861. He was then residing in Canada, and claimed that he wrote the book in order to secure money to ransom three of his children who were still slaves in Kentucky. The attempt at fictional effects, especially the use of conversation, does not suggest too strongly that Campbell was really the author.

The narratives published between 1840 and 1865 of Negroes who apparently did nothing else deserving public notice except to get out of slavery run into the hundreds. Many are no more than thumb-nail sketches, such as one finds in Benjamin Drew's *The Refugee: or, The Narratives of Fugitive Slaves in Canada* (1856). The book contains about four hundred pages of brief "life stories," which Drew claimed he had gathered in the course of a tour in Canada West. He said: "While his informants talked, the author wrote: nor are there in the whole volume a dozen verbal alterations which were not made at the moment of writing, while in haste to make the pen become a tongue for the dumb." The antislavery newspapers abound in such cameo biographies, most of them told in the first person as true records of the words of the fugitives. Adequately representative of the whole mass is a single one, "Narrative of James Curry, a Fugitive Slave," which appeared in the *Liberator* for January 10, 1840. The story, even then growing old, of a slave's hardships and adventurous flight to freedom, it was prefaced with the following note:

There are, there can be, no narratives of more absorbing interest, than those of runaway slaves from this land of republican tyranny. The one which occupies so large a portion of our present number is recited in a very artless manner, and will repay a careful perusal. It is a real case, and no fiction, as written down from the lips of the self-emancipated bondman by a talented female, who will accept our thanks for the favor she has done us in communicating it for publication in the Liberator.

Narratives of a similar *genre* came in a flood of pamphlets, and some assumed the proportions of sizable vol-

umes. Most of them are monotonous, full of repetition, badly written, and roughly printed. But a few are readable. The
Narrative of Henry Box Brown (1849) relates Brown's
unique experience in winning his way to freedom by submitting to be "sent by express" from Richmond to Philadelphia "packed in a box three feet long and two feet wide."
The story of his romantic escape provided enough publicity
to make him a lecturer on the abolition platform,[32] and
inspired some lover of the minstrel song, "Uncle Ned," to
compose a ballad, one stanza of which is:

> Brown laid down the shovel and the hoe,
>   Down in the box he did go;
> No more slave work for Henry Box Brown,
>   In the box by express he did go.[33]

Perhaps no two slaves in their flight for freedom ever
thrilled the world so much as did William and Ellen Craft,
a young couple married according to the rites of slavery.
Ellen was so fair that she could pass as white, and William
was black. During the Christmas holidays of 1848 they left
Macon, Georgia, where they were bound to different masters,
she disguised in man's clothes as a young planter, and he
as the accompanying servant. The ruse succeeded, and the
two reached the safety of the Underground Railroad at
Philadelphia. They became heroes, about whom speeches
were made and poems were written. According to one report
President Polk declared after the passage of the Fugitive
Slave Law that he would employ military force for their
capture.[34] But they fled to England, where they were put
to school in an institution founded by Lady Byron for the
benefit of children of rural districts.[35] The story of the
Crafts was ideal for a "narrative," but it seems not to have
been told in book form until it appeared in London in 1860

as *Running a Thousand Miles for Freedom*. The *Narrative of the Life of Moses Gandy* (1844) has an interest in that it was penned by George Thompson, the celebrated English Abolitionist, who claimed in the preface that he "carefully abstained from casting a single reflection or animadversion" of his own. Linda Brent's story, *Incidents in the Life of a Slave Girl* (1861), is fairly readable, probably because of the "editing" of Lydia Maria Child. But of all the narratives of this class the least dull perhaps is the work of an anonymous biographer, whose unusual subject matter is suggested by the full title of his book, *Twelve Years a Slave; Narrative of Solomon Northrup, a Citizen of New York, Kidnapped in Washington City in 1841, and Rescued in 1853, from a Cotton Plantation near the Red River in Louisiana*. The book, published in 1853, does not seem too long, even though it contains more than three hundred pages. A perusal of it makes one realize that the narratives of fugitives would have been more effective if they had been written as pure biographies and not as "dictated" or "edited" autobiographies. The absurd style in which the "dictated" autobiography might be written is apparent in the opening of L. A. Chamerovzow's rendering of *Slave Life in Georgia: A Narrative of the Life, Sufferings, and Escape of John Brown* (1855):

My name is John Brown. How I came to take it, I will explain in due time. When I was in slavery, I was called Fed. Why I was so named, I cannot tell.

Such unrealistic expression is a distinguishing mark of a typical "dictated" autobiography, the category in which the majority of the narratives of obscure fugitives belong.

The publication of the life stories of Negroes was not confined to accounts of fugitives. In 1849, there appeared in Philadelphia the *Religious Experience and Journal of Mrs. Jarena Lee,* "revised and corrected from the original manuscript, written by herself." Her distinction was that she defied the regulations and in spite of her sex became a preacher in the African Methodist Episcopal Church. *A Narrative of the Life of Noah Davis: Written by Himself at the Age of Fifty-Four* was published in Baltimore about 1859. Davis had been a slave and published his book in order to "raise sufficient means to free his last two children from slavery." But, possibly because he was living in Baltimore and wished to sell his *Narrative* there, slavery is scarcely referred to in it. Davis presents himself as a meek and gentle soul, interested in no topic in the world besides religion. We can probably accept as really of Negro authorship *An Autobiography, with Details of a Visit to England* (1862), by Jeremiah Asher, a Baptist preacher who had charge of colored congregations in Providence and Philadelphia. With ample internal evidence indicating actual Negro authorship is *A Narrative of the Life and Travels of Mrs. Nancy Prince, Written by Herself,* the first edition of which was published in 1850. It is a naïve description of the impressions received by an American Negro woman during a sojourn of several years in Russia, where she claimed her husband was a servant in the Czar's household. It contains also an account of a visit to Jamaica. Several years before the publication of the *Narrative* Mrs. Prince had lectured in New England on the "manners and customs of Russia."[36] And she was the author of at least one open letter, published in the *Liberator* for September 17, 1841.

A final group of the biographies of the period includes those which were published as authentic fact accounts, but which were in reality pure works of fiction created by white writers. It is impossible to draw the line between the true

and the fictional in even the most honest of the biographies.
The deception which could be resorted to in the name of
antislavery propaganda has been shown in the discussion of
A Narrative of the Life and Adventures of Charles Ball,
reprinted in its original form as late as 1853, and brought
out with slight changes in 1858 as *Fifty Years in Chains.*[37]
The occasional unscrupulousness of even such an organization as the American Anti-Slavery Society is seen in the
fact that the spurious *Narrative of James Williams,* which
it had suppressed in 1838, was in 1841 advertised as again
for sale among its publications.[38] A Negro known as James
Williams and not the amanuensis, John G. Whittier, was
responsible for its misrepresentation.[39] But it is not likely
that any Negro whatsoever had anything to do with the
Life and Opinions of Julius Melbourn, published at Syracuse in 1847 and reissued in an enlarged edition in 1851.
The parts of the book ascribed to Melbourn and the parts
designated as contributed by the editor, Jabez D. Hammond,
are dangerously alike in style. Melbourn is presented as a
cultivated free mulatto who lived in Raleigh, North Carolina, from his birth in 1790 until he took up his residence in
England in 1835. The account of his life throughout bears
the face of fiction. Yet its truthfulness as actual autobiography was apparently unquestioned at the time the book was
published.[40]

The *Autobiography of a Female Slave* (1857) is still
rated as a genuine "slave narrative" by those, it must be
assumed, who have only looked at the title and have never
read the book. How it could have been accepted as a true
history by the *Liberator* in 1857 is difficult to determine.[41]
For the account is a pale tale of blacks and mulattoes parad-
ing as the creatures of sentimental romance. The author
was Mattie Griffiths, a young Kentucky woman, who, accord-

ing to Lydia Maria Child, turned Abolitionist after she had read the speeches of Charles Sumner, freed her slaves, and refused to accede to the wishes of her relatives to deny publicly that she had written the *Autobiography of a Female Slave*.[42] Even more excitingly fictional than the first work of its *genre*, Aphra Behn's *Oronooko*, is *The Life and Adventures of Zamba, an African Negro King; and His Experiences of Slavery in South Carolina*, published in London in 1847 as "written" by Zamba and "corrected and arranged" by Peter Neilson. The pictures of slavery which it presents are possibly true to fact; but the stereotyped adventure plot taxes the reader's credulity beyond all reason.[43] Kate E. R. Pickard, for a time engaged as a teacher in a school in Tuscumbia, Alabama, published in 1856 a lengthy book founded no doubt on actual events, but worked up into a stirring tale of action. It was called *The Kidnapped and the Ransomed, Being the Personal Recollections of Peter Still and His Wife "Vina," after 40 Years of Slavery*. The appropriateness of Peter Still's story for fictional treatment is conveniently suggested by Kate E. R. Pickard's own summary:

Kidnapped, in his early childhood, from the doorsteps of his home in New Jersey; more than forty years a slave in Kentucky and Alabama; his unsuccessful appeal to the great Henry Clay; his liberation through the generosity of a Jew; his restoration to his mother by the slightest threads of memory; the yearning of his heart for his loved ones; the heroic but disastrous attempt of Conklin to bring his wife and children to him—wherever these incidents of his life were detailed they seldom failed to draw from the hand of the listener some contribution towards the exorbitant sum demanded for the liberation of his family.

Seth Conklin, a sort of Benjamin Lundy of the fifties, is the principal figure in the most thrilling episode in the story;

and, perhaps to give verisimilitude to the effect of the whole, a biographical sketch of Conklin, the work of William Howard Furness, is tacked on at the end.

The final, and perhaps the most significant, statement which should be made regarding the biographies of obscure Negroes, whether real or imagined, is that they were commercially successful. That they provided antislavery propaganda must not be ignored. But that they sold rapidly is a surer reason for their great abundance.

II

This is not true of the verse produced by Negroes in the United States between 1840 and 1865. Little of it exhibits the facile talent for versifying found in the poems of Phillis Wheatley and George Moses Horton, but in thought it shows a remarkable growth over the efforts of earlier Negro poets. With few exceptions, those who produced it were already before the public, or were destined to become prominent, as teachers, preachers, and racial leaders. They did not publish poems to be traded for bread. Their verses were their offering to the fight against slavery and for the uplift of their race.

A number whose writings have been discussed were the authors of occasional verse. Reference has been made to William Wells Brown's "Fling Out the Anti-Slavery Flag," which was prefixed to the 1849 London edition of his *Narrative*.[44] The meters are irregular but not unsingable; and the thought compares favorably with that of the average abolition hymn. Frederick Douglass' orations contain passages which are verse-like in their marching rhythms; and in at least one of his speeches, that on the Dred Scott Decision, delivered in New York in May, 1857, he introduced two riming stanzas, apparently of his own composition, in which he tried to express the possible effect of a general insurrection of slaves in the South.

> The fires thus kindled, may be revived again;
> The flames are extinguished, but the embers remain;
> One terrible blast may produce an ignition,
> Which shall wrap the whole South in wild conflagration.
>
> The pathway of tyrants lies over volcanoes;
> The very air they breathe is heavy with sorrows;
> Agonizing heart-throbs convulse them while sleeping,
> And the wind whispers Death, as over them sweeping.[45]

Such phrasing as

> The pathway of tyrants lies over volcanoes,

which is certainly poetic in suggestiveness, is found frequently in Douglass' prose.[46] Quotations have been given from the hymns which Sojourner Truth was reputed to have composed and sung. There exists also a doggerel poem, "The Slave's Parting Hymn," supposedly composed by Josiah Henson while he was still in slavery.[47]

In the *Liberator* for May 28, 1841, there appeared "An Original Poem Composed for the Soiree of the Vigilant Committee of Philadelphia, May 7, 1841." The author was Daniel Alexander Payne, whose work as a Negro educator, church historian, and author of reminiscences belongs to the period following the Civil War.[48] Born free in Charleston, South Carolina, in 1811, Payne received a fair education in his boyhood, and in 1829 opened a school for the colored in his native city. In 1835, after the passage of laws in South Carolina forbidding the instruction of blacks, the school was closed; and four years later Payne was settled in the North as a minister in the African Methodist Episcopal Church. His rise was so rapid that in 1852 he was created a bishop.[49] His *Liberator* poem shows that he had within him the promise of unusual intellectual development if not of more than ordinary poetic skill. The opening lines suggest the dignity of Phillis Wheatley and at the same time a vigor which none of her verses attain:

> Rise, God of Freedom! From thy throne of light,
> Stretch forth thy arm of uncreated might;
> In dire confusion cause thy foes to fly,
> Chased by the lightning of thy frowning eye.
> Long have they scorned and mocked thy regal crown,
> Despised thy laws, and cast thine image down:
> O, hasten then, in thine appointed hour,
> And crush to nought the proud oppressor's power.

The remaining six stanzas are none the less direct in expression and smooth in rhythm. If there is no original imagination in the poem, there is at least a firm control of the emotion. Other verse which Payne produced early in his career and introduced occasionally into his later prose writings is similar in kind.[50]

Charles L. Reason, at one time a professor in Central College, for many years a teacher in the city of New York, and a trusted drafter of resolutions for colored conventions,[51] owes his place in Negro literature to two rather ambitious odes. The first, a tribute to Clarkson called "Freedom," occupies eight pages of Alexander Crummell's *A Eulogy on the Life and Character of Thomas Clarkson* (1847). It surveys in strained and grandiose manner the human battle for liberty from the days of the ancient Greeks to Toussaint L'Ouverture's struggles in San Domingo and Clarkson's fight against slavery. The laudatory lines addressed directly to Clarkson end with:

> Well hast thou fought, great pioneer!
> The snows of age upon thy head,
> Were Freedom's wreaths; by far more dear
> Than finest sculpture o'er the dead.

The second ode, "Hope and Confidence," was published in
the *Autographs for Freedom* for 1854.[52]   Whatever central
theme the poem has is brought out in the concluding stanza:

> Yes! Truth opes within a pure sun-tide of bliss,
>   And shows in its every calm flood,
> A transcript of regions where no darkness is,
> Where Hope its conceptions may realize,
>   And Confidence sleeps in the Good.

Such lines, by no means Reason's worst, show that he was
less a poet than Payne.   Both were plodding versifiers, but
Payne was at least smooth and lucid.   Fortunately, Reason
left a few short prose pieces which prove that he could
think directly and write with clearness.[53]

One of Reason's colleagues at Central College, George B.
Vashon, was a more natural poet and a better technician in
verse.   Vashon was one of the first colored graduates of
Oberlin College to gain distinction as a racial leader.[54]   His
work as a teacher and as a lawyer left him little time for
writing poetry; but two of his efforts which have come down
to us are good enough to make us regret that he did not
write more.

The idea of the first, "Vincent Ogé," published in
abridged form in the *Autographs for Freedom* for 1854,[55]
was probably suggested to Vashon during a trip to the West
Indies which he took in 1847.[56]   The poem contains approximately four hundred lines, and presents the effect of completeness.   Whatever abridgments were made at the time of
publication were no doubt slight.   Vashon was more happy
in the selection of a subject than most of his predecessors
among the Negro poets had been.   He was himself a mulatto,[57] and he turned to the career of a Haytian mulatto
hero, Vincent Ogé, for his story.   Ogé, educated in France,
was executed at Cap Français on March 12, 1791, for having

stirred up a rebellion of mulattoes in Sainte Dominigue, who, fired by European revolutionary ideas, made up their minds to gain the recognition of citizenship from the French governmental authorities. To the Haytians he is a national martyr, second only perhaps to Toussaint L'Ouverture.[58] Vashon in his poem attempted to suggest the story of Ogé's insurrection and death rather than to relate it as a direct narrative.

The poem opens with an elaborate and not ineffective simile, in which an unsuccessful revolution for freedom is likened to a twilight, at first with the colorful glories of the sunset skies and then with the quick closing in of night. The simile is followed by a description of the tropical richness of nature in Hayti. Ogé is introduced as standing

> mid this array
> Of matchless beauty, but his brow
> Is brightened not by pleasure's play.

In spite of nature, in which he takes a romantic delight, he is ill at ease, because the revolution in France has crossed to Hayti, and as yet, although he feels that his people are crushed, he has taken no part in it. His mother is brought in as the force which pushes him out of lethargy into action.

> "Go forth," she said, "to victory;
> Or else, go bravely forth to die!
> Go forth to fields where glory floats
> In every trumpet's cheering notes!
> Go forth, to where a freeman's death
> Glares in each cannon's fiery breath!
> Go forth and triumph o'er the foe;
> Or, failing that, with pleasure go
> To moulder on the battle plain,
> Freed ever from the tyrant's chain!"

He follows her command, and leads a battle, in which he is defeated and taken captive. Judged with the "mock'ry of

legal doom," he is sentenced to die.   But in his death he is
a martyr.

> Thy coming fame, Ogé, is sure;
> Thy name with that of L'Ouverture,
> And all the noble souls that stood
> With both of you in time of blood,
> Will live to be the tyrant's fear—
> Will live, the sinking soul to cheer!

Vashon's models were obviously Byron and Scott. Ogé
appears as another Childe Harold, filled with Nordic melancholy, having nothing of African exuberance and nothing
of Gallic gayety.   The mother, as though she had stepped
from one of Scott's verse romances, says to her sons on the
eve of battle,

> "But if your hearts should craven prove,
> Forgetful of your zeal—your love
> For rights and franchises of men,
> My heart will break; but even then,
> Whilst bidding life and earth adieu,
> This be the prayer I'll pray for you:
> 'Passing from guilt to misery,
> May this for aye your portion be,—
> A life dragged out beneath the rod,
> An end, abhorred of man and God,
> As monument, the chains you nurse,—
> An epitaph, your mother's curse!' "

She is more interestingly drawn than Ogé, but her character
is marked with nothing which we can distinguish as Negro.
The descriptive passages at the opening of the poem are
reminiscent of the quiet verse of *Childe Harold*.   There are,
however, appropriate and effective changes in the rhythm,
and before we have reached the end we have heard echoes
of *The Destruction of Sennacherib* and of *The Lady of the*

Lake. Vashon often shows himself a feeble imitator of his masters. Such lines as

> Rights and franchises of men

are frequent. When grammar gets in the way of meter, grammar is likely to be sacrificed, as in the line,

> For the land of the Gauls had arose in its might.

There are too many absurd images, introduced, we might suppose for the sake of rime, such as,

> As monument, *the chains you nurse,—*
> An epitaph, your mother's curse!

Yet there is much graceful music in the poem, and some interesting imagery. Vashon undoubtedly had talent. In "Vincent Ogé" he attempted a more ambitious poem than any American Negro before him had tried. He was not so skillful in his imitation of Byron and Scott as Phillis Wheatley had been in her imitation of Pope; but "Vincent Ogé," based on the life of a Negro hero and inspired by the abolition spirit which in the fifties was pushing the Negro forward, is far more readable than any poem which came from her pen.

"A Life-Day," apparently never printed except in Daniel Alexander Payne's *The Semi-Centenary and the Retrospection of the African Meth. Episcopal Church* (1866), is less ambitious than "Vincent Ogé," but the verse is richer and more finished. Vashon claimed that the poem was founded upon "incidents which took place in one of our southern states," and that the judge referred to in the story "figured as a provisional governor in President Johnson's plan of reconstruction."[59] In the opening of the poem a southern slaveowner is pictured as lying on his bed stricken with yellow fever, deserted by all of his relatives. The only person who remains with him is a female slave. She nurses him to recovery; and, impressed by her faithfulness, he marries her. Their union, blessed by two children, is harmonious and happy. But the man dies. His relatives then return; and, claiming that his marriage has been illegal, they assert their rights to his property. They are sustained by the courts, and thus the wife and children of the man become the property of the despised relatives. The situation is a hackneyed one in antislavery literature. But it is perhaps nowhere portrayed with more natural emotion than in Vashon's brief poem.

A Negro Presbyterian minister, Elymas Payson Rogers, who was for a number of years in charge of a church in Newark, New Jersey, published in 1856 a political satire in verse, *The Repeal of the Missouri Compromise Considered.* It was written in 1854, and was read extensively in public before it was printed and circulated as a pamphlet.[60] Rogers, who was of unmixed African blood, died in 1861 in Africa, where he had gone in the interests of colonization.[61] He was referred to by one of his contemporaries as a "logical" if not a "fluent and easy" speaker.[62] While he may have lacked fluency in the pulpit and on the lecture platform, he was evidently at ease in expressing himself in octosyllabic couplets.

The Repeal of the Missouri Compromise Considered begins:

> 'T is done! the treach'rous deed is done,
> Eternal infamy is won
> By legislators, wh've decreed
> The direful and unrighteous deed—

and then moves on with the steadiness of a ticking metronome throughout its twenty-four pages. As carefully as Phillis Wheatley measured the syllables of her verse, her finished work is no smoother than that of Rogers. The dominating effect of his poem is monotony. Political satire had been given a new verse idiom in Lowell's *Biglow Papers;* but Rogers, ignoring what interest he might have aroused with a little dramatization and Negro dialect, imitated the older forms, which were still abundantly represented in the newspaper verse of his day. Whatever story there is in his poem is brought out by dialogue and by personification. The following lines describe the condition of the country in 1820, at the time of the passage of the Missouri Compomise:

> "I want the land," was Freedom's cry;
> And Slavery answered, "So do I!
> By all that's sacred, I declare
> I'll have my just and lawful share.
> The Northern cheek should glow with shame,
> To think to rob me of my claim;
> And if my claim you dare deny,
> I'll knock the Union into Pi!"
> The Northern faces did not glow,
> Because they were composed of dough:
> But such a tall and horrid threat,
> Their equilibrium upset.

As vigorous a passage as the poem contains is the following speech of the South, represented as having become boastful after the enactment of the Fugitive Slave Law:

> "I'll show my power the country through,
> And will the factions north subdue;
> And Massachusetts shall obey,
> And yield to my increasing sway.
> She counts her patriotic deeds,
> But scatters her disunion seeds;
> She proudly tells us of the tea
> Sunk by her worthies in the sea,
> And then she talks more proudly still
> Of Lexington and Bunker Hill;

> But on that hill, o'er patriots' graves,
> I'll yet enroll my negro slaves.
> I may have trouble, it is true,
> But still I'll put the rebels through,
> And make her statesmen bow the knee,
> Yield to my claims, and honor me.
> And though among them I shall find
> The learned, the brilliant, and refined,
> If on me they shall e'er reflect,
> No senate chamber shall protect
> Their guilty pates and heated brains,
> From hideous gutta percha canes."

Except for the digressions which extol the work of Frederick Douglass and other colored Abolitionists, there are few hints in the poem that the author was a Negro. Rogers no doubt intended to make of it a verse satire of general interest. As such, it is comparatively weak. But, because of its intellectuality and thoughtful workmanship, it is a noteworthy contribution to Negro literature, such a work as one might scarcely expect from an American Negro of the fifties.

Possibly the only barber in America who has ever published a volume of verse was James M. Whitfield, a Negro born in Massachusetts but resident most of his life in Buffalo, New York. In 1853, he published a volume of fair size, *America, and Other Poems,* the favorable public recognition of which seems to have encouraged him to put away his razors and to enter vigorously the fight for the uplift of his race. A believer in the theory that the promise of the Negro could be fulfilled only outside the borders of the United States, he took an active part in the Colored Colonization Convention of 1854, defended its program against the attacks of Frederick Douglass, and accepted as his special mission the promotion of the emigration of blacks to Central America, working hand in hand with James Theodore Holly, who, as we have seen, was a promoter for emigration to Hayti.[63] His public life apparently allowed him little free time to write poetry, but his one volume is enough to give him a distinguished place among the Negro poets of his period.

America, and Other Poems was dedicated to Martin R. Delany, who shortly before the publication of the book was interested in the scheme for Central American colonization for which Whitfield was later to be the chief promoter.[64] The anonymous author of the introduction, possibly Whitfield himself, wrote:

"Another book of poetry," exclaims the reader; "and that, too, by one of the proscribed race, whose lot has been ignorance and servitude." . . . We do not claim that the poetry is of the highest order; but we do claim that it would be creditable to authors of greater pretensions than the humble colored man, who hath wrought it amid the daily and incessant toil necessary for the maintenance of a family, who are dependent upon the labor of his hands for support. . . . He is uneducated, not entirely, but substantially.

However limited his education might have been, Whitfield knew how to write distinctly from the Negro's point of view. The strongest controversial poems in the volume, "America," "Lines on the Death of John Quincy Adams," and "How Long," are versified versions of the doctrines to which the Negro antislavery orators, such as Remond, Douglass, and Ward, were giving voice. "America" might be taken as representative. The main theme is expressed in the first four lines—

> America, it is of thee,
> Thou boasted land of liberty,—
> It is to thee I raise my song,
> Thou land of blood, and crime, and wrong.

Regarding the Negroes who took part in the Revolution to establish the independence of America, it is said:

> . . . they fought, as they believed,
>   For the inherent rights of man;
> But mark how they have been deceived
>   By slavery's accursed plan.

The aspiration of the Negro of the eighteenth century has given way to the feeling that—

> The aerial piles which fancy reared,
>   And hopes too bright to be enjoyed,
> Have passed and left his young heart seared,
>   And all his dreams of bliss destroyed.

An echo of Douglass' bitter condemnation of a Christianity which in America preaches brotherhood and promotes slavery is heard in such a stanza as:

> Here Christian writhes in Bondage still,
>   Beneath his brother Christian's rod,
> And pastors trample down at will,
>   The image of the living God.

After more than a hundred lines of pessimistic contemplation and resentment, "America" ends with a prayer of courage—the courage of a Garrisonian nonresistant:

> Father! before thy throne we come,
>   Not in the panoply of war,
> With pealing trump, and rolling drum,
>   And cannon booming loud and far;
> Striving in blood to wash out blood,
>   Through wrong to seek redress for wrong;
> For while thou'rt holy, just and good,
>   The battle is not to the strong;
> But in the sacred name of peace,
>   Of justice, mercy, love, and truth,
> We pray and never mean to cease,
>   Till weak old age and fiery youth,

> In freedom's cause their voices raise,
>   And burst the bonds of every slave;
> Till, north and south, and east and west,
>   The wrongs we bear shall be redressed.

Although he included in his volume several hymns, and verses on the dedication of churches, Whitfield was not always full of religious faith.   Perhaps the most interesting of his poems, "The Misanthropist," is a cry of doubt and hopelessness.   The poet presents himself as one who cannot be gay, who sees his life as barren as the ocean.

> And I have felt that there was traced
>   An image of my inmost soul
> In that dark, dreary, boundless waste.

Whatever he reads tells of intrigue and hate; the history of religion is an account of warfare.   He concludes:

> But mine must still the portion be,
> However dark and drear the doom,
> To live estranged from sympathy,
> Buried in doubt, despair, and gloom;
> To bare my breast to every blow,
> To know no friend, and fear no foe,
> Each generous impulse trod to dust,
> Each noble aspiration crushed,
> Each feeling struck with withering blight,
> With no regard for wrong or right,
> No fear of hell, no hope of heaven,
> Die all unwept and unforgiven,
> Content to know and dare the worst,
> Which mankind's hate, and heaven's curse,
> Can heap upon my living head,
> Or cast around my memory dead;
> And let them on my tombstone trace,
> "Here lies the Pariah of his race."

When Whitfield wrote the poem, he was probably looking at himself through Byron's Childe Harold.   But because

"The Misanthropist" is one of the earliest attempts made by an American Negro to portray in bold and uncringing verse the pathos of his social isolation, it is important in the development of Negro literature.

Whitfield had not only read Byron. His "To A. H." and "Ode for Music," each to a great extent a catalogue of classical allusions, hint strongly that he was familiar with Thomas Gray. But for most of his poems it is easy to find models in the antislavery newspapers. His reading did not quite unmake his native imagination, seen all too rarely in such racy lines as,

> Where the wild waste of waters yell,
> Through caverns deep and dark as hell.

Except for encouraging him to indulge too freely in alliteration, evident at its extremest in such a line as,

> Of princely pomp and priestly pride,

his imitation of other poets seems to have affected little his Negro feeling for the music of language. His verse always moves with sound if not with thought. If his education had been even less unsubstantial, his work would possibly have been more natural, and therefore better. Like many of the early American Negro poets, he suffered from having a little learning.

The best known Negro poet of the period, Frances Ellen Watkins, was not the most talented nor the most promising. However, her more meritorious later poetry and fiction, to be discussed in a succeeding chapter, attach interest to her beginnings as a short story writer and to her one important volume of verse issued before 1865, *Poems on Miscellaneous Subjects,* originally published in 1854 with a preface by William Lloyd Garrison, and reprinted at least in 1857, 1858, 1864, and 1871.[65] According to numerous biographical sketches, Frances Ellen Watkins was born free in Baltimore in 1825, attended a colored school in her native city, and about 1851 took up teaching, in which she was engaged for three or four years in Ohio and Pennsylvania. From the time of the publication of *Poems on Miscellaneous Subjects* until her death, in 1911, she was before the Negro public as a writer, lecturer, and reformer, known after her marriage in 1860 as Frances E. W. Harper.[66]

Poems on Miscellaneous Subjects is made up almost entirely of narrative pieces.   Slavery is the dominating theme.   In "The Slave Mother," which, like most of Mrs. Harper's early verse, shows strongly the influence of Longfellow, we have the frequently told tale of a mother's parting from the child who has been placed in the hands of a slave trader.   "The Slave Auction" relates a similar story.   The experience of Mrs. Stowe's Eliza Harris in crossing the Ohio on ice floes with the bloodhounds at her heels is celebrated in a ballad, called "Eliza Harris," which suggests Whittier as well as Longfellow.[67]   "The Fugitive's Wife" describes the despair and fear of a slave woman whose husband is planning a dash for liberty.   "The Tennessee Hero" tells of a Negro who "had heard his comrades plotting for liberty and rather than betray them had received seventy hundred and fifty lashes and then died."   A second "The Slave Mother" is the story of a fleeing woman who murders her baby when she realizes that she is to be caught and taken back into slavery.   One stanza, remindful of the simplicity of a folk ballad, gives to the piece an appropriate mood:

> Winter and night were on the earth,
>   And feebly moaned the shivering trees,
> A sigh of winter seemed to run
>   Through every murmur of the breeze.

And if Mrs. Harper had not stopped the story before the end in order to insert her own comment, she would have made of it an effective antislavery ballad.   Perhaps the best lines in the volume are contained in "Rizpah, the Daughter of Ai," one of a few poems which are based on Biblical rather than on abolition themes:

> The jackal crept out with a stealthy tread,
> To batten and feast on the noble dead;
> The vulture bore down with a heavy wing
> To dip his beak in life's stagnant spring.
>
> The hyena heard the jackal's howl,
> And he bounded forth with a sudden growl,
> When Rizpah's shriek rose on the air
> Like a tone from the caverns of despair.[68]

Most of the stories in *Poems on Miscellaneous Subjects*, whether antislavery or Biblical, were told and retold by the abolition versifiers of the forties and fifties. Mrs. Harper was in no sense the least skillful among them.   But that she was better known than the other Negro poets who were writing in the fifties is probably best explained by the fact that she was on the lecture platform circulating her books among her audiences just as many other Negro lecturers of the time were circulating the stories of their lives.[69]

III

One other work published by Mrs. Harper before 1865, "The Two Offers," deserves mention.[70] It is a prose tale, about a cultivated white woman who gives up marriage in order to devote her life to the liberation of the slave. As fiction and as argument, it is most weak.   Its one distinction is that it is probably the American Negro's first attempt at the short story form.[71]

At the end of Mrs. Harper's *Poems on Miscellaneous Subjects* are three essays in prose, "Christianity," "The

Colored People of America," and "Breathing the Air of Freedom." Although they are unpardonably platitudinous, they are better as essays than "The Two Offers" is as a story. Reference has been made to many other brief pieces written by Negroes of the period which can best be classified as essays. But it seems that there was only one book written by an American Negro between 1840 and 1865 which was avowedly issued as a collection of essays.

It was published at Hartford in 1841, and was called *Essays; Including Biographies and Miscellaneous Pieces in Prose and Poetry*. The author, Ann Plato, was introduced to the public in a brief preface by the Reverend James W. C. Pennington, who praised her as a devout member of his church in Hartford. One poem in the book hints that she might have been a school teacher, and another that her father was of Indian extraction.[72] She was spiritually a near relative of Phillis Wheatley; the writings of the two reveal the same gentle femininity. But artistically Ann Plato was akin to Jupiter Hammon. She was steeped in old-fashioned Connecticut Puritanism, and she let it out in hesitating and timid prose discussions of such subjects as religion, education, benevolence, obedience, and death. One of the essays, "Diligence and Negligence," is in the form of an allegory and shows an inkling of original imagination. The biographies promised in the title are on Hartford personages "noted for their piety." The poems, which occupy thirty-nine of the one hundred and twenty pages of the volume, are either half-afraid musings on deathbeds and graveyards or a monotonous repetition of the following confession, given in "Advice to Young Ladies":

> At thirteen years I found a hope,
> And did embrace the Lord;
> And since, I've found a blessing great,
> Within his holy word.

It is no wonder that the Abolitionists neglected Ann Plato. The one antislavery piece in her book, "To the First of August," a poem celebrating the freeing of the slaves in the British West Indies, has the girlish restraint which marks all of her work and which shows that she was useless in the fight for emancipation.

Most of the prose fiction produced by Negroes of the period has been considered in the discussion of the work of William Wells Brown, Martin R. Delany, and Mrs. Harper. There remains one important book, *The Garies and Their Friends,* which was published in London in 1857. The identity of the author, Frank J. Webb, seems still to be a mystery. However, he has on good authority been classed as a colored man,[73] and certainly there is an abundance of internal evidence in *The Garies* indicating that the author had such an intimate knowledge of Negro life in Philadelphia during the middle of the nineteenth century as a white man could scarcely have obtained.

In the first edition of *The Garies and Their Friends* an introduction by Harriet Beecher Stowe promised on the title-page was replaced by a note by Lord Brougham stating that Mrs. Stowe's manuscript had arrived too late to be printed with the book. In the second edition the promised introduction appeared, and along with it the interesting dedication: "To the Lady Noel Gordon, this book is, by her permission, most affectionately inscribed, with profound respect, by her most grateful friend, the Author."

As the work of an American Negro, the book was worthy of such patronage. While it lacks the verve and narrative force of Brown's *Clotel,* it is far more subjectively emotional. The scene of most of the action is Philadelphia; the time is from about 1830 to 1855; and the theme is race prejudice. The plot concerns the destinies of two families, one being unmistakably Negro, and the other, the Garies, consisting of a wealthy white Southerner and his colored wife and their near-white children. The Garies come to Philadelphia, where they hope to enjoy the peace that has been denied them in the South. Their first difficulty is in finding a minister who will legalize their marriage. Then, when it is discovered that Mrs. Garie is not white, their children are dismissed from the school to which they have been admitted. Finally, the rumor spreads that Mr. Garie is an Abolitionist. One evening a mob gathers around his house.

"What do you all want—why are you on my premises creating this disturbance?" cried Mr. Garie.

"Come down and you'll soon find out. You white-livered Abolitionist, come out, damn you! We are going to give you a coat of tar and feathers, and your black wench nine-and-thirty. Yes, come down, come down!" shouted several, "or we'll come after you."

In the fray which follows Garie is killed, and his wife, forced into a woodhouse, gives birth during the night to a child and dies. The rest of the story traces the fortunes of the Garie children. The son, who has been sent to a school in the country where no one knows that he is colored, grows to manhood and wins the affections of an unsuspecting white girl. But his past turns up, and she is not permitted to see him again.

He was now completely removed from the society in which he had so long been accustomed to move; the secret of his birth had become widely known, and he was avoided by his former friends and sneered at as a "nigger." His large fortune kept some two or three whites about him, but he knew they were leeches seeking to bleed his purse, and he wisely avoided their society.

He was very wretched and lonely; he felt ashamed to seek

the society of colored men now that the whites despised and rejected him, so he lived apart from both classes of society, and grew moody and misanthropic.

He becomes a Hamlet, unable to adjust himself to life, and rails against circumstance until disease comes on and death delivers him.   The Negro family which is throughout the story contrasted with the Garies fights on, and, in spite of poverty and oppression, attains a certain happiness.

Such blunt simplicity as is found in the passages here quoted from Webb is not typical of his style.   He was altogether too conscious of the fact that he was writing a novel. There is power in his story, but it is all but lost in melodrama and sentimentality.   Moreover, there are long passages which are hopelessly tedious and dull.   But he undoubtedly felt the pathos of his characters, and at times revealed it with poignancy. When a really noteworthy American Negro novel is written, it will probably be on the theme which Webb attempted.

CHAPTER VII

BIOGRAPHY, HISTORY, SOCIOLOGICAL TREATISES, ORATORY, AND THEOLOGY, 1865–1900

I've got to walk my lonesome valley,
I've got to walk it for myself;
Nobody else can walk it for me,
I've got to walk it for myself.

Jesus walked His lonesome valley,
He had to walk it for Himself;
Nobody else could walk it for Him;
He had to walk it for Himself.

—Quoted in John Wesley Work's *Folk Songs of the American Negro*, 1915.

I

With the end of slavery came also the end of the abolition agitation which had in mushroom fashion accomplished much towards the intellectual and cultural advancement of the Negro. An American Frederick Douglass could not have arisen except under the conditions which prevailed in the North during the twenty years preceding the Civil War. But there was a pathos in the superior Negro's ambitions during the feverish time of abolition agitation. It lay in the fact that he was so encouraged, so praised, so puffed up that he could not be critical of himself. Much of what he published should never have been put on paper, much less in print. That he was not ready to distinguish between the valuable and the worthless may be understood by any one who examines the 1859 volume of the *Anglo-African*.[1] The last period of his authorship which we shall study, that extending from the close of the Civil War to the end of the nineteenth century, gave him what all the hullabaloo made over him by the Abolitionists could never effect. It taught him how to estimate what he could do and what he could not do. Therefore it is the determining period in the history of American Negro literature. It gave us studies about Negro life such as whites could never produce. More than anything else, it revealed to us the beauty and richness of Negro folklore. It decided once and for all that the Negro was to make strong and worthy contributions to American art. It convinced us that we can with just reason look forward to the American Pushkin or Dumas.

It was a period of as grave social and political problems as any disintegrated racial group ever faced. All Negroes in the United States were now free; all were nominally citizens. But as a whole they were in the most dismal ignorance. The story of how in the broken South they fell a prey to every type of sordid political exploitation is a familiar one. All the world knows how the carpetbaggers dealt with them, and how the Ku Klux Klan worked upon their primitive superstitions. The masses of the southern Negroes knew nothing but slavery, and as freedmen they were defenceless in the hands of their traducers. Their own leaders and their white friends, in the South as well as in the North, realized that as their condition of servitude had been wiped out their state of ignorance must be eradicated. Education was their first necessity. The more than four million blacks of the South who in 1870 could neither read nor write had to be fitted for the citizenship which had been granted them.[2] The great program of teaching the Negro to adjust himself to his civil and political rights was begun, we might say, with the organization of the Freedmen's Bureau in 1865.[3] Missionaries from the churches, promoters of free public schools, and wealthy philanthropists entered the work ;[4] and such was the progress of Negro education that by 1900 substantially more than half of the colored population of the country above the age of ten was not counted as illiterate.[5]   Between 1865 and 1900 more than sixty colleges and universities, not including the greater number of normal and industrial schools and theological seminaries, were established for the exclusive training of Negroes.[6]   It has been shown by a careful survey that between 1870 and 1879 there were 313 Negroes who were graduated from American colleges, that there were 736 during the next ten years, and that the last decade of the nineteenth century saw the number increased to 1,126.[7] Many counted in these numbers came from the leading colleges and universities. Edward A. Bouchet, the first Negro to be made a member of the Phi Beta Kappa Society, received the degree of Doctor of Philosophy from Yale in 1876. At least five other Negroes before the year 1900 were awarded the same degree by Boston University, Syracuse University, Harvard, and the University of Pennsylvania.[8]

The Negro church, always a strong force in the intellectual development of the race, showed a growth equally as remarkable as that of the schools. By the beginning of the present century there were probably few Negro communities in the United States, whether rural or urban, without some sort of religious organization. The two sects which had always appealed most strongly to the Negro mind, the Methodist and the Baptist, expanded with enormous numbers. The membership of only one Methodist body, the African Methodist Episcopal Church, grew from 172,806 in 1876 to 688,354 in 1901.[9] According to a trustworthy estimate, the Negro Baptists increased at the rate of 33,000 each year from 1870 to 1894, with a grand total of 1,604,310

in the latter year.[10] Negro representation in the other de-
nominations showed a proportionate development.[11]

With his own schools and his own churches, the Negro
of the South settled in isolated communities, much as the
Negro of the North had done three-quarters of a century
earlier.   By 1900, he had attained throughout the country
at least a degree of economic independence.   He had his
own business houses, his own professional men; and he was
in a measure socially self-reliant.[12]   His fraternal organizations developed and prospered.[13]   In 1870, he had at least
ten newspapers; in 1880, thirty-one; and in 1890, one hundred and fifty-four.[14]   After 1872 he had, to a great extent
as his own, a national magazine which has survived until
our day, the *Southern Workman,* published by the Hampton
Institute.[15]   Another monthly periodical of broad scope
which was to survive without interruption, the *A. M. E.
Church Review,* literary as well as religious in its policies,
came into being in 1884.[16] Throughout the period the large
national church organizations maintained their own publishing houses.[17]

During the last decade of the nineteenth century the
Negro began manifesting evidences that his initial period in
adjusting himself to the conditions of free life in America
was reaching its end.   What had been expended on his
education and uplift was beginning to bear fruit.   White
America slowly awoke to the realization that black America
had in spite of slavery, social degradation, and abuse developed a sort of general culture out of which there might
come something of permanent value.   Joel Chandler Harris
and the Fisk Jubilee Singers had charmed the world with
the beauty of Negro tales and music; and the mad scramble,
still unabated, to collect Negro folklore was started.[18]
William E. Burghardt Du Bois emerged as one of America's

eminent sociologists.   Booker T. Washington set America
and Europe to talking about whàt he was accomplishing as
an educator at Tuskegee.   Alexander Crummell founded the
American Negro Academy, and its interesting publications
were begun.[19]   Arthur A. Schomburg set about his difficult
task of assembling an exhaustive library of books by and
about the Negro.[20]   Charles W. Chesnutt began his serious
career as a writer by publishing a story in the *Atlantic
Monthly*.[21]   Henry Ossawa Tanner, the son of an African
Methodist bishop, completed in 1897 a painting, "The Res-
urrection of Lazarus," which was purchased by the French
government to be included among the few specimens which
represent America in the Luxembourg collection.[22]   The
poetry of Paul Laurence Dunbar was brought to the attention of the American public by none other than William
Dean Howells.

The following statement was made by Howells in his
introduction to Dunbar's *Lyrics of Lowly Life* (1896):

> I think I should scarcely trouble the reader with a special
> appeal in behalf of this book, if it had not specially appealed
> to me for reasons apart from the author's race, origin, and
> condition.   The world is too old now, and I find myself too
> much of its mood, to care for the work of a poet because he is
> black, because his father and mother were slaves, because he
> wàs, before and after he began to write poems, an elevator-boy.
> These facts would certainly attract me to him as a man, if I
> knew him to haƭe a literary ambition, but when it came to his
> literary art, I must judge it irrespective of these facts, and
> enjoy or endure it for what it was in itself.

In the history of American Negro literature this statement
is most significant.   It was a recognition by the man who in
the nineties was popularly regarded as America's leading
critic that Negro literature had at last emerged as a distinct
unit in American culture.   The Negro artist was to be

judged by the same standards which the white artist was
obliged to meet.   The masses of blacks were still in a state
of ignorance and economic misery.   But another class,
represented in considerable numbers in all of the northern
cities and throughout the South and Southwest, had grasped
every opportunity for education, enlightenment, and cultural
advancement.   They were on the intellectual plane where
they were not to be judged as Negroes, but as producers,
pure and simple.   A general public, white and black, was to
read what they wrote, often without knowing that they
were colored.   Sure criticism was to be meted out to them;
they welcomed it, and became critics of themselves.   Tons
of printed stuff flowed from their pens.   And from it all we
are able to cull a body of writing which forms a contribution to American literature not to be ignored.

II

Negro writers, whether of the group of racial leaders
or of the masses, continued to publish accounts of their
lives, as they had done for a hundred years.   Small pamphlet autobiographies, badly written and cheaply printed,
although not so numerous as in the days of abolition agitation, still came in abundance.   Indeed, we shall probably
have "slave narratives" as long as any Negro who was once
a bondman is still alive.   Typical of those of the pamphlet
sort which appeared between 1865 and 1900 is *The Life and
Adventures of James Williams,* published in Sacramento in
1873.   Williams' power of invention was in one respect as
great as that of the earlier James Williams who deceived
Whittier into accepting as true a life story which proved to
be a product of Negro imagination.[23]   While the later James
Williams was not so vivid, he was certainly more versatile.

He crowded into the miserable pamphlet relating the story of his experiences descriptions of hairbreadth escapes from dangers on land and sea, essays on the comparative merits of Catholicism and Protestantism, and ventures into verse, of which the following is representative:

> Then well may I say, in the Garden of Eden,
>   There was beauty.
> In the Garden of Eden, Beauty awoke and spoke to Beauty.
> And from the word, there was beauty.
> In the Garden of Eden, Beauty became
>   A living mortal.[24]

A characteristic of much Negro history, from William C. Nell's *The Colored Patriots of the American Revolution* (1855) to John W. Cromwell's *The Negro in American History* (1914), is that the historian seems to arrive at a point beyond which he cannot go without bringing before us in catalogue order the main facts in the careers of illustrious members of his race. Perhaps the most comprehensive Negro biographical dictionary is William J. Simmons' *Men of Mark*, published in 1887. It is most voluminous, and to one who has the time to check its numerous errors still useful as a clue to information.[25] Simmons, as his title indicates, dealt only with "men of mark." An interesting work presenting lives of lesser figures is Octavia V. Rogers Albert's *The House of Bondage, or, Charlotte Brooks and Other Slaves* (1890). Mrs. Albert's accounts, all of them brief, hark back to the spirit of grievance found in the narratives so frequently printed in the antislavery newspapers. More modern in tone and no doubt more trustworthy for the facts presented, are the numbers of authors' autobiographical essays prefacing books on church history, collections of sermons, and volumes of verse.

But the Negro literature of the period is not unrepresented by a type of biography which was a sure mark of development. Besides such a lengthy study as the *Life and Times of Frederick Douglass,* discussed in an earlier chapter,[26] several other biographical works of distinction by or about Negroes were published between 1865 and 1900. Reference has been made to the reprinting of the *Narrative of Sojourner Truth, Northern Slave* (1850) in 1875, 1883, and 1884, each time with elaborate augmentation.[27] In 1886, Sarah H. Bradford published her *Harriet, the Moses of Her People,* an informing and very readable life of another Negro heroine of abolition and Civil War fame, Harriet V. Tubman.[28] A biography replete with facts dealing with the place of the Negro in the abolition crusade is the *Life and Public Services of Martin R. Delany* (1883), the work of Frances E. Rollin Whipper, a colored woman, who wrote under the name of Frank A. Rollin.[29] The work of seven other Negro biographers of the period, Elizabeth Keckley, Henry Ossian Flipper, Daniel Alexander Payne, Charles W. Chesnutt, Archibald H. Grimké, John Mercer Langston, and Booker Taliaferro Washington, merits a more detailed examination.

The unusual portrait of Mary Todd Lincoln which Elizabeth Keckley gives in *Behind the Scenes; or, Thirty Years a Slave, and Four Years in the White House* (1868) makes of the book, ostensibly an autobiography, a work of singular importance. Elizabeth Keckley's part in writing the book was probably little more than providing the facts,[30] and furnishing the letters from Mrs. Lincoln which make up a considerable body of the work.[31] But if Elizabeth Keckley did not do the actual writing, she put herself so much into the dictation that we feel from the beginning to the end that we are face to face with "Madame Keckley," as Lincoln

called her, "formerly a slave, but more recently modiste
and friend to Mrs. Abraham Lincoln," and withal a spirited
woman, blessed with an ingenious African wit. She gives
briefly the necessary facts about herself. We are told of
her birth in Virginia; of her thirty years of slavery in that
state, in North Carolina, and in St. Louis; of her learning
to be a dressmaker and of her earning through her skill
enough money to pay for the freedom of herself and the
mulatto son whom she had borne to a North Carolina
planter; of her marriage to a worthless man and of her
separation from him; of her pride in her son while he was
a student at Wilberforce and of her sorrow over his death
in battle; and finally of her winning her way into the
intimacies of the Lincoln household in the White House.
Abraham Lincoln himself rarely enters the scene. When he
does, it is likely to be in a homely picture, such as the
following observation made when Elizabeth Keckley among
several other White House servants was accompanying the
Lincolns on their celebrated visit to Virginia after the fall
of Richmond:

On our return to City Point from Petersburg the train moved
slowly, and the President, observing a terrapin basking in the
warm sunshine on the wayside, had the conductor stop the train,
and one of the brakemen bring the terrapin in to him. The movements of the ungainly little animal seemed to delight him, and
he amused himself with it until we reached the James River,
where our steamer lay. Tad stood near, and joined in the
happy laugh with his father.

Mrs. Lincoln, on the other hand, is almost constantly with
us; she is really the central figure of the book. We see her
in her temperamental moods; we laugh inwardly with her
"modiste" at her when she is displaying her strange passion
for elaborate dress; we pity her neuroticism. Elizabeth

Keckley does not present herself as really a servant to Mrs. Lincoln; she is rather a confidante. If we can trust her statement, she was the one person whom Mrs. Lincoln wished to see after the assassination of her husband. The friendship between the former first lady of the land and her colored servant reaches its test in the final chapters, which treat of the pitiful attempt which the two make in New York to auction off Mrs. Lincoln's White House wardrobe as Eugénie had auctioned her imperial gowns in Paris. The servant's devotion and faithfulness stand the test. If she had been Mrs. Lincoln's intimate confidante, she was now her consoler. And she claimed that it was to offer consolation that she wrote *Behind the Scenes,* produced certainly in the simple idiom of an uneducated servant even though penned by an unknown hand. The book appeared at the time of the deluge of publications on the Lincolns, and seems to have been lost in the flood.[32] As a portrait of Mary Todd Lincoln which came from an unexpected source, it deserved a better fate.[33]

Considerable comment in *Behind the Scenes* is devoted to Elizabeth Keckley's feelings toward race prejudice. She was a Negro woman proud of her color, and she lost no opportunity to push her race forward. The two men presented as most willing to help the widowed and poverty-stricken Mrs. Lincoln out of her financial straits were colored men, Frederick Douglass and Henry Highland Garnet.[34] In many respects, the book is a study of the unhappy social position of the Negro.

That subject is given main place in another very readable autobiography, Henry Ossian Flipper's *The Colored Cadet at West Point* (1878). Flipper was not the first Negro who was entered at West Point, but he was the first to remain until he received an Army commission.[35] Ap-

pointed by a Georgia Congressman in 1872 and admitted to
the Academy in 1873, he was graduated in 1877; and a few
months after he was stationed at Fort Sill, Indian Territory,
his autobiography, "written by request, transcribed from
notes taken at West Point," was published in New York.
The beginning, told in the third person, is affected and
awkward; but soon the formality of the third person is
dropped, and the account moves intimately. Every statement seems to be exact. Documentation, in the form of
letters and newspaper clippings, is generously provided.
Flipper was graduated forty-fifth in a class of eighty-five.
One wonders at times in reading the story of his experiences
how he could have done so well. For he insists most upon
picturing himself as enduring a solitary existence. Such a
lament as the following occurs again and again:

Alas! What a trial it is to be socially ostracized, to live in
the very midst of life and yet be lonely, to pass day after day
without saying perhaps a single word other than those used in
the section-room during a recitation. How hard it is to live
month after month without even speaking to woman, without
knowing or feeling the refining influence of her presence! What
a miserable existence.

Once the lament turns into very bad verse.

> Oh! 'T is hard, this lonely living! To be
> In the midst of life so solitary,
> To sit all the long, long day through and gaze
> In the dimness of gloom, all but amazed
> At the emptiness of life, and wonder
> What keeps sorrows and death asunder.
> 'T is the forced seclusion most galls the mind,
> And sours all joys which it may find.
> 'T is the sneer, tho' half hid, is better still,
> And makes dormant anger to passion's will.
> But oh! 'T is harder yet to bear them all
> Unangered and unheedful of the thrall,

To list the jeer, the snarl, and epithet
All too base for knaves, and e'en still forget
Such words were spoken, too manly to let
Such baseness move the nobler intellect.
But not the words, nor e'en the dreader disdain
Move me to anger or resenting pain.
'T is the thought, the thought most disturbs my mind,
'T is that ever-recurring thought awakes
My anger.

In spite of the lament, there is a certain self-assurance in these doggerel lines, the self-assurance that made Flipper a success at West Point. He wrote his book as a message to his race. As a pariah at West Point, he was naturally unhappy. But the military precision with which he told his story shows that courage was the keynote of his character rather than a sentimental brooding over his outcast state.

Among the autobiographical sketches and personal memoirs produced by ministers of the period Bishop Daniel Alexander Payne's *Recollections of Seventy Years* (1888) is the most outstanding. Reference has been made to Payne's verse, his main contribution to Negro literature before 1865.[36] But he had not only by that year stamped his individuality on his race as a maker of smooth and thoughtful verses; he had already become prominent as a minister and social organizer of marked ability.[37] His writings on theology and education will be considered later in this chapter. But of all his work his *Recollections of Seventy Years* comes nearest perhaps to the attainment of genuine literary merit.

The book was published when Payne was seventy-seven years of age. He had really been working on it since his childhood, and could not have given it a more appropriate title. The poems which he had composed from time to time, notes which he had filed away, conversations which he had

recorded on scraps of paper, and copies of letters which
he had written are brought freely into the story of his life
and make of it something of a journal.   He had probably
known intimately more Negro leaders and had been in close
contact with more racial movements, educational and social
as well as religious, than any other person alive in 1888.
Therefore, in recording the events of his own life he was
producing a social history of the Negro race in the United
States during the nineteenth century.   There was much of
the scholarly in Payne's mentality; during his boyhood in
Charleston and later at the Gettysburg Seminary he had had
the privilege of a careful and severe tutelage.[38]   Frederick
Douglass padded his *Life and Times* with oratory; Payne
kept his *Recollections of Seventy Years* close to facts, most
of which, if they are not stated as his own observations,
are accurately documented.   Compactness is the salient
characteristic of his style.   Such a paragraph as the following, occurring in the chapter in which he tells of his thirteen
years as president of Wilberforce University, is suggestive
of his manner of stating things:

I paid a visit to the Hermitage, the home of Gen. Andrew
Jackson, about twelve miles east of Nashville.   The day was
stormy; in many places the road was in a very bad condition,
and the crossings at Mill Creek and Stone's Bridge were awful,
the rebels having destroyed the bridges over both streams.   We
approached the Hermitage through an avenue lined with red
cedars.   It is of brick, with porticoes on the north and south
sides, those on the south sustained by Corinthian pillars of wood
painted white, and the northern by Doric columns.   The ashes
of General Jackson were sleeping in a flower-garden to the
east of his residence in a sepulcher of native sandstone quarried
on his own plantation, and built in the form of a Grecian
temple.   Here also lie the ashes of his wife, for whom it was
built.   His adopted son was absent at this time in search of the
body of one of his sons, a captain in the rebel army, who had

died near Atlanta, Ga., of wounds received in battle. Neither George Washington nor Andrew Jackson left a son to inherit their fortunes or their honors. Their relatives by their wives were all rebels, and used their influence and their energies for the overthrow of that very government which both labored to establish and perpetuate.

The quotation shows the vividness with which Bishop Payne as an aged man remembered the details of his life. His *Recollections* is undoubtedly a faithful record of a leader who is rightly regarded as one of the makers of his race.[39] It is an important source book for the student of Negro life during the critical years when the Negro civilization which exists in America was being built up.

Among the Negro leaders who became prominent in national politics after the Civil War, John Mercer Langston is the one about whom we know most. *From the Virginia Plantation to the National Capitol* (1894), a volume running well beyond five hundred pages, is a detailed account of his remarkable career. Whether Langston himself wrote it is a question. His printed speeches, which will be discussed later, prove that he could have written it in even a better style than that in which it was produced.[40] The copyright was secured in his own name, and the book has been generally accepted as a pure autobiography.[41] But the account is told in the third person, and there is not that natural modesty which one expects in the self-written memoir. In whatever way it came into being, it is an illuminating work, bearing such a relation to the political problems of the Negro as Payne's *Recollections of Seventy Years* bears to the educational and religious problems. It traces Langston's life from the year of his birth, 1829, until after he had made his first speech at the national Capitol in 1891 as a Representative in Congress from Virginia. We see him as a boy in Ohio, as a student at Oberlin, as one of the first Negro lawyers in the West, as an educator at Howard University and Virginia Institute, as Minister to Hayti, and finally as a' Congressman. As in Payne's *Recollections,* there is much in the book which is of value to the student of the social history of the Negro. For example, a chapter on the place of the Negro in the early history of Oberlin College provides information which is perhaps nowhere else obtainable. Moreover, there are many pages in *From the Virginia Plantation to the National Capitol* which afford interesting reading.

Langston no doubt lost the sympathy of many members of his race by giving up his work as an educator in order to struggle to become a nondescript member of Congress long after Reconstruction had proved that the Negro's work as a leader in national politics was for years to come to be negligible.[42] A more notable Negro educator of the period, Booker T. Washington, adhered to a social doctrine which was the direct opposite to that of Langston. Washington's prime message to his race was, "Begin at the bottom." Because of the program of industrial education to which he devoted his life, it has been claimed that his theories involved too great a compromise with white prejudice to admit of the highest cultural progress of the colored race.[43] Whether we defend him or oppose him, we must agree that he is today the most generally respected and admired of all the American Negroes of the past, not excepting Frederick Douglass.

Booker T. Washington's writings were put together in the rush of an extremely active life. Their literary merit dwindles when compared with that of other less well known Negroes among both his predecessors and contemporaries. However, because of his popularity, his autobiography, *Up from Slavery,* is the one book by a Negro which has become a sort of American classic.

Up from Slavery was originally published as a serial in the *Outlook,* where it was begun in November, 1900, and completed the following April. Lyman Abbott, then in control of the *Outlook,* introduced it to his readers with an editorial, in which he said, "The story of such a life is more romantic than fiction: it is indeed philosophy teaching by example."[44]   Booker T. Washington had been a famous man since the delivery of his widely quoted address at the opening of the Cotton States Exposition at Atlanta, Georgia, on September 18, 1895. He summed up the idea of the address in a simile which caught the public fancy—"In all things that are purely social we can be as separate as the fingers, yet one as the hand in all things essential to mutual progress." This sentence became a text for all of his later argument on the Negro problem. It expressed a sentiment which the great American public, South as well as North, could accept, and its author won such an esteem as had never before been accorded an American colored man. When *Up from Slavery* appeared, there were hosts of readers to receive it. As soon as the last chapters had been printed in the *Outlook,* it was issued in book form. Many editions, including one arranged for the use of school children, have followed.[45]   Today it is possibly as familiar to American readers as Franklin's *Autobiography.* And its reputation is not confined to America.[46]

Few who read it realize that it is only one of many Negro autobiographies and that it is by no means the best among them. Washington gives an account of his birth in a dismal Virginia slave cabin, of his sordid childhood in a West Virginia salt-mining town, of his struggling days as a student at Hampton Institute, of his beginnings as a teacher, of his difficulties and ultimate triumph at Tuskegee, and of his modesty in receiving the plaudits of an admiring world, white as well as black. There is less of the really interesting in such a career than there is in the lives of Gustavus Vassa, Frederick Douglass, and Daniel Alexander Payne. Much in *Up from Slavery* does not belong in one's memoirs. Page after page makes the reader feel that Washington wrote the book in order to plead for funds for the upbuilding of Tuskegee rather than to give a true portrait of himself. There is in the book too obvious an attempt to please everybody. Certain conciliatory passages make the lover of justice long for the "big stick" of a Frederick Douglass. The style is too pedagogical. The reader is too often made to feel that he is a child being taught his lessons. Such extreme simplicity, frequently of the monosyllabic type, does not, as we shall see, mark the style of Washington's purely sociological writings and certainly not of his oratory.

But in one great respect *Up from Slavery* shows an advance in Negro literature. Its excellence lies in its sincerity. If it is not the most interesting, nor the most powerful, nor the most literary, it is the most believable of all the Negro autobiographies. It has been often said that the Negro is by nature histrionic, that in the presence of whites he is always acting. This was certainly not true of Booker T. Washington. He knew that he was writing *Up from Slavery* mainly for a white public, but he did not assume a pose. One reads the book as he would any other account of an American arising from the depths to the heights. He sees the tremendous problems at Tuskegee, and he recognizes in them universal problems. He loses sight of the fact that he is reading about a race different from his own. This is Washington's greatest stylistic accomplishment, to be attributed no doubt to his natural honest straight-forwardness. He felt a pride in his color; he had no defenses to make for it. He is concerned with relating the plain facts of his life and with describing and promoting the program of his educational work. He suggests his sincerity and the secret of it in the following passage, in which he refers to his beginnings at Tuskegee:

As I look back now over that part of our struggle, I am glad that we had it. I am glad that we endured all those discomforts and inconveniences. I am glad that our students had to dig out the place for their kitchen and dining room. I am glad that our first boarding-place was in that dismal, ill-lighted, and damp basement. Had we started in a fine, attractive, convenient room, I fear we would have "lost our heads" and become "stuck up." It means a great deal, I think, to start off on a foundation which one has made for one's self.

Up from Slavery presents the most honest portrait which any American Negro had by 1900 drawn of his real self. But if the reader of the book wishes more thrilling accounts of the lives of Negroes as told by themselves, such accounts may be had.

Little need be said about Booker T. Washington's other biographical works. *The Story of My Life and Work* (1900), published "to be sold by subscription," is an earlier version of *Up from Slavery*. *Working with the Hands* (1904) and *My Larger Education* (1911), issued as sequels to *Up from Slavery,* are devoted mainly to descriptions of the work which Washington was carrying on at Tuskegee. *Frederick Douglass* (1907) is an eloquent tribute to his greatest predecessor among the American Negroes. In writing it Washington evidently intended to interpret Douglass rather than to add new information to what was already known about him. For there is little in the book

which might not have been derived from Douglass' autobiographies and from Frederic May Holland's *Frederick
Douglass: the Colored Orator,* which had been published in
1891. The style is in the manner of Washington's historical and sociological writings, which will be examined later.

There had appeared in 1899 another *Frederick Douglass,*
the work of Charles W. Chesnutt, the Negro novelist.
Those who read the book, written in a finished style of
which Booker T. Washington was in no sense master, probably never realized that the author was a colored man. Like
Washington's study of Douglass, it is mainly interpretative.
If Mr. Chesnutt had not published excellent short stories
and novels,[47] he would still be entitled to a place of importance in Negro literature. For his *Frederick Douglass* is to
be classed among the most thoughtfully constructed and
carefully written works which the American Negro produced before the end of the nineteenth century.[48]

Charles W. Chesnutt was not the only Negro of the
nineties who wrote biography which demanded research
and skilled workmanship. For the "American Reformers"
series of lives Archibald H. Grimké, a colored man who
had been born in Charleston, South Carolina, in 1849, who
had been educated at Lincoln University and Harvard,
where he received a law degree in 1874, and who had worked
on newspapers in Boston,[49] was called upon to provide two
works. The first, *William Lloyd Garrison, the Abolitionist,*
was published in 1891. This was followed one year later
by *The Life of Charles Sumner, the Scholar in Politics.*
The author's aim in writing the two books, as he stated it
in the second, was "to give a comprehensive view of the
forces, moral and political, which combined to achieve the
downfall of slavery." For the *Garrison* he admitted his
indebtedness to "that storehouse of anti-slavery material,

the story of the life of William Lloyd Garrison by his children." The *Sumner* is likewise made up mainly of material drawn from earlier biographical studies, particularly from the opening volumes of Edward L. Pierce's *Memoir and Letters of Charles Sumner.*[50] Mr. Grimké wrote in an impassioned style. Emotion too often clouded his sense of accurate expression. However, his *Garrison* and *Sumner* were a worthy contribution to the "American Reformers" biographies. While they lack the supply of added information on the antislavery movement which Frederic May Holland put into his *Frederick Douglass,* belonging to the same series, they are as well written and perhaps more readable. There is nothing in either, except possibly an extreme sympathy for the subject treated, to hint that the author was a Negro. In their work as biographers Charles W. Chesnutt and Archibald H. Grimké showed that colored men were taking their places in American literature simply as writers and not as Negroes who were to be looked upon by the curious as venturing into strange fields.[51]

III

Booker T. Washington said in the opening chapter of *The Story of the Negro* (1909),

It seemed to me that what I had put into the book "Up from Slavery," was, in a very definite way, an epitome of the history of my race, at least in the early stages of its awakening and in the evolution through which it is now passing.

The long line of Negro autobiographies extending from Briton Hammon's *Narrative* to Booker T. Washington's *Up from Slavery* gives undoubtedly a better understanding of the progress of the American Negro than the writings of the avowed historians. However, the work of colored historians between 1865 and 1900 was by no means negligible. By the latter year the racial leaders showed that they were as interested in delving into their past as they were in studying their contemporary social problems. And in both their historical and their sociological treatises they began to discard the old manner of spreading propaganda and to adopt the usages of scientific investigation.

But throughout the period there was still an abundance of the type of history represented by the antislavery writings of William C. Nell and William Wells Brown. The work of Joseph T. Wilson well illustrates the persistence of a history that is more gossip and vituperation and puffed defense than a record and thoughtful organization of facts. Wilson, a native of Virginia, a resident of Massachusetts, and an adventurer in the South Seas and in South America,[52] was at the beginning of the Civil War living in Chili. Upon hearing of the hostilities in the United States, he, according to his own statement, hastened back to this country and "fell into the ranks with the first Negro soldiers that left the Touro Building at New Orleans, in November, 1862, and marched out on the Opelousas road, to serve in defense of the Union."[53] Later transferred to a Massachusetts regiment, he fought throughout the war;[54] and after the restoration of peace he seems to have engaged in teaching.[55] His first extensive effort at history, *Emancipation: Its Course and Progress from 1481 B. C. to A. D. 1875,* was published in 1882.[56] It is an attempt at a general survey of Negro history, and as such is of incomparably less value than Brown's *The Rising Son.* In the year in which *Emancipation* was published Wilson was chosen by the post of the Grand Army of the Republic to which he belonged to write a history of the part which his regiment had played in the Civil War. Six years later, in 1888, his *Black Phalanx,* a lengthy volume devoted to the general subject of the American Negro soldier, was published. Two lengthy chapters give a résumé of the Negro's services in the Revolution and War of 1812, most of the information in which might have been drawn from Nell's *The Colored Patriots of the American Revolution.* The rest of the book deals with the Negro in the Civil War. In that it is long enough to afford the free citation of official documents, letters, and newspaper comment, it is an improvement over Brown's *The Negro in the American Rebellion.* But Wilson was a less skilled writer than Brown, and more illiterate. One finds again and again in the *Black Phalanx* such a paragraph (spelling and grammar reported verbatim) as the following:

> The laurels won by the Phalanx in the Southern States, notwithstanding the "no quarter" policy, was proof of its devotion to the cause of liberty and the old flag, which latter,—though until within a short period had been but a symbal of oppression to the black man,—Cailloux had reddened with his life's blood, and Carney, in a seething fire, had planted on the ramparts of Wagner. The audacious bravery of the Phalanx wrung from Generals Banks and Gillmore congratulatory orders, while the loyal people of the nation poured unstinted praises. Not a breach of discipline marred the negro soldier's record; not one cowardly act tarnished their fame. Grant pronounced them gallant and reliable, and Weitzel was willing to command them.

In spite of its wordiness, the book found readers.[57]

As much a hodgepodge of interesting data as Wilson's *Black Phalanx* is William Still's *The Underground Rail Road* (1872). The book contains almost eight hundred pages, adequately summed up in the explanatory title:

> A record of facts, authentic narratives, letters, &c., narrating the hardships, hair breadth escapes and death struggles of the slaves in their efforts for freedom, as related by themselves

and others, or witnessed by the author; together with sketches
of some of the largest stockholders, and most liberal aiders and
advisers of the road.

Still was as illiterate as Wilson, but he was at least able to
write direct narration.[58]

Still's work as a historian is more justifiable than that
of Wilson, for there is no other book exactly like *The
Underground Rail Road*. However, there was no reason
why either *Emancipation* or *Black Phalanx* should have
been published. The former was hardly off the press before
the appearance of George Washington Williams' *History of
the Negro Race in America, from 1619 to 1880* (1883) ; and
simultaneously with the publication of *Black Phalanx* came
Williams' *A History of the Negro Troops in the War of
the Rebellion* (1888).[59]

The first of Williams' books, issued in two volumes,[60]
appeared under the imprint of G. P. Putnam's Sons, and the
second under that of Harper & Brothers. Works on Negro
history written by a Negro were at last recognized by eminent American publishers as worthy of their sponsorship.
And Williams deserved the distinction of seeing his books
brought before the public in a dignified manner.

He had tried many things and had achieved various successes before he won enduring gratitude from his people as
their first serious historian. Born in Pennsylvania in 1849
of mixed Negro, German, and Welsh ancestry, with a
Lutheran mother and a Unitarian father, he had practically
completed a secondary school course at an academy in
Massachusetts when the Civil War broke out. By reporting
himself as older than he really was, he was allowed to enlist
in the Union Army ; and when mustered out in 1865 he was
a sergeant-major. He was in Texas at the time, and the lure
of more warfare drew him into Mexico, where he joined

the forces recruited to oust Maximilian. When he left the
Mexican army, after a few months, he was a lieutenant-
colonel. From 1868 to 1874 he seems to have spent most
of his time in theological seminaries, and in the latter year
began his career as a Baptist minister. From preaching
he turned first to newspaper work, then to governmental
clerkships in Washington, and finally to the study of law in
Cincinnati. He was admitted to the bar, became interested
in politics, and in 1877 was elected to the Ohio Legislature.
Such varied pursuits offered a strange but not altogether
unfitting preparation for his work as a historian.[61]

Williams, perhaps in temperament more like Frederick
Douglass than like any other of his celebrated Negro predecessors, possessed a practical, fact-loving mind and a passion
for oratory. He had been trained in theological seminaries,
and at the time of writing his histories he was still to a
degree a religionist. Yet in recording his conclusions regarding his race he followed as axiomatic a principle which
he stated as follows:

I am alive to the fact, that, while I am a believer in the Holy
Bible, it is not the best authority on ethnology. As far as it
goes, it is agreeable to my head and heart.[62]

And as he freed himself from Biblical explanations concerning the origins of races, he also freed himself to a great
extent from what must have been his natural predilection
to extol too highly the rôle which the Negro had played in
civilization. An anonymous English reviewer said of Williams' first historical work:

The materials have been collected with great care; official documents in most cases printed in full; and though a member of
an oppressed race cannot be expected to write calmly about the
wrongs of his people, there is no needless or offensive vituperation. The style is clear and straightforward, with a few

Americanisms here and there, some of which will be new to
many of his readers on this side, as the verb "to enthuse,"
meaning "to inspire enthusiasm."[63]

Such a conclusion regarding Williams' attitude towards his
subject is sound enough. But it is impossible to accept his
style as "clear and straightforward." He was too oratorical
to resist the temptation to play with words, and therefore
made the *History of the Negro Race in America* far too
long.[64]

His aim in writing the work he stated as follows:

I became convinced that a history of the Colored people in
America was required, because of the ample historically trustworthy material at hand; because the Colored people themselves
had been the most vexatious problem in North America, from
the time of its discovery down to the present day; because that
in every attempt upon the life of the nation whether by foes
from without or within, the Colored people had always displayed
a matchless patriotism and an incomparable heroism in the
cause of Americans; and because such a history would give
the world more correct ideas of the Colored people, and in-
cite the latter to greater effort in the struggle of citizenship and
manhood. The single reason that there was no history of the
Negro race would have been a sufficient reason for writing
one.[65]

In order to give an idea of the sort of people who were first
sold as slaves to the Virginia colonists, he devotes the opening of the work to what he calls "Preliminary Considera-
tions," in reality a summary more romantic than historical,
a compromise between the Biblical and the scientific. He
also gives in this section an account of African achievements
in modern civilization, discussing at length what Western
ideas had accomplished in the organization of life in Liberia
and Sierra Leone. The second part of the book traces the
history of slavery in America during the seventeenth and

eighteenth centuries, each colony being taken up in turn. The third part, which ends the first volume, treats of the Negro during the Revolution. The fourth part, perhaps the weakest, deals with what has since been called "the neglected period of antislavery," the period extending from about 1800 to 1830. Williams here falls upon the easy resource of devoting much space to the services of the Negro in the War of 1812. The fifth part is a lively treatment of antislavery agitation in the thirties and forties. The sixth part is entitled "The Period of Preparation," and deals with the aspects of slavery which precipitated the Civil War, to which the seventh part is devoted. The eighth part is a study of the Negro's first decade of freedom. The book ends with a rather pessimistic section, called "The Decline of Negro Governments." Yet it is felt by Williams as only a period of temporary depression. In the very last paragraph of the book he says:

Race prejudice is bound to give way before the potent influences of character, education, and wealth. And these are necessary to the growth of the race. Without wealth there can be no leisure, without leisure there can be no thought, and without thought there can be no progress. The future work of the Negro is twofold: subjective and objective. Years will be devoted to his own education and improvement in America. He will sound the depths of education, accumulate wealth, and then turn his attention to the civilization of Africa. . . . In the interpretation of *History* the plans of God must be concerned, *"For a thousand years in Thy sight are but as yesterday when it is passed, and as a watch in the night."*

Williams evidently felt in writing the book that the whole past of the African was as a "watch in the night." He said in the preface of the second volume:

After seven years I am loath to part with the saddest task ever committed to human hands! I have tracked my bleeding countrymen through the widely scattered documents of American history; I have listened to their groans, their clanking chains, and melting prayers, until the woes of a race and the agonies of centuries seem to crowd upon my soul as a bitter reality. Many pages of this history have been blistered with my tears; and, although having lived but little more than a generation, my mind feels as though it were cycles old.

In reading the work we too feel that we have the Negro with his centuries of oppression crowding upon us "as a bitter reality." Such emotional effect was Williams' highest stylistic achievement and at the same time his chief pitfall. He was too articulate.[66] But in the maze of words, too often ungrammatically strung together, there are facts, supported by letters, legal statutes, and official documents; indeed, there is enough accurate information in the book for a masterly history. Much might be said against Williams' taste, but little against his industry in research.[67] Like Douglass, Williams loved the concrete and objective as well as the oratorical. Although the *History of the Negro Race in America* appeared almost half a century ago, it is still perhaps the most comprehensive general history of the American Negro. Many fields which it surveys rapidly and inadequately have been treated in scholarly manner by specialized historians. It is exceedingly old-fashioned and needs to be superseded.[68] But its place in the development of Negro literature is most important. Only two among Williams' predecessors stand out as possibly better writers of prose: Alexander Crummell was a surer master of English style, and Frederick Douglass possessed a greater talent for oratorical expression. None of the books by Crummell and Douglass were taken seriously by the literary world at the time they were published. However, Williams' *History of the Negro Race in America* was recognized with lengthy reviews, some of which were most favorable, in a number of the leading American and English magazines. Because of its widespread appeal and practical usefulness it deserved the attention which it gained.

Immediately after the publication of the *History of the Negro Race in America*, before Williams had received his first royalties from the work, he settled in Boston; and, although oppressed by extreme poverty, he began collecting material for a book on the Negro in the Civil War.[69] The work was completed by 1886,[70] but was not published until two years later, when it appeared as *A History of the Negro Troops in the War of the Rebellion, 1861–1865*. The task which confronted Williams in getting the book ready for the press he himself has suggested:

From the first to the last there were 178,975 Negro soldiers in the United States Volunteer army, and of this number 36,847 were killed, wounded, and missing. They participated in four hundred and forty-nine battles, and served in nearly every military department of the United States. Besides this large military force, there were at least one hundred and fifty thousand Negro laborers in the Quartermaster and Engineering departments.[71]

Although, in spite of the advice of a number of his critics, he had not outgrown his weakness for oratory, he met the demands of recording the history of these large and scattered units most admirably. After a preliminary survey, fortunately brief, of the Negro's part in ancient and modern European warfare, he studies in detail the various Negro organizations which rendered actual service in the Civil War. He himself no doubt had a share in much that he wrote about, but he rarely enters the scene. The story is developed mainly with documented facts. Still the reader never loses sight of Williams' attitude towards his subject, which he expressed as follows:

The part enacted by the Negro soldier in the war of the Rebellion is the romance of North American history. It was midnight and noonday without a space between; from the Egyptian darkness of bondage to the lurid glare of civil war; from clanging chains to clashing arms; from passive submission to the cruel curse of slavery to the brilliant aggressiveness of a free soldier; from a chattel to a person; from the shame of degradation to the glory of military exaltation; and from deep obscurity to martial immortality. No one in this era of fraternity and Christian civilization will grudge the Negro soldier these simple annals of his trials and triumphs in a holy struggle for human liberty. Whatever praise is bestowed upon his noble acts will be sincerely appreciated, whether from former foes or comrades in arms. For by withholding just praise they are not enriched, nor by giving are they thereby impoverished.[72]

Despite such an attitude, there is not in the book that consistent cheap glorification of the Negro which marks such an earlier work as Brown's *The Negro in the American Rebellion.* All such treatises Williams ignored. He was justified in doing so, for his book is of another *genre.* Notwithstanding its wordiness, it is, because of the array of facts which it presents, respectable history, a worthy supplement to his earlier more general study of the Negro.

Probably the most widely read general history of the American Negro which has been published is Booker T. Washington's *The Story of the Negro,* issued in two volumes in 1909. It was Washington's one extended venture into the field of history. The work no doubt satisfied his aim, which was obviously no more than to provide a popular account of the Negro's oppression and achievements in the Western world. Williams' *History of the Negro Race in America* might have been the source for practically all of the facts which it contains. The book would not be named here except for the fact that it was the production of a man whose main literary achievements came before the year

1900. It is enough to say that, except for the conversational charm of the style, it is not the sort of history to be given serious consideration in Negro literature as a production of the year 1909.

For the Negro had already shown that he was able to write such history as the modern world accepts as strong. In 1896, William E. Burghardt Du Bois published as the first volume of the *Harvard Historical Studies* his monograph, *The Suppression of the African Slave Trade to the United States of America, 1638–1870*. Dr. Du Bois said modestly in his preface, "I . . . trust that I have succeeded in rendering by this monograph a small contribution to the scientific study of slavery and the American Negro." Time has proved that his confidence was more than justifiable. The book is still considered the authoritative study of the field to which it is devoted. The historical method employed is that of the strictest scholarship. The style is that of the scholar who is seeking the effect of accuracy and truth. But there is a certain charm in the sense of logic with which the study is planned, in the discrimination with which the facts are grouped, and in the freedom from bias which we associate with all sound history. An estimate made by an enthusiastic unnamed reviewer at the time the book was published is worthy of quotation:

His story of the suppression of the slave-trade is told with simplicity, directness, and convincing force, and in an interesting style rarely found in monographs. We have failed to note in the book a single important statement of fact for which specific authority is not adduced; but there is an entire absence of anything like pedantry, and irrelevant matter has been rigidly excluded. That this study will long remain the authoritative work on the subject which it treats may be confidently predicted. And after all the discussion over the probable future of the negro in this country, it is matter of profound significance and

great encouragement that a member of the race which, scarcely
more than a generation ago, was openly bought and sold and
hunted in our streets, should have traced, out of abundant
knowledge and with unbiased mind, the course of our national
connection with that unholy traffic, from its beginning to its
close, in a volume which is an honor alike to its author, to the
university whose approval it has received, and to American
historical scholarship.[73]

*The Suppression of the African Slave Trade to the United
States* was by far the greatest intellectual achievement which
had by 1900 come from any American Negro. It taught
the colored man that if he were to be considered a historian
he had to produce work which could meet the requirements
of high standards. It prepared the way for a number of
specialized historical studies of excellence which have come
from American Negroes during the past thirty years.

IV

Dr. Du Bois' varied career as a man of letters belongs
properly to the twentieth century. His one extended work,
besides *The Suppression of the African Slave Trade to the
United States,* important in Negro literature before 1900 is
The Philadelphia Negro, which appeared in 1899 as the
fourteenth volume in the *Publications of the University of
Pennsylvania: Series of Political Economy and Public Law.*
It was as revolutionary in Negro sociological studies as
*The Suppression of the African Slave Trade to the United
States* was in history. We have seen that every colored
writer from Jupiter Hammon on down, unless he was
steeped in religious mysticism, had something to say about
the social conditions of his race. With the exception of a
few brief essays, such as those which James McCune Smith
published in the fifties,[74] little of what was written was

based on thoughtful investigation. Although valuable conclusions were often reached, they were arrived at through
obvious assumptions. In writing *The Philadelphia Negro*
Dr. Du Bois assumed nothing. The book is a lucid report
of an extensive and painstaking examination of the life of
the Negro in the city in which he had probably achieved
most. The body of the work is made up of tabulated statements of what had been discovered regarding the physical
conditions of the Philadelphia Negro, where he had come
from, his conjugal and family relationships, the extent of
his education, his occupations, his church and social organizations, his economic status, his crimes, his tendency towards
and freedom from alcoholism, his contact with the whites,
and his exercise of the right of citizenship. Dr. Du Bois
said in his preface:

> It is my earnest desire to pursue this particular form of
> study far enough to contribute a fair basis of induction as to
> the present condition of the American Negro. If, for instance,
> Boston in the East, Chicago and perhaps Kansas City in the
> West, and Atlanta, New Orleans, and Galveston in the South,
> were studied in a similar way, we should have a trustworthy
> picture of Negro city life. Add to this an inquiry into similarly
> selected country districts, and certainly our knowledge of the
> Negro would be greatly increased.

This program of investigation was never carried out as out-
lined. But Dr. Du Bois himself followed *The Philadelphia
Negro* with his valuable work in directing the researches
reported in the *Atlanta University Studies*. And he perhaps more than any one else prepared the way for the
intensive work which the Negro has done in recent years
in studying scientifically the actual living conditions of his
race.

One does not expect readability in a book like *The Philadelphia Negro*, to a great extent a compendium of statistical

tables.   In the works which he published before 1900 Dr.
Du Bois had little opportunity for the display of that richness of style which his later publications have proved is his
by a heritage of nature.   While no other Negro who wrote
on racial problems between 1865 and 1900 was his equal as
a scientific thinker and as an unbiased recorder of facts, a
number produced sociological treatises which meet the interests of the general reader.

Among these, probably no one was a more skilled stylist
than T. Thomas Fortune, one of the most celebrated of the
Negro journalists of the period.   Fortune was born in Florida in 1856.   His father was a politician, for a time during
the Reconstruction régime a member of the Florida Legislature.   Through his influence the boy was for a period employed as a page in the Florida Senate, and early decided
that the northern carpetbagger was "oily, mercenary, cow-
ardly . . . a gambler, a drunkard, a libertine."[75]   Schooling
of an irregular sort, including two years at Howard University, seems to have been of less importance in training him
for his future career than work in a printing office.[76]   The
year 1882 found him in New York, editor of the *Globe,* a
Negro daily.   From this time until the year of his death,
1928, he was prominently identified with American Negro
journalism, advocating always the policy of Negro independence in politics.

Fortune's first book, *Black and White: Land, Labor, and
Politics in the South* (1884), is an economic study of the
southern Negro as he stood two decades after freedom.   The
thesis is stated as follows:

That the colored people of this country will yet achieve an
honorable status in the national industries of thought and activity I believe, and try to make plain. . . . My purpose is to show
that poverty and misfortune make no invidious distinctions of

"race, color, or previous condition," but that wealth unduly centralized oppresses all alike; therefore, that the labor elements of the whole United States should sympathize with the same elements in the South, and in some favorable contingency effect some unity of organization and action, which shall subserve the common interest of the common class.

In defending his argument for organized labor, Fortune lays bare the actual situation of the southern Negro in his relations to the landowning whites. The picture presented is a pessimistic one, but it is enlivened by witty comment, such as the following:

The South is weighted down with debt, almost as poor as the proverbial "Job's turkey," and yet she supports a dual school system to gratify a *prejudice*.

The Negro is urged to prepare himself to join forces with the working classes at large by seeking training in the industries and by learning the dignity of labor. That such a scheme for the salvation of the colored race is practicable Fortune is confident. He says in his conclusion:

I know it is not fashionable for writers on economic questions to tell the truth, but the truth should be told, though it kill. . . . The hour is fast approaching when the laboring classes of our country, North, East, West, and South, will recognize that they have a *common cause, common humanity,* and a *common enemy;* and that, therefore, if they would triumph over wrong and place the laurel wreath upon triumphant justice, without the distinction of race, or of previous condition, *they must unite!* And unite they will, for a "fellow feeling makes us wond'rous kind." When the issue is properly joined, the rich, be they black, or be they white, will be found upon the same side; and the poor, be they black or be they white, will be found on the same side.

Although his doctrines were socialistic, Fortune did not believe that the organization of Negro labor and the union of white and black working classes could be effected through any sort of political party affiliation. His second volume, *The Negro in Politics* (1885), is a spirited attack on Frederick Douglass' tenet that for the colored American "the Republican party is the ship, all else is the ocean." The mood of Fortune's attack is suggested by the following:

The history of the race since 1865 should teach us that there is no more tricky and slimy thing in the catalogue of duplicity and cowardice than the average politician; and yet we are supremely ignorant in this matter and hasten with a glibness, the outgrowth of ignorance, to brand as a traitor any man of us who has the intelligence and the courage to protest against the broken promises, the sugar-coated capsules, of political mountebanks.

Fortune comments upon the progress which the Negro has manifested since his emancipation, but adds:

. . . when it comes to politics; when it comes to an issue as to who shall control our ballot; when it reduces itself to who shall say what measure of right and justice the colored man shall have, how he should secure it, and in what manner, then the race quakes like Mount Aetna when Jupiter turns over, and rushes pell-mell into the arms of some white ward-heeler or national white trickster, trimmer, or demagogue, to shield it from the wrath impending—or, oftener, apprehended to be impending!

His final message to his people is that they need not be Republicans nor Democrats, but "simply men," conscious of their powers.

Both *Black and White* and *The Negro in Politics* were published before Fortune had reached his thirtieth year. Both show the radicalism of youth. But the general scheme of reform proposed in each was defended with sound reason as well as with enthusiastic fervor. There is a sparkle in his journalistic way of saying things which harks back to the incendiarism of David Walker and Henry Highland

Garnet.[77]   His prose well reflects the imagination out of which grew some creditable verse.[78]

Fortune said in 1884, when Booker T. Washington was in the pioneer period of his work at Tuskegee, "I do not inveigh against higher education; I simply maintain that the sort of education the colored people of the South stand most in need of, is *elementary* and *industrial*."[79]   Washington said in 1900, "In the summer of 1900, with the assistance of such prominent colored men as Mr. T. Thomas Fortune, who has always upheld my hands in every effort, I organized the National Negro Business League, which held its first meeting in Boston, and brought together a large number of colored men who are engaged in various lines of trade in different parts of the United States."[80]   In such movements as the formation of the National Negro Business League Fortune saw his dream of organized Negro labor partially realized.[81]   In spite of the progress which had already been made in industrial education at the time Fortune wrote *Black and White,* neither he nor any one else was able to prophecy how phenomenal its growth would be during the next twenty years.   The man most responsible for that extraordinary development was, as all the world knows, Booker T. Washington.   We have seen that *Up from Slavery* suffers as autobiography because of its overabundance of argument for industrial education.   For all of his public addresses and for all of his writings Washington had one theme—the training of colored youth in practical trades.

One of the earliest of his many magazine articles on industrial education which were to appear in standard periodicals was "The Awakening of the Negro," published in the *Atlantic Monthly* for September, 1896.[82]   This article was reprinted as a chapter in Washington's first and, with the possible exception of *Up from Slavery,* most important book, *The Future of the American Negro,* published in 1899. The work is a generalized discussion of industrial education for the Negro, as it had been thought about in the days of antislavery agitation,[83] and as it had been studied and experimented with since the founding of Hampton Institute in 1867. The argument shows no logical sequence of development; one in reading the book might as well begin with the last chapter as the first. Wherever he reads, he is amused by lively illustrative incident, he is warmed by Washington's sincerity and fervor, and he is not often repelled by that child-like simplicity of style which makes much of *Up from Slavery* passable as juvenile entertainment. Washington knew the effectiveness of advertising an idea by repeating it. Even though he is telling over and over again the same thing, he varies his expression so that we read on without weariness. The sense of humor which made Washington delightful on the platform guides him in some of his happiest comment, as in the following bit of irony:

Within the last thirty years—and, I might add, within the last three months,—it has been proven by eminent authority that the Negro is increasing in numbers so fast that it is only a question of a few years before he will far outnumber the white race in the South, and it has also been proven that the Negro is fast dying out, and it is only a question of a few years before he will have completely disappeared. It has also been proven that education helps the Negro and that education hurts him, that he is fast leaving the South and taking up his residence in the North and West, and that his tendency is to drift toward the low lands of the Mississippi bottoms. It has been proven that education unfits the Negro for work and that education makes him more valuable as a laborer, that he is our greatest criminal and that he is our most law-abiding citizen. In the midst of these conflicting opinions, it is hard to hit upon the truth.

Except possibly in his work on the peasantry of other lands, *The Man Farthest Down; a Record of Observation and Study in Europe* (1913), Washington said in *The Future of the American Negro* all that he was ever to say in his numerous sociological treatises, of which the most important are *Education of the Negro* (1900),[84] *Tuskegee and Its People* (1905), and *The Negro in Business* (1907).[85]   And the pleasingly popular style in which Washington wrote *The Future of the American Negro* he never improved upon.

In occasional magazine articles on sociological problems William Saunders Scarborough, a native of Georgia, a graduate of Oberlin with the class of 1875, and most of his life a member of the faculty of Wilberforce University, of which he was president from 1908 until the year of his death, 1926,[86] expressed views on the education and destiny of the Negro which were often at great variance from the views of Booker T. Washington.   Representative of Scarborough's sociological essays are "The Educated Negro and Menial Pursuits," a refutation of the charge that Negroes educated in the humanities were obliged to resort to trades upon leaving college, and "The Negro and Our New Possessions," a defense of the idea that the Philippines, Hawaii, and Porto Rico were lands to which the educated Negro could migrate and develop in a self-sufficient manner.   Both essays were published in the *Forum,* the first in 1898 and the second in 1901.[87]   But Scarborough is more interesting in Negro literature as the first recognized classical scholar which the race produced in the United States.   He was the author of a Greek grammar, published in 1881,[88] and of a treatise on Aristophanes' *The Birds,* presented as a paper in 1886 before the American Philological Association.[89]   He is also of significance in Negro literature before 1900 because of his efforts to make known the importance to American art of African folklore.[90]

V

Much of the Negro oratory published between 1865 and 1900 was, as we might expect, on sociological problems. Enfranchisement, disfranchisement, the denial of civil rights, theories concerning education, the eternal question of prejudice against color, the Ku Klux Klan, lynching, entanglements of party politics, theology—all such topics are found discussed by Negroes in speeches which were published in newspapers, in records of Congress, in pamphlets, and in volumes. There were now a dozen Negro orators where there had been one before, and the eradication of slavery only broadened the range of subjects upon which they had occasion to speak. Yet oratory was the one field of literature in which the Negro made no advancement after 1865. Frederick Douglass, trained in the traditions of the art when it was at its prime in America, remained until his death, in 1895, the unrivalled orator of his race. And his successor has never arisen.

Most of the speeches delivered by Negroes who served in Congress during the Reconstruction years add little more than volume to Negro literature.[91] From the colored Congressmen who expressed themselves during the long continued debate over the Civil Rights Bill we might expect sincere passion if not eloquence. Spurred on by the enthusiasm of such supporters as Charles Sumner, they had every opportunity of showing the best that was in them as speakers from the platform. But in most of their efforts we find neither passion nor eloquence, only commonplaceness.

A notable exception is a speech delivered by Robert Brown Elliott, Congressman from South Carolina, before the House of Representatives on January 6, 1874.[92] Elliott, born in Boston in 1842, educated in England, where he was graduated from Eton College in 1859, took up his residence in South Çarolina at the close of the Civil War, and was in 1870 and again in 1872 elected to Congress.[93] His defense of the Civil Rights Bill does not convince us that he was a sincere benefactor of his race rather than a clever politician; but it is with no denial oratory in the preferred nineteenth-century style. The peroration is so fervid and sparkling that it deserves quotation:

The results of the war, as seen in reconstruction, have settled forever the political status of my race. The passage of this bill will determine the civil status, not only of the Negro, but of any other class of citizens who may feel themselves discriminated against. It will form the cap-stone of that temple of liberty, begun on this continent under discouraging circumstances, carried on in spite of the sneers of monarchists and the cavils of the pretended friends of freedom, until at last it stands in all its beautiful symmetry and proportions, a building the grandest which the world has even seen, realizing the most sanguine expectations and the highest hopes of those who, in the name of equal, impartial, and universal liberty, laid the foundation stones.

The Holy Scriptures tell us of an humble hand-maiden who long, faithfully, and patiently gleaned in the rich fields of her wealthy kinsman; and we are told further that at last, in spite of her humble antecedents, she found complete favor in his sight. For over two centuries our race has "reaped down your fields." The cries and woes which we have uttered have "entered into the ears of the Lord of Sabaoth," and we are at last politically free. The last vesture only is needed—civil rights. Having gained this, we may, with hearts overflowing with gratitude, and thankful that our prayer has been granted, repeat the prayer of Ruth: "Entreat me not to leave thee, or return from following after thee; for whither thou goest, I will go; and where thou lodgest, I will lodge; thy people shall be my people, and thy God my God; where thou diest, will I die, and there will I be buried; the Lord do so to me, and more also, if aught but death part thee and me."

The *Congressional Record* reported that the speech was followed by "great applause"; as exemplification of extraordinary skill in word juggling it deserved such a reception.[94]

A less sonorous performance as oratory, but a convincing expression of deeply felt convictions, is a brief and simple address delivered before the Senate on March 31, 1876, by Blanche K. Bruce, Senator from Mississippi from 1875 to 1881.[95] Bruce—who lived the first twenty years of his life as a slave; who, after leaving his master at the beginning of the Civil War, taught school in Mark Twain's home town, Hannibal, Missouri; who later studied at Oberlin College; and who, having entered politics in the state of Mississippi, was in 1874 raised from the position of a county sheriff to that of United States Senator[96]—has been often proclaimed the most deserving of the Negroes who served in Congress during the Reconstruction régime.[97] The speech referred to was occasioned by the introduction of a resolution in the Senate calling for the appointment of a committee to investigate alleged illegal voting practices in Mississippi. It is in reality another plea for civil rights. The hopefulness and trust which have made the modern Negro what he is are epitomized in the following paragraph:

I have confidence, not only in my country and her institutions, but in the endurance, capacity and destiny of my people. We will, as opportunity offers and ability serves, seek our places, sometimes in the literary arts, science and the professions. More frequently mechanical pursuits will attract and elicit our efforts; more still of my people will find employment and livelihood as the cultivators of the soil. The bulk of this people—by surroundings, habits, adaptation, and choice will continue to find their homes in the South and constitute the masses of its yeomanry. We will there, probably of our own volition and more abundantly than in the past, produce the great staples that will contribute to the basis of foreign exchange, and in giving the nation a balance of trade, and minister to the wants and comforts and build up the prosperity of the whole land. Whatever our ultimate position in the composite civilization of the Republic and whatever varying fortunes attend our career, we will not forget our instincts for freedom nor our love for country.

John Mercer Langston, whose autobiography, *From the Virginia Plantation to the National Capitol,* has been discussed, was in Congress long enough to deliver at least one important speech, a protest against the disfranchisement of the blacks in the southern states.[98] However, it is not representative of Langston's strongest achievements in oratory. He began his career as a public speaker as early as 1855, when, at the age of twenty-six, he delivered an address at an anniversary meeting of the American Anti-Slavery Society, having been introduced to his audience by William Lloyd Garrison as a "young graduate of Oberlin College."[99] A volume of his "selected speeches and addresses," entitled *Freedom and Citizenship,* was published in 1883. The speeches included cover the years from 1858 to 1880, and afford an interesting sidelight on the specific problems which faced the Negro leaders during that period. An 1858 address is entitled "The World's Anti-Slavery Movement: Its Heroes and Its Triumphs"; one delivered in 1865 is called "Citizenship and the Ballot: the Relations of the Colored American to the Government and Its Duty to Him"; one for 1874 is "Equality before the Law," a discussion of the political and civil status of the American Negro before and after the adoption of the Thirteenth Amendment; one for 1877, called "The Other Phase of the Reconstruction," is an argument that the Republican program for the readjustment of the South is entirely pacific; and an 1879 address, "The Exodus," is an economic study of the problem of Negro

emigration from the South. In all these, Langston sees the
adopted policies of the Republican Party as the strongest
safeguards for the welfare of the Negro. Although few of
them were delivered as party speeches, they are none the
less political. Even in the eulogistic addresses included in
the volume, on Richard Allen, on Charles Sumner, and
on the Negro soldiers who died in the Civil War, Langston
is the politician.

Each of the speeches in *Freedom and Citizenship* is firm
in structure and harmonious in mood. Langston loved
generalization too well, he was perhaps too meticulous in
being a safe Republican, to resort to the bold assertion that
arouses excitement. We find instead of intimate observations and enlivening anecdotes in his speeches the free
citation of legal statutes and authoritative decrees. His
aim as an orator was evidently to be logical rather than
emotional. He was far more white than black, and we can
look in vain in his writings for evidences of that vague and
elusive quality which we often feel in works by Negroes and
which we accept as an African heritage.

There was a nobler urge than the desire for political
recognition which stirred the Negro to appear on the lecture
platform between 1865 and 1900 as a pleader for his race.
The work of educating the emancipated slaves and the fast
increasing colored population rested to a great extent upon
philanthropic aid and general good will. The primary need
was money, and the enormous sums of it which were required could be obtained most easily, not from federal and
state governmental sources, but from individuals and private
organizations. But potential helpers had to be persuaded
that their contributions would go towards the advancement
of a cause which would promote widespread benefit.

In the eighties, Joseph C. Price, who was born in North

Carolina in 1854 of a slave father and a free mother, who was graduated as the valedictorian from Lincoln University in 1879, and who was ordained a Methodist minister in 1880,[100] founded and maintained Livingstone College in North Carolina mainly through funds which he obtained from philanthropists by appealing to them from the lecture platform in this country and in England,   One of Price's few extant speeches, *Education and the Race Problem,* delivered before the National Education Association in 1890, is of a sincerity and warmth which prophecy that if the author had not been cut off by death when he was only forty he might have become a formidable rival of the most popular Negro orator of the period, Booker T. Washington.[101]

Within almost exactly seven months after the death of Frederick Douglass, Booker T. Washington delivered at the opening of the Cotton States Exposition in Atlanta the oration which made him internationally known and which determined the line of his future activity. From 1895 to the year of his death, 1915, he lectured far and wide; and the main purpose of every address which he gave was to spread enlightenment on the movement for industrial education and to gain financial support for the advancement of his work at Tuskegee. The number of his speeches which were published at the time of delivery in the press of the country must run into the hundreds. But as an orator he did not become a successor of Frederick Douglass. The composition of a speech was never to Washington a fine art. One might search in vain among his addresses for a work so thoughtfully constructed, so skillfully formed with definite beginning and middle and end, as Douglass' *John Brown.* Washington belonged to the modern school of orators. To him success in the art of public speech meant holding an audience by informal and pleasing talk. Such material as makes up his orations is found in *The Future of the American Negro* and in *Up from Slavery*. Whether as a writer or as a speaker, he appeared before the public with a positive singleness of purpose: he would prove to the world that in the experiments in industrial education being carried on at Tuskegee, Hampton, and other schools lay the hope of redemption for the American Negro. He was a spokesman for a theory and not, as Frederick Douglass had been, the wise, farseeing spokesman of the many theories that promised the welfare of the Negro.

It has been said that Washington showed no development in style in his books on sociological problems; this is likewise true of his oratory. Three of the speeches which he delivered during his first two years as a famous man are his most celebrated and probably his best. Each, because of its brevity and simplicity and sincerity, might be compared with Lincoln's "Gettysburg Address." The first, the "Cotton States Exposition Address," is illustrative of Washington's tendency to sum up the entire thought of a discourse in one appropriate simile.

A ship lost at sea many days suddenly sighted a friendly vessel. From the mast of the unfortunate vessel was seen a signal: "Water, water; we die from thirst!" The answer from the friendly vessel at once came back: "Cast down your bucket where you are." A second time the signal, "Water, water; send us water!" ran up from the distressed vessel, and was answered: "Cast down your bucket where you are." The captain of the distressed vessel, at last heeding the injunction, cast down his bucket, and it came up full of fresh, sparkling water from the mouth of the Amazon River. To those of my race who depend upon bettering their condition in a foreign land, or who underestimate the importance of cultivating friendly relations with the Southern white man, who is his next door neighbor, I would say: "Cast down your bucket where you are"—cast it down in making friends in every manly way of the people of all races by whom we are surrounded.[102]

The second, the "Harvard Alumni Dinner Address," delivered on June 24, 1896, the day Washington received the honorary degree of Master of Arts from Harvard, shows the graceful ease with which he could on any occasion whatsoever bring in the subject of industrial education.

If through me, an humble representative, seven millions of my people in the South might be permitted to send a message to Harvard—Harvard that offered upon death's altar young Shaw, and Russell, and Lowell, and scores of others, that we might have a free and united country—that message would be, "Tell them that the sacrifice was not in vain. Tell them that by habits of thrift and economy, by way of the industrial school and college, we are coming. We are crawling up, working up, yea, bursting up. Often through oppression, unjust discrimination, and prejudice, but through them all we are coming up, and with proper habits, intelligence and property, there is no power on earth that can permanently stay our progress."[103]

And in the third of these celebrated orations, the "Robert Gould Shaw Monument Address," delivered in Boston on May 31, 1897, Washington displays what seems to have been his genius for selecting the telling anecdote.

Not many days ago, in the heart of the South, in a large gathering of the people of my race, there were heard from many lips praises and thanksgiving to God for his goodness in setting them free from physical slavery. In the midst of that assembly a Southern white man arose, with gray hair and trembling hands, the former owner of many slaves, and from his trembling lips there came the words: "My friends, you forget in your rejoicing that in setting you free, God was also good to me and my race in setting us free."[104]

Little need be said about the later orations. Talks given to the students at Tuskegee, many of which were printed in

Character Building (1902) and *Putting the Most into Life*
(1906), are marked with a didacticism and a childlike idiom
which have been pointed out as weaknesses in the style of
Up from Slavery. Such addresses as *The Education and
Industrial Emancipation of the Negro*, delivered at the
Brooklyn Institute of Arts and Sciences on February 22,
1903, and published as a pamphlet at Tuskegee the same
year, and the lectures included in the volume, *The Negro in
the South, His Economic Progress in Relation to His Moral
and Religious Development* (1907), the joint work of Washington and William E. Burghardt Du Bois, are in substance
and in style much like the series of articles which make up
The Future of the American Negro.

Perhaps an orator of the modern school needs no more
than a clear message and the power to entertain with arrest-
ing stories and ingenious comparisons.[105] Endowed in ample
measure with this equipment, convinced with all his being
that his program of reform had the highest value, and
blessed with that happy understanding of human nature
which enabled him to make his hearers laugh or cry at his
will, Booker T. Washington, appearing before the most
intellectual as well as the most humble audiences, won his
way into the American heart, white and black. What he
was saying from the lecture platform he was saying also in
books and magazine articles, both of which came in a steady
stream from 1899 to 1912. He and one of his contemporaries, Paul Laurence Dunbar, whose career as poet and
novelist is to be discussed in the succeeding chapter, had by
1900 popularized, we might say, Negro literature. They
made it known to thousands where before it had been known
to tens. They achieved what the most ardent defender of
the Negro could scarcely have hoped for at the time of the
emancipation of the slaves.

VI

Most of the writings which have been considered in this chapter were addressed to white readers. In order to find out what the Negro between 1865 and 1900 was saying exclusively to his own people, it is best for us to turn to the publications of the religious leaders. It was in his church that the Negro was least restrained in dealing with the varied problems which affected his race. In his ventures into abstract theological reasoning he often showed a sense of logic which the world at large has been too willing to deny him. And in his numerous works on church history he added knowledge of great value to the student of the social development of the colored race.

Alexander Crummell, who, as we have seen, was the strongest advocate of Negro independence of mind who arose during the period of abolition agitation, lived on until near the end of the nineteenth century and never ceased to preach the doctrine of Negro self-reliance. The founding of the American Negro Academy was a fitting climax for the career of a man who felt that the most important lesson which the American Negro needed to learn was pride in his African past. Crummell's message is in our own day having its fullest effect. But it was not falling on barren ground before 1900. In such pamphlets as Bishop B. T. Tanner's *The Negro's Origin* (1869), *The Color of Solomon—What?* (1895), and *The Descent of the Negro* (probably 1898), we have a serious, if not scientific, attempt to prove that the Negro was not a mere servant and observer in the ancient civilizations which whites are wont to consider as exclusively white. Bishop H. M. Turner's *The Black Man's Doom* (1896), containing his own comment and speeches by Frederick Douglass and Robert G. Ingersoll on "the two barbarous and cruel decisions of the United States Supreme

Court, declaring the Civil Rights Act unconstitutional and disrobing the colored race of all civil protection," is a spirited appeal, coming certainly from a militant clergyman, for the Negro to learn pride and, if necessary, defiance. Milder in tone but none the less sure as messages designed to make the Negro conscious of his racial accomplishments are such works as the Reverend James C. Embry's *Our Father's House* (1893) and Bishop W. J. Gaines's *The Negro and the White Man* (1897).

What the Negro preachers of the time had to say on social problems is mainly of value in Negro literature because of the freedom and boldness with which they said it. The publications on the immediate problems of the church present a style of a different type, equally interesting. There is a medieval picturesqueness in the imagination shown in Bishop John B. Small's *The Human Heart Illustrated by Nine Figures of the Heart, Representing the Different Stages of Life, and Two Death-Bed Scenes: the Wicked and the Righteous* (1898). Bishop Levi Jenkins Coppin's defense of infant baptism, *The Relation of Baptized Children to the Church* (1890), has twistings of logic which the New England divines might have envied. Another unusual bit of fantastic reasoning is Harrison Berry's crude pamphlet, *The Foundation of Atheism Examined, with an Answer to the Question, "Why Don't God Kill the Devil?"* (1882). To cite the writings of the Reverend T. G. Steward along with a pamphlet of the illiterate Berry might seem out of place. Steward, well educated, was master of a forceful style, and in some of his works exhibited sound thinking as well as a display of erudition;[106] but his *Genesis Re-read* (1882), an attempt to reconcile the Biblical story of creation and the theory of evolution, and his *The End of the World* (1888), an extravagant prophecy, present in pompous language the same kind of scholastic quibbling which Berry produced in vulgar idiom. This is likewise true of Bishop J. W. Hood's painstaking *The Plan of the Apocalypse* (1900), the result, we are told in the introduction, of a lifetime's study of the *Book of Revelation*. A more modern and probably more useful sort of theological problem is treated in the Reverend J. W. Stevenson's *How to Get and Keep Churches Out of Debt* (1886).

The specimens of pulpit oratory published by Negroes of the period range from Crummell's admirable *The Greatness of Christ* (1882), still one of the American Negro's highest stylistic achievements,[107] to the Reverend John Jasper's typical "negro sermon," *The Sun Do Move!* (1882). It is a regrettable fact that the name of Jasper as a Negro preacher is probably more widely known in America today than the name of Crummell.[108] It is a fact so regrettable that it is tragic. *The Sun Do Move!*, with its quaint reasoning and picturesque dialect, is not an unimportant contribution to Negro literature; but it is far less typical of the Negro pulpit oratory of the period than Crummell's *The Greatness of Christ*. Many years before Bishop Hood produced his *Plan of the Apocalypse*, he published a volume of sermons, *The Negro in the Christian Pulpit* (1884), which, because of a straightforward message and a simple style, is an approach to the excellence of the sermons of Crummell. Unimportant when compared with Bishop Payne's other writings, but examples of sound doctrinal explanation, are the two discourses which make up *Sermons Delivered by Bishop Daniel A. Payne* (1888). In the specimens included in *Sermons and Addresses by the Late Rev. Bishop Singleton T. Jones, D.D.* (1892) one finds a richness in word picturing which the talented orator might envy. Jones was as staunchly Methodist as the Reverend Charles

B. W. Gordon was Baptist. Gordon's *Select Sermons* (1889) is a series of discourses delivered evidently for the purpose of defending the tenets of Baptist faith. Whatever relief Gordon gives us from unemotional pleading is found in the profuse quotation of doggerel poems of his own making. The Reverend E. M. Brawley showed that the Negro Baptists were masters of a higher type of oratory in a compilation of sermons by various ministers which he published about 1890 as *The Negro Baptist Pulpit.*

A more interesting and enduring type of Negro pulpit oratory is found in such works as the Reverend B. F. De Costa's *Three Score and Ten, the Story of St. Philip's Church* (1889), a sermon presenting a historical survey of Episcopalianism among the Negroes of the city of New York. It conveniently introduces us to the most valuable writings of the Negro preachers. Most of their treatises on race problems and most of their sermons have been deservedly forgotten. But their studies in church history will probably long remain what they are today, rich sources for the student of the social history of the Negro.

In the sixties came Bishop Payne's *The Semi-Centenary and the Retrospection of the African Meth. Episcopal Church* (1866) and Bishop Benjamin T. Tanner's more formidable but less readable *An Apology for African Methodism* (1867). There were no other important church histories until the eighties, when there appeared the Reverend A. Wayman's *My Recollections of African M. E. Ministers* (1881), a series of interesting biographical sketches; Bishop Tanner's *An Outline of Our History and Our Government* (1884), a question and answer textbook; Bishop John Jamison Moore's *History of the A. M. E. Zion Church, in America* (1884), a sort of companion volume to Tanner's *Apology;* and two books dealing with the beginnings of the Negro Baptist church, the Reverend James M. Simms's *The First Colored Baptist Church in North America* (1888) and the Reverend E. K. Love's *History of the First African Baptist Church* (1888). In the nineties there was a flood of church histories, the most important being Bishop Wesley J. Gaines's *African Methodism in the South* (1890); Bishop Payne's crowning work, *History of the African Methodist Episcopal Church* (1891); a challenge to it from the Zion branch of Methodism, Bishop J. W. Hood's *One Hundred Years of the African Methodist Episcopal Zion Church* (1895); an account from the Southern Methodists, the Reverend C. H. Phillips' *The History of the Colored Methodist Episcopal Church in America* (1898); a survey of contemporary Baptist activities, the Reverend A. W. Pegues' *Our Baptist Ministers and Schools* (1892); and a history of a Philadelphia church which had tried successfully the experiment of sponsoring industrial education, the Reverend Matthew Anderson's *Presbyterianism: Its Relation to the Negro* (probably 1897).

With the possible exception of Payne's definiteness, Tanner's really romantic affectation (in his *Apology for African Methodism* he repeatedly resorts to such perversity as using the Latin *et* for the English *and*), and Anderson's scholarly control of his material, there is little in the style of any one of these books which distinguishes it as in any way of literary interest. Payne's *History of the African Methodist Episcopal Church* is readable. Like his *Recollections of Seventy Years,* it is a compendium of live facts collected by a man who always saw things straight and who had probably seen more than any other member of his race. From the time he produced his earliest verse, more than half a century before he published his *History,* he put into his expression a simple straightforwardness which pleases a reader. But whether the other church historians provided interest or not, they imparted information. If not in itself the last word, it is an excellent clue. More than any other body of writing, the Negro church histories give us an intimate view of the society of the socially isolated blacks. There is no better evidence that the Negro by 1900 had become awake to his cultural potentialities than the quantity of church history which he had by that year produced. He was alert and assiduous in studying the institution which he could call peculiarly his own. He showed that Alexander Crummell's plea for Negro pride was being heard.

CHAPTER VIII

FICTION AND POETRY, 1865–1900

Little David, play on your harp,
Hal-le-lu! Hal-le-lu!
Little David, play on your harp,
Hal-le-lu!

Little David was a shepherd boy,
He killed Goliath, and he shouted for joy.

Joshua was the son of Nun;
He never did stop till his work was done.

Jes' wait till I get on the mountain top;
Gwine to make my wings go flip-pi-ty flop.

—From William Eleazar Barton's
*Old Plantation Hymns: a Collection
of Hitherto Unpublished Melodies of
the Slave and the Freedman,* 1899

I

In 1867, Lorenzo D. Blackson, an illiterate colored
Methodist preacher, who, according to his own statement,
was born in Delaware in 1817, published a book which he
called *The Rise and Progress of the Kingdoms of Light and
Darkness; or, The Reigns of Kings Alpha and Abadon.*
Whatever he intended it to be, it is such a work of the
imagination as no American Negro had before produced.
Book cataloguers have appropriately listed it as "the Negro's
Pilgrim's Progress." Bunyan probably inspired it, but it is
only to a slight degree imitative of him or of any one else.
It is the product of what seems to have been a pure African

temperament. Blackson said of himself at the close of one division of the book:

I must here end the first part of my story, and for its defects the kind reader must excuse the humble author, as purity of motives is his highest aim. He therefore hopes that you will the more readily excuse the defects of this little work, when you learn that he is but a poor colored man, who has never went to school twelve months in his life, and whose opportunities have been and still are very small, as he has hitherto labored each day for bread for himself and family, and much of what he here presents to the reader has been written at night after ending his day's labor.

He did not need to offer apologies; for, although the story is disjointed, the reasoning childlike, and the grammar atrocious, the work as a whole is a revelation of imaginative playfulness. From the beginning to the end it is charmingly folkloristic.

The story opens as follows:

A certain King, whose power is beyond description, at a period called the beginning of time, formed a kingdom on a small part of his dominion known by the name of Earth; which, although it contains many millions of square miles, yet it is very small when compared with the whole of his dominion, which is without bounds.

This king, known as Alpha, creates Adam and Eve and places them in charge of Earth. All goes well until King Abadon, *alias* Satan, who has been driven out of Heaven along with the wicked angels whom he had led in a revolt against King Alpha, succeeds in tempting Adam and Eve to disobedience.

So now gentle reader, you plainly may discover how greatly these two had transgressed, in breaking the just laws of such a kind sovereign, who had favored them so greatly, yet although they had transgressed, he did not deal with them as their crime deserved, but had mercy upon them, and suffered them to still remain on his earthly dominion. . . . Then did the King of Light appoint his servant Conscience as a dictator to them, to remind them of their duty to him as their rightful sovereign. So Mr. Conscience made known to them how greatly they had sinned in breaking the laws of their most merciful King.[1]

Then follow in quick order the story of Cain and Abel, a description of the Flood, and an account of the appearance on Earth of King Alpha, now identified as Christ. The two kings declare war against each other. Among Alpha's chief advisers are Mr. Truth, Mr. Confession, Mr. Repentance, and Mr. Faith, "who was Mr. Truth's companion and friend, and without him there was no petition acceptable to King Alpha, for without Mr. Faith it was impossible to please King Alpha." Abadon's leading warriers are Mr. Untruth, Mr. Malice, Mr. Anger, Mr. Revenge, Lust-of-the-Flesh, and Lust-of-the-Eye. The two armies are drawn up in battle formation, and there are skirmishes, in one of which King Alpha is struck by a soldier of Abadon, named Death, and remains lifeless for three days. After he comes to, he engages in an encounter of revenge and gets possession of Death's keys. Thus, with intermittent fighting, the centuries pass. Abadon has recruited his army with forces drawn from heathen lands and with "the Popish, the Mormon, the Unitarian, and Universal regiments." Alpha's divisions have become classified as "the Lutheran, the Quaker, the Presbyterian, the Baptist, the Episcopalian, the Congregational, and more latterly the Methodist, the Abolition, and the Union." The time shifts into the distant future. Abadon, with Gog and Magog as his chief generals and all the unbelievers who have ever lived as his soldiers, makes one last desperate attack upon the city of Zion. Alpha, followed by the true Christians of all epochs and all lands, valiantly meets the attack, and Abadon is triumphantly vanquished.

After the story as thus outlined has been told in more than two hundred and fifty pages of prose, Blackson tacks on a summary of the whole written in verse, of which a typical stanza is:

> In length, all dressed in armor bright,
> 'T will be a very pretty sight.
> When music all begins to play,
> I think the saints will shout that day.

Then, as a final word, he says:

Adieu. Your brother in Christ, L. D. B.

P. S. If life lasts, I may address you again, the Lord willing. Amen.

If he ever "addressed" us again, there seems to be no record of what he said. There was apparently only one edition of *The Rise and Progress of the Kingdoms of Light and Darkness*, and no notice whatsoever of the book from those who might have appreciated the rare imagination put into it. Even in the passages in which Blackson halts the story to air his knowledge of geography or preach a little sermon to the newly emancipated slaves, there is the charm of an unexpected image at every turn. That Christ and Satan are made so militant in the story, that there is so much ado over the organization and equipment of armies, that one meets so frequently such expressions as "ground our arms at Jesus' feet," is no doubt due to the fact that most of the book was written while all America was thinking and talking warfare. The effect of the Civil War on the mind of a simple and obscure member of the race over which it was fought is perhaps nowhere else so picturesquely revealed. That the English is so faulty adds to the effectiveness of the book; it is not written in dialect, but it is in a fitting idiom. Both matter and style are of such stuff as has given the originality and charm which distinguish the Negro folk song. The story of Kings Alpha and Abadon came too early. The feeling of whoever reads it today is likely to be regret that the Lord seems to have been unwilling for Blackson to "address" us again.

There could scarcely be such a reaction towards most of the other novels and short stories and poems published by American Negroes between 1865 and 1900. Blackson succeeded in writing an unusual and remarkable work of the imagination without knowing what he was about. The majority of his contemporaries who produced fiction and poetry were usually too self-conscious of what they were trying to accomplish. However, their work marks a distinct and great advancement in Negro literature. Blackson's *Rise and Progress of the Kingdoms of Light and Darkness* was, on the other hand, an accident, which might have turned up in the eighteenth century as well as in 1867.

The Negro fiction writers of the period evidently saw only three possible things to do in creating a short story or a novel. First, they might explore the primitive Negro mind, not as Blackson had done, but as Joel Chandler Harris and Thomas Nelson Page were doing. Second, they might disregard their race entirely, and, as Dumas had done in France, write romances about the whites. And third, they might follow the example set by William Wells Brown and Frank J. Webb and devote themselves to stories of propaganda defending the Negro against prejudice and social discrimination.

In his last book, *My Southern Home,* published in 1880, William Wells Brown showed that he understood the fictional value of Negro folklore.[2] The book was to a great extent developed with such materials as Joel Chandler Harris and Thomas Nelson Page were in the later eighties and nineties to make universally popular. The rising young Negro writers of fiction did not fail to realize that these materials were their own peculiar heritage. While they seem to have ignored Brown, they leaned heavily upon Harris and Page. Chief among them was Charles W. Chesnutt, easily the most gifted and the most important. Mr. Chesnutt, who was born in Cleveland, Ohio, in 1858, was in 1927 awarded the Spingarn Medal for his "pioneer work as a literary artist depicting the life and struggle of Americans of Negro descent."[3] He passed his early childhood in Cleveland, and has been a regular resident of that city since 1887, the year in which he was admitted to the Ohio bar. However, he had before taking up the practice of law and work as a court stenographer lived for a long period in North Carolina, where he received most of his schooling and where he was for nine years engaged in teaching.[4] He had also for a few months worked on newspapers in the city of New York.[5] His experiences and observations in the South furnished him the raw material for most of his fictional works, the first of any importance being a short story, "The Goophered Grapevine," published in the *Atlantic Monthly* for August, 1887, and the last being a novel, *The Colonel's Dream*, issued in 1905.[6] In addition to his short stories and novels, he is the author of a biography, *Frederick Douglass* (1899),[7] and of a number of sociological articles and essays.[8] Admirable as his study of Douglass is, and thoughtful as his comment on the Negro problem is, it is his work in fiction that determines the high place which he holds in Negro literature. His greatest originality, as we shall see later, was shown in his stories on the color line in America. But his most artistic work is that which was done in imitation of Harris and Page, or that which is in no way related to the Negro.

Mr. Chesnutt's *The Conjure Woman* (1899),[9] a collection of seven short stories, most of which had been previously published in magazines,[10] has a framework similar in some respects to that of *Uncle Remus, His Songs and Sayings* and in other respects to that of *In Ole Virginia*. A gentleman residing in northern Ohio, interested in grape culture, finds it necessary on account of the health of his wife to seek a warmer climate. He goes to North Carolina, purchases a plantation, continues to grow grapes, and incidentally learns much about the folklore and customs of the Negro natives from a series of tales related to him by Uncle Julius McAdoo, the aged colored man whom he employs as a coachman. Uncle Julius, "not entirely black," has the clever sense of self-protection which we find in Harris' Uncle Remus and the sentimentality about events "which happen' befo' de wah" that marks the characters of Page's narrators. However, Uncle Julius is an individual, not an imitation of a type. While he is an old-fashioned southern Negro, he does not fail to recognize that his northern employer feels a different interest in him from that which had been shown him by his former masters. And perhaps no other Negro in American literature has exhibited such a familiarity with the ways of conjurers. Each of Uncle Julius' tales, all of which were possibly founded by Mr. Chesnutt on genuine folklore, has something to do with some mysterious "conjure person," usually Aunt Peggy, who has the power to do such things as "goopher" a vineyard in order to prevent the slaves from stealing the scuppernongs.

She sa'ntered 'round' 'mongs' de vimes, en tuk a leaf fum dis one, en a grape-hull fum dat one; en den a little twig fum here, en a little pinch er dirt fum dere,—en put it all in a big black bottle, wid a snake's toof en a speckle hen's gall en some ha'rs fum a black cat's tail, en den fill' de bottle wid scuppernon' wine. W'en she got de goopher all ready en fix', she tuk'n went out in de woods en buried it under de root uv a red oak tree, en den come back en tole one er de niggers she done goopher de grapevimes, en a'er nigger w'at eat dem grapes 'ud be sho ter die inside'n twel' mont's.

Most of the space in each tale is devoted to Uncle Julius' descriptions of the curious things which result from conjure. But it is not delight in exercising his imagination which guides him; there is a practical motive back of what he relates. And he usually gets what he wishes.

His stories are too carefully put together to give the impression of spontaneous reality which one gains from a typical Uncle Remus tale. Moreover, Uncle Julius' dialect is labored. It is easy to see that Mr. Chesnutt had not had a lifelong familiarity with the speech of the southern Negro. But the imperfections are comparatively so slight and the general interest so great that *The Conjure Woman* measures up well with its more illustrious prototypes. A critic, who in spite of investigation apparently did not know that Mr. Chesnutt was a colored man, wrote of *The Conjure Woman* a few months after it was published:

When a book is favorably reviewed from Maine to California, when the stories in it are said to be "fresh, vivid, dramatic sketches," in "new and delightful vein," when the narrator of these stories, Uncle Julius, is called not only "a cousin once removed," but "own brother" to Uncle Remus, a new character in whose portrait "there is not a line out of place,"— we are naturally led to inquire who is the creator of this character, shrewd, and at the same time naïf as a child.[11]

A sincere work of art, *The Conjure Woman* was positive evidence that Negro literature was coming of age.[12]

There is nothing in *The Conjure Woman* to indicate that

the author was colored. Mr. Chesnutt was one of three American Negroes who in the nineties came before the public as men of letters irrespective of race. The biographies of Archibald H. Grimké have been discussed.[13] Paul Laurence Dunbar was the third who showed that there was finally to be no such thing in America as a separate Negro literature in the sense that there is a separate Negro church or a separate Negro journalism.

When Dunbar died, in 1906, he was in his thirty-fourth year. According to all accounts, his parents, both of whom had been slaves, were of pure African blood. He was born in Dayton, Ohio, grew to manhood there, and always considered that city his permanent home. In the public high school in Dayton from which he was graduated in 1891 he was editor-in-chief of the school paper, president of a literary society, and in his senior year the class poet.[14] The year following his graduation he was working as an elevator-boy, sending postage for the return of rejected manuscripts, and boldly asking editors if they would buy stories of a patterned sort.[15] During that same year he got ready for the press his first volume of poems, *Oak and Ivy*, which was privately printed in 1893. It seems to have attracted no more than local attention.[16] However, his next volume, *Majors and Minors*, dated 1895 but actually not published until 1896,[17] got into the hands of Robert G. Ingersoll and James A. Herne; the former wrote a warm letter of congratulation to Dunbar, and the latter dispatched a copy of the book to William Dean Howells.[18] Impressed especially by the excellence of Dunbar's dialect verse, Howells gave the book a lengthy review, not only favorable but enthusiastic, in his "Life and Letters" column in *Harper's Weekly*, June 27, 1896. With the merit of his work thus recognized, Dunbar secured a standard publisher for his third volume,

Lyrics of Lowly Life, which appeared in 1896 with the
well-known introduction by Howells.[19] The book went
through repeated editions,[20] and made Dunbar a famous
man, generally regarded in this country and in England as
the first American Negro "to feel the negro life aesthetically
and express it lyrically."[21] The discussion of his verse and
of his career as a poet belongs to another part of this chapter.
Since he owed his livelihood mainly to royalties received
from his books and magazine publications, and since he
showed unusual skill in narrative verse, it was inevitable
that he should have returned to the prose fiction which he
was attempting as early as 1892. And it was natural that
he should have done what Mr. Chesnutt first did; that is,
follow the trend determined by popularity and write on
Negro folk types in the manner of Harris and Page.

Dunbar's first collection of short stories, *Folks from
Dixie* (1898), contains some of his most characteristic and
best work as a writer of fiction. There is no such framework for the grouping of the stories as Mr. Chesnutt was to
use in *The Conjure Woman.* Whatever unity the book as
a whole has is told by the title, *Folks from Dixie;* the
characters, not all of them colored, are either still in Dixie
or once lived there. Two of the stories, "The Ordeal at
Mt. Hope," an argument for industrial education, and "At
Shaft 11," an indirect plea for the Negro to stay out of
labor unions, were designed for more than entertainment.
The rest are pure tales. "The Colonel's Awakening," the
scene of which is laid in Virginia, follows so closely Page's
method of extracting pathos out of the portrayal of the
love and devotion of a faithful Negro servant that it might
fit well into *In Ole Virginia.* A similar blending of kindliness and romance and sentimentality is in "A Family Feud,"
a tale of ante-bellum days on two Kentucky plantations.

The majority of the stories in the volume, however, show an indebtedness to Harris rather than to Page. Dunbar's knowledge of plantation life in Kentucky probably came from his mother, who passed her childhood and early womanhood as a slave and who was throughout most of Dunbar's life his constant companion.[22]   At any rate, he had derived from some source a penetrating understanding of the primitive Negro's superstitions, religious zeal, romance, humor, and language. The following exhortation addressed by a preacher to a willful girl in "Annie 'Lizer's Stumblin' Block" gets to the very heart of Negro folk feeling:

"You see, honey," Uncle Eben went on, "when you starts out on de Christian jou'ney, you's got to lay aside evry weight dat doeth so easy beset you an' keeps you f'om pergressin'; y' ain't got to think nothin' 'bout pussunal 'dornment; you's jes' got to shet yo' eyes an' keep open yo' hea't an' say, Lawd, come; you must n't wait fu' to go to chu'ch to pray, nuther, you mus' pray anywhar an' ev'rywhar. Why, when I was seekin', I ust to go 'way off up in de big woods to pray, an' dere's whar de Lawd answered me, an' I'm a-rejoicin' to-day in de powah of de same salvation. Honey, you's got to pray, I tell you. You's got to brek de backbone of yo' pride an' pray in earnes'; an' ef you does dat, you'll git he'p, fu' de Lawd is a praar-heahin' Lawd an' plenteous in mussy."

It is such talk that makes *Folks from Dixie* a memorable volume. And it was his intimate knowledge of the folk ways of Negroes which enabled Dunbar to do some of the strongest work found in his later volumes of short stories, *The Strength of Gideon* (1900), *In Old Plantation Days* (1903), and *The Heart of Happy Hollow* (1904).

At the time of its appearance *Folks from Dixie* was by far the most artistic book of fiction which had come from an American Negro. But it was within a year superseded by Mr. Chesnutt's *The Conjure Woman*. Dunbar was certainly more skillful than Mr. Chesnutt as a recorder of dialect, and he perhaps got closer to the real heart of the plantation Negro. However, he created no such character as Uncle Julius, and he never attained Mr. Chesnutt's mastery of treating a folk tale from a subtle and intellectual point of view. Dunbar's stories appealed to the readers of such periodicals as *Lippincott's Magazine,* while Mr. Chesnutt's met the requirements of the more critical *Atlantic Monthly* public.

Among the American writers who have been unable to judge what they could and could not do Dunbar is conspicuous. In 1898, the year of *Folks from Dixie,* he published his first novel, *The Uncalled.*[23] It was to a certain extent autobiographical, an exposition of Dunbar's own ordeal in deciding whether he ought to enter the ministry.[24] Since he was really writing about a personal experience, one cannot help wondering why he did not put himself into the story as a colored man. The action deals with the conflict in the mind of a white youth living in a small Ohio town who feels that he should not become a preacher but who is forced by circumstances into a seminary and then into the pulpit. There is not a single Negro character in the book. As a story about whites written by a Negro it introduces us to the second type of fiction which the Negro of the period attempted. Such a type Dunbar should have painstakingly avoided. All of the bubbling spontaneity which he showed in his tales on blacks is replaced in *The Uncalled* by cheap conventional story-telling, with echoes of Dickens and the popular magazine, and with an English which is often downright faulty. The book came as a great disappointment to Dunbar's admirers.[25] Despite its weakness, it seems to have had some commercial success,[26] and in 1900 Dunbar published a second novel in which all of the characters are whites, *The Love of Landry*. It is a story of Easterners, all treacly sentimentalists, who think that they find the sublime beauty of reality on a Colorado ranch. It was, if that is possible, even a poorer performance than *The Uncalled*. However, in the career of Dunbar *The Love of Landry* has a peculiar interest, in that the idea of the story was suggested to him while he was in the mountains of Colorado fighting the first stages of the disease, tuberculosis, which was after a struggle of more than five years to claim him.[27]

Dunbar's third novel, *The Fanatics* (1901), is a more successful treatment of white types. While it is a romance of the Civil War, emphasis is not on battle scenes, but on how the struggle affects a small Ohio town which is made up of sympathizers for the South as well as for the North. There is exciting narrative from the beginning. However, interest does not become strong until the "contrabands" come pouring in from across the Ohio River with their queer songs and delightful dialect. Yet entirely too little is made of them. With the exception of a minor character, who provides an interesting climax for the ending of the tale, the Negro appears for no more than atmosphere.

A more realistic attempt to write stories in which the Negro is absent altogether, or else is of trivial importance, was made by Paul Laurence Dunbar's wife, who as Alice Moore brought out in 1895 a privately printed volume of poems, essays, and narrative sketches, called *Violets, and Other Tales*, and who as Alice Dunbar published in 1899 *The Goodness of St. Rocque, and Other Stories*. She writes at the present time under the name of Alice Dunbar Nelson, and is perhaps best known as the compiler of a book of orations by Negroes, *Masterpieces of Negro Eloquence* (1914). Mrs. Nelson was born and reared in New Orleans, and the characters in her stories were probably based on real New Orleans types. *Violets, and Other Tales,* with the exception of three sketches—"Titee," "A Carnival Jungle," and "Little Miss Sophie," all reprinted in *The Goodness of St. Rocque*—is one of those lifeless privately printed things which most authors who ever do anything better would like to destroy. But the second volume, inspired undoubtedly by George Washington Cable, has some excellent material handled with pleasing effect. The persons introduced are usually either Creole or French, and what they do seems to be determined by place, the New Orleans of traditional romance. Perhaps the best piece in the book is "M'sieu Fortier's Violin," a tender little story of an aged musician who loses his position as a player in the opera orchestra. One of M'sieu Fortier's speeches suggests the dialect which gives to the volume its main charm:

"Minesse," he said one day to the white cat,—he told all his troubles to her; it was no use to talk to Ma'am Jeanne, she was too deaf to understand,—"Minesse, we are gettin' po'. You' pere, git h'old, an' hees han's dey go no mo' rapidement, an' dere be no mo' soirees dese day. Minesse, eef la saison don' hurry up, we shall eat ver' lil' meat."

While the flavor of such a passage is very remindful of Cable, it has an individuality. Mrs. Nelson found types in New Orleans which her master had neglected, and she treated them in sketches which are frail and at the same time redolent of a delicate sympathy.

As in the other kinds of fiction produced by Negroes of the period, Mr. Chesnutt excelled in stories dealing with whites. Yet among all his serious tales there seems to be only one in which the Negro does not appear. That is a short story, "Baxter's Procrustes," published in the *Atlantic Monthly* for June, 1904. It is not only Mr. Chesnutt's most artistic achievement, but perhaps the best short story which any American Negro has as yet written.   Indeed, it is so good that one wonders why it has been forgotten, why anthologists of the short story have invariably passed it by. It is a subtle satire, developed with a perfectly balanced intellectual humor, on the dilettantism of curio and book collectors.   We are introduced in the beginning to the Bodleian Club, a group of American gentlemen who if they had lived in England in the eighteenth century would have been called humorous.   They are entirely too aesthetic for us to look upon them as Pickwickian.   A condition of membership is that any person who is invited must possess a specimen of rare pipe manufacture which he is willing to donate to the Club at the time of his reception.   But the collection of pipes is by no means the Club's chief pride. Every Bodleian knows the value of an antique book and a precious binding.   Moreover, every Bodleian is a poet. Baxter, so enigmatic that he often dumbfounds his colleagues, but withal considered one of the brainiest of Bodleians, announces that he is on the point of finishing a poem, which he calls "Procrustes."   The members of the Club engage to add the work to their publications, and to dress it with a cover which will in every way reflect the true Bodleian taste.   The anticipated evening arrives when the beautiful "Procrustes," fresh from the hands of the world's most artistic binder, is ready for distribution.   All the Bodleians are assembled, each eagerly awaiting his copy. And a guest is present, an Englishman.   "Procrustes" is handed to him, and he is stupid enough to cut the leaves. It is discovered that the pages are blank.   Then the president of the Club, with an equanimity becoming a Bodleian, rises to congratulate Baxter.   He says:

His Procrustes, from the collector's point of view, is entirely logical, and might be considered as the acme of bookmaking. To the true collector, a book is a work of art, of which the contents are no more important than the words of an opera. Fine binding is a desideratum, and, for its cost, that of the Procrustes could not be improved upon. The paper is above criticism. The true collector loves wide margins, and the Procrustes, being all margin, merely touches the vanishing point of the perspective.

The story is, of course, a bagatelle, but as such it is almost flawless. Mr. Chesnutt had leaned upon Harris and Page in writing the stories which make up *The Conjure Woman*. If he leaned upon any one of his contemporaries in creating "Baxter's Procrustes," it was upon Henry James. Whoever reads the story is bound to regret that the author was a year after its publication to relinquish writing permanently.

Two of the stories in Paul Laurence Dunbar's *Folks from Dixie*, "The Ordeal at Mt. Hope" and "At Shaft 11," have been pointed out as dealing with social problems. They belong to the third field in which the Negro novelists and short story writers between 1865 and 1900 ventured, that of fiction offering comment on the social status of the Negro, especially in relation to the white man. It was, as we might expect, the field in which the Negro was most voluminous, and, if not most pleasing, most vigorous. It was also the field in which he was most original.

In his later collections of short stories Dunbar dwelt more and more on racial problems. He said in the foreword to *The Heart of Happy Hollow*:

Happy Hollow; are you wondering where it is? Wherever Negroes colonize in the cities or villages, North or South, wherever the hod carrier, the porter, and the waiter are the society men of the town; wherever the picnic and the excursion are the chief summer diversion, and the revival the winter time

of repentance, wherever the cheese cloth veil obtains at wed-
dings, and the little white hearse goes by with black mourners
in the one carriage behind, there—there—is Happy Hollow.
Wherever laughter and tears rub elbows day by day, and the
spirit of labour and laziness shake hands, there—there—is
Happy Hollow.

But Happy Hollow was not to Dunbar a place for nothing
more than sentimental tears and spontaneous laughter.   It
had its serious side, its sense of wronged justice, its tragedy.
In a story of an educated colored youth's ruthless disillusion-
ment, "One Man's Fortune," included in *The Strength of
Gideon,* a white lawyer is made to say:

The sentiment of remorse and the desire for atoning which
actuated so many white men to help Negroes right after the
war has passed off without being replaced by that sense of plain
justice which gives a black man his due, not because of, nor
in spite of, but without consideration of his color.

The idea thus expressed was a guiding principle for Dunbar
in writing stories on such themes as Negroes exploited by
unscrupulous politicians, the economic relations existing between whites and blacks, and the effect of city life on
country-bred Negroes.   The deep pathos of the truth which
it expresses is brought out with force in two stories on
lynching, "The Tragedy at Three Corners," in *The Strength
of Gideon,* and "The Lynching of Jube Benson," in *The
Heart of Happy Hollow.*

But Dunbar's most complete and profound study of the
true reality of Happy Hollow came in his fourth and last
novel, *The Sport of the Gods,* published in book form in
1902.[28]   It is at the same time his most interesting and most
imperfect novel.   The title hints that Dunbar might have
been reading Thomas Hardy, and the story itself more than
once shows a naturalistic view of life.[29]   Berry Hamilton,

who had been a slave, has remained in the South, and at the opening of the action is presented as a butler, living happily in a pretty cottage with his wife and two children— Kitty, who is being trained as a housekeeper, and Joe, who expects to become a barber. A theft of a large sum of money is committed in the house of Berry's employer; and the innocent colored butler is accused, given a mock trial, and sent to prison for a long term. His wife and children, turned from their home and treated as outcasts by blacks as well as whites, are forced to go somewhere, and they decide upon New York. What happens to them in the city is summarized by Dunbar as follows:

Whom the gods wish to destroy they first make mad. The first sign of the demoralization of the provincial who comes to New York is his pride at his insensibility to certain impressions which used to influence him at home. First, he begins to scoff, and there is no truth in his views nor depth in his laugh. But by and by, from mere pretending, it becomes real. He grows callous. After that he goes to the devil very cheerfully.

Kitty is green enough to be seduced by the first man she meets, but laments her folly, turns hard and practical, and succeeds as a member of a black theatrical troupe. Joe succumbs to the allurements of the Banner Club, "an institution for the lower education of the colored youth . . . a social cesspool." He works in a barber's shop, makes money, and spends it on a colored actress whom he meets at the Club. His paramour finally grows tired of him, and in a fit of jealous rage he strangles her. His punishment is imprisonment for life. The mother, thinking that since her husband is in the penitentiary she is automatically divorced, marries a gambler, who beats her in order to force her to support him when he is out of luck. Such is the situation which his children and wife are in when Berry Hamilton is released from prison and comes to New York in search of them, the truth having been divulged that he has paid the penalty for the crime of a degenerate white man.

The tragedy is attributed not so much to the wiles of the city as to the ignorant Negro's helplessness when in the clutches of circumstance aggravated by an unfair social system. The novel is structurally about as bad as it could be. A half happy ending is dragged in, and no temptation to submit to melodrama is resisted. Plausibility is in many situations strained to the shattering point. The style is nervous and uneven, typical of that which one might expect from the mind of a man who is suffering from tuberculosis.[30] But there are many patches which are intense, serious, and telling. The description of the first evening which the country Hamiltons spend at a Negro theatre in New York is an effective blending of the Dickensian and the bitter. The horrid tinsel of life as it is portrayed in the Banner Club is saved from the nauseating and repelling only by a grim sort of humor. For example, a minor character, called Sadness, perhaps the first embodiment of the spirit of the blues which appeared in Negro literature, says on one occasion to Joe, who in a drunken stupor has just revealed the terrible secret that his father is a convict:

For a fellow who has had for a full year the advantage of the education of the New York clubs, you are strangely young. Let me see, you are nineteen or twenty now—yes. Well, that perhaps accounts for it. It's a pity you weren't born older. It's a pity most men aren't. They would not have to take so much time and lose so many good things learning. Now, Mr. Hamilton, let me tell you, and you will pardon me for it, that you are a fool. Your case isn't half as bad as nine-tenths of the fellows that hang around here. Now, for instance, my father was hung. . . . Oh, yes, but it was done with a very good rope and by the best citizens of Texas, so it seems that I really ought to be very grateful to them for the distinction they conferred upon my family, but I am not. I am ungratefully sad.

One of Sadness' friends, a white newspaper reporter who spends his evenings drinking at the Banner Club, is equally philosophical and interesting until he turns detective and solves in unbelievable manner the secret of Berry Hamilton's innocence.   It is the portrayal of such characters as these that caused an anonymous critic at the time of Dunbar's death to refer to *The Sport of the Gods* as a compendium of information for the average American.[31]   If it was a revelation to white America, it was a sermon to all America. Dunbar usually lost himself as an artist when he felt strongly the urge to preach,[32] and *The Sport of the Gods* suffers extremely as a specimen of pure fiction.   But with the exception of certain perfectly executed short stories, such as "Jimsella" in *Folks from Dixie* and "The Finding of Zach" in *The Strength of Gideon*,[33] it is of all Dunbar's work in prose the book in which the modern reader would probably find greatest interest.

Dunbar's poetry, as we shall see later, reveals that there was little bitterness in his nature.   Moreover, he was a writer with a broad public to please.   Bold and uncompromising fiction on the Negro problem was not to be expected from him.   For that we have to turn to Mr. Chesnutt.   But before considering Mr. Chesnutt's stories of the color line we should give at least passing attention to a few works by less important writers.

Frances E. W. Harper, whose antislavery poetry has been discussed,[34] published in 1893, towards the end of her career as an author of poor stories and fair verse, a full-length novel, *Iola Leroy; or, Shadows Uplifted*.   In a note at the end of the book she says:

From threads of fact and fiction I have woven a story whose mission will not be in vain if it awakens in the hearts of our countrymen a stronger sense of justice and a more Christlike humanity in behalf of those whom the fortunes of war threw, homeless, ignorant, and poor, upon the threshold of a new era.

The story, recounting the adventures of a quadroon during the Civil War, is so crowded with incidents and with characters that the reader is likely more than once to lose track of what the action is about. The mission for which Mrs. Harper destined *Iola Leroy* was no doubt better fulfilled by a novel which appeared in 1894, *Appointed,* the work of Walter H. Stowers, whose pen name was "Sanda."[35]   It is the story of the friendship between a cultivated and ambitious young colored man, John Saunders, and his white employer's son, Seth Stanley. The opening scenes, laid in Detroit, are tedious. But the action in time shifts to the South, and the interest is heightened. The culminating episodes, describing the lynching of John Saunders for no other reason than that he has struck a white man in self-defense, have emotion and power. *Appointed* was probably the first of many stories written by Negroes which describe the horrors of lynching. The following suggests how Stowers brought out the terror of the situation:

> The mob itself was a motley one. It seemed that the riff-raff of the town had suddenly blown together to whirl and twist around a moving center and vent its fury in loud curses and threatenings as it surged along, with each individual part of it endeavouring to get nearer to the center. Here and there were respectable appearing persons who were urging on the others, and who were the most industrious in keeping up the passions of the mob by their loud and persistent crying of "Hang him! String him up to the nearest lamp post. Where's a rope? Damn the nigger!" They acted like party whips in keeping their members in line and ready for action, or rather like devils urging on their imps to malicious acts and tortures.

There has probably never been in fiction a truly realistic picture of a lynching scene. But the exaggeration of *Ap-*

pointed is as nothing compared with the wild portrayal of injustice, cruelty, and brutality found in *Contending Forces, a Romance Illustrative of Negro Life North and South* (1900), by Pauline E. Hopkins. The story is as complicated and as difficult to keep straight as Mrs. Harper's *Iola Leroy,* but there is so much sensationalism that the reader's morbid curiosity impels him to read on to the end. The author claimed rightly that the "fire and romance" of Negro history had been unrecognized by Anglo-Saxons.[36]   Her weakness as a writer was that she tried to crowd enough fire and romance for forty books into one four-hundred-page volume.

The *Conjure Woman* proved Mr. Chesnutt's power to follow with remarkable skill and originality a passing fashion in literature.   It is, almost as much as "Baxter's Procrustes," a work which the unknowing reader is obliged to regard as a white man's production.   This cannot be said of Mr. Chesnutt's other important works of fiction.   In form they are imitative, and often not of such good models as were employed for *The Conjure Woman.*   But because they are strong social studies presented undeniably from the Negro's point of view, they make up an original contribution to American literature.   If they had been as artistically done as *The Conjure Woman* and "Baxter's Procrustes," they would deserve a place of genuine distinction in American fiction.[37]   It is regrettable that they include no more than one volume of short stories, *The Wife of His Youth, and Other Stories of the Color Line* (1899), and three novels, *The House behind the Cedars* (1900), *The Marrow of Tradition* (1901), and *The Colonel's Dream* (1905).[38]

What makes *The Wife of His Youth, and Other Stories of the Color Line* a unified book is that each story in the volume, whether comic or tragic, presents a crucial situation in the life of the American Negro resulting from racial prejudice. In one of the stories, "The Web of Circumstance," a naturalistic tale based on the identical motivating situation which Dunbar was to use in *The Sport of the Gods*, the author halts the action and says:

Some time, we are told, when the cycle of years has rolled around, there is to be another golden age, when men will dwell together in love and harmony, and when peace and righteousness shall prevail for a thousand years. God speed the day, and let not the shining thread of hope become so enmeshed in the web of circumstance that we lose sight of it; but give us here and there, and now and then, some little foretaste of this golden age, that we may the more patiently and hopefully await its coming!

But on almost every page of the book prejudice is pictured as so monstrous that patience and hope seem futile. That it can be as venomous for human happiness when it comes from Negroes themselves as when it come from whites is shown in "The Wife of His Youth," a superbly constructed short story developed around the dilemma of a wealthy and refined colored man, almost white, who is called upon to decide whether he will acknowledge the faithful black wife of his youth in slavery or marry an accomplished woman of his own caste and tastes.[39] The terrible sacrifices which prejudice can demand are brought out forcibly in "Her Virginia Mammy" (a tale suggestive of Cable's *Mme. Delphine*) and in "The Sheriff's Children," a story of tragic intensity of the struggle between a white man and his mulatto son. Even in the one sentimental story in the book, "The Bouquet," about a little girl who is not allowed to go to the funeral of the white teacher whose memory she adores, and in the humorous tales, particularly "Uncle Wellington's Wives," about a North Carolina plantation

Negro who goes to the North and marries an Irish washer-woman, the tragic sting of prejudice is felt.

In Mr. Chesnutt's novels "the shining thread of hope" becomes still more "enmeshed in the web of circumstance." The action of all three is laid in the South, and the outlook on the life portrayed in each is decidedly naturalistic. *The House behind the Cedars* presents a beautiful and sensitive heroine, Rena Walden, who, although classed as colored, is so white that her Negro identity is easily mistaken. In her struggle to live her life conscientiously and honestly she has to contend with the low ambitions of her mulatto mother, she has to take into account the position of a brother who is "passing" successfully as a white lawyer, and she has to fight the violent passions of a characterless and vulgar mulatto who wishes to marry her and of a quick-tempered southern white man who determines to make her his mistress after he discovers that she is colored. She weakens before the hopelessness of her struggle and dies, having recognized just before her end that the one person in the world who has been honorable and unselfish in his devotion to her is a simple-souled and yet heroic black man. *The Marrow of Tradition* strikes deeper into the social complications created by the color line and studies jointly the relationship existing between two sisters, one white and one mulatto, and the consequences resulting from a crime committed by a depraved young white man when he is disguised as his own kind and faithful colored servant. The involved action culminates in a race riot, probably suggested to Mr. Chesnutt by the riots in Wilmington, North Carolina, in 1898.[40] *The Colonel's Dream*, the most poignantly tragic and yet perhaps the most realistic of the three books, is the story of a dreamer's attempts at reform in a southern town, which is crushed equally by a harsh economic system and by an

ever seething racial hatred.   Henry French, born and reared
in North Carolina and made a colonel in the Confederate
Army at the age of nineteen, has after years of hard struggle
in New York accumulated a large fortune.   He has no ties
in the South, but an indefinable something seems to be drawing him back to the scene of his youth.   Accompanied by his
little motherless son, he returns to his home town, for what
he tells himself is to be no more than a vacation.   But the
sordidness of life there convinces him that he has something
to do with his remaining years and with his money.   He
must stir the South out of its slavishness to the traditions
which are destroying it.   In the fight which he makes for
reform, all the odds are against him.   In the end there is
nothing for him to do except admit his defeat and feel a
hopelessness and despair for his native land.

The description of the event which makes him recognize
his failure, which awakens him from his "dream," is one
of Mr. Chesnutt's strongest pieces of writing.   The colonel's
little son and the lovable, old-fashioned colored man who
takes care of him are killed by a railway train while the
aged servant is trying to rescue the boy from the tracks.
The colonel, as a mark of respect and devotion for the
faithful Negro, has his body buried in the white cemetery
of the town beside the grave of the child.   A few nights
after—

Long the colonel lay thinking, after he retired to rest, and
the muffled striking of the clock downstairs had marked the
hour of midnight ere he fell asleep.   And he had scarcely dozed
away, when he was awakened by a scraping noise, as though
somewhere in the house a heavy object was being drawn across
the floor.   The sound was not repeated, however, and thinking
it some trick of the imagination, he soon slept again.

As the colonel slept this second time, he dreamed of a
regenerated South, filled with thriving industries, and thronged

with a prosperous and happy people, where every man, having enough for his needs, was willing that every other man should have the same; where law and order should prevail unquestioned, and where every man could enter, through the golden gate of hope, the field of opportunity, where lay the prizes of life, which all might have an equal chance to win or lose.

For even in his dreams the colonel's mind did not stray beyond the bounds of reason and experience. That all men would ever be equal he did not even dream; there would always be the strong and the weak, the wise and the foolish. But that each man, in his little life in this our little world might be able to make the most of himself, was an ideal which even the colonel's waking hours would not have repudiated.

Following this pleasing thread with the unconscious rapidity of dreams, the colonel passed, in a few brief minutes, through a long and useful life to a happy end, when he too rested with his fathers, by the side of his son, and on his tomb was graven what was said of Ben Adhem: "Here lies one who loved his fellow men," and the further words, "and tried to make them happy."

Shortly after dawn there was a loud rapping at the colonel's door:

"Come downstairs and look on de piazza, Colonel," said the agitated voice of the servant who had knocked. "Come quick, suh."

There was a vague terror in the man's voice that stirred the colonel strangely. He threw on a dressing gown and hastened downstairs, and to the front door of the hall, which stood open. A handsome mahogany burial casket, stained by earth and disfigured by rough handling, rested upon the floor of the piazza, where it had been deposited during the night. Conspicuously nailed to the coffin lid was a sheet of white paper, upon which were some lines rudely scrawled in a handwriting that matched the spelling:

"*Kurnell French:* Take notis. Berry yore ole nigger somewhar else. He can't stay in Oak Semitury. The majority of the white people of this town, who dident tend yore nigger funarl, woant have him there. Niggers by their selves, white

people by their selves, and them that lives in our town must bide by our rules. By order of
"Cumity."

Since Mr. Chesnutt saw his material in such clearly out-lined plots and was able to create such episodes as that which ends *The Colonel's Dream,* he could have written, one is con-vinced, more artistic novels. William Dean Howells could not have praised *The House behind the Cedars, The Marrow of Tradition,* and *The Colonel's Dream* as he praised *The Conjure Woman* and *The Wife of His Youth.*[41] The novels are valuable and original as social studies. It was a high idealism that prompted Mr. Chesnutt to write them and thus jeopardize in a way his career as an artist. But as fiction they lack that harmony and sure workmanship which make of "Baxter's Procrustes" a little masterpiece. They are complicated with too many sub-plots, they contain numerous characters roughly sketched and few definitely portrayed, they are made too nervous with spasmodic suspense and mi-nor climaxes, they emphasize to too great an extent the flam-boyant and theatrical, and they are weighed down with propaganda. With all their imperfections, they hold a by no means insignificant place in the field of American fiction to which they belong. If in execution they are not so good as Cable's *The Grandissimes* and Page's *Red Rock,* they are much better than Dixon's *The Leopard's Spots.*

II

Poetry, always the form in which the Negro writer was most himself or most skillfully imitative, flourished between 1865 and 1900 as never before. In Paul Laurence Dunbar it reached its highest plane. But contemporary with Dunbar and immediately preceding him was a fairly numerous group of Negro poets who attempted almost every type of verse.

Jupiter Hammon and George Moses Horton as authors of a primitive poetry, frequently like the folk song in its effect, had at least three interesting successors. Reference has been made to Lorenzo D. Blackson's versified summary of the story told in *The Rise and Progress of the Kingdoms of Light and Darkness*. In the same year in which Blackson's book appeared, 1867, B. Clark, an uneducated mulatto living in York, Pennsylvania,[42] published *The Past, Present, and Future, in Prose and Poetry*, a volume made up of forty pages of chaotic and unimaginative prose about the destiny of the human race and more than a hundred pages of verse, produced, we are told, during the author's odd moments of leisure.[43] Its very crudeness makes it strange, and therefore interesting. For example, in a ballad version of the Biblical story of Haman we have this stanza:

> How many thousands, since that day
> Have built a gallows, so that they
>   Some one might hang!
> But, to their horror and surprise,
> They've found, with all their deep disguise,
>   Themselves have swang.

The obvious imitations of Longfellow are at times surprisingly smooth in sound, as:

> Winds echo through the trees,
>   And are unseen,
> Though we may feel the breeze
>   Ever so keen.

> So deeds, however kind,
>   When they are past,
> Are driven from the mind,
>   Like the rude blast.

Although Clark's moments for reading and writing might have been infrequent, he familiarized himself in a way with ballads, acrostics, paraphrases, epitaphs, odes, and hymns, and imitated them with reckless abandon. He was more varied than another poet of his kind, Islay Walden, but he was not so intimate in telling us about himself. Walden, born a slave in North Carolina, was apparently as natural a versifier as George Moses Horton. We are told that at the time in his life when all the knowledge he had of poetry had been derived from hearing hymns sung in church he composed the following on the burial of an ox:

> Poor old Dick,
> He died quick!
> He died all in a minute.
> Here is a shaft thirty feet,
> And we have thrown him in it.
>
> He was red,
> And he is dead!
> The buzzards may forsake him;
> For he is buried thirty feet,
> Where they can never get him.[44]

After the end of the Civil War had made him free, Walden came to the North, and wandered, it seems, through Pennsylvania and New Jersey, "trading rimes for bread." A church in New Brunswick, New Jersey, became sufficiently interested in him to subscribe the funds necessary to send him to Howard University.[45] He was a student there when, probably in 1873, he published his first volume, *Walden's Miscellaneous Poems, Which the Author Wishes to Dedicate to the Cause of Education, and Humanity.*[46] A second volume, *Walden's Sacred Poems,* was published at New Brunswick in 1877. It was made up of uninteresting hymns written in perfectly executed meters, and proves that education had spoiled whatever poet there had been in Walden. In his earlier volume he had in his own brusque manner given delightful glimpses of his character. In "One to Love" he assures us that he could never be a Mormon, that one woman would be a satisfying paradise for him. An echo of the slavishness which he has not been able to shake off is a tender little versified letter addressed to a "child living in North Carolina" whom he in his boyhood had been required to "tend and pet." He feels no resentment towards those who had held him in bondage; his one concern is whether the child had become a Christian. But he is most interesting when he is begging, as in the following stanzas from "Wish for an Overcoat," which he dedicated to his "wants and necessities":

> Oh! had I now an overcoat,
>   For I am nearly freezing;
> My head and lungs are stopped with cold,
>   And often I am sneezing.
>
>   .   .   .   .   .
>
> Then, look down upon my feet,
>   For there my boots are bursting,
> With upturned heels and grinning toes,
>   With tacks which long were rusting.

Verse not primitive enough to be of interest and not good enough to be of value was produced in abundance. Charlotte L. Forten, one of the first of her race to awake to the beauties of Negro folk song,[47] attained some recognition from her people as a poet.[48] Elijah W. Smith was in the seventies praised for his newspaper verse.[49] James Madison Bell, a chief helper of John Brown in preparing for the Harper's Ferry raid,[50] is remembered as the author of two poems celebrating Lincoln's Emancipation Proclamation, *The Day and the War* (San Francisco, 1864) and

The Progress of Liberty (San Francisco, 1866), and of an ode written on the final ratification of the Fifteenth Amendment, *The Triumph of Liberty* (Detroit, 1870). All three were reprinted in 1901 along with many more smooth and platitudinous verses in *The Poetical Works of James Madison Bell*, prefaced with an interesting biographical sketch by Bishop B. W. Arnett. J. Willis Menard, the first Negro to be elected to Congress,[51] published in 1879 *Lays in Summer Lands,* a collection of forty-six poems, the titles of which suggest a personal quality which is unfortunately lacking. In 1895, Eloise A. Bibb brought out a volume, entitled *Poems,* of which little can be said except that the verse is neat and prim. Introduced to the public by Booker T. Washington, Mary Weston Fordham published in 1897 *Magnolia Leaves: Poems,* containing a number of old-fashioned Puritan elegies and verses on a variety of subjects. One poem in the book, "The Washerwoman," is notable as a clever imitation of Thomas Hood. A typical stanza is:

> With hands all reddened and sore,
>   With back and shoulders low bent,
> She stands all day, and part of the night,
>   Till her strength is well-nigh spent.
> With her rub-rub-rub,
>   And her wash, rinse, shake,
> Till the muscles start and the spirit sinks,
>   And the bones begin to ache.

T. Thomas Fortune, whose work as a journalist and essayist on sociological topics has been discussed,[52] published in 1905 *Dreams of Life; Miscellaneous Poems,* most of the specimens in which, including nature pieces, love lyrics, elegiac verses, and long narratives, had been undoubtedly written many years before and had possibly been published in newspapers. The fast journalistic movement of Fortune's style in prose gives way in verse to a struggle with the demands of meter and rime.   At the rare moments when he is at ease he is likely to be trite and grandiose, as in the opening lines of a sonnet addressed to Edgar Allan Poe:

> Not one of all Columbia's tuneful choir
> Has pitched his notes to such a matchless key,
> As Poe—the wizard of the Orphic lyre.

"Dukalon," one of the narrative poems included in *Dreams of Life,* is a sentimental idyl, written in *terza rima,* of two lovers who hold clandestine meetings on the banks of the St. John's River in Florida.   Another, "The Bride of Ellerslee," is a story of the struggle between the English and the Spanish for the possession of Florida.   Since Fortune was born in that state and, according to his own declaration, "loved it above all others,"[53] it was natural for him to use it as a setting for his poems.   But it is not so easy to explain why Albery A. Whitman, the most talented and the most significant of all the American Negro poets between Phillis Wheatley and Paul Laurence Dunbar, chose Florida as the whole or partial scene of his three most ambitious efforts.

Whitman, whose photographs reveal a face in which Caucasian features dominate over African, was born in 1851. Although he was a slave until 1863,[54] he wrote as follows of his early life:

I was bred to the plow.   Amid the rugged hills, along the banks of Green River in Kentucky, I enjoyed the inestimable blessings of cabin life and hard work during the whole of my early days. I was in bondage,—*I never was a slave,*—the infamous laws of a savage despotism took my substance—what of that?[55]

By the time he was twenty-five years of age he had taught school and had become a minister of some prominence in the African Methodist Episcopal Church.[56]   In 1877, he published his first long poem, *Not a Man, and Yet a Man.* Predilection to alcohol seems to have been the obstacle which prevented his rise in the church.[57]   This frailty, combined with ill health and poverty,[58] must have made his years as an itinerant preacher in Ohio and Kansas indeed hard.   But the courage and optimism of his poems indicate that he lived all of his life in such a world of denial as he had created for himself during his childhood in slavery.   He had the soul of a poet.   The best known of his works, *The Rape of Florida,* appeared in 1884.   It was reprinted with slight alterations the following year as *Twasinta's Seminoles; or, The Rape of Florida,* and again in 1890 in a volume with the same title, in which were included also a reprint of *Not a Man, and Yet a Man* and a collection of apparently hitherto unpublished short poems grouped into a special section called *Drifted Leaves.*   The last publication, *An Idyl of the South,* came in 1901.

Not a Man, and Yet a Man contains more than two hundred and fifty closely printed pages, and is therefore to be classed among the more lengthy American poems.   As a work of metrical imitations it is a veritable *tour de force,* reverting back in its effect to an eighteenth-century American poem, Timothy Dwight's *Greenfield Hill,* which Whitman probably did not know.   In easy couplets which seem to repeat rather than echo the music of Goldsmith's *The Deserted Village,* the opening of the poem introduces us to Rodney, a heroic slave, the property of Sir Maxey, the richest man in a town of the Middle West, called Saville, where life is pioneer and yet idyllic.   We are next taken to an Indian village, in reading the description of which we might almost be deceived into believing that we hear the exact trochaics of Longfellow's *Hiawatha.*   In verse following Whittier's *Snow-Bound* and Longfellow's *Paul Revere's Ride*, we are told of how Sir Maxey's daughter, Dora, is taken captive by the Indians, of how Rodney rescues her and wins her affections, and of how her father, outraged at the thought of her love for his black slave, scorns the promise which he had made to give her as wife to the man who would save her from her captors. Rodney is turned over to a slave trader to be sold into the far South. We next find him on a plantation in Florida, where he forgets his infatuation for Dora in a real love, that for Leona, a Creole slave. After a stirring chain of events, the slave lovers win their way to Canada and freedom. The happenings in Florida are told in the measures of Scott's *Lady of the Lake*, scarcely disguised even in such occasional dialect passages as the following:

> In yonder room is Rodney tied,
> Where stands a locust on dis side.
> De white folks sell him in de morn,
> An' he'll be left yer, shore's yer born,
> Go see him, gal, bid him farewell,
> An' tell him what yer's got to tell,
> An' I'll stand here, de outside by,
> An' keep watchout wid open eye.

The conclusion, in the hexameters of Longfellow's *Evangeline*, shows Rodney and Leona in Canada, where chance throws them under the protection of Dora, who has discovered that what she had interpreted as love for Rodney was after all admiration for his heroism and sympathy for his lot. Because the varying music of so many well-known unrelated poems is incorporated into it, *Not a Man, and Yet a Man* seems complicated. The plot is in reality well unified, and the characterization is adequately consistent.

In the dedication of *The Rape of Florida*, addressed to Bishop H. M. Turner, Whitman wrote:

. . . in essaying the "stately verse," mastered only by Spenser, Byron, and a' very few other great poets, I may seem to have "rushed in where angels fear to tread." To this view of the matter, I will say by way of defense: some negro is sure to do everything that any one else has ever done, and as none of the race have executed a poem in the "stately verse," I simply *venture in.*

The poem relates only indirectly to the Negro. It is a story, crowded with love and romance and adventure, of the expulsion from Florida of a group of Seminoles, who were occasionally the benefactors of runaway slaves who fled to them in their swamps. The interest of the poem lies in Whitman's use of the Spenserian stanza as he had learned it from Byron. Sound means so much in the book that the story is difficult to follow. Whitman claimed that William Cullen Bryant said of him,

> The stuff's in him of robust manliness;
> He is a poet, singing more by ear
> Than note.

In turn, he addressed the memory of Bryant in *The Rape of Florida* as follows:

> O! shade of our departed sire of song!
> If what to us is dim be clear to thee,
> Hear while my yet rude numbers flow along!
> If spirit may a mortal's teacher be,
> Stand thou near by and guidance offer me!
> That, like thy verses, clear as summer blue,—
> Bright mirrors of the peaceful and the free,
> Reflecting e'er the good, the great and true;
> So mine may be, and I my pleasing task pursue.[59]

It is needless to comment on how the music of such a stanza approaches that of Byron's *Childe Harold.* And in the narrative portions of *The Rape of Florida* the nearness to Byron's sound is felt all the more strongly.

In "The Octoroon," the poem which makes up the major part of Whitman's last volume, *An Idyl of the South,* the influence is evidently that of Tennyson. The plot concerns a Florida slave girl, to all appearances white, who is loved by the son of her master. Whitman put enough straightforward drama into the action for us to follow it without being continually reminded that we are hearing a reproduction of the music of another poet. The work is almost original.

This is also true of a number of the short poems. The one which Whitman claimed was his earliest composition,[60] "My Mountain Home," suggests Whittier; but there is a subjectivity in it which draws the reader's attention away from its possible models. Because Whitman told us that as a child he tried to "scribble down what the birds and beasts were saying, and what even the dumb rocks were thinking,"[61] the lyric, the thought of which is suggested by the following stanza, means more than skillful imitation:

> My home was 'mong the mountains blue,
>   Close by a friendly stream
> Whose mossy banks my childhood knew—
>   Whose waves were childhood's dream.

That Whitman excelled as a writer of the dialect verse which in the eighties was becoming popular is shown in the following from "Tobe's Dream":

> Sally Ann's er cookin' ob de hoe cake bread,
> De chilluns am er playin' in de flo',
> De ham meat's er fryin' wid a mighty good smell,
> An' it makes de darky smile mighty sho'.
> An' it's home time, sun down,
> Time for de heart ter feel lite,
>   Home time, sun down,
> An' de darky bids care good-night.

Probably the strongest of the short poems, "Bells of Time," was obviously modelled after Poe and Tennyson; but it was so skillfully put together that it seems something new. The opening stanza is adequately illustrative:

> Ring! ring! ring! in thy dusty halls,
>   O Bells of Time,
> Calling the morn of life,
>   Banging the noon of life,
> Tolling the eve of life,
>   Ring! ring! O Bells of Time.

Whitman's talent is as baffling to explain as that of Phillis Wheatley. Both belong to the mocking-bird class of poets. In the discussion of Phillis Wheatley's work given in the first chapter of this book, she was compared with "Blind Tom," the mimic pianist. The comparison fits Whitman as well. His gift for hearing and reproducing the music of words must be considered a sort of genius. He was proud enough to declare:

I have yielded to the firm belief that the Negro has a future: I abhor the doctrine that he is but a cipher in the sum of the world's greatness—a captive in the meshes of dominating influences. . . . The time has come when all the "Uncle Toms" and "Topsies" ought to die. Goody-goodness is a sort of man worship: ignorance is its inspiration, fear its ministering spirit, and beggary its inheritance.[62]

But when he set out to be the unyielding bard of his race, he had nothing new to sing. He showed far less originality in thought than many a less talented Negro had shown. Indeed, he did exactly what Phillis Wheatley had done a century before. And what was said of her must be said of him: if his power of creation had equalled his skill in mimicry, he would stand as an ornament in American literature rather than as a curiosity.

If the author of a little book entitled *Catoninetales; a Domestic Epic,* published in 1891, was really, as its sponsors claimed, Hattie Brown, "a young lady of color lately deceased at the age of 14," Albery A. Whitman was not the only Negro who in recent years showed a talent related to that of Phillis Wheatley. A one-page memoir prefacing the poem claims that Hattie Brown was born in Georgia, that her parents were "field hands," and that her knowledge of verse came from hearing the daughters of "her mistress" read poetry. The versified stories which make up *Catoninetales,* each supposed to be an episode in one of the nine lives of a cat, named Kok Robyn, are obscured by nonsense notes and bizarre typography. Once detached and examined, they seem naïve enough to be accepted as the work of a child's imagination. But the book as a whole is such an oddity that one is inclined to regard it as no more than a publisher's hoax.

The one Negro poet immediately preceding Dunbar who experienced anything like general popularity was Frances E. W. Harper. Her rise as a writer of verse has been discussed,[63] and reference has been made to the prose fiction which she attempted late in life. A twentieth edition of her *Poems on Miscellaneous Subjects,* published originally in 1854 with an introduction by William Lloyd Garrison, was issued in 1871. In that same year she brought out a new volume of short pieces, entitled *Poems.* It was said in 1878 by one who was closely associated with her in her reform work, William Still, that fifty thousand copies of these two books had been sold to those who had heard her lectures.[64] Selections from these earlier publications along with many new pieces similar in character make up Mrs. Harper's last volume, also entitled *Poems,* published in 1900. However popular her lyrics and sentimental ballads might have been, they continued to the end to be feeble echoes, particularly of Longfellow.

But in the longer narrative forms she did more interesting work. *Sketches of Southern Life,* originally published in 1872, and reprinted, each time with additions, in 1888 and 1896, presents in a connected series of poems two characters whom one remembers, Aunt Chloe and Uncle Jacob. Aunt Chloe is the narrator, and a very rambling one. While she does not speak in dialect, her idiom is true to the life of the primitive Negro. She says in "The Deliverance," in describing the conduct of the slaves on her plantation when they hear that they are free:

> We just laughed, and danced, and shouted,
>   And prayed, and sang, and cried,
> And we thought dear Uncle Jacob
>   Would fairly crack his side.

She has a homely Negro wit that sees straight through the farce of the black man in national politics, and her vigorous comment on Johnson and Grant is a charming display of honest common sense. One regrets that *Sketches of Southern Life* contains pieces, mainly on reform topics, in which Aunt Chloe is not the narrator and in which Uncle Jacob, a pleasing old mystic, is not on hand to warn and exhort. In creating these two characters Mrs. Harper perhaps did more than any other Negro poet before Dunbar in getting close to the reality of primitive Negro life.

However, in her most consistently even piece of work, that which shows her highest achievement as a versifier, she has nothing to say about the Negro. It is *Moses: a Story of the Nile,* published as early as 1869.[65] The poem was obviously written to be read in public, and the opening hints that Mrs. Harper might have intended to make of it a drama.

In a scene, the setting for which the reader is left to con-
struct for himself, Moses discloses to the Princess who has
reared him his determination to lead his people out of
Egypt.   She at first protests, but because she loves Moses as
though he were her own child she finally agrees to his departure.   After this opening scene the dramatic form is
dropped, and the rest of the poem is a straight narrative of
the life adventures of Moses.   The verse, often metrically
uneven, is the most natural which Mrs. Harper produced.
In passages admitting of prettiness, as in the description of
how angels come down from heaven and bury Moses, there
is a delicate charm:

> And when the grave was finished,
> They trod with golden sandals
> Above the sacred spot,
> And the brightest, fairest flowers
> Sprang up beneath their tread.
> Nor broken turf, nor hillock,
> Did e'er reveal that grave,
> And truthful lips have never said,
> "We know where he is laid."

The poem is significant in Negro literature because one who
reads it is not constantly aware of imitation.   Mrs. Harper
must yield place to Albery A. Whitman as the most talented
Negro poet between Phillis Wheatley and Paul Laurence
Dunbar.   But of all Dunbar's predecessors who were not
primitive and spontaneous singers Mrs. Harper came nearest to producing a fairly extensive body of verse which has
a certain originality.

The publication in 1896 of Dunbar's *Lyrics of Lowly
Life* is the greatest single event in the history of American
Negro literature.   Dunbar incorporated into the book the
best selections from his earlier volumes, *Oak and Ivy* (1893)

and *Majors and Minors* (1895), both referred to above. How the work, introduced to the public by William Dean Howells, was received has been pointed out. As we have seen, Dunbar divided his interests during the remainder of his brief career between fiction and poetry. Although some of his short stories were thoughtfully conceived and admirably constructed, and although one of his novels, *The Sport of the Gods,* contains such material as should be an inspiration to Negro fiction writers for years to come, his verse is the work which distinguishes him as the universally recognized outstanding literary figure who had by 1900 arisen from the ranks of the American Negro. And *Lyrics of Lowly Life* is in all respects his happiest and most significant volume.

"Ere Sleep Comes Down to Soothe the Weary Eyes," the poem which opens the volume, is a song of the man who sees in the "waking world a world of lies," a theme possibly inspired by Shelley, whom Dunbar counted as his favorite poet.[66] But the book is not a lyrical arraignment of society. Whether the thought is gay or melancholy, the verse is overflowing with the feeling that,

> A song is but a little thing,
>   And yet what joy it is to sing!
> In hours of toil it gives me zest,
> And when at eve I long for rest;
> When cows come home along the bars,
>   And in the fold I hear the bell,
> As night, the shepherd, herds his stars,
>   I sing my song, and all is well.[67]

One poem after another in the volume proves that Dunbar was a master of spontaneous melody. There is never intricacy of thought nor of imagery, but there is always the song that arouses mood. It was Shelley the melodist and not

Shelley the humanitarian whom Dunbar worshipped. And
he was natural and sincere enough to distinguish between
thoughtful influence and slavish dependence. He came as
near to Shelley in "The Rising of the Storm" as in any
poem he wrote, but the following stanzas indicate that he
was not submitting to downright imitation:

> Far out in the night,
> On the wavering sight
> I see a dark hull loom;
> And its light on high,
> Like a Cyclop's eye,
> Shines out through the mist and gloom.

> Now the waves well up
> From the earth's deep cup,
> And fall on the sea and shore,
> And against the pier
> The waters rear
> And break with a sullen roar.

Most of the pieces in *Lyrics of Lowly Life* are in Shelley's
English. Many of the subjects—including definitions of
life, the mysteries of love and passion, the appeal of nature,
and the premonitions of death—are such as one finds often
treated in the lyrics of Shelley. If the volume had contained no more, it would be accounted merely a collection
of gentle sentiments sung in pure melody, far superior, to
be sure, to anything which any other American Negro poet
had done, but not sufficiently strong to be considered a
contribution of merit to American literature.

Fortunately, the volume contains a number of selections
written in what Howells called the Negro's "own accent of
our English."[68] The dialect poems justify the term "lowly
life" used in the title. The first which one comes upon is
"Accountability," a monologue of an old "darky" who has

stolen "one ob mastah's chickens" and who tries to rational-
ize the morality of the deed. A few pages farther on appears "An Ante-Bellum Sermon," in which is heard:

> Now ole Pher'oh, down in Egypt,
>   Was de wuss man evah bo'n,
> An' he had de Hebrew chillun
>   Down dah wukin' in his c'on;
> 'T well de Lawd got tiahed o' his foolin,'
>   An' sez he: "I'll let him know—
> Look hyeah, Moses, go tell Pher'oh
>   Fu' to let dem chillun go."

A little later comes the familiar "Banjo Song," with the
characteristic stanza,

> Oh, de music o' de banjo,
>   Quick an' deb-lish, solemn, slow,
> Is de greates' joy an' solace
>   Dat a weary slave kin know!
> So jes' let me hear it ringin',
>   Dough de chune be po' an' rough,
> It's a pleasure; an' de pleasures
>   O' dis life is few enough.

Next appears as true a pastoral as American poetry probably has to offer, "Song of Summer," the delightful folk
imagery of which is illustrated by the following stanza:

> Squir'l a-tippin' on his toes,
>   So's to hide an' view you;
> Whole flocks o' camp-meetin' crows
>   Shoutin' hallelujah.
> Peckahwood erpon de tree
>   Tappin' lak a hammah;
> Jaybird chattin' wif a bee,
>   Tryin' to teach him grammah.

Too infrequently, follow more poems in the language which
the Negro's unguided habits fashioned out of English. The

soul of the black laborer satisfied with little is expressed
with a pure art in "When de Co'n Pone's Hot."

> When de cabbage pot is steamin',
>   An' de bacon good an' fat,
> When de chittlins is a-sputter'n',
>   So's to show you whah dey's at;
> Tek away yo' sody biscuit,
>   Tek away yo' cake an' pie,
> Fu' de glory time is comin',
>   An' it's 'proachin' mighty nigh,
> An' you want to jump an' hollah,
>   Dough you know you'd bettah not,
> When yo' mammy says de blessin',
>   An' de co'n pone's hot.

"When Malindy Sings," inspired, we are told, by the singing
of the poet's mother,[69] is another true expression of Negro
character.

> She jes' spreads huh mouf and hollahs,
>   "Come to Jesus," twell you hyeah
> Sinnahs' tremblin' steps and voices,
>   Timid-lak a-drawin' neah;
> Den she tu'ns to "Rock of Ages,"
>   Simply to de cross she clings,
> An' you fin' yo' teahs a-drappin'
>   When Malindy sings.

Equally expressive of the true nature of the lowly Negro
are "Discovered" and "A Coquette Conquered," humorous
love poems; "The Deserted Plantation," a sentimental song
of reminiscence, suggestive of the mood of Thomas Nelson
Page's "Marse Chan"; "Signs of the Times," a pastoral
of autumn; and "The Party," an hilarious descriptive poem.

The dialect poems in *Lyrics of Lowly Life* made the
book the artistic, as well as the popular, success which it
became. They made the reputation of Dunbar. After all,

the teacher who meant most to him was not Shelley, but James Whitcomb Riley. His friendship with Riley was begun as early as 1892,[70] and probably as sincere a personal poem as he ever wrote was "James Whitcomb Riley," ostensibly presented from a western farmer's point of view.[71] It is a fitting criticism of Dunbar's own dialect poems. His aim, like Riley's, was to sing songs of his people that "come closest to your heart," that depend upon "human feelin'" and not upon "trim an' skillful phrases," that tell us "the same ol' things our souls have longed to know," that present a lesson "so good an' low that the humblest one kin reach it," and that "thrill with honest passion." His admiration for Riley led him to include in *Lyrics of Lowly Life* "After a Visit," "The Spellin' Bee," "A Confidence," and a few other pieces written in the dialect of the middle western white farmer. Entertaining, humorous, and highly musical, they might easily be mistaken for Riley's own work. Therefore, there is little excuse for their existence. But in applying Riley's methods to the Negro, Dunbar achieved genuine originality. His strongest predecessors in the writing of Negro dialect verse, Sidney Lanier, Irwin Russell, and Joel Chandler Harris, were detached from their material; Dunbar was a part of his. His realism is better than theirs because it was inspired by sincere feeling and not by the search for novelty; his music appeals to us as more natural because we do not in any way have to associate it with white singers. His Negro dialect verse is today generally accepted as the best which has been written in America. It deserves that consideration, and will probably maintain it. For the picturesque and poetic Negro language which Dunbar knew so well is rapidly passing away; he preserved a record of it at the right time.

A type of pure English verse which Dunbar should have

cultivated more intensively is represented in *Lyrics of Lowly Life* by such pieces as "Frederick Douglass," undoubtedly more eloquent than any memorial poem produced by any one of Dunbar's Negro predecessors; "The Colored Soldiers," a stirring tribute to the colored men who fell in the Civil War; and "Ode to Ethiopia," perhaps the most significant of the poems which are not in dialect. It opens with:

> O Mother Race! to thee I bring
> This pledge of faith unwavering,
>   This tribute to thy glory.

And the concluding stanza is:

> Go on and up! Our souls and eyes
> Shall follow thy continuous rise;
>   Our ears shall list thy story
> From bards who from thy root shall spring,
> And proudly tune their lyres to sing
>   Of Ethiopia's glory.

The gravest charge which can justly be brought against Dunbar as the author of *Lyrics of Lowly Life* is that he too often forgot the pledge which he made to his race in "Ode to Ethiopia." He was endowed by nature "to sing of Ethiopia's glory," but he crowded his first important volume with songs which have little relation to himself and none to his own people. Such songs can be estimated as no more than pretty exercises.[72]

He was twenty-four years old when *Lyrics of Lowly Life* was published, and youthfulness might have been accepted as a reason for the shortcomings of the book. But Dunbar never fulfilled its unusual promise. As we have seen, recognition as a poet prepared the way for the attainment of an ambition which he had long cherished, that for publishing prose fiction. Editors of magazines and publishers of books lured him into the quick production of short stories, novels, and made-to-order verses. Lecture bureaus engaged him for platform readings. The Dunbar who in the obscurity of Dayton had produced *Lyrics of Lowly Life* and *Folks from Dixie* now felt called upon to write for a wide public, made up mainly of whites who were curious to know what a black man of letters could accomplish. But the hardest obstacle which the artist in Dunbar had to combat was a natural physical frailty, finally distinguished as tuberculosis. Three volumes of verse followed *Lyrics of Lowly Life*: in 1899 came *Lyrics of the Hearthside;* in 1903, *Lyrics of Love and Laughter;* and in 1905, *Lyrics of Sunshine and Shadow.*[73] In spite of the odds which he had to fight against in writing the verse included in these volumes, no one of them falls below the standards which he set for himself in *Lyrics of Lowly Life*. Each, containing pure lyrics, occasional verses on the Negro written in straight English, and dialect poems, is similar in arrangement to the earlier volume. While his prose fiction was being printed in the popular magazines, his verse was appearing usually in such periodicals as the *Century, Harper's*, the *Outlook, Current Literature,* the *Bookman,* and the *Atlantic Monthly*. That he held himself true to the poet within him during the hectic nine years of life which were allotted him after his first great success is a sure mark of Dunbar's genius. If he had in the first place made poets of the soil, such as Burns and Riley, his exclusive masters, and if he had turned his back against popularity, his career would possibly be one of the most singular which American literature has to record.

But it is unfair criticism to expect too much of a Negro poet who lived in the United States in the days when Dunbar lived. The more one considers his work in verse, the more one wonders at his accomplishment. One of his most talented successors among the Negro poets, Countée Cullen, has most aptly expressed a truth which applies to Dunbar more perhaps than to any other Negro singer who has arisen in America:

> Yet do I marvel at this curious thing:
> To make a poet black, and bid him sing.

The number of the *Outlook* for November 3, 1900, contained the first installment of Booker T. Washington's *Up from Slavery*, Charles W. Chesnutt's short story, "The Sway-backed House," and a sonnet on Frederick Douglass by Paul Laurence Dunbar. Earlier in the same year William Dean Howells had published in the *Atlantic Monthly* a critical essay on Mr. Chesnutt's stories,[14] in the conclusion of which he said:

With Mr. Booker T. Washington the first American orator of our time, fresh upon the time of Frederick Douglass; with Mr. Dunbar among the finest of our poets; with Mr. Tanner, a black American, among the only three Americans from whom the French government ever bought a picture, Mr. Chesnutt may be well willing to own his color.

Such acclaim of Negro creators is ample evidence that at the end of the nineteenth century American Negro literature arrived at its majority. In spite of the gravest obstacles, the "jubilee" spirit of its makers had urged it on until it stood out as a production worthy of serious consideration in American art.

CHAPTER IX

CONCLUSION

For dear the bondsman holds his gifts
  Of music and of song:
The gold that kindly nature sifts
  Among his sands of wrong;

The power to make his toiling days
  And poor home-comforts please;
The quaint relief of mirth that plays
  With sorrow's minor keys.

> —From John Greenleaf Whittier's "At Port Royal, 1861," *Atlantic Monthly*, February, 1862

The history of American Negro literature as we have traced it is a story which, except in detached and unrelated parts, has never before been told. Few realize that at the end of the nineteenth century the American Negro had a literature which had been a hundred and forty years in the making. Booker T. Washington's *Up from Slavery* and Paul Laurence Dunbar's lullabies are still popular. Yet when Charles W. Chesnutt's *The Conjure Woman* was reprinted in 1929, it was reviewed in one of America's most distinguished critical journals as a new work. Phillis Wheatley is remembered by college students who take courses in early American literature as a poetic oddity of the eighteenth century. Frederick Douglass is possibly recalled by students of American history as an orator who in the days of abolition agitation was often compared with such giants of the lecture platform as Charles Sumner and Wendell Phillips. But there exists little written by Phillis Wheatley and Frederick Douglass which is not now out of print. Gustavus Vassa, Lemuel B. Haynes, William Wells Brown, Alexander Crummell, Albery A. Whitman, Frances E. Watkins Harper, and many others whose writings we have considered are comparatively unknown to the world today, black as well as white. The literature consciously produced by the American Negro before the end of the nineteenth century has been all but buried in the recent past.

While it was being formed by the comparatively few Negroes of the North, a literature of a different sort was being created by the hordes of blacks, slaves and freedmen, of the South. Even though this folk literature may not be known by name, it is felt by every American. It is a part of our national individuality. We can only with difficulty imagine what our poetry, fiction, drama, music, and dance would be without it.

The primitive Negro is still dancing new dances, singing new songs, and telling new tales. He probably began expressing himself in this manner as soon as he arrived at Jamestown in 1619.

But his songs seem to have been wholly unrecognized in America during the seventeenth and eighteenth centuries. There is an approach to folk expression in the poems of Jupiter Hammon and in the verse incorporated in Gustavus Vassa's *Life*.[1] According to Sir George Grove, "as early as 1782 melodies ascribed to the American blacks were being printed in Britain."[2] These melodies have apparently not been identified. Certainly as early as 1798 one African folk song had been translated into English and had been printed. In his *Travels in the Interior Districts of Africa*, published in London in that year, Mungo Park tells of a stormy night which he passed in a hut where a group of black women were spinning cotton.

They lightened their labour by songs, one of which was composed extempore; for I myself was the subject of it. It was sung by one of the young women, the rest joining in a sort of chorus. The air was sweet and plaintive, and the words, literally translated, were these.—"The winds roared, and the rains fell.—The poor white man, faint and weary, came near and sat under our tree.—He has no mother to bring him milk; no wife to grind his corn.—*Chorus*. Let us pity the poor white man; no mother has he, &c., &c."[3]

The song, apparently an interesting example of communal authorship and of the Negro's characteristic method of developing a theme with a solo part and a chorus, pleased the English fancy when Park reported it in his native country. The Countess of Devonshire adapted the words to meters, and her version was set to music by G. G. Ferrari.[4] Both Park's original and the Countess of Devonshire's arrangement were freely reprinted in the American antislavery newspapers, not as an example of the Negro's musical and verse-making talent but of the kindliness of his nature.[5] And the Countess of Devonshire was not the only one who was stirred to make a metrical arrangement of Park's transcript. An anonymous versifier published an entirely different adaptation of it in the issue for April 20, 1827, of the American Negro's first newspaper, *Freedom's Journal*.

In the late twenties, two Negro dances, the "Zip Coon" and the "Long Tail Blue," became popular on the American variety stage.[6] In 1832, another dance, the "Jim Crow," which seems to have originated in Cincinnati, was introduced to New York.[7] A blending of the plantation Negro's song, dance, and tale, and of the white variety actor's invention, the "Jim Crow" became a fad. A life of its supposed maker, a Louisville Negro claimed to have been called Jim Crow, was published in Philadelphia in 1837 with the telling title-page:

Life of Jim Crow, Showing How He Got His Inspiration as a Poet; The Number of Fathers Who Claimed Him When He Got Up in the World, Though None Would Claim Him Before; the Magic Spring "Way in de Woods ob Ole Kentuck," Where de Little Fairy Told Him of His Futur Greatness and Consequence in de World; His Interview with Gineral Jackson, with a Whole Basket Full of Incidents Which Befel Him before He Made His Grand Jump on the Stage!—Written by Himself.

There have been preserved many stanzas of the "Jim Crow" song, of which the following, taken from the *Life of Jim Crow,* is typical:

> If I was de president ob
> Dese United States,
> I'd eat molasses all de day
> An' swing upon de gate.
>
> An' wheel about an' turn about
> An' do jis so,
> An' eb'ry time I wheel about
> I jump Jim Crow.

There is probably as much white creation in such a stanza as Negro imagination and rhythm. But the following fancies, also taken from the *Life of Jim Crow,* can be traced to real folk origin:

> I come to a riber
> An' couldn't get across,
> So I gib half a dollar
> For an' ole blind hoss.
>
> Snake baked a hoe cake,
> An' set de frog to watch it;
> De frog fell asleep,
> An' de lizard come an' cotch'd it.

What Negro tunes have meant to the dance and popular music from "Zip Coon," "Long Tail Blue," "Jim Crow,"

and the songs of Stephen Collins Foster to "Rainbow round
My Shoulder," "Get Happy," George Gershwin's *Rhapsody
in Blue,* and Ernst Krenek's *Jonny Spielt Auf* is known to
the whole world.

Possibly because of its association with the flippant
American minstrelsy of the time, the antislavery agitators
either ignored the Negro folk song or frowned upon it.
Harriet Beecher Stowe in *Uncle Tom's Cabin* casually
quoted refrains from spirituals,[8] and once introduced what
she called "one of those unmeaning songs, common among
slaves."

> Mas'r see'd me cotch a coon,
>   High, boys, high!
> He laughed to split—d' ye see the moon?
>   Ho! ho! ho! boys, ho!
> Ho! yo! hi-e! oh!

In his collection of antislavery songs, *The Liberty Minstrel*
(1844), George W. Clark included "Song of the Coffle
Gang," the words of which he attributed to "the Slaves."

> O gracious Lord! when shall it be,
> That we poor souls shall all be free?

Lord, break them slavery powers—will you go along with me?
Lord, break them slavery powers—go sound the jubilee.

Another song in the book, supposedly written by "a Colored
Man," is more folkloristic.

> If e'er I reach the Northern shore,
> I'll n'er go back, no, never more;
> I think I hear these ladies say,
> We'll sing for Freedom night and day.
>
> Sinner! man! why don't you repent?
> For the judgment is rolling around!
> For the judgment is rolling around!

In a later collection of abolition hymns compiled by Clark, *The Harp of Freedom* (1856), appears a slave song which was at least partially real.

> Oh, when we go back home where we were born,
> We'll sing our songs both night and morn,
>   Case de day of slavery's gone,
>   Way down in de Car'lina state.
>
> *Oh, den by and by we do hope to meet um,*
> *By and by we do hope to meet um*
>   *Way down in de Car'lina state.*
>
> Oh, thar lives father, and thar lives mother,
> Thar lives sister, and thar lives brother;
>   When shall we all meet each other,
>   Way down in de Car'lina state?

Frederick Douglass commented on the melancholy and gay singing of the slaves, and in his autobiographies of 1845 and 1855 quoted two of their songs.[9] William Wells Brown,[10] Martin R. Delany,[11] and other abolition writers, white as well as colored, showed that they had Negro folk songs stored away in their memories.[12]

But it might be said that the true Negro folk song was given no just artistic appreciation until Thomas Wentworth Higginson published in the *Atlantic Monthly* for June, 1867, his "Negro Spirituals," in which he recorded the words of thirty-six hymns and two secular songs. In the same year came *Slave Songs of the United States,* containing the music as well as the words of more than a hundred melodies, collected and arranged for publication by William Francis Allen, Charles Pickard Ware, and Lucy McKim Garrison. In the seventies and eighties the Negro schools, particularly Fisk University and Hampton Institute, took up the work of preserving the songs and of making known their beauty.

So popular were the interpretations of the Fisk Jubilee Singers in the United States and in Europe that the religious songs of the Negro, commonly called spirituals, are still sometimes referred to as "jubilees." The name fits well the optimism which most of them express. However, the genuine artistic worth of the Negro's folk song was not positively proved until Anton Dvořák's *Symphony from the New World, Op. 95,* was performed for the first time in Carnegie Hall in the city of New York on December 15, 1893. Since that work was heard, no one has doubted the originality and richness of the musical ideas contained in the Negro's plantation melodies. Today the spiritual finds a place of dignity on concert programs. And its charm lies in the poetic suggestiveness of its words as well as of its music.

If the Negro had given us no spirituals, no work songs, no ballets, no reels, no shouts, no street cries, no blues, we should still be intimately familiar with his primitive mind. For from the time Gustavus Vassa's *Life* was published in London in 1789 the Negro's superstitions, exotic customs, idiosyncrasies of character, tales about animals and ghosts and voodoo wonders, and delightful distortion of the English language have had a place in American literature. The talk and antics allotted to Bones and Tambo on the minstrel stage formed a travesty of the primitive Negro's character and ways which the world is still too unwilling to look beyond. But while minstrelsy was being developed, a serious interpretation of the Negro folk mind was being given in the slave narratives and to a certain extent in antislavery fiction. One can probably gain a truer impression of the primitive Negro from a reading of the *Narrative of the Life and Adventures of Henry Bibb* (1849), *Narrative of Sojourner Truth, Northern Slave* (1850), George Moses

Horton's *Naked Genius* (1865), and Lorenzo D. Blackson's *The Rise and Progress of the Kingdoms of Light and Darkness* (1867) than from all the blackface shows which were staged when minstrelsy was in its flower. In the eighties and nineties the folk tales of the Negro were made universally popular in the journalistic and not always too correct versions of Joel Chandler Harris.[13] Br'er Rabbit, a portrait begun by the Negro folk in Africa and completed on the Georgia plantations, emerged as a distinguished character in American fiction. In the writings of Harris, Sidney Lanier, Irwin Russell, Thomas Nelson Page, Paul Laurence Dunbar, Charles W. Chesnutt, and others, the plantation Negro's customs and language and stories attained a dignity in literature which the Negro's songs had attained in music. And what Negro folklore means to the American writer of today is seen in such works as Langston Hughes's *The Weary Blues*, James Weldon Johnson's *God's Trombones*, Dubose Heyward's *Porgy*, and Marc Connelly's *The Green Pastures*.

The Negro folk have shown in their songs that they can be intensely subjective. Practically all of the spirituals are properly to be thought of as lyrics. A number of them express a depth of religious feeling which puts to shame most makers of hymns. It would be difficult to find resignation to divine guidance more convincingly sung than in "I Lay Dis Body Down."[14] Thomas Wentworth Higginson said in introducing the song into his "Negro Spirituals":

"I lie in de grave and stretch out my arms." Never, it seems to me, since man first lived and suffered, was his infinite longing for peace uttered more plaintively than in that line.

Perhaps in the folk lyricism of all peoples there is nothing more imaginative and musically melancholy. But there are many spirituals more picturesque in details, more playfully childlike in mingling the real and the mystic, and more intimate in revealing personal feeling. A notable example is "Little David, Play on Your Harp,"[15] with the concluding "jubilee" fancy:

> Jes' wait till I get on the mountain-top;
> Gwine to make my wings go flip-pi-ty flop.

Alike in character are the universally admired "Swing Low, Sweet Chariot," "Nobody Knows de Trouble I've Seen," "All God's Chillun," and "Steal Away to Jesus." One instinctively feels the wonder of the mind which sees the religious in such a picture as:

> Yonder come Peter wid a fan in his han',
> Walkin' on de watah like a nat'l man.[16]

Most of the Negro's blues and work songs are intimately subjective. Even without the air of the lugubrious Methodist-like hymn to which it is sung, the melancholy of the following plantation blues, which probably had its origin in the bottoms of the Mississippi River, is felt:

> Up de riber,
> Fur's I c'n see,
> No boat's a-comin'
> But de *Laura Lee*.
> I mus'n go,
> I mus'n go,
> I mus' hoe
> Dis cot'n row.[17]

The following work song, chanted angrily to a sort of recitative, reflects in unmistaken manner the dissatisfaction which its makers felt in the task to which it refers:

> Did you eber, eber, eber,
> In y'r life, life, life,

See de Debil, Debil, Debil,
An' his wife, wife, wife,
Diggin' tatahs on a col' an' frosty mornin'?[18]

The primitive Negro has rarely told a story in song in
which he has not brought in an expression of his own feelings. "To the Pines," sung by Negroes in North Carolina,
is probably as complete a ballad as one finds in Negro folk
literature, and yet it is to a great extent lyrical.

To the pines, to the pines,
Where the sun never shines,—
I shiver when the cold wind blo-o-ows.

The longest train I ever saw
Was six and a half miles long;
The engine was pulling up a three-mile grade,
The cab had never left town.

Last Saturday night a week ago,
My gal got killed by that train;
Her head was caught in the drivin' wheel,
Her body has never been found.

"My gal, my gal, where'd you get them shoes,
And that dress you wear so fine?"
"I got them shoes from a railroad man,
And the dress from a man in the mine."

Look down, look down, that long steel track
Where you and I must go.
The long steel rails and the short cross bars,—
I'll walk my way back home.

To the pines, to the pines,
Where the sun never shines,—
I shiver when the cold wind blo-o-ows.[19]

It is remarkable that the Negro's imagination has built both
indecent ballads and spirituals around such a situation and
such a picture as are suggested by the following:

"Who's been here since I's been gone?"
"A big, black nigger wid a derby on."

But the tendency to mingle the narrative and the lyrical is perhaps best represented by the number of songs which have some reference to John Henry, the Robin Hood, or Paul Bunyan, of the American Negro folk.[20] "The Nine-Pound Hammer," which seems to have originated in North Carolina, is an interesting example.

"Roll on, Buddy, don't you roll so slow."
"Babe, how can I roll,
When the wheels won't go-o-o?"

Nine-pound hammer
Kill John Henry,
Ain't a-goin' to kill me, ain't a-goin' to kill me.

Nine-pound hammer,
Little too heavy,
A-swingin' from the side, a-swingin' from the side.

Goin' o'er the mountain
For to see my darlin',
An' I ain't a-comin' back, an' I ain't a-comin' back.

Take this hammer
To the captain,
An' tell him I'm gone, an' tell him I'm gone.

"Roll on, Buddy, don't you roll so slow."
"Babe, how can I roll,
When the wheels won't go-o-o?"[21]

The primitive Negro has an extraordinary instinct for dramatization. An interesting example is his explanation of what takes place when owls are heard hooting early in the morning. Mr. Owl has spent the night foraging. Shortly after dawn he starts on his leisurely way home. He and

Mrs. Owl dislike company, and yet they have many relations who are in the habit of visiting them. When the husband is still a mile away from his nest, the following conversation between him and his wife is heard:

> "Who-oo-oo-oo's there?
> Who-oo-oo-oo's there?"

> "Jack, Jack, an' his wife,
> An' Lord knows who all!
> Jack, Jack, an' his wife,
> An' Lord knows who all!"[22]

When this little story is interpreted by the imaginative plantation Negro, the crustiness of dissatisfaction in Mrs. Owl's reply is sounded with full force. Another illustration of the Negro's skill in dramatizing a situation is his description of what is heard when bloodhounds are pursuing a fleeing slave. The dogs call out in deep-throated voices:

> "How o-o-old are you?
> How o-o-old are you?"

And the Negro's fast beating feet reply:

> "Twenty-one, twenty-two!
> Twenty-one, twenty-two!"[23]

Above all things, the Negro folk have shown a genius for expressing themselves musically. Their poems and tales are intermingled with melody and the dance. Perhaps few trained versifiers have ever fashioned the sound of words to action more ingeniously than the primitive bard, or group of singers, who created the well known spiritual, "De Ol' Ark's a-Moverin'." Although it is ten times more effective when it is heard sung, it is suggestive enough when read on the printed page.

Oh, de ol' ark's a-moverin', a-moverin', a-moverin',
   De ol' ark's a-moverin',
   And I'm goin' home.
   De ol' ark she reel,
   De ol' ark she rock,
De ol' ark she landed on de mountain-top.
Oh, de ol' ark's a-moverin', a-moverin', a-moverin',
   De ol' ark's a-moverin',
   And I'm goin' home.

The folk literature of the Negro proves that he is emotional, imaginative, musical. It proves that he is expressive by nature. We are so familiar with it in our everyday American life that we have with difficulty been able to see in it more than the commonplace. Now we are beginning to realize that it is perhaps America's most precious artistic heritage. We are beginning to estimate the debt which we owe to its creators.

It is a legacy to all America, but particularly to the Negroes themselves. The story of their sufferings and triumphs, their melancholy and gaiety, their despair and patience, is embedded in their traditional songs and tales.

Will the Negro artist working deliberately prove himself worthy of being called a descendant of those who created this folk literature?

This question, it seems, is answered by what the American Negro, in the face of apparently insurmountable obstacles, had accomplished in forming a consciously produced literature by the end of the nineteenth century. His achievements during the past thirty years, especially in poetry and fiction, have shown a sure and steady advancement. He has not yet written an enduring masterpiece, but that could scarcely be expected of him. If his consciously produced literature shows nothing else, it shows tenacity of purpose.

The Negro author is determined to hold on. If his evolution continues, he will in time write works which will fulfill the promise of the creation of his folk ancestors.

There is no reason to feel that his evolution will not continue. The "jubilee" spirit which preserved him through a long period of such degradation as few races have ever experienced will continue to preserve him. There is something within him, undoubtedly a racial inheritance, which stirs him to strive to "get on the mountain-top." With our American social organization such as it is, much is denied him. But literature and the related arts are open freely to him. It is in them that he has his best opportunity to "rise and shine."

NOTES

CHAPTER I

1. See Chapter IX.
2. *Winthrop's Journal,* ed. James Kendall Hosmer, 1908, I, 260; *Connecticut as a Colony and as a State,* ed. Forrest Morgan, 1904, I, 504; Samuel Greene, *History of the State of Rhode Island,* 1894, I, 240; *Narratives of New Netherland, 1609-1664,* ed. J. Franklin Jamison, 1909, pp. 129-130; Edward Raymond Turner, *The Negro in Pennsylvania,* 1911, pp. 1-4; Edward McCrady, *The History of South Carolina under the Proprietary Government,* 1897, p. 151; John Spencer Bassett, *Slavery and Servitude in the Colony of North Carolina,* 1896, pp. 15-16; Charles C. Jones, Jr., *The History of Georgia,* 1883, I, 111-112, 423-426; and Benjamin Brawley, *A Short History of the American Negro,* 1913, pp. 5-12.
3. W. O. Blake, *The History of Slavery and the Slave Trade,* 1857, p. 378.
4. The term *Negro* as used throughout this book is to be understood in the American sense; that is, as meaning one who is wholly or partially of African ancestry.
5. See Benjamin Brawley, *A Social History of the American Negro,* 1921, pp. 21-26.
6. See Carter G. Woodson, *The Education of the Negro Prior to 1861,* 1915, pp. 23-24.
7. See Edward Channing, *A History of the United States,* 1924, II, 376-398.
8. "Diary of Cotton Mather, 1681-1706," *Massachusetts Historical Society Collections,* VII (Seventh Series), 176-177 (1911).
9. In his *The Negro Christianized: an Essay to Excite and Assist That Good Work, the Instruction of Negro Servants in Christianity* (1706) Mather claimed a little more for the Negroes. He suggested that they might be useful as teachers of the small children of their masters.
10. C. F. Pascoe, *Classified Digest of the Records of the Society for the Propagation of the Gospel in Foreign Parts with Much Supplementary Information,* 1893, p. 24.

11. Slave advertisements appearing in early newspapers are an interesting commentary on the education of eighteenth-century Negroes. Some are spoken of as able to read and write; a few are recommended for superior attainments, such as ability to speak two languages, or to play several musical instruments. But nothing whatever is said of the literacy of the great majority of those who are offered for sale. *Cf.* "Eighteenth Century Slave Advertisements," *Journal of Negro History*, I, 163-216. (Apr., 1916).

12. Gustavus Vassa, *The Interesting Narrative of the Life of Olaudah Equiano, or Gustavus Vassa*, 1789, II, 5.

13. See Chapter II.

14. This is likewise true of the educational programs of such friends of the Negro as Isaac Tatem and Anthony Benezet, whose main aim in the schools which they organized was to teach the Negro enough to get him ready to enjoy the privileges of freedom. See Woodson, *op. cit.*, p. 53.

15. See Prince D. S. Mirsky, *Pushkin*, 1926, Chapter I.

16. Antonius Gulielmus Amo, *Tractatus de arte sobrie et accurate philosophandi* . . . , 1738, title-page. *Cf.* Henri Grégoire, *De la littérature des nègres*, 1808, pp. 198-202.

17. *Ibid.*, pp. 223-225.

18. Edward Long, *History of Jamaica*, 1774, II, 475.

19. *Ibid.*, II, 475-480. See T. H. MacDermott, "From a Jamaica Portfolio—Francis Williams," *Journal of Negro History*, II, 147-160 (Apr., 1917).

20. *Ibid.* See also Grégoire, *op. cit.*, p. 237.

21. *Letters of Ignatius Sancho*, ed. Joseph Jekyll, 1782, "Memoir."

22. See Thomas Jefferson's favorable comment on Sancho's *Letters* in "Notes on Virginia," *The Writings of Thomas Jefferson*, Monticello Edition, 1904, II, 196-197.

23. Ottabah Cugoano, *Thoughts and Sentiments on the Evil and Wicked Traffic of Slavery and Commerce of the Human Species*, 1787, pp. 11-12. See Grégoire, *op. cit.*, pp. 215-223.

24. *American Museum*, V, 61-62 (Jan., 1789).

25. *American Museum*, V, 62-63 (Jan., 1789); J. P. Brissot de Warville, *New Travels in the United States*, 1792, pp. 157-158.

26. See W. B. Hartgrove, "The Negro Soldier in the American Revolution," *Journal of Negro History*, I, 130-131 (Apr., 1916).

27. See Oscar Wegelin, *Jupiter Hammon*, 1915, pp. 7-19.

28. Jupiter Hammon, *An Address to the Negroes in the State of New-York*, 1787, p. 4.

29. *Ibid.*, p. 6.

30. A note by the printers to each of the 1787 editions of his *Address* includes the following statement: "The manuscript wrote in his own hand is in our possession. We have made no material alterations in it, except in the spelling, which we found needed considerable correction."

31. See Wegelin, *op. cit.*, p. 11.

32. One of his pieces in verse, "A Poem for Children with Thoughts on Death," seems to be a Methodist commentary on the rigid Calvinism expounded in that portion of *The Day of Doom* which describes the last judgment of children who have died in infancy and who are not of "God's Elect."

33. Hammon, *op. cit.*, p. 4.

34. *Cf.* Wegelin, *op. cit.*, pp. 18, 48.

35. There were two editions of the *Address*, in New York and Philadelphia, in 1787, and a third, in New York, in 1806.

36. See Chapter IX.

37. Hammon probably got the idea for the poem from Phillis Wheatley's "On Being Brought from Africa to America," included in her *Poems on Various Subjects* (1773).

38. Credit for resurrecting Jupiter Hammon must be given to Oscar Wegelin, whose first published account of Hammon appeared in the *Literary Collector* for August, 1904, in an article entitled " Was Phillis Wheatley America's First Negro Poet?"

39. *Cf. The Book of American Negro Poetry*, ed. James Weldon Johnson, 1922, pp. xxvii-xxviii.

40. Whitefield died on September 30, 1770. In the *Massachusetts Spy* for the following October 11, Phillis Wheatley's elegy was advertised as "this day was published." At least five other editions of the elegy are dated 1770.

41. The main source for the great number of biographical sketches of Phillis Wheatley is the "Memoir" which prefaces the 1834 edition of her *Poems*, published by George W. Light, Boston. It appeared as anonymous, but was positively identified by Light in 1864 as the work of Margaretta Matilda Odell, a "relative of the mistress of Phillis," who claimed that the facts

contained in the "Memoir" were derived from grand-nieces of "Phillis's benefactress and corroborated by a grand-daughter of that lady." See Charles Deane, *Letters of Phillis Wheatley,* 1864, pp. 8-9. The account by Margaretta Matilda Odell was the basis of the best known early biography of Phillis Wheatley, B. B. Thatcher's *Memoir of Phillis Wheatley, a Native African and a Slave* (1834).

42. This letter was prefixed to the first edition (London, 1773) of Phillis Wheatley's *Poems on Various Subjects,* and was reprinted in several subsequent editions. It is here quoted as it appeared in the first edition.

43. Quoted from the original manuscript, in Phillis Wheatley's own handwriting. The manuscript, dated 1767, is in the Schomburg Collection of the New York Public Library. The poem, in revised and improved form, appears in *Poems on Various Subjects,* pp. 15-16.

44. Deane, *op. cit.,* p. 13.

45. N. B. Shurtleff, "Phillis Wheatley, the Negro-Slave Poet," *Boston Daily Advertiser,* Dec. 21, 1863. Shurtleff's brief but authoritative sketch was reprinted in Deane, *op. cit.,* pp. 9-11.

46. The exact time of her stay abroad has not been determined. A poem on her departure from Boston, "A Farewell to America," is dated Boston, May 7, 1773. The dedication of *Poems on Various Subjects* is dated Boston, June 12, 1773. It is very probable that she was in London the following July (see below, Chapter I, Note 48). We know from a letter which she wrote to Obour Tanner on October 30, 1773, that she had by then been back in America for some time.

47. *Poems of Phillis Wheatley,* 1834, "Memoir."

48. In the library of Harvard College there is a copy of Milton's *Paradise Lost,* on the flyleaf of which appears the inscription in Phillis Wheatley's handwriting: "Mr. Brook Watson to Phillis Wheatley, London, July—1773." Below is appended the following statement: "This Book was given by Brook Watson, formerly Lord Mayor of London, to Phillis Wheatley—and after her death was sold in payment of her Husband's debts.—It is now presented to the Library of Harvard University at Cambridge, by Dudley L. Pickman of Salem. March, 1824." *Cf.* E. S. Abdy, *Residence and Tour in*

America, 1835, I, 165, and Arthur A. Schomburg's "Appreciation" in Chas. Fred. Heartman's edition of Phillis Wheatley's *Poems and Letters*, 1915.

49. *Poems of Phillis Wheatley*, 1834, "Memoir."

50. Negotiations for the publication were under way as early as November, 1772 (see the letter by John Wheatley published in the volume). The first English notice of the book which I have found is in the *Monthly Review*, XLIX, 457-459 (Dec., 1773), and the first American notice seems to be that in the *Boston Gazette*, Jan. 24, 1774.

51. Shurtleff, *loc. cit.*

52. The poem was published in the *Pennsylvania Magazine* for April, 1776. Washington's reply to the letter was dated February 2, 1776. In it he said: "If you should ever come to Cambridge, or near headquarters, I shall be happy to see a person so favored by the muses, and to whom Nature has been so liberal and beneficent in her dispensations."

53. *A Volume of Records Relating to the Early History of Boston, Containing Boston Marriages from 1772 to 1809*, 1903, p. 441.

54. *Poems of Phillis Wheatley*, 1834, "Memoir."

55. For the discovery of this poem, apparently never reprinted and evidently unknown to Chas. Fred. Heartman when he published in 1915 his collected edition of Phillis Wheatley's *Poems and Letters*, I am indebted to Mr. Lyon N. Richardson, of Western Reserve University.

56. In the *Boston Magazine*, Sept., 1784, p. 462, appears the following editorial note, the poem referred to being "To Mr. and Mrs. *******, on the Death of Their Infant Son": "The poem, in page 488, of this number, was selected from a manuscript Volume of Poems, written by Phillis Peters, formerly Phillis Wheatley—and is inserted as a specimen of her Work: should this gain the Approbation of the Publick, and sufficient encouragement be given, a Volume will be shortly Published, by the printers hereof, who receive subscriptions for said work."

57. *Independent Chronicle* (Boston), Dec. 9, 1784.

58. *Cf.* Chas. Fred. Heartman, *Phillis Wheatley*, n. d. (1915?), p. 35. A "Poem on Providence," listed by Mr. Heartman as possibly published in an unidentified magazine in 1772 is in all probability a reprint of "Thoughts on Providence," in-

cluded in *Poems on Various Subjects.* I have been unable to identify the magazine from which the leaves containing the poem, now in the Boston Public Library, were cut. But the style of print is that of no period earlier than the nineteenth century. And that a quotation from John Wheatley's letter published in *Poems on Various Subjects* accompanies the poem proves almost conclusively that its publication followed rather than preceded that of the volume.

59. As in the case of "To Mr. and Mrs. *******, on the Death of Their Infant Son," I am indebted for the discovery of these two poems, neither of which seems to have been known by editors of Phillis Wheatley, to Mr. Lyon N. Richardson.

60. *Cf. Ebony and Topaz, a Collectanea,* ed. Charles S. Johnson, 1927, p. 78. The poem, "To a Gentleman on a Voyage to Great Britain for the Recovery of His Health," reprinted in *Ebony and Topaz* as having been located in Daniel Ricketson's *History of New Bedford,* 1858, had been included in *Poems on Various Subjects,* and had been reprinted in the *Liberator,* Oct. 13, 1832.

61. The "Proposals" occupy a full column on the front page of the *Evening Post and the General Advertiser,* Oct. 30, 1779, and were reprinted in the same paper Nov. 6, 27, and Dec. 4, 11, and 18, 1779.

62. One title listed, "To Lieut. R--------- D-------- of the Navy," possibly refers to the verses "addressed to a gentleman of the navy" which Phillis Wheatley had in 1774 and 1775 published in the *Royal American Magazine.*

63. What is possibly a manuscript copy of one of the letters promised, "To the Right Hon. Wm. E. of Dartmouth, Sec. of State of N. America," is in the library of the Massachusetts Historical Society. The letter, dated October 10, 1772, was addressed to the Earl of Dartmouth to accompany a copy of the poem which Phillis Wheatley inscribed to him and later included in *Poems on Various Subjects.*

64. *Poems of Phillis Wheatley,* 1834, "Memoir."

65. Quoted from the 1772 broadside. The elegy with a few changes appears in *Poems on Various Subjects* as "To a Clergyman on the Death of His Lady."

66. *Poems on Various Subjects,* 1773, p. 31.

67. Although there is no apparent inconsistency in the style,

it is stated in *Poems on Various Subjects* that the latter part
of this adaptation is the work of another hand.

68. *Poems on Various Subjects*, p. 74. See above, Note 63.

69. *Poems on Various Subjects*, p. 18.

70. *Cf.* James Weldon Johnson, *op. cit.*, p. xxiv.

71. *Poems of Phillis Wheatley*, 1834, "Memoir."

72. *Cf.* Katherine Lee Bates, *American Literature*, 1898,
pp. 78-79.

73. In the Schomburg Collection of the New York Public
Library there are two volumes of the 1773 edition of Shenstone's
Works in Verse and Prose, on the flyleaf of each of which is
the inscription in Phillis Wheatley's handwriting: "May
Eveleigh to Phillis Wheatley, Sept. 24, 1774."

74. *Proceedings of the Massachusetts Historical Society,
1863-64,* VII, 166-167 (1864).

75. Two of the poems, "Ode to Neptune" and "Hymn to
Humanity," are done in the manner of the hymns of Addison
and Watts. "A Farewell to America," perhaps her most graceful achievement in versification, is written in the simple meter
of the ballad. The elegy on Whitefield has the music of Gray's
Elegy Written in a Country Churchyard.

76. See Chapter VIII.

77. See James M. Trotter, *Music and Some Highly Musical
People,* 1879, pp. 143-146. For interesting early accounts of
Bethune's strange musicianship, see the *Liberator,* Mar. 16,
1860, and *Frederick Douglass' Paper*, Mar. 30, 1860.

78. *Poems on Various Subjects,* p. 116.

79. *Ibid.*, p. 51.

80. *Ibid.*, p. 66.

81. *Ibid.*, p. 80.

82. *Ibid.*, p. 107.

83. *Ibid.*, p. 109.

84. Grégoire, *op. cit.*, p. 190.

85. Briton Hammon's owner might have been General John
Winslow (1703-1774), a resident of Marshfield. See Maria
Whitman Bryant, *Genealogy of Edward Winslow of the May-
flower and His Descendants from 1620 to 1865*, 1915, pp. 37-40.

86. *Monthly Review*, LXXIII, 399 (Nov., 1785).

87. *Ibid.*

88. Because, it may be assumed, of his indifference toward

the welfare of his own people, the name of Marrant, like that of Jupiter Hammon, was not kept alive by the early Negro leaders. It was not until recently, when Arthur A. Schomburg reprinted the *Sermon*, that interest in him was in any way reawakened.

89. *American Museum*, I, 463-465 (June, 1787).

90. *Ibid.*, IV, 414-417; 509-512 (Nov. and Dec., 1788).

91. *Cf.* Carter G. Woodson, *Negro Orators and Their Orations*, 1915, p. 14; Grégoire, *op. cit.*, pp. 212-215.

92. In the *American Museum*, VI, 77-80 (July, 1789), there is "A Letter on Slavery," by a "Free Negro." It is a stronger and a more radical invective than the essay by "Othello," and is written in a more ingenious and subtle style, the pompousness of "Othello" being replaced by a poignant and trenchant idiom. The author was in all probability a Negro. Although he has been repeatedly referred to as American, there is little reason to classify him as such. The article is accompanied by the following editorial note: "This letter was originally published in England, where the number of Negroes is considerably increased, since the late war in America." There is a possibility that the author was one of the many American Negroes who went to England during the Revolution, but the equivocal note of the editor of the *American Museum* does not furnish sufficient evidence to support this view. Internal evidence in "A Letter" suggests that the author was a native of the West Indies. *Cf.* Woodson, *Negro Orators and Their Orations*, p. 25.

93. The account of Molly Welsh as the grandmother of Banneker was first printed in the *Proceedings of the Maryland Historical Society for 1854*, the data having been furnished by Martha E. Tyson, a daughter of George Ellicott. This version of Banneker's ancestry was given in more elaborate detail in *Banneker, the Afric-American Astronomer*, edited from the posthumous papers of Martha E. Tyson and published in 1884. According to an earlier account, that of John B. H. Latrobe, published in the *Proceedings of the Maryland Historical Society for 1837*, Banneker's "father was a native of Africa, and his mother the child of natives of Africa; so that to no admixture of the blood of the white man was he indebted for his peculiar and extraordinary abilities." Mrs. Tyson's con-

clusions certainly seem to be more tenable than Latrobe's, since her father was so closely associated with Banneker. *Cf.* Henry E. Baker, "Benjamin Banneker, the Negro Mathematician and Astronomer," *Journal of Negro History*, III, 99-119 (Apr., 1918); and Will W. Allen, *Banneker, the Afro-American Astronomer*, 1921, Chapter I.

94. See M. D. Conway, "Benjamin Banneker," *Atlantic Monthly*, XI, 79-84 (Jan., 1863); and Carter G. Woodson, *The Negro in Our History*, 1927, pp. 137-140.

95. Benjamin Banneker, *Copy of a Letter from Benjamin Banneker, to the Secretary of State, with His Answer*, 1792, p. 3.

96. *Ibid.*, p. 9.

97. *Ibid.*, p. 11. Jefferson was rather contradictory in his statements regarding Banneker. In a letter to Joel Barlow, dated October 8, 1809, he wrote: "I have a long letter from Banneker, which shows him to have had a mind of very common stature indeed. . . . We know that he had spherical trigonometry enough to make almanacs, but not without the suspicion of aid from Ellicott, who was his neighbor and friend, and never missed an opportunity of puffing him." See *The Writings of Thomas Jefferson*, Monticello Edition, 1904, XII, 322. See also *Writings of Thomas Jefferson*, ed. Paul Leicester Ford, 1899, V, 379.

98. *Cf.* Woodson, *The Negro in Our History*, pp. 138-140.

99. Tyson, *Banneker, the Afric-American Astronomer*, p. 53.

100. *Ibid.*

101. Allen, *op. cit.*, pp. 62-63.

102. Grégoire, *op. cit.*, p. 427.

103. I have referred to Belinda's picture of her childhood life in her "Petition of an African." It is too brief and generalized to be classed with Vassa's.

104. This and all other quotations given from Vassa's *Life* are taken from the 1789 edition.

105. *Monthly Review*, LXXXII, 551-552 (June, 1789).

CHAPTER II

1. See Henry Noble Sherwood, "Paul Cuffe," *Journal of Negro History*, VIII, 153-229 (Apr., 1923).

2. See Henry Noble Sherwood, "Paul Cuffe and His Con-

tribution to the American Colonization Society," *Proceedings of the Mississippi Valley Historical Association*, VI, 370-402 (1912-1913).

3. *Cf.* Henry Wilson, *Rise and Fall of the Slave Power in America,* 1872, pp. 208-222.

4. Benjamin Brawley, *A Short History of the American Negro,* 1924, p. 40.

5. The figures are from the United States official census reports.

6. John Spencer Bassett, *Slavery in the State of North Carolina,* 1899, pp. 73-74.

7. Carter G. Woodson, *The Education of the Negro Prior to 1861,* 1915, pp. 93-150.

8. See the *Emancipator,* Oct. 27, 1836.

9. Carter G. Woodson, *History of the Negro Church,* 1921, pp. 85-86.

10. Richard Allen, *The Life . . . of the Rt. Rev. Richard Allen,* 1880, pp. 18-25.

11. Woodson, *History of the Negro Church,* pp. 93-99.

12. Carter G. Woodson, *The Negro in Our History,* 1922, p. 144.

13. *Minutes and Proceedings of the First Annual Convention of the People of Color,* 1831; John W. Cromwell, *The Negro in American History,* 1914, pp. 27-47.

14. *Liberator,* June 1, 1833.

15. *Mirror of Liberty,* Aug., 1838.

16. *Cf.* Louis H. Fox, *New York City Newspapers, 1820-1850,* 1927, p. 45.

17. *Liberator,* Mar. 26, 1831; *Genius of Universal Emancipation,* XI, 497 (Apr., 1831).

18. *Genius of Universal Emancipation,* XI, 497 (Apr., 1831).

19. *Ibid.*

20. George F. Bragg, *Richard Allen and Absalom Jones,* 1915, pp. 10-11.

21. *Freedom's Journal,* Nov. 2, 1827.

22. It was reprinted in Allen, *op. cit.,* pp. 33-69.

23. "Some Letters of Richard Allen and Absalom Jones to Dorothy Ripley," *Journal of Negro History,* I, 436-443 (Oct., 1916).

24. Allen, *op. cit.,* "Preface."

25. Richard Allen and Absalom Jones, *A Narrative of the Proceedings of the Black People*, 1794, p. 24.

26. See William Douglass, *Annals of St. Thomas' Church*, 1862, pp. 119-121.

27. See above, Chapter II, Note 23.

28. Daniel Alexander Payne, *Recollections of Seventy Years*, 1888, pp. 100-101.

29. Daniel Coker, *A Dialogue between a Virginian and an African Minister*, 1810, "Appendix"; Daniel Alexander Payne, *History of the African Methodist Episcopal Church*, 1891, p. 90.

30. *Journal of Daniel Coker*, 1820, "Letter to the Maryland Colonization Society."

31. See Martin R. Delany, *The Condition, Elevation, Emigration, and Destiny of the Colored People of the United States*, 1852, p. 130.

32. See the verse tributes to Forten in the *Liberator*, Jan. 15, 22, 1841.

33. S. H. Gloucester, *A Discourse Delivered on the Occasion of the Death of Mr. James Forten*, 1842, p. 18.

34. *Ibid.* See also the abridgment of Robert Purvis' eulogy, printed in William C. Nell, *The Colored Patriots of the American Revolution*, 1855, pp. 166-181. A tribute containing biographical information was published in the *Liberator*, Apr. 8, 1842.

35. Douglass, *op. cit.*, pp. 124-125.

36. See Alice Adams, *The Neglected Period of Anti-Slavery in the United States*, 1908, p. 92, and Carter G. Woodson, *Negro Orators and Their Orations*, 1925, pp. 42-43.

37. Adams, *loc. cit.*

38. *Liberator*, Sept. 16, 1853.

39. *Liberator*, Aug. 23, 1834.

40. See the *Pennsylvania Freeman*, Mar. 29, 1838, and the *Emancipator*, Apr. 14, 1838.

41. Letters by Purvis are to be found in the *Liberator*, Aug. 23, 1834, Nov. 30, 1841, Sept. 16 and Dec. 16, 1853, and Aug. 28, 1862; in the *Pennsylvania Freeman*, Nov. 17, 1841; and in the *National Anti-Slavery Standard*, Dec. 2, 1841.

42. *Liberator*, Apr. 5, 1834.

43. *Emancipator*, Aug. 24, 1837; *Liberator*, Oct. 9, 1840.

44. I have been unable to locate a number later than that

for December, 1839. The publication was possibly continued into the forties.

45. *Colored American*, Sept. 9, 16, 23, 30, 1837.

46. See the *Emancipator*, July 4, 1839.

47. See Douglass, *op. cit.*, pp. 123-124.

48. *Ibid.*

49. *Emancipator,* July 4, 1839.

50. See J. B. Wakeley, *Lost Chapters Recovered from the Early History of American Methodism,* 1858, pp. 438-461.

51. *Ibid.*

52. *African Repository*, X, 186-188 (Aug., 1834) ; *Colored American,* Mar. 4, Apr. 22, 1837; Nell, *op. cit.*, p. 321.

53. *Mirror of Liberty*, Jan., 1839.

54. *Ibid.*

55. Joseph Sidney, another young New York Negro, published also in 1809 *An Oration, Commemorative of the Abolition of the Slave Trade.*

56. The *Address* was partially reprinted in *Freedom's Journal,* Aug. 10, 1827.

57. Letters by Paul are to be found in the *Liberator,* Jan. 14 and Aug. 25, 1832; June 22 and Nov. 23, 1833; and Apr. 12, 1834. Accounts of the unpleasantness experienced in America by Mrs. Nathaniel Paul, an English woman, are given in the *Liberator,* Oct. 15, 1841, and Mar. 17, 1853.

58. *Colored American,* Oct. 14, 1837.

59. The account of the attack on Wright is reported in the *Emancipator,* Oct. 20, 1836.

60. *Colored American,* Aug. 12, 1837.

61. Theodore S. Wright and Samuel E. Cornish, *The Colonization Scheme,* 1840, p. 1.

62. *Liberator,* Sept. 24, 1831; *Minutes and Proceedings of the First Annual Convention of the People of Color,* 1831, pp. 6-8.

63. See letter of Russwurm dated February 26, 1827, printed in Carter G. Woodson, *The Mind of the Negro as Reflected in His Letters Written during the Crisis, 1800-1860,* 1926, p. 3.

64. *Liberator,* Apr. 16, 30, 1831.

65. See the *Colored American,* Jan. 27, 1838.

66. See the *African Repository,* XXVII, 324-325 (Nov., 1851).

67. David Ruggles, *The "Extinguisher" Extinguished,* 1834, p. 7.

68. *Ibid.,* p. 45.

69. See the *National Anti-Slavery Standard,* Aug. 13, 1840, and the *Emancipator,* Aug. 30, 1840.

70. *Liberator,* Dec. 21, 1849.

71. If more numbers of the *Mirror of Liberty* were issued, they are apparently no longer in existence. And there seems to be no references to them. However, in a letter to the *Emancipator,* Jan. 23, 1840, Ruggles expressed the hope that his health would permit his continuing the *Mirror,* thereby intimating possibly that the magazine had appeared throughout 1839.

72. *National Anti-Slavery Standard,* Apr. 6, 1843; *Liberator,* Dec. 21, 1849.

73. This couplet was used as a motto for an open letter by Ruggles published in the *Liberator,* Aug. 13, 1841. For a high tribute to Ruggles' character see Nell, *op. cit.,* Wendell Phillips' "Introduction."

74. The journal and the letters form a major part of the "Cuffe Manuscripts," now in the possession of the Free Public Library of New Bedford, Massachusetts. Besides the journal and letters, there are included in the manuscripts a number of documents bearing on Cuffe's life, especially on his work as a Colonizationist. With the exception of copious extracts from the manuscripts quoted in Henry Noble Sherwood's "Paul Cuffe," *Journal of Negro History,* VIII, 155-229 (Apr., 1923), little from Cuffe's journal and letters has been printed.

75. See Woodson, *The Negro in Our History,* pp. 143-145.

76. *Walker's Appeal in Four Articles,* ed. Henry Highland Garnet, 1848, p. v.

77. *Ibid.,* p. vi. See the *Liberator,* Jan. 29, 1831.

78. *Genius of Universal Emancipation,* XI, 15 (Apr., 1830).

79. See the *Liberator,* Jan. 22, 1831, and Garnet's introduction to his edition of the *Appeal.*

80. *Greensborough Patriot,* as quoted in the *Liberator,* Jan. 29, 1831.

81. *Ibid.* See also Adams, *op. cit.,* pp. 93-94, and Samuel J. May, *Some Recollections of the Anti-Slavery Conflict,* 1869, pp. 133-134.

82. *Walker's Appeal,* ed. Garnet, p. vi.

83. *Liberator,* Jan. 29, 1831.

84. H. Easton, *A Treatise on the Intellectual Character and Civil and Political Condition of the Coloured People of the United States,* 1837, p. 26.

85. *Report of a Concert in Behalf of the Oppressed,* 1836, p. 8.

86. See the *Liberator,* Nov. 11, 1843.

CHAPTER III

1. See Chapter I.

2. Reprinted, each time with additional comment, in 1835 and 1896.

3. *A Narrative of the Life and Adventures of Venture, a Native of Africa,* edition of 1896, notes.

4. *Ibid.,* p. 32.

5. *Narrative of . . . Ukawsaw Gronniosaw,* 1814, "Dedication."

6. The authorship has been attributed to Joseph Mitchell, who is named on the title-page as "the publisher" (see the card catalogue of the New York Public Library); and to William Walker, who is credited in the preface with having "collected and arranged" the facts (see Ralph Leslie Rusk, *The Literature of the Middle Western Frontier,* 1926, II, 293).

7. See Chapter I.

8. The pamphlet, published without date, takes Bayley's life up to 1836, and in the 1839 edition of Mott's *Biographical Sketches* it is referred to as having been printed.

9. *Anecdotes and Memoirs of William Boen,* 1834, p. 12.

10. The author of *Memoirs of Eleanor Eldridge* and of a "sequel," *Eleanor's Second Book* (1839), has been identified as Frances Whipple Greene. See *Rhode Island Historical Tracts, No. 11,* ed. Sidney S. Rider, 1889, Part I. For this information I am indebted to Miss Bella Gross of the Columbia University Library.

11. *Pennsylvania Freeman,* Jan. 24, 1839.

12. *Liberator,* Dec. 7, 1838.

13. It was reprinted in the *Emancipator,* Aug. 23 to Oct. 18, 1838.

14. See John Herbert Nelson, *The Negro Character in American Literature*, 1926, p. 66.

15. *Liberator*, Feb. 17, 1837.

16. *Cf.* Nelson, *op. cit.*, p. 61.

17. Another interesting fictive narrative published during the period is the *Life of Jim Crow* (1837). See Chapter IX.

18. *Emancipator*, Aug. 30, 1838. Also, a manuscript letter from Whittier to an unnamed "Friend," dated March 6, 1886. The letter is now in the Schomburg Collection of the New York Public Library.

19. Whittier is definitely referred to as early as Jan. 25, 1838, as the recorder of the story. See the *Emancipator* for that date. In the frequent allusions to the book from this time on he is usually named as the amanuensis.

20. It was being reprinted serially in the *Michigan Observer* by September, 1838. See the *Pennsylvania Freeman*, Sept. 13, 1838.

21. *Emancipator*, Aug. 30, 1838.

22. The attack on the authenticity of the *Narrative* was sponsored mainly by J. B. Rittenhouse, editor of the *Alabama Beacon*. See the *Beacon* for Mar. 29, Apr. 5, and July 26, 1838. For replies of leaders in the American Anti-Slavery Society see the *Emancipator*, Aug. 16, 23, 30, Sept. 20, and Oct. 25, 1838.

23. *Emancipator*, Oct. 25, 1838; *Liberator*, Nov. 2, 1838.

24. The letter (referred to above, Chapter III, Note 18) has never, so far as I know, been printed. The engraving by Patrick Reason, a New York Negro, which accompanied the published *Narrative* was made from the portrait mentioned by Whittier. See the *Narrative of James Williams*, 1838, "Editor's Note." Whittier was confused about the time of his meeting with Williams; as shown above, it was in the early winter of 1838.

25. *Emancipator*, Feb. 8, 1838; *Pennsylvania Freeman*, Mar. 29, 1838.

26. *Emancipator*, Aug. 30, 1838.

27. He should not be confused with a Jamaican James Williams who published an autobiography in England in 1838, nor with a James Williams who published an account of his work as an agent of the Underground Railroad in San Francisco in 1873.

28. See the comment in the *Liberator*, Mar. 9, 16, 1838; in

the *Emancipator,* Apr. 12, 1838; and in the *Herald of Freedom,* June 23, July 7, 1838.

29. See the *Liberator,* Jan. 22, 29, 1841. See also the "Catalogue of Anti-Slavery Publications in America from 1750 to 1863" in *The Proceedings of the American Anti-Slavery Society, 1864.*

30. A third English edition was published in 1839, and a fourth in 1848.

31. *Pennsylvania Freeman,* Apr. 5, 1838.

32. See the *Liberator,* Mar. 30, 1838. According to a poster advertising a speech which Roper was to deliver in Hull, England, on October 9, 1839, he was the year following the publication of the *Narrative* a student at University College, London.

33. *Liberator,* Mar. 30, 1838.

34. *Narrative of the Adventures and Escape of Moses Roper from American Slavery,* Edition of 1839, p. vii.

35. According to the *Liberator,* Mar. 30, 1838, Roper was so fair that when he was in Boston in 1835 he was "duly warned to train in the militia."

36. *Liberator,* Mar. 30, 1838.

37. See Chapter II.

38. See the *Liberator,* Dec. 5, 1833; Jan. 4, 1834; June 27, 1835; and Mar. 11, June 16, 1837.

39. A volume of Boyd's poems, interesting as imitations of Milton, was published in London in 1834. One of his best pieces, "The Vanity of Life," appeared in the *Liberator,* Feb. 16, 1833. Two poems by the "Colored Female of the Barbadoes" were published in the *Emancipator,* Sept. 27, 1837.

40. The book was copyrighted in the "Northern District of New York."

41. Testimonials regarding his character from two citizens of Zanesville are given in his book.

42. For interesting anecdotes regarding Cannon's queer character, see A. W. Wayman, *My Recollections of African M. E. Ministers,* 1881, pp. 7-10.

43. Stephen B. Weeks, "George Moses Horton: Slave Poet," *Southern Workman,* XLIII, 571-577 (Oct., 1914).

44. *Ibid.* See also Collier S. Cobb, *An American Man of Letters,* a reprint from the *University of North Carolina Magazine* for October, 1909.

45. See Kemp P. Battle, *History of the University of North Carolina,* 1907, I, 603-605.

46. *Ibid.*

47. George Moses Horton, *Poems by a Slave,* 1837, second preface. See also Weeks, *loc. cit.*

48. See the *Greensboro Daily News,* Nov. 24, 1929.

49. It is expressly stated in the preface of Horton's 1829 volume that some of his verses had "found their way into the Boston newspapers."

50. *Liberator,* Mar. 29, 1834.

51. See Cobb, *loc. cit.*

52. George Moses Horton, *Naked Genius,* 1865, "Introduction."

53. Weeks, *loc. cit.*

54. *Ibid.*

55. Cobb, *loc. cit.*

56. Horton, *Naked Genius,* "Introduction."

57. Battle, *loc. cit.*

58. Arthur A. Schomburg, *Bibliographical Checklist of American Negro Poetry,* 1916, p. 23.

59. *Cf.* Weeks, *loc. cit.*

60. Another poem printed in Battle's *History,* "The Pains of a Bachelor's Life," appears in slightly different form in *Naked Genius* as "The Cheerless Condition of Bachelorship."

61. See Cobb, *loc. cit. Cf.* Weeks, *loc. cit.*

62. Horton, *Naked Genius,* pp. 1, 160.

63. *Cf.* Schomburg, *loc. cit.*

64. See Weeks, *loc. cit.*

65. *Cf.* W. H. Morse, "Lemuel Haynes," *Journal of Negro History,* IV, 22-23 (Jan., 1919). See Timothy Mather Cooley, *Sketches of the Life and Character of the Rev. Lemuel Haynes, A. M.,* 1839, pp. 1-29.

66. Cooley, *op. cit.,* p. 30.

67. *Ibid.,* p. 41.

68. *Ibid.,* p. 61.

69. *Ibid.,* p. 39.

70. *Ibid.,* p. 275.

71. *Ibid.,* p. 96.

72. *Ibid.,* pp. 167-168.

73. *Ibid.,* p. 127.

74. *Colored American,* Apr. 8, 1837.
75. Cooley, *op. cit.,* p. 73.
76. *Ibid.,* p. 77.
77. *Colored American,* Mar. 11, 1837.
78. See Chapter IV.
79. Cooley, *op. cit.,* pp. 46-61.
80. *Ibid.,* p. 34.

Chapter IV

1. *National Anti-Slavery Standard,* Feb. 25, 1847.
2. See Alexander Crummell, *The Eulogy on Henry Highland Garnet, D.D.,* 1882. Crummell and Garnet were students at the Noyes Academy when it was broken up.
3. See William G. Allen, *The American Prejudice. against Color,* 1853, Chapter II.
4. *Liberator,* Feb. 19, 1841.
5. Frank A. Rollin, *Life and Public Services of Martin R. Delany,* 1883, p. 69.
6. See Carter G. Woodson, *The Education of the Negro Prior to 1861,* 1915, p. 277.
7. *African Repository,* XLV, 298 (Oct., 1869).
8. Rollin, *op. cit.,* p. 39.
9. Frederic May Holland, *Frederick Douglass: the Colored Orator,* 1891, p. 226.
10. Samuel Ringgold Ward, *The Autobiography of a Fugitive Negro,* 1855, p. 235.
11. *African Repository,* XXIX, 82-83 (Mar., 1852). See also the *National Anti-Slavery Standard,* July 1, 1847.
12. *Negro Population, 1790-1915,* 1918, p. 57.
13. Woodson, *op. cit.,* pp. 271-273.
14. See Carter G. Woodson, *The Negro in Our History,* 1927, p. 274.
15. "Declaration of the American Anti-Slavery Society," adopted at the convention held December 6, 1833. Printed in *The Anti-Slavery Almanac for 1836.*
16. *Pennsylvania Freeman,* Sept. 20, 1838.
17. Ward, *op. cit.,* pp. 31, 50.
18. *Liberator,* June 5, 1840.
19. *Liberator,* Jan. 28, 1842.
20. William Wells Brown, *The Rising Son,* 1874, p. 460.

21. Typical letters of Remond are to be found in the *Liberator*, Sept. 25, Oct. 16, 30, 1840; May 21, 1841; Mar. 11, 1842; Sept. 22, 1843; Apr. 18, June 9, 1845; and in the *National Anti-Slavery Standard*, Oct. 1, 1840. Typical speeches are wholly or partially reported in the *Liberator*, July 9, Nov. 19, 1841; June 23, 1854; July 10, 1857; Mar. 21, 1858; July 20, Aug. 1, 1860; and in the *National Anti-Slavery Standard*, Jan. 1, 1858.

22. *Liberator*, Nov. 19, 1841.

23. *Liberator*, Sept. 22, 1843.

24. Frederick Douglass, *Life and Times*, 1892, pp. 269-270. See also John Wallace Hutchinson, *Story of the Hutchinsons*, 1896, I, 70.

25. *Narrative of the Life of Frederick Douglass*, 1845, p. iv.

26. *Cf.* Holland, *op. cit.*, p. 8.

27. *Ibid.*, pp. 161-165.

28. See the *Rochester American*, Dec. 9, 1853, and the *Liberator*, Jan. 27, 1854.

29. Douglass, *Life and Times*, p. 327.

30. Typical letters are to be found in the *Liberator*, Sept. 26, Oct. 3, 10, 24, Nov. 28, 1845; Jan. 16, 30, Feb. 27, May 15, June 26, Aug. 28, Nov. 27, 1846; Jan. 29, Apr. 30, June 4, 11, 1847; and in the *National Anti-Slavery Standard*, Oct. 15, 1846; July 23, Aug. 10, Sept. 9, 23, 1847.

31. The letter was first printed in the *Liberator*, Nov. 27, 1846. For press comment regarding it see the *Liberator*, Jan. 1, 1847.

32. *People's Journal* (London), Apr. 24, 1847; *National Anti-Slavery Standard*, July 8, Sept. 30, 1847, and Jan. 27, 1848. See above, Chapter IV, Note 27.

33. Typical early speeches are in the *Liberator*, Feb. 6, 27, May 29, and July 3, 1846. Others are to be found in Frederick Douglass, *My Bondage and My Freedom*, 1855, pp. 407-418.

34. Quoted in the *Liberator*, May 30, 1845.

35. From a featured review in the New York *Tribune*, June 10, 1845. For varied press opinion on the *Narrative*, see the quotations given in the *Liberator*, May 23, 30, June 6, 20, 1845, and in the *National Anti-Slavery Standard*, June 19, 1845.

36. *Liberator*, Nov. 12, 1847. The translation, made by S. K. Parkes, appeared in Paris at the beginning of 1848 as *Vie de Frédéric Douglass*.

37. Garrison himself considered the attack absurd. See the *Liberator,* Jan. 29, 1847.

38. For varied press notices regarding *My Bondage and My Freedom,* see *Frederick Douglass' Paper,* June 20, 1856.

39. See the *Liberator,* June 17, 1842.

40. *Liberator,* Jan. 27, 1843.

41. *Liberator,* Nov. 17, 1843.

42. Quoted in the *Liberator,* Feb. 23, 1844, from the *Herald of Freedom.*

43. Quoted in the *Liberator,* Aug. 1, 1845, from the *Liberty Press* (Utica).

44. Typical of the verse tributes are the poems published in the *Liberator,* July 11, 1845; Mar. 27, May 1, Nov. 27, Dec. 4, 1846; Jan. 15, Feb. 5, May 14, Nov. 19, 1847; and in the *National Anti-Slavery Standard,* May 27, 1847.

45. Printed in the *Liberator,* June 8, 1849.

46. The pamphlet bears no publication date.

47. An interesting development resulting from Douglass' precipitated flight in 1859 was that for a lecture for which he had been engaged in Concord Henry David Thoreau appeared as his substitute. See the *Atlas and Bee* (Boston), Nov. 2, 1859, and the *Liberator,* Nov. 4, 1859.

48. For an earlier reply to Thompson's attack see the *Liberator,* Jan. 2, 1852.

49. A more direct and stronger appeal for Negro enlistments is *Men of Color, to Arms!* Written as a speech but possibly never spoken, it was printed as a broadside in 1863.

50. Holland, *op. cit.,* p. 313.

51. Douglass, *Life and Times,* p. 328.

52. *People's Journal* (London), Apr. 24, 1847; *Liberator,* June 4, 25, July 9, 23, Aug. 20, Sept. 24, 1847; *National Anti-Slavery Standard,* July 8, 1847, Jan. 27, 1848. See above, Chapter IV, Note 32.

53. *National Anti-Slavery Standard,* Sept. 30, 1847; Douglass, *My Bondage and My Freedom,* p. 395.

54. The last issue of *Douglass' Monthly* which I have been able to locate is that for November, 1861. Douglass himself referred to it as still being published in March, 1863 (see *Life and Times,* p. 414).

55. See the *North Star,* Aug. 11, 1848.

56. See the *Liberator*, July 4, 1851.
57. Douglass, *Life and Times*, p. 325.
58. *National Anti-Slavery Standard*, Jan. 27, 1848.
59. *Frederick Douglass' Paper*, May 18, 1860.
60. *North Star*, Dec. 22, 1848.
61. Manuscript letter from Douglass to I. C. Kendall, dated Jan. 3, 1854. In the New York Public Library.
62. Douglass, *Life and Times*, p. 324.
63. See Janet Marsh Parker, "Reminiscences of Frederick Douglass," *Outlook*, LI, 552-553 (Apr. 6, 1895).
64. Douglass, *Life and Times*, p. 324.
65. *Frederick Douglass' Paper*, May 18, 1860.
66. See the *Liberator*, Sept. 5, 1856. For the attack of a Negro on Douglass, see the letter by Robert Purvis published in the *Liberator*, Sept. 16, 1853.
67. *Liberator*, July 4, 1851.
68. Manuscript, in the library of the New York Historical Society.
69. Typical magazine articles are "The Color Line," *North American Review*, CXXXII, 567-577 (June, 1881); "The Condition of the Freedmen," *Harper's Weekly*, XXVII, 782-783 (Dec. 8, 1883); "The Future of the Colored Race," *North American Review*, CXLII, 437-440 (May, 1886); and "Reminiscences," *Cosmopolitan*, VII, 376-382 (Aug., 1889).
70. William Wells Brown, *Narrative of William W. Brown, a Fugitive Slave*, 1848, p. 26. The *St. Louis Times*, the paper for which Brown claimed he worked, was published from June, 1829, to some time in 1832, and Lovejoy was connected with it from 1828 to 1831. See William Hyde, *Encyclopaedia of the History of St. Louis*, 1899, III, 1313, 1363, and Henry Tanner, *History of the Rise and Progress of the Alton Riots*, 1878, pp. 3-5.
71. Josephine Brown, *Biography of an American Bondman*, 1856, p. 6.
72. *Ibid.*, pp. 45-50.
73. See *Douglass' Monthly*, IV, 469 (June, 1861).
74. Letters of this nature are to be found in the *National Anti-Slavery Standard*, Nov. 7, 1844; Jan. 30, 1845; Nov. 12, 1846; Feb. 11, 1847; Mar. 10, 31, Apr. 21, 1855; and in the *Liberator*, Nov. 2, 23, 1849; Feb. 8, 1850; Feb. 7, 1851; June 3,

1853; Sept. 22, Oct. 20, 1854; Aug. 17, Oct. 23, 1855; Oct. 30, Nov. 6, 20, 1857; Sept. 23, 1859.

75. The letter was published in the *Liberator*, Dec. 14, 1849.

76. Published in the *Liberator*, July 12, 1850.

77. Josephine Brown, *op. cit.*, p. 95.

78. *Liberator*, July 30, 1847; Feb. 11, 1848.

79. *Liberator*, Oct. 20, 1848; June 1, 1849.

80. Josephine Brown and a sister were placed by their father in a seminary in France in 1851, and later in a school in London. In 1854 both were schoolmistresses in England. See the *Liberator*, May 26, 1854.

81. *National Anti-Slavery Standard*, July 13, 1848.

82. William Wells Brown, *Three Years in Europe*, 1852, "Memoir" by William Farmer; Josephine Brown, *op. cit.*, pp. 82-83, 96-99; *Liberator*, May 26, 1854.

83. Josephine Brown, *op. cit.*, p. 83.

84. Brown probably got the song and the note from the *Liberator*, May 20, 1848.

85. See Levi Gaylord, "A Scene at New Orleans," *Liberator*, Sept. 21, 1838. See also the *Liberator*, Feb. 3, 1854. Early political enemies of Jefferson had not ignored the scandal (see William Cullen Bryant, *The Embargo; or, Sketches of the Times*, 1808).

86. Josephine Brown, *op. cit.*, pp. 96-99.

87. *Liberator*, Sept. 22, 1854.

88. Various press notices were reprinted in the *Liberator*, Jan. 12, 1855.

89. *Ibid.* See also the *Liberator*, Feb. 3, 1854.

90. William Wells Brown, *The Black Man*, 1863, "Preface."

91. There are a number of references to *Miralda*, and it is very possible that it was published serially in an antislavery newspaper or as a pamphlet.

92. William J. Simmons, *Men of Mark*, 1887, pp. 447-450.

93. William Wells Brown, *The Escape*, 1858, "Author's Preface."

94. Manuscript letter from Brown, written at Hartford, Nov. 29, 1857. In the Schomburg Collection of the New York Public Library.

95. See Chapter VII.

96. *Cf.* Holland, *op. cit.*, pp. 184-185.

97. Ward, *op. cit.*, p. 7.

98. *Ibid.*, p. 33. See also the *Liberator*, Feb. 27, 1852. *Cf.* John Herbert Nelson, *The Negro Character in American Literature*, 1926, p. 63.

99. Ward, *op. cit.*, p. 3.

100. *Ibid.*, p. 49. *Cf.* Brown, *The Black Man*, p. 284.

101. Ward, *op. cit.*, p. 32.

102. *Ibid.*, p. 33.

103. See I. Garland Penn, *The Afro-American Press*, 1892, p. 72.

104. *North Star*, Dec. 15, 1848.

105. *Ibid.*

106. *Anti-Slavery Reporter*, III (Third Series), 280 (Apr., 1855).

107. *Ibid.*, I (Third Series), 155 (July, 1853).

108. See Brown, *The Black Man*, p. 284.

109. The antislavery papers contain numerous excerpts from his speeches. A brief address on Daniel Webster and the Fugitive Slave Law, delivered in Faneuil Hall, Boston, was printed in the *Liberator*, Apr. 5, 1850.

110. Frederick Douglass, *Two Speeches*, [1857?], p. 7.

111. Ward, *op. cit.*, "Dedication."

112. There are numerous references to a pamphlet by Ward, *Reflections on the Gordon Rebellion*, published in Jamaica in 1866. I have been unable to locate a copy. For the probable date of Ward's death I am indebted to unpublished information gathered by Mr. Frank Cundall, of the Institute of Jamaica, Kingston, Jamaica.

CHAPTER V

1. Samuel Ringgold Ward, *The Autobiography of a Fugitive Negro*, 1855, p. 37.

2. See Martin R. Delany, *The Condition, Elevation, Emigration, and Destiny of the Colored People of the United States*, 1852, pp. 110-147.

3. William C. Nell, *The Colored Patriots of the American Revolution*, 1855, p. 10.

4. *Liberator*, December 18, 1846.

5. An account of Nell's break and subsequent quarrel with Douglass was reported in the *Liberator*, Sept. 30 and Dec. 16, 1853.

6. *National Era*, July 22, 1847.

7. See Chapter II.

8. Typical of Nell's published letters are those in the *Liberator*, Feb. 11, 1848, Mar. 23, 1862, Jan. 16, 1863, and Dec. 29, 1865.

9. *Colored American*, Sept. 9, 26, 1837.

10. William Wells Brown, *The Rising Son*, 1874, pp. 453-454.

11. See the note by William C. Nell in the *Liberator*, Sept. 8, 1854, on the reception of Smith into the New York Geographical Society and of John V. De Grasse, a Negro physician of Boston, into the Massachusetts Medical Society. See also Marshall Hall, *The Two-Fold Slavery of the United States*, 1854, p. 109. Hall, an English physician, said of Smith, "I can bear this testimony, that he is amongst the best informed physicians of the United States."

12. *Liberator*, June 1, 1838; *Colored American*, June 9, 1838; *Herald of Freedom*, June 9, 1838.

13. Smith's name does not appear in the paper as an editor after May 18, 1839. His resignation was announced in the number for June 22, 1839.

14. Reprinted in the *Liberator*, Feb. 16 and 23, 1844.

15. *Anglo-African*, 1, 5-17 (Jan., 1859).

16. *Liberator*, September 8, 1854.

17. Alexander Crummell, *The Eulogy on Henry Highland Garnet, D.D.*, 1882, p. 6.

18. Frank A. Rollin, *Life and Public Services of Martin R. Delany*, 1883, p. 39.

19. *Ibid.*, pp. 40-50.

20. The unpublished records of the Harvard Medical School show that Delany was a student there for the year 1851-52.

21. See Chapter VII.

22. W. P. and F. J. Garrison, *William Lloyd Garrison, 1805-1879: The Story of His Life Told by His Children*, 1885-1889, III, 193-194.

23. Rollin, *op. cit.*, p. 81. *Cf.* the *Liberator*, May 21, 1852.

24. See Rollin, *op. cit.*, pp. 327-367.

25. See Fanny Jackson-Coppin, *Reminiscences of School Life*, 1913, pp. 155-156.

26. See I. Garland Penn, *The Afro-American Press*, 1891, p. 52.

27. *National Anti-Slavery Standard,* Jan. 27, 1848.

28. William G. Allen, *The American Prejudice against Color,* 1853, p. 7.

29. See the *Anti-Slavery Reporter,* I (Third Series), 280 (Dec. 1, 1853).

30. Suggestive of his letters are those published in the *Liberator,* Jan. 9, 1852, Nov. 20, 1852, and July 22, 1853.

31. Manuscript letter from Glasgow, written at Edinburgh, June 3, 1859. In the Schomburg Collection of the New York Public Library.

32. See Jackson-Coppin, *op. cit.,* p. 157.

33. In a second publication, *The Review of the Revolutionary Elements of the Rebellion* (1868), Putnam identified himself as a colored man.

34. See A. W. Wayman, *My Recollections of African M. E. Ministers,* 1881, p. 51.

35. William T. Catto, *A Semi-Centenary Discourse,* 1857, p. 87.

36. William Douglass, *Sermons Preached in the African Protestant Episcopal Church of St. Thomas,* 1854, "Dedication." See George F. Bragg, *Men of Maryland,* 1914, pp. 47-54.

37. The speech was reported in the *Liberator,* May 22, 1840.

38. *Liberator,* May 22, 1840.

39. Henry Highland Garnet, *A Memorial Discourse,* 1865, James McCune Smith's "Introduction," p. 20; Crummell, *op. cit.,* p. 12.

40. Garnet, *op. cit.,* Smith's "Introduction," p. 52.

41. *Cf.* Crummell, *op. cit.,* p. 22. See the *North Star,* Dec. 15, 1848; *Douglass' Monthly,* IV, 557 (Nov., 1861); and the *Liberator,* Dec. 8, 1843, and Apr. 27, 1860.

42. Crummell, *op. cit.,* p. 13; Garnet, *op. cit.,* Smith's "Introduction," p. 40.

43. Penn, *op. cit.,* pp. 52, 83-88.

44. See "Letter from John Hooker," *Liberator,* June 20, 1851.

45. *Ibid.*

46. *Ibid.*

47. See John W. Cromwell, *The Negro in American History,* 1914, pp. 241-242.

48. James Theodore Holly, *A Vindication of the Capacity of the Negro Race for Self-Government,* 1857, "Preface."

49. *Ibid.*, "Advertisement."

50. See Robert J. Love, *Is Bishop Holly Innocent?*, 1883.

51. Cromwell, *op. cit.*, p. 242.

52. Crummell, *op. cit.*, p. 10.

53. Manuscript letter, undated, to Crummell from John Jay. In the Schomburg Collection of the New York Public Library. See Alexander Crummell, *The Shades and the Lights of a Fifty Years' Ministry*, [1894?], pp. 8-9.

54. *Ibid.*

55. *Ibid.*

56. See Cromwell, *op. cit.*, pp. 130-138.

57. Crummell, *The Shades and the Lights of a Fifty Years' Ministry*, p. 14.

58. *Ibid.*, p. 18. Also manuscript letters to Crummell from Thomas Fry, at one time Fellow and Tutor in Lincoln College, Oxford, dated July 15, 1848, and from Elizabeth D. Bland, dated Dec. 6, 1850. The letters are in the Schomburg Collection.

59. A reprint was published by the Massachusetts Colonization Society in 1857.

60. *African Repository*, XXXVII, 194 (July, 1861) and XXXVIII, 127 (Apr., 1862).

61. Manuscript letters to Crummell from George T. Downing, dated Apr. 19, 1860, and from Wm. A. Tyson, undated. In the Schomburg Collection.

62. I have not been able to locate a pamphlet copy of "Hope for Africa."

63. *African Repository*, XL, 257-267, 289-296 (Sept. and Oct., 1864); XLIV, 257-263 (Sept., 1867).

64. *African Repository*, XLVIII, 55-61, 162-168, 234-238 (Feb., June, and Aug., 1872).

65. Manuscript letter to Crummell from Thomas Kelton, an English clergyman, dated June 20, 1870. In the Schomburg Collection.

66. Manuscript letter to Crummell from William Croppinger, of the American Colonization Society, dated June 8, 1864. In the Schomburg Collection.

67. Manuscript letter to Crummell from James McCune Smith, undated, in the Schomburg Collection. See B. F. De Costa, *The Story of St. Philip's Church*, 1889, p. 38.

68. See William E. Burghardt Du Bois, *The Souls of Black Folk*, 1903, pp. 215-228.

69. The manuscripts, containing many sermons which were never printed, were collected by Mr. Arthur A. Schomburg, and now form a part of the Schomburg Collection of the New York Public Library.

70. See Arthur A. Schomburg, "Jupiter Hammon, before the New York African Society," *Amsterdam News,* Jan. 22, 1930.

71. See Penn, *op. cit.,* pp. 36-39. See also Frederick G. Detweiler, *The Negro Press in the United States,* 1922, p. 39.

72. The *Anglo-African* for 1859 was issued in a bound volume, which is not rare. I have also seen the numbers for January, February, and March, 1860. According to Penn, *op. cit.,* pp. 118-119, the publication was continued until 1861, the year of Thomas Hamilton's death.

73. *Liberator,* Dec. 31, 1858.

74. *Anglo-African,* I, 400 (Dec., 1859).

75. See lists of contributors, the pieces of a number of whom were signed with pseudonyms when published, in the *Anglo-African* for January, February, and March, 1860.

76. The number contains a rare engraving of Aldridge in the rôle of Titus Andronicus.

77. *Cf.* William Wells Brown, *The Rising Son,* 1874, p. 444.

78. *Cf.* Charles S. Johnson, "The Rise of the Negro Magazine," *Journal of Negro History,* XIII, 7-21 (Jan., 1928).

79. See Chapter VI.

80. See Johnson, *loc. cit.*

CHAPTER VI

1. See Chapters I and III.

2. See Chapters IV and V.

3. See Chapter III.

4. *National Anti-Slavery Standard,* Feb. 25, 1847. See Chapter IV.

5. Charles Edward Stowe, *Life of Harriet Beecher Stowe,* 1889, pp. 149-153.

6. See Fred Landon, "Henry Bibb, A Colonizer," *Journal of Negro History,* V, 437-447 (Oct., 1920).

7. Henry Bibb, *Narrative of the Life and Adventures of Henry Bibb,* 1849, "Preface."

8. Josiah Henson, *An Autobiography of Josiah Henson,* 1878, p. 156.

9. Harriet Beecher Stowe, *A Key to Uncle Tom's Cabin,* 1853, pp. 26-27.

10. What seems to have been an English edition of the *Life* was evidently published in 1852. I have been unable to locate a copy. See Josiah Henson, *Father Henson's Story of His Own Life,* 1858, pp. 203-204.

11. Harriet Beecher Stowe, *loc. cit.*

12. See the *Liberator,* Apr. 11, 1851, and *Father Henson's Story of His Own Life,* pp. 182-186.

13. In the 1878 edition of *An Autobiography* (p. 242) there is an advertisement of a "young people's illustrated edition" of *Uncle Tom's Story of His Life,* by John Lobb, with a preface by the Earl of Shaftesbury and "An Address to the Young People of Great Britain by Uncle Tom." It is stated that the book contains "notices of slave-life and incidents and anecdotes of Mr. Henson's personal history, received from himself, which have never before been published." I have not seen a copy. *Cf. Journal of Negro History,* III, 1-21 (Jan., 1918).

14. *An Autobiography of Josiah Henson,* p. 157.

15. Harriet Beecher Stowe, *op. cit.,* pp. 13-21.

16. *Narrative of the Sufferings of Lewis Clarke,* 1845, J. C. Lovejoy's "Preface."

17. *Ibid.,* pp. 39-40.

18. *Cf.* John Herbert Nelson, *The Negro Character in American Literature,* 1926, pp. 64-65.

19. For press comment regarding her lectures see the *Liberator,* Sept. 15, Oct. 6, 1854, and Aug. 17, 1855.

20. *Narrative of Sojourner Truth,* 1855, p. 197.

21. See Chapter II.

22. See Newman I. White, *American Negro Folk-Songs,* 1928, p. 463.

23. See John W. Cromwell, *The Negro in American History,* 1914, pp. 113-114.

24. See William Wells Brown, *The Rising Son,* 1874, pp. 531-532.

25. See the *Liberator,* May 5, 1854.

26. The letters were printed in the *Liberator,* Apr. 27, 1860, as copied from the *Syracuse Standard.*

27. There was a third edition in 1861.

28. I have not seen a copy of the original edition, which was probably issued in 1854 or 1855.

29. *Liberator*, Sept. 17, 1841.

30. See the *Liberator*, Oct. 1, 1841, Jan. 14, July 8, 1842, and Aug. 11, 1843.

31. *Liberator*, Oct. 1, 1841.

32. See the *Liberator*, May 31, 1850.

33. *Narrative of the Life of Henry Box Brown*, English Edition, 1851, "Appendix."

34. *Liberator*, Sept. 20, 1851.

35. *Liberator*, Oct. 22 and Dec. 17, 1852. See Josephine Brown, *Biography of an American Bondman*, 1856, pp. 75-81.

36. See the *Liberator*, Mar. 8, 1839.

37. See Chapter III.

38. See the *Liberator*, Jan. 22, 29, 1841.

39. See Chapter III.

40. See the extracts of press notices reprinted in the *Liberator*, Aug. 20, 1847.

41. See the review in the *Liberator*, Jan. 23, 1857.

42. *Letters of Lydia Maria Child*, 1883, pp. 90, 132.

43. *Cf.* Nelson, *op. cit.*, pp. 66-67.

44. See Chapter IV.

45. Frederick Douglass, *Two Speeches*, n. d., p. 34.

46. *Cf.* Frederic May Holland, *Frederick Douglass: the Colored Orator*, 1891, p. 259.

47. Quoted in *An Autobiography of Josiah Henson*, pp. 218-219.

48. See Chapter VII.

49. Daniel Alexander Payne, *Recollections of Seventy Years*, 1888, pp. 1-141.

50. See Chapter VII. According to Martin R. Delany, *The Condition, Elevation, Emigration, and Destiny of the Colored People of the United States*, 1852, p. 125, Payne published in 1850 "a small volume of his productions, *Pleasures and Other Miscellaneous Poems*, issued from the press of Sherwood & Company, Baltimore." I have been unable to locate a copy, and have seen no references to the work in Payne's autobiographical writings.

51. Manuscript letter from Reason to Alexander Crummell,

dated May 12, 1873. In the Schomburg Collection of the New York Public Library.

52. *Autographs for Freedom*, II, 221-229 (1854).

53. Typical of Reason's prose are "The Colored People's Industrial College," *Autographs for Freedom*, II, 11-15 (1854), and "Caste Schools," *Liberator*, Jan. 4, 1850.

54. William Wells Brown, *op. cit.*, p. 476. See John M. Langston, *From the Virginia Plantation to the National Capitol*, 1894, pp. 74-76.

55. *Autographs for Freedom*, II, 44-60 (1854).

56. Delany, *op. cit.*, pp. 119-120.

57. William Wells Brown, *The Black Man*, 1863, pp. 223-227.

58. See H. P. Davis, *Black Democracy*, 1928, p. 34.

59. See Daniel Alexander Payne, *The Semi-Centenary and the Retrospection of the African Meth. Episcopal Church*, 1866, pp. 172-175.

60. E. P. Rogers, *The Repeal of the Missouri Compromise Considered*, 1856, "Preface."

61. Brown, *The Black Man*, p. 274.

62. *Ibid.*, p. 272. Cf. *Minutes of the Second Presbyterian and Congregational Convention*, 1858, pp. 15-19.

63. See Carter G. Woodson, *The Mind of the Negro as Reflected in Letters Written during the Crisis, 1800-1860*, 1926, pp. 500-502. See also Cromwell, *op. cit.*, pp. 42-43.

64. See Chapter V.

65. The reprint of 1871 was published as a twentieth edition. There are several references to a verse pamphlet, called *Forest Leaves*, published by Frances Ellen Watkins in the early fifties. I have not located a copy.

66. William Still, *The Underground Rail Road*, 1878, pp. 755-780; George F. Bragg, *Men of Maryland*, 1914, pp. 64-79; Monroe N. Work, *The Negro Year Book*, 1925, p. 218. See Chapter VIII.

67. "Eliza Harris" was printed in *Frederick Douglass' Paper*, Dec. 25, 1853.

68. "The Tennessee Hero," the second "The Slave Mother," and "Rizpah" are among the six pieces added to *Poems on Miscellaneous Subjects* in the 1857 and later editions.

69. See Still, *op. cit.*, p. 799; *Frederick Douglass' Paper*, Mar. 11, 1865; and the *Liberator*, Mar. 3, 1865.

70. Published in the *Anglo-African,* I, 288-291, 311-313 (Sept. and Oct., 1859).

71. *Eventide: A Series of Tales and Poems,* published in Boston in 1854 as the work of "Effie Afton," has been attributed to Mrs. Harper (see William Cushing, *Initials and Pseudonyms, First Series,* 1885, p. 7). I have seen no mention of the work in any of the numerous biographical sketches on Mrs. Harper. Moreover, there seems to be no internal evidence to support the claim that she wrote the book and published it under a pseudonym.

72. Ann Plato, *Essays,* 1841, pp. 92, 110-112.

73. See the card catalogue of the Schomburg Collection of the New York Public Library.

CHAPTER VII

1. See Chapter V.

2. See *Negro Population, 1790-1915,* 1918, p. 33.

3. Paul Skeel Peirce, *The Freedmen's Bureau,* 1904, pp. 75-86; Laura Josephine Webster, "The Operation of the Freedmen's Bureau in South Carolina," *Smith College Studies in History,* I, 67-119 (Jan., 1916); L. P. Jackson, "The Educational Efforts of the Freedmen's Bureau and Freedmen's Aid Societies in South Carolina, 1862-1872," *Journal of Negro History,* VIII, 1-41 (Jan., 1923); and Carter G. Woodson, *The Negro in Our History,* 1927, pp. 589-591.

4. See Booker T. Washington, *The Story of the Negro,* 1909, II, 114-148.

5. *Negro Population, 1790-1915,* p. 409.

6. Monroe N. Work, *The Negro Year Book,* 1925, pp. 325-341.

7. *Ibid.,* p. 299.

8. *Ibid.*

9. *The Negro Church,* "Atlanta University Publications," *No. 8,* ed. W. E. Burghardt Du Bois, 1903, p. 126.

10. *Ibid.,* p. 111.

11. *Ibid.,* pp. 138-153. See Carter G. Woodson, *The History of the Negro Church,* 1921, pp. 286-299.

12. Washington, *op. cit.,* II, 196-259.

13. *Ibid.,* II, 148-171; *Economic Co-operation among Negro*

Americans, "Atlanta University Publications," *No. 12,* ed. W. E. Burghardt Du Bois, 1907, pp. 109-128; and Arthur A. Schomburg, *Masonic Truths,* n. d., pp. 5-43.

14. I. Garland Penn; *The Afro-American Press,* 1891, pp. 112-114.

15. It was said in the *Southern Workman,* XXIX, 1 (Jan., 1900): "The Southern Workman, founded by General Armstrong in 1872 and published monthly by the Hampton Normal and Agricultural Institute, is a sixty-four page magazine devoted to the interests of the black and red races of this country, and to the work done for them at this school. Each number contains information about some of the school's 1031 graduates, who have since. 1868, taught more than 130,000 children in 18 states in the South and West."

16. See Chapter V.

17. *The Negro Church,* ed. Du Bois, pp. 115, 121, 127, 133, 146.

18. See Chapter IX.

19. The Academy was organized on March 5, 1897. The objects as stated were: (1) The Promotion of Literature, Science, and Art; (2) The Culture of a Form of Intellectual Taste; (3) The Fostering of a Higher Education; (4) The Publication of Scholarly Works; (5) The Defense of the Negro against Vicious Assaults.

20. See *The New Negro,* ed. Alain Locke, 1925, pp. 231-238.

21. Mr. Chesnutt's "The Goophered Grapevine," included in *The Conjure Woman* (1899), was originally published in the *Atlantic Monthly,* LX, 254-260 (Aug., 1887). See Chapter VIII.

22. See Benjamin Brawley, *The Negro in Literature and Art,* 1929, pp. 141-148.

23. See Chapter III.

24. I might name as other pamphlet "narratives" of more than usual interest *The Life of James Mars, a Slave* (1866), Jacob Stroyer's *Sketches of My Life in the South* (1879), and *Life of Isaac Mason, as a Slave* (1893).

25. A Negro work similar in arrangement is James M Trotter's *Music and Some Highly Musical People* (1878)

26. See Chapter IV.

27. See Chapter VI.

28. Sarah H. Bradford had in 1869 published the briefer *Scenes in the Life of Harriet Tubman.* For references to Harriet V. Tubman's work as an agent of the Underground Railroad see Woodson, *The Negro in Our History,* p. 235.

29. See Fanny Jackson-Coppin, *Reminiscences of School Life,* 1913, p. 157.

30. See Elizabeth Keckley, *Behind the Scenes,* 1868, p. 320.

31. *Ibid.,* pp. 332-371.

32. I have seen no references to Elizabeth Keckley in writings on Lincoln and Mrs. Lincoln. *Behind the Scenes* is, however, usually classed with the Lincoln biographies. See George Thomas Ritchie, *A List of Lincolniana in the Library of Congress,* 1903, p. 39, and William H. Smith, *A Priced Lincoln Bibliography,* 1906, p. 32.

33. Another colored servant's observations in the household of a president of the United States are to be found in Paul Jennings' brief and uninteresting *A Colored Man's Reminiscences of James Madison* (1865).

34. Keckley, *op. cit.,* pp. 313-324.

35. Henry Ossian Flipper, *The Colored Cadet at West Point,* 1878, p. 35.

36. See Chapter VI.

37. See John W. Cromwell, *The Negro in American History,* 1914, pp. 115-126.

38. Daniel Alexander Payne, *Recollections of Seventy Years,* 1888, pp. 14-18, 56-71.

39. See Cromwell, *loc. cit.*

40. See Cromwell, *op. cit.,* pp. 155-164.

41. *Cf.* Brawley, *op. cit.,* p. 107.

42. Because of a contest over his election, Langston actually served in Congress only from September 23, 1890, to March 3, 1891. See *Biographical Dictionary of the American Congress, 1774-1927,* 1928, pp. 1202-1203.

43. See *Anthology of American Negro Literature,* ed. V. F. Calverton, 1929, pp. 16-17.

44. *Outlook,* LXVI, 533-534 (Nov. 3, 1900).

45. W. C. Jackson's *Boy's Life of Booker T. Washington,* 1922, based on *Up from Slavery,* is issued in a school edition.

46. There was an English edition in 1902. Translations appeared in German and Spanish by 1902, and in French by 1903.

47. See Chapter VIII.

48. Charles W. Chesnutt's *Frederick Douglass* appeared in the "Beacon Biographies," among the contributors to which were such scholars and critics as W. P. Trent, Edward Everett Hale, Jr., Ellery Sedgwick, and Norman Hapgood.

49. *Who's Who in America,* 1924, XIII, 1387.

50. *Cf.* the *Nation,* LXIV, 435-436 (June 9, 1892).

51. Mr. Grimké is the author of a considerable number of historical and sociological essays, contributed mainly to the "Occasional Papers" of the American Negro Academy, of which he was president from 1903 to 1919. Among the more valuable of the essays are *Right on the Scaffold, or, The Martyrs of 1822,* 1901, and "Meaning and Need of the Movement to Reduce Southern Representation," in *The Negro and the Elective Franchise,* 1905.

52. W. T. Andrews and J. W. Cromwell, *In Memoriam: Tally R. Holmes, of South Carolina, and Col. Joseph T. Wilson, of Virginia,* 1891, pp. 7-8.

53. Joseph T. Wilson, *Black Phalanx,* 1888, "Preface."

54. Andrews and Cromwell, *loc. cit.*

55. Wilson, *op. cit.,* 503-508.

56. It is a copious enlargement of a pamphlet with the same title published in 1881.

57. Besides the 1888, there were 1892 and 1897 editions.

58. There was a revised and enlarged edition of *The Underground Rail Road* in 1878.

59. Two other historians of the type of Wilson and Still should be named: John Wallace, author of *Carpetbag Rule in Florida* (1888); and Edward Augustus Johnson, author of *A School History of the Negro Race in America* (1891) and of *History of Negro Soldiers in the Spanish-American War and Other Items of Interest* (1899).

60. Before the end of 1883 there was also a "popular" one-volume edition.

61. The facts regarding Williams as here given were taken mainly from William J. Simmons, *Men of Mark,* 1887, pp. 549-556. According to Simmons, they were obtained directly from Williams.

62. George W. Williams, *History of the Negro Race in America,* 1883, I, iv.

63. *Westminster Review,* CXX, 254 (July, 1883).

64. *Cf.* the *Spectator,* LVI, 808-810 (June 23, 1883).

65. Williams, *op. cit.,* "Preface."

66. *Cf.* the *Literary World,* XIV, 72-73 (Mar. 10, 1883).

67. *Cf.* the *Academy,* XXIV, 107-108 (Aug. 18, 1883).

68. *Cf.* Brawley, *op. cit.,* p. 108.

69. Manuscript letters, dated Feb. 28, June 1, and June 9, 1883, from Williams to Mrs. S. R. Putnam. In the Schomburg Collection of the New York Public Library.

70. George W. Williams, *A History of the Negro Troops in the War of the Rebellion, 1861-1865,* 1888, "Preface."

71. *Ibid.,* p. 324.

72. *Ibid.,* pp. xiii-xiv.

73. *Nation,* LXIII, 498-500 (Dec. 31, 1896).

74. See Chapter V.

75. T. Thomas Fortune, *The Negro in Politics,* 1885, p. 36.

76. Simmons, *op. cit.,* pp. 785-791.

77. See Chapters III and V.

78. See Chapter VIII.

79. T. Thomas Fortune, *Black and White,* 1884, pp. 81-82.

80. Booker T. Washington, *Up from Slavery,* 1901, p. 316.

81. *Cf.* T. Thomas Fortune, "The Race Problem: the Negro Will Solve It," *Belford's Magazine,* V, 489-495 (September, 1890), and "The Negro's Place in American Life at the Present Day," in *The Negro Problem,* 1903, pp. 213-234.

82. *Atlantic Monthly,* LXXVIII, 322-328. (Sept., 1896).

83. See above, Chapter II, Note 64, and Chapter VI, Note 53. See also Frederick Douglass, *Life and Times;* 1892, pp. 353-357, and Frederic May Holland, *Frederick Douglass: The Colored Orator,* 1891, pp. 220-221.

84. A monograph of forty-four pages contributed by the State of New York to the United States educational exhibit at the Paris Exposition in 1900.

85. See B. F. Riley, *Life and Times of Booker T. Washington,* 1916, pp. 231-241.

86. *Who's Who in America,* 1926, XIV, 1685.

87. *Forum,* XXVI, 434-441 (Nov., 1898), XXXI, 341-349 (May, 1901).

88. *First Lessons in Greek; Adapted to the Greek Grammars of Goodwin and Hadley, and Designed as an Introduction to Xenophon's Anabasis and Similar Greek,* 1881.

89. Printed in 1886 as a pamphlet, entitled *The Birds of Aristophanes, a Theory of Interpretation.*

90. See Chapter IX.

91. A number of speeches delivered by Negroes in Congress have been reprinted from the *Congressional Globe* and the *Congressional Record* in Carter G. Woodson, *Negro Orators and Their Orations,* 1925, pp. 262-410.

92. *Congressional Record* . . . Forty-Third Congress, First Session, 1874, II, 407-410.

93. *Biographical Directory of the American Congress,* p. 941. See Cromwell, *op. cit.,* pp. 179-187.

94. Equally flamboyant in style is Elliott's eulogy on Charles Sumner, published in a pamphlet entitled *Sumner Memorial Meeting: Oration Delivered in Faneuil Hall, April 14, 1874, under the Auspices of the Colored Citizens of Boston, with the Address of Edward G. Walker, President of the Meeting, and a Sketch of the Proceedings,* 1874.

95. *Congressional Record* . . . Forty-Fourth Congress, First Session, 1876, IV, 2101-2104.

96. *Biographical Directory of the American Congress,* p. 751.

97. See Washington, *Up from Slavery,* p. 86, and Cromwell, *op. cit.,* pp. 164-170.

98. *Congressional Record* . . . Fifty-First Congress, Second Session, 1891, XXII, 1479-1482. See above, Chapter VII, Note 42.

99. The speech is given in full in John Mercer Langston, *From the Virginia Plantation to the National Capitol,* 1894, pp. 151-155.

100. Cromwell, *op. cit.,* pp. 171-178.

101. *Cf.* Brawley, *op. cit.,* p. 53.

102. The "Cotton States Exposition Address," which has been many times printed, was given in authorized form in Washington's *Up from Slavery,* pp. 218-225.

103. Washington quoted the "Harvard Alumni Dinner Address" in full in his *The Story of My Life and Work,* 1900, pp. 210-212.

104. Washington, *The Story of My Life,* pp. 236-242.

105. *Cf.* Washington, *Up from Slavery,* the chapter entitled "The Secret of Success in Public Speaking," pp. 238-266.

106. Anticipatory of Steward's serious historical work, *The Haitian Revolution, 1791-1804; or, Sidelights on the French Revolution*, 1914, was his *How the Black St. Domingo Legion Saved the Patriot Army in the Siege of Savannah, 1779*, published in 1899 as the seventh number in the *Occasional Papers of the American Negro Academy*.

107. See Chapter V.

108. *The Sun Do Move!* has been several times reprinted. Jasper has been made the subject of two full-length biographies, E. A. Randolph's *The Life of Rev. John Jasper*, 1884, and William E. Hatcher's *John Jasper, the Unmatched Negro Philosopher and Preacher*, 1908.

CHAPTER VIII

1. Blackson's account of the fall of man was, as the summary indicates, probably drawn from *Paradise Lost*. It is needless to say that there is no evidence of a borrowing from Milton's style.

2. See Chapter IV.

3. Benjamin Brawley, *The Negro in Literature and Art*, 1929, pp. 80-81.

4. *Who's Who in America*, 1930, XVI, 507; *Current Literature*, XXIV, 416 (Oct., 1900).

5. Carolyn Shipman, "The Author of *The Conjure Woman*, Charles W. Chesnutt," *Critic*, XXXV, 632-634 (July, 1899).

6. Besides his serious work, Mr. Chesnutt during his career as a writer contributed stories to the popular magazines. See Shipman, *loc. cit.*

7. See Chapter VII.

8. Typical of his sociological treatises are "A Plea for the American Negro," *Critic*, XXXVI, 160-163 (Feb., 1900), an attack on Booker T. Washington's defense of industrial education; "A Defamer of His Race," *Critic*, XXXVIII, 350-352 (Apr., 1901), an attack on William Hannibal Thomas' *The American Negro;* and "The Disfranchisement of the Negro," in *The Negro Problem*, 1903, pp. 77-125.

9. An edition, provided with an introduction by Joel E. Spingarn, was issued in 1929. It had by that time, like all the rest of Mr. Chesnutt's books, been long out of print.

10. The stories in the volume previously published include "The Goophered Grapevine," *Atlantic Monthly*, LX, 254-260 (Aug., 1887); "Po' Sandy," *Atlantic*, LXI, 605-611 (May, 1888); "The Conjurer's Revenge," *Overland Monthly*, XIII (New Series), 623-629 (June, 1889); and "Hot-Foot Hannibal," *Atlantic*, LXXXIII, 49-56 (Jan., 1899).

11. Shipman, *loc. cit.*

12. An "Uncle Julius" story not reprinted in *The Conjure Woman* is "Dave's Neckliss," *Atlantic Monthly*, LXIV, 500-508 (Oct., 1889).

13. See Chapter VII.

14. Lida Keck Wiggins, *The Life and Works of Paul Laurence Dunbar*, 1907, pp. 25-32.

15. Manuscript letter from Dunbar to the American Press Association, dated September 13, 1892. In the Schomburg Collection of the New York Public Library.

16. See Wiggins, *op. cit.*, pp. 33-35.

17. *Ibid.*, p. 49.

18. *Ibid.*, p. 55.

19. Howells' "Introduction" was reprinted in the *Bookman*, XXIII, 185-186 (Apr., 1900); in Wiggins, *The Life and Works of Paul Laurence Dunbar*, 1907; and in *The Complete Poems of Paul Laurence Dunbar*, 1913.

20. There was an English edition in 1897.

21. Paul Laurence Dunbar, *Lyrics of Lowly Life*, 1896, W. D. Howells' "Introduction."

22. See John W. Cromwell, *The Negro in American History*, 1914, pp. 188-194.

23. Before it was issued in book form, it had appeared in *Lippincott's Magazine*, LXIV, 579-669 (May, 1898).

24. Brawley, *op. cit.*, p. 67.

25. See Grace Isabel Colbron, "Across the Colour Line," *Bookman*, VIII, 338-341 (Dec., 1898).

26. It was reissued by the original publishers in 1903.

27. *Bookman*, XII, 512 (Jan., 1901).

28. The story had previously appeared in *Lippincott's Magazine*, LXVII, 515-594 (May, 1901). It was published in England in 1902 as *The Jest of Fate*.

29. *Cf.* John Chamberlain, "The Negro as Writer," *Bookman*, LXX, 603-611 (Feb., 1930).

30. *Cf.* the *Athenaeum,* Nov. 29, 1902.

31. *Bookman,* XXIII, 185-186 (Apr., 1906).

32. Dunbar's purely sociological essays, typical of which is "Negro Life in Washington," *Harper's Weekly,* XLIV, 32 (Jan. 13, 1900), are superficial and weak. *Cf.* Brawley, *op. cit.,* p. 74.

33. *Cf.* Brawley, *op. cit.,* pp. 73-74.

34. See Chapter VI.

35. For the identification of "Sanda" as Walter H. Stowers I am indebted to Mr. Arthur A. Schomburg.

36. Pauline E. Hopkins, *Contending Forces,* 1900, "Preface."

37. *Cf.* Chamberlain, *loc. cit.*

38. Two other strong stories of the color line never published in book form should be named: "The Sway-backed House," *Outlook,* LXVI, 588-593 (Nov. 3, 1900), and "The March of Progress," *Century,* LXI, 422-428 (Jan., 1901).

39. "The Wife of His Youth" was originally published in the *Atlantic Monthly,* LXXXII, 55-61 (July, 1898).

40. *Cf.* Brawley, *op. cit.,* p. 79.

41. W. D. Howells, "Mr. Charles W. Chesnutt's Stories," *Atlantic Monthly,* LXXXV, 699-701 (May, 1900).

42. B. Clark, *The Past, Present, and Future,* 1867, pp. 1-2.

43. *Ibid.*

44. *Walden's Miscellaneous Poems,* 1873, "Introduction."

45. *Walden's Sacred Poems,* 1877, William R. Taylor's "Introduction."

46. I have not seen a copy of the first edition of *Walden's Miscellaneous Poems.* The second edition, evidently including all the poems in the first and as many more, was published in 1873. See *Walden's Miscellaneous Poems,* 1873, p. 47.

47. *Liberator,* Dec. 12, 1862; William Francis Allen, Charles Pickard Ware, and Lucy McKim Garrison, *Slave Songs of the United States,* 1867, pp. xxxvii, 4.

48. See William Wells Brown, *The Rising Son,* 1874, pp. 475-476.

49. *Ibid.,* pp. 552-553.

50. *The Poetical Works of James Madison Bell,* 1901, B. W. Arnett's "Biographical Sketch."

51. See Carter G. Woodson, *Negro Orators and Their Orations,* 1925, pp. 263-267.

52. See Chapter VII.

53. T. Thomas Fortune, *Dreams of Life*, 1905, "Preface."

54. William J. Simmons, *Men of Mark*, 1887, p. 1122.

55. Albery A. Whitman, *The Rape of Florida*, 1884, p. 4.

56. Albery A. Whitman, *Not a Man, and Yet a Man*, 1877, "Preface."

57. Daniel Alexander Payne, *Recollections of Seventy Years*, 1888, p. 238.

58. Simmons, *op. cit.*, p. 1126.

59. Whitman, *The Rape of Florida*, Canto I.

60. Albery A. Whitman, *Twasinta's Seminoles*, 1890, p. 87.

61. Whitman, *The Rape of Florida*, p. 6.

62. *Ibid.*, pp. 3-4.

63. See Chapter VI.

64. William Still, *The Underground Rail Road*, 1878, p, 779.

65. A second edition is dated 1869. I have not seen a first edition.

66. Manuscript letter from Dunbar to Alexander Crummell, dated November 1, 1894. In the Schomburg Collection.

67. Dunbar, *Lyrics of Lowly Life*, p. 4, the first stanza of "The Poet and His Song."

68. *Ibid.*, p. xviii.

69. Brawley, *op. cit.*, p. 72.

70. See Wiggins, *op. cit.*, p. 29.

71. See *The Complete Poems of Paul Laurence Dunbar*, 1913, p. 287.

72. *Cf.* the *Academy*, LI, 625 (June 19, 1897).

73. Interestingly illustrated "gift-book" editions of poems by Dunbar, made up almost entirely of selections from the volumes named, include the following: *Poems of Cabin and Field* (1899); *Candle-Lightin' Time* (1901); *When Malindy Sings* (1903); *Li'l' Gal* (1904); *Howdy, Honey, Howdy* (1905); *Joggin' Erlong* (1906); *Chris'mus Is a' Comin'* (1907); and *Speakin' o' Christmas* (1914). *Cf.* Andrew M. Burris, "Bibliography of Works by Paul Laurence Dunbar, Negro Poet and Author, 1872-1906," *American Collector*, V, 69-73 (1927).

74. Howells, *loc. cit.*

CHAPTER IX

1. See Chapter I.

2. George Grove, *Dictionary of Music and Musicians*, ed. A. Fuller Maitland, 1904-1907, III, 361.

3. Mungo Park, *Travels in the Interior Districts of Africa, in the Years 1795, 1796 and 1797*, 1798, p. 198.

4. *Ibid.*, "Appendix."

5. The song was reprinted in America as early as 1800. See the *Columbian Phoenix, or Boston Review*, I, 350-352 (June, 1800).

6. *Putnam's Monthly*, V, 72-79 (Jan., 1853).

7. *Ibid.*

8. See motto for Chapter IV.

9. See Chapter IV.

10. See Chapter IV and motto for Chapter V.

11. See Chapter V and motto for Chapter III.

12. See Newman I. White, *American Negro Folk-Songs*, 1928, pp. 454-465.

13. *Cf. The New Negro*, ed. Alain Locke, 1925, pp. 238-271.

14. See motto for Chapter I.

15. See motto for Chapter VIII.

16. Traditional in Texas.

17. Traditional in Texas.

18. Traditional in Alabama.

19. MS. of Miss Alberta L. Pierson, of Columbus, Ohio.

20. See Guy B. Johnson, *John Henry, Tracing Down a Negro Legend*, 1929, pp. 18-19.

21. MS. of Miss Alberta L. Pierson.

22. Traditional in Texas.

23. Traditional in Alabama. *Cf.* E. C. Perrow, "Songs and Rhymes from the South," *Journal of American Folklore*, XXVIII, 129-190 (Apr.-June, 1915).

BIBLIOGRAPHIES

The bibliographies which follow form a brief record, necessarily representative rather than exhaustive, of American Negro literature as it existed at the end of the nineteenth century.

Works known to be by white authors are marked with an asterisk. Pseudonyms are indicated by quotation marks.

Unless otherwise specified, references are, so far as is known, to first editions. In case of important changes in later editions, separate entries are made.

If no finding place is indicated, it is to be understood that a work named is not rare or that at least one edition of it is in the Schomburg Collection of the New York Public Library, probably the most complete existing assembly of books by and about the Negro. Other libraries are either named in full or designated by the following abbreviations: AAS (American Antiquarian Society); BA (Boston Athenaeum); BPL (Boston Public Library); CHS (Connecticut Historical Society); ColU (Columbia University); CorU (Cornell University); LOC (Library of Congress); MHS (Massachusetts Historical Society); MdHS (Maryland Historical Society); NYHS (New York Historical Society); NYPL (New York Public Library); PHS (Pennsylvania Historical Society); UTS (Union Theological Seminary); and YU (Yale University).

I. THE BEGINNINGS OF NEGRO AUTHORSHIP, 1760-1790

A. Poetry

ANONYMOUS. The Negro's Prayer. In A. Mott, Editor, *The Life and Adventures of Olaudah Equiano; or Gustavus Vassa, the African,* 1829, p. 36.

BANNEKER, BENJAMIN. A Rimed Problem. In Will W. Allen, *Banneker, the Afro-American Astronomer,* 1921, pp. 62-63.

HAMMON, JUPITER. An Address to Miss Phillis Wheatly [*sic*], Ethiopian Poetess, in Boston, Who Came from Africa at Eight Years of Age, and Soon Became Acquainted with the Gospel of Jesus Christ. Broadside. Hartford, 1778. CHS

—— A Dialogue, Entitled, The Kind Master and Dutiful Servant. In Jupiter Hammon, *An Evening's Improvement,* n. d., pp. 23-28. NYHS

—— An Evening Thought: Salvation by Christ with Penetential [*sic*] Cries: Composed by Jupiter Hammon, a Negro Belonging to Mr. Lloyd, of Queen's Village, on Long Island, the 25th of December, 1760. Broadside. N. p., n. d. [1760?]. NYHS

—— A Poem for Children with Thoughts on Death. In Jupiter Hammon, *A Winter Piece,* n. d., pp. 23-24. CHS

VASSA, GUSTAVUS. Miscellaneous Verses, or Reflections on the State of My Mind during My First Convictions; of the Necessity of Believing the Truth, and Experiencing the Inestimable Benefits of Christianity. In Gustavus Vassa, *The Interesting Narrative of the Life of Olaudah Equiano, or Gustavus Vassa, the African,* 1789, II, 155-159.

WHEATLEY, PHILLIS. An Elegiac Poem, on the Death of That Celebrated Divine, and Eminent Servant of Jesus Christ, the Late Reverend and Pious George Whitefield, Chaplain to the Right Honourable the Countess of Huntingdon, &c., &c. . . . 8 pp. Boston, 1770. NYHS

—— An Elegy Sacred to the Memory of That Great Divine, the Reverend and Learned Dr. Samuel Cooper, Who Departed This Life December 29, 1783, Aetatis, 59. 8 pp. Boston, 1784. NYHS

—— His Excellency General Washington. *Pennsylvania Magazine, or American Monthly Museum,* II, 193 (Apr., 1776). NYPL

—— Liberty and Peace, a Poem. 4 pp. Boston, 1784. NYHS

—— Philis's [*sic*] Reply to the Answer in Our Last by the Gentleman in the Navy. *Royal American Magazine,* II, 34-35 (Jan., 1775). BPL

—— Poem Addressed, by Philis [*sic*], (a Young Affrican [*sic*], of Surprising Genius) to a Gentleman of the Navy, with His Reply. *Royal American Magazine,* I, 472-473 (Dec., 1774). NYPL

—— Poems and Letters. First Collected Edition. Edited by Chas. Fred. Heartman, with an Appreciation by Arthur A. Schomburg. 111 pp. New York, n. d. [1915].

—— Poems on Various Subjects, Religious and Moral. 124 pp. London, 1773.

―――― Thoughts on His Excellency Major General Lee Being Betray'd into the Hands of the Enemy by the Treachery of a Pretended Friend. *Proceedings of the Massachusetts Historical Society, 1863-64,* VII, 166-167 (1864).

―――― To Mrs. Leonard, on the Death of Her Husband. Broadside. N. p., n. d. [Boston, 1771?]. PHS

―――― To Mr. and Mrs. *******, on the Death of Their Infant Son. *Boston Magazine,* Sept., 1784, p. 488. BPL

―――― To the Hon'ble Thomas Hubbard, Esq; on the Death of Mrs. Thankfull Leonard. Broadside. Boston, 1773. PHS

―――― To the Rev. Mr. Pitkin on the Death of His Lady. Broadside. Boston, 1772. NYHS

B. Prose

BANNEKER, BENJAMIN. Benjamin Banneker's Pennsylvania, Delaware, Maryland and Virginia Almanack and Ephemeris, for the Year of Our Lord, 1792 ... 48 pp. Baltimore, n. d. [1791]. NYPL

―――― Banneker's Almanack, and Ephemeris for the Year of Our Lord, 1793 ... 44 pp. Philadelphia, n. d. [1792]. NYPL

―――― Benjamin Banneker's Pennsylvania, Delaware, Maryland and Virginia Almanack and Ephemeris. For the Year of Our Lord, 1794 ... 48 pp. Baltimore, n. d. [1793]. MHS

―――― Benjamin Banneker's Pennsylvania, Delaware, Maryland, and Virginia Almanac, for the Year of Our Lord 1795 ... 34 pp. Philadelphia, n. d. [1794]. NYHS

―――― Banneker's Maryland, Pennsylvania, Delaware, Virginia, Kentucky, and North Carolina Almanack and Ephemeris, for the Year of Our Lord 1796 ... 36 pp. Baltimore, 1795. MdHS

―――― Banneker's Virginia, Pennsylvania, Delaware, Maryland and Kentucky Almanack and Ephemeris, for the Year of Our Lord 1797 ... 44 pp. Richmond, 1796. AAS

―――― Copy of a Letter from Benjamin Banneker, to the Secretary of State, with His Answer. 12 pp. Philadelphia, 1792. NYPL

―――― Same, with a Biographical Sketch of Banneker. 15 pp. Philadelphia, 1792. NYHS

BELINDA. Petition of an African. *American Museum,* I, 463-465 (June, 1787). UTS

HAMMON, BRITON. A Narrative of the Uncommon Sufferings and Surprizing Deliverance of Briton Hammon, a Negro Man. 14 pp. Boston, 1760. NYHS

HAMMON, JUPITER. An Address to the Negroes in the State of New-York. 20 pp. New York, 1787. NYHS

—— An Evening's Improvement. Shewing, the Necessity of Beholding the Lamb of God. To Which Is Added, a Dialogue, Entitled, The Kind Master and Dutiful Servant. 28 pp. Hartford, n. d. NYHS

—— A Winter Piece: Being a Serious Exhortation, with a Call to the Unconverted: and a Short Contemplation on the Death of Jesus Christ. . . . 24 pp. Hartford, n. d. CHS

MARRANT, JOHN. Journal of John Marrant. 106 pp. London, 1789. Library of Mr. Arthur B. Spingarn, New York, N. Y.

—— A Narrative of the Lord's Wonderful Dealings with John Marrant, a Black. . . . Taken down from His Own Relation, Arranged, Corrected, and Published by the Rev. Mr. Aldridge. 40 pp. London, 1785.

—— A Sermon; Preached on the 24th Day of June, 1789, Being the Festival of St. John the Baptist, at the Request of the Right Worshipful the Grand Master, Prince Hall, and the Rest of the Brethren of the African Lodge of the Honourable Society of Free and Accepted Masons in Boston. 16 pp. Boston, 1789.

"OTHELLO." An Essay on Slavery. *American Museum*, IV, 414-417, 509-512 (Nov. and Dec., 1788). ColU

VASSA, GUSTAVUS. The Interesting Narrative of the Life of Olaudah Equiano, or Gustavus Vassa, the African. Written by Himself. 2 vols. London, 1789.

WHEATLEY, PHILLIS. Letter . . . to His Excellency Geo. Washington. *Pennsylvania Magazine, or American Monthly Museum*, II, 193 (Apr., 1776). NYPL

—— Letters of Phillis Wheatley, the Negro-Slave Poet of Boston. Edited by Charles Deane. 19 pp. Boston, 1864. NYPL

—— Letters to Obour Tanner. *Proceedings of the Massachusetts Historical Society, 1863-64,* VII, 267-279 (1864).

—— Poems and Letters. First Collected Edition. Edited by Chas. Fred. Heartman, with an Appreciation by Arthur A. Schomburg. 111 pp. New York, n. d. [1915].

II. Writings of the Pioneer Racial Leaders, 1790-1840

A. Pennsylvania Group

ALLEN, RICHARD. Letter on Colonization. *Freedom's Journal,* Nov. 2, 1827. CorU

———— The Life, Experience, and Gospel Labors of the Rt. Rev. Richard Allen, to Which Is Annexed the Rise and Progress of the : African Methodist Episcopal Church in the United States. . . . 69 pp. N. p., n. d. [1880]. ColU

ALLEN, RICHARD, and ABSALOM JONES. A Narrative of the Proceedings of the Black People, during the Late Awful Calamity in Philadelphia, in the Year 1793; and a Refutation of Some Censures Thrown upon Them in Some Late Publications. By A. J. and R. A. 24 pp. Philadelphia, 1794. NYPL

———— Some Letters of Richard Allen and Absalom Jones to Dorothy Ripley. *Journal of Negro History,* I, 436-443 (Oct., 1916).

ALLEN, RICHARD, and JACOB TAPISCO. The Doctrine and Discipline of the African Methodist Episcopal Church. 192 pp. Philadelphia, 1817.

ANONYMOUS. Letters from a Man of Colour, on a Late Bill before the Senate of Pennsylvania. 11 pp. N. p. [Philadelphia?], 1813.

FORTEN, JAMES. Letter to William Lloyd Garrison. *Liberator,* Sept. 17, 1841.

FORTEN, JAMES and RUSSELL PARROTT. An Address to the Humane and Benevolent Inhabitants of the City and County of Philadelphia. In *Minutes of the Proceedings of a Special Meeting of the Fifteenth American Convention, Held in Philadelphia, December 10, 1818,* n. d., pp. 69-72.

FORTEN, JAMES, JR. An Address Delivered before the Ladies' Anti-Slavery Society of Philadelphia, on the Evening of the 14th of April, 1836. 16 pp. Philadelphia, 1836. LOC

GLOUCESTER, JOHN. Address of John Gloucester to the First African Church. In William T. Catto, *A Semi-Centenary Discourse* . . . , 1857, pp. 56-57.

JONES, ABSALOM. A Thanksgiving Sermon, Preached January 1, 1808, in St. Thomas's, or the African Episcopal Church,

Philadelphia; on Account of the Abolition of the African Slave Trade. 24 pp. Philadelphia, 1808. NYPL

JONES, ABSALOM, and RICHARD ALLEN. A Narrative of the Proceedings of the Black People, during the Late Awful Calamity in Philadelphia, in the Year 1793; and a Refutation of Some Censures Thrown upon Them in Some Late Publications. By A. J. and R. A. 24 pp. Philadelphia, 1794. NYPL

—— Some Letters of Richard Allen and Absalom Jones to Dorothy Ripley. *Journal of Negro History*, I, 436-443 (Oct., 1916).

PARROTT, RUSSELL. An Address on the Abolition of the Slave Trade Delivered . . . 1st of January, 1816. 12 pp. Philadelphia, 1816. NYHS

PARROTT, RUSSELL, and JAMES FORTEN. An Address to the Humane and Benevolent Inhabitants of the City and County of Philadelphia. In *Minutes of the Proceedings of a Special Meeting of the Fifteenth American Convention, Held in Philadelphia, December 10, 1818*, n. d., pp. 69-72.

PURVIS, ROBERT. Appeal of Forty Thousand Citizens Threatened with Disfranchisement to the People of Pennsylvania. 18 pp. Philadelphia, 1838.

—— Eulogy on the Life and Character of James Forten, Delivered at Bethel Church, Philadelphia, March 30, 1842. In William C. Nell, *The Colored Patriots of the American Revolution*, 1855, pp. 166-181.

—— Letter on Frederick Douglass. *Liberator*, Sept. 16, 1853.

—— Letter to Hon. S. C. Pomeroy, Colonization Agent. *Liberator*, Sept. 12, 1862.

—— Speeches and Letters by Robert Purvis. Published by the Request of the Afro-American League. 23 pp. N. p., n. d.

—— A Tribute to the Memory of Thomas Shipley, the Philanthropist, Delivered at St. Thomas' Church, Nov. 23rd, 1836. 18 pp. Philadelphia, 1836. NYHS

SAUNDERS, PRINCE. An Address Delivered at Bethel Church, Philadelphia; on the 30th of September, 1818. Before the Pennsylvania Augustine Society, for the Education of People of Colour. . . . To Which Is Annexed the Constitution of the Society. 12 pp. Philadelphia, 1818.

—— Haytian Papers. A Collection of the Very Interesting Proclamations and Other Official Documents; Together with Some Account of the Rise, Progress, and Present State of the Kingdom of Hayti. 228 pp. London, 1816. NYPL

—— Same. 156 pp. Boston, 1818. NYPL

—— A Memoir Presented to the American Convention for Promoting the Abolition of Slavery, and Improving the Condition of the African Race, December 11th, 1818 . . . 19 pp. Philadelphia, 1818.

TAPISCO, JACOB, and RICHARD ALLEN. The Doctrine and Discipline of the African Methodist Episcopal Church. 192 pp. Philadelphia, 1817.

WHIPPER, WILLIAM. An Address, on Non-Resistance to Offensive Aggression. *Colored American*, Sept. 9, 16, 23, 30, 1837. NYHS

—— Eulogy on William Wilberforce, Esq. Delivered . . . on the Sixth of December, 1833. 35 pp. Philadelphia, n. d.

WHIPPER, WILLIAM, Editor. The National Reformer. Philadelphia. Vol. I, Nos. 1-12, Sept. 1838-Apr., 1839; Sept., 1839-Dec., 1839. PHS

B. New York Group

CORNISH, SAMUEL E. My Friends Will Please Notice. *Colored American*, Aug. 12, 1837. NYHS

CORNISH, SAMUEL E., and THEODORE S. WRIGHT. The Colonization Scheme, Considered in Its Rejection by the Coloured People. 26 pp. Newark, 1840.

CORNISH, SAMUEL E., Editor. The Colored American (called originally the Weekly Advocate). New York (after June 2, 1838, New York and Philadelphia). Mar. 4, 1837 (Vol. I, No. 9)–Dec. 29, 1838 (Vol. II, No. 45). CorU, LOC, NYHS, NYPL

—— Rights for All. New York. May 29 (Vol. I, No. 1), June 12, Aug. 7, Sept. 18, Oct. 9 (Vol. I, No. 6), 1829. AAS

CORNISH, SAMUEL E., and JOHN B. RUSSWURM, Editors. Freedom's Journal. New York. Mar. 30 (Vol. I, No. 3)-Sept. 14 (Vol. I, No. 27), 1827. NYHS, CorU

CORNISH, SAMUEL E., and JAMES McCUNE SMITH, Editors. The Colored American. New York and Philadelphia. Jan. 12-May 18, 1839. NYHS, NYPL, CorU

HUGHES, BENJAMIN F. Eulogium on the Life and Character of William Wilberforce, Esq. 16 pp. New York, 1833.

PAUL, NATHANIEL. An Address Delivered on the Celebration of the Abolition of Slavery in the State of New York, July 5, 1827. 24 pp. Albany, 1827.

———— Letter from Rev. Nathaniel Paul. *Liberator,* June 22, 1833.

———— Letter to William Lloyd Garrison. *Liberator,* Aug. 25, 1832.

RAY, CHARLES B., Publisher. The Colored American. New York. May 30, Aug. 15, 1840, Mar. 13, 1841. LOC, NYHS

RUGGLES, DAVID. An Antidote for a Poisonous Combination Recently Prepared by a "Citizen of New York," *alias* Dr. Reese, Entitled, "An Appeal to the Reason and Religion of American Christians," &c. Also, David Meredith Reese's "Humbugs" Dissected. 32 pp. New York, 1838.

———— The "Extinguisher" Extinguished, or, David M. Reese, M.D., Used Up. 48 pp. New York, 1834.

———— Letter. *Liberator,* July 14, 1843.

———— Letter to William Lloyd Garrison. *Liberator,* July 22, 1844.

RUGGLES, DAVID, Editor. The Mirror of Liberty. New York. Aug., 1838, Jan. 1839. NYHS

RUSSWURM, JOHN B. Letter to the *United States Gazette. Liberator,* Apr. 30, 1831.

RUSSWURM, JOHN B., Editor. Freedom's Journal. New York. Sept. 21, 1827 (Vol. I, No. 28)-Mar. 21, 1828 (Vol. I, No. 52); Dec. 12, 1828 (Vol. II, Whole No. 89); Jan. 2, 1829 (Vol. II, Whole No. 92); Feb. 14, 1829 (Vol. II, Whole No. 98). NYHS

RUSSWURM, JOHN B., and SAMUEL E. CORNISH, Editors. Freedom's Journal. New York. Mar. 30 (Vol. I, No. 3)-Sept. 14 (Vol. I, No. 27), 1827. NYHS, CorU

SIDNEY, JOSEPH. An Oration, Commemorative of the Abolition of the Slave Trade in the United States. Delivered before the Wilberforce Philanthropic Association, in the City of New York, on the Second of January, 1809. 20 pp. New York, 1809. NYHS

SIPKINS, HENRY. An Oration on the Abolition of the Slave Trade; Delivered in the African Church in the City of New York, January 2, 1809. 21 pp. New York, 1809.

SMITH, JAMES McCUNE, and SAMUEL E. CORNISH, Editors. The Colored American. New York and Philadelphia. Jan. 12-May 18, 1839. NYHS, NYPL, CorU

WILLIAMS, PETER, JR. A Discourse, Delivered on the Death of Capt. Paul Cuffe, before the New York African Institution, in the African Methodist Episcopal Zion Church, October 21, 1817. 16 pp. New York, 1817.

—— Discourse Delivered in St. Philip's Church, for the Benefit of the Coloured Community of Wilberforce, in Upper Canada; on the Fourth of July, 1830. 16 pp. New York, 1830.

—— Letter to the Citizens of New York. *African Repository*, X, 186-188 (Aug., 1834). ColU

—— An Oration on the Abolition of the Slave Trade; Delivered in the African Church in the City of New York, Jan. 1, 1808. 28 pp. New York, 1808.

WRIGHT, THEODORE S. Address, before the Convention of the New York State Anti-Slavery Society, on the Acceptance of the Annual Report, Held at Utica, Sept. 20, 1837. *Colored American,* Oct. 14, 1837. NYHS

—— An Address to 3,000 Colored Citizens of New York Who Are the Owners of 120,000 Acres of Land in the State of New York, Given to Them by Gerrit Smith, of Peterboro . . . 20 pp. New York, 1846.

—— Letter to Dr. Alexander, of the Princeton Theological Seminary. *Emancipator,* Oct. 20, 1836. NYPL

WRIGHT, THEODORE S., and SAMUEL E. CORNISH. The Colonization Scheme, Considered in Its Rejection by the Coloured People. 26 pp. Newark, 1840.

C. New England Group

CUFFE, PAUL. A Brief Account of the Settlement and Present Situation of the Colony of Sierra Leone, in Africa. 12 pp. New York, 1812. Free Public Library, New Bedford, Mass.

—— Extracts from the Journal and Letters of Paul Cuffe. In Henry N. Sherwood, "Paul Cuffe," *passim, Journal of Negro History,* VIII, 155-229 (Apr., 1923).

EASTON, HOSEA. A Treatise on the Intellectual Character and Civil and Political Condition of the Coloured People of the United States, and the Prejudice Exercised Towards Them. 56 pp. Boston, 1837.

HALL, PRINCE. A Charge Delivered to the African Lodge, June 24, 1797, at Metonony, Mass. 8 pp. N. p., n. d.

LEWIS, R. B. Light and Truth, Collected from the Bible and Ancient and Modern History, Containing the Universal History of the Colored and the Indian Races, from the Creation of the World to the Present Time. 400 pp. Boston, 1844. (Copyrighted in 1836).

WALKER, DAVID. Walker's Appeal, in Four Articles; Together with a Preamble, to the Coloured Citizens of the World, but in Particular and Very Expressly to Those of the United States of America. . . . 80 pp. Boston, 1829.

——— Same, with Additions. 88 pp. Boston, 1830. ColU

D. Miscellaneous

ANONYMOUS. Minutes and Proceedings of the First Annual Convention of the People of Colour, Held by Adjournment in the City of Philadelphia, from the Sixth to the Eleventh of June, Inclusive, 1831. 20 pp. Philadelphia, 1831.

BRADLEY, JAMES. Letter, on the Conditions of the Coloured People of Cincinnati. *Herald of Freedom*, Mar. 7, 1835.

COKER, DANIEL. Journal of Daniel Coker, a Descendant of Africa, from the Time of Leaving New York in the Ship Elizabeth, Capt. Sebor, for . . . Africa, in Company with Three Agents and about Ninety Persons of Color. . . . 52 pp. Baltimore, 1820.

III. BIOGRAPHY, POETRY, AND MISCELLANEOUS WRITINGS, 1790–1840

A. Biography

ANONYMOUS. Anecdotes and Memoirs of William Boen, a Coloured Man, Who Lived and Died near Mount Holly, New Jersey. To Which Is Added the Testimony of Friends of Mount Holly Monthly Meeting concerning Him. 18 pp. Philadelphia, 1834. NYHS

——— Incidents in the Life of Solomon Bayley. 8 pp. Philadelphia, n. d. NYPL

"JIM CROW." Life of Jim Crow. . . . Written by Himself. 24 pp. Philadelphia, 1837.

*"MR. FISHER." Slavery in the United States: a Narrative of the Life and Adventures of Charles Ball, a Black Man. 400 pp. Lewiston, Pa., 1836. LOC

——— Same. 517 pp. New York, 1837.

*GREENE, FRANCES WHIPPLE. Memoirs of Eleanor Eldridge. 128 pp. Providence, 1838.

——— Eleanor's Second Book. 128 pp. Providence, 1839.

GRONNIOSAW, JAMES ALBERT UKAWSAW. A Narrative of the Most Remarkable Particulars in the Life of James Albert Ukawsaw Gronniosaw, an African Prince. As Related by Himself. 32 pp. Leeds, 1814.

*HILDRETH, RICHARD. The Slave: or, Memoirs of Archy Moore. 2 vols. Boston, 1836.

JOHNSTONE, ABRAHAM. The Address of Abraham Johnstone, a Black Man, Who Was Hanged at Woodbury, in the County of Gloucester and State of New Jersey on Saturday the the [sic] 8th Day of July Last; to the People of Colour. . . . 47 pp. Philadelphia, 1797. NYPL

*"LADY OF BOSTON." Memoir of Mrs. Chloe Spear, a Native of Africa, Who Was Enslaved in Childhood, and Died in Boston, January 3, 1815. . . . Aged 65 Years. iii, 108 pp. Boston, 1832. NYHS

*LESTER, CHARLES E. Chains and Freedom: or, The Life and Adventures of Peter Wheeler, a Colored Man Yet Living. 260 pp. New York, 1839.

*MITCHELL, JOSEPH, Publisher. The Missionary Pioneer; or, A Brief Memoir of the Life, Labours, and Death of John Stewart, (Man of Colour,) Founder under God of the Mission among the Wyandotts at Upper Sandusky, Ohio. 96 pp. New York, 1827.

ROPER, MOSES. Narrative of the Adventures and Escape of Moses Roper, from American Slavery; with a Preface by the Rev. T. Price, D.D. 193 pp. London, 1837.

"A RUNAWAY SLAVE." Recollections of Slavery. Emancipator, Aug. 23, 30, Sept. 6, 13, 20, 27, Oct. 4, 11, 18, 1838. NYPL

Venture. A Narrative of the Life and Adventures of Venture, a Native of Africa; but Resident above Sixty Years in the United States of America. 24 pp. New London, 1798.

Williams, James. Narrative of James Williams, an American Slave, Who Was for Several Years a Driver on a Cotton Plantation in Alabama. 108 pp. New York, 1838. (Recorded by John G. Whittier.)

B. Poetry

"Ada." My Country. *Liberator,* Jan. 4, 1834.

——— The Slave. *Liberator,* Mar. 11, 1837.

——— The Slave Girl's Farewell. *Liberator,* June 27, 1835.

Anonymous. The Black Beauty. *Freedom's Journal,* June 8, 1827. NYHS

Cannon, N. C. The Rock of Wisdom; an Explanation of the Sacred Scriptures . . . To Which Are Added Several Interesting Hymns. 144 pp. N. p., 1833.

Horton, George Moses. Hope of Liberty. 22 pp. Raleigh, N. C., 1829. NYHS

——— Naked Genius. 160 pp. Raleigh, N. C., 1865. BA

——— Pains of a Bachelor's Life. In Kemp P. Battle, *History of the University of North Carolina,* 1907, I, 604-605. NYPL

——— Pleasures of a Bachelor's Life. In Kemp P. Battle, *History of the University of North Carolina,* 1907, I, 604. NYPL

——— Poems by a Slave. 23 pp. Philadelphia, 1837. (A reprint of *Hope of Liberty.*) NYPL

——— Verses Addressed to Horace Greeley. In Collier Cobb, *An American Man of Letters,* 1909, pp. 7-8. NYPL

C. Miscellaneous

Cannon, N. C. The Rock of Wisdom; an Explanation of the Sacred Scriptures . . . to Which Are Added Several Interesting Hymns. 144 pp. N. p., 1833.

Haynes, Lemuel B. The Character and Work of a Spiritual Watchman Described. A Sermon Delivered at Hinesburgh, February 23, 1791. At the Ordination of the Rev. Reuben Parmerlee. 22 pp. Litchfield, n. d. NYHS

―――― The Important Concerns of Ministers, and the People of Their Charge, at the Day of Judgment. Illustrated in a Sermon, Delivered at Rutland, Orange Society, August 22d, 1797, at the Interment of the Rev. Abraham Carpenter, Their Worthy Pastor. 26 pp. Rutland, 1798.

―――― A Letter, to the Rev. Hosea Ballou . . . In *An Interesting Controversy between Rev. Lemuel Haynes . . . and Rev. Hosea Ballou . . .* , 1805, pp. 13-23.

―――― Letters, Sayings, and Extracts from Sermons and Addresses. In Timothy Mather Cooley, *Sketches of the Life and Character of the Rev. Lemuel Haynes, A. M.,* 1839, *passim.*

―――― Mystery Developed; or, Russell Colvin, (Supposed to be Murdered), in Full Life, and Stephen and Jesse Boorn, His Convicted Murderers Rescued from Ignominious Death by Wonderful Discoveries. 48 pp. Hartford, 1820.

―――― The Nature and Importance of True Republicanism. 24 pp. N. p., 1801.

―――― The Substance of the Rev. Lemuel Haynes' Sermon Delivered at Rutland, (West Parish,) Oct. 28th, 1804. Occasioned by the Sudden and Much Lamented Death of the Late Rev. Job Swift, D.D. In Job Swift, *Discourses on Religious Subjects,* 1805, pp. 23-32.

―――― Universal Salvation, a Very Ancient Doctrine: with Some Account of the Life and Character of Its Author; a Sermon Delivered at Rutland, West Parish, Vermont, in the Year 1805. In *An Interesting Controversy between Rev. Lemuel Haynes . . . and Rev. Hosea Ballou . . .* , 1805, pp. 3-7. (*Universal Salvation,* available in many different editions, was being reprinted as late as 1860.)

IV. WRITINGS OF THE LEADING NEGRO ANTI-SLAVERY AGENTS, 1840-1865

BROWN, WILLIAM WELLS. The American Fugitive in Europe. Sketches of Places and People Abroad; with a Memoir by the Author. 320 pp. Boston, Cleveland, and New York, 1855. (The American edition, enlarged, of *Three Years in Europe,* London, 1852.)

—— The American Slave Trade. *Liberty Bell,* 1848, pp. 231-238.

—— The Black Man: His Antecedents, His Genius, and His Achievements. 288 pp. New York and Boston, 1863.

—— Same, enlarged. 312 pp. Boston, 1863.

—— Clotel; or, The President's Daughter. A Narrative of Slave Life in the United States. 245 pp. London, 1853.

—— Clotelle: A Tale of the Southern States. 104 pp. Boston, 1864.

—— Clotelle; or, The Colored Heroine, a Tale of the Southern States. 114 pp. Boston, 1867.

—— A Description of William Wells Brown's Original Panoramic Views of the Scenes in the Life of an American Slave, from His Birth in Slavery to His Death, or His Escape to His First Home of Freedom on British Soil. 5, 48 pp. London, 1849. BPL

—— The Escape; or, A Leap for Freedom. A Drama in Five Acts. 52 pp. Boston, 1858. BPL

—— Fling Out the Anti-Slavery Flag. In *Narrative of William W. Brown, a Fugitive Slave,* London, 1849, p. ii.

—— A Lecture Delivered before the Female Anti-Slavery Society of Salem, at Lyceum Hall, Nov. 14, 1847. . . . Reported by Henry M. Parkhurst, Phonographic Reporter. 22 pp. Boston, 1847.

—— Letter. *National Anti-Slavery Standard,* Jan. 30, 1845. NYHS

—— Letter from Darlington, England. *Liberator,* Feb. 8, 1850.

—— Letter from Glasgow. *Liberator,* Feb. 7, 1851.

—— Letter from London, Oct. 12, 1849. *Liberator,* Nov. 2, 1849.

—— Letter from London, Aug. 29, 1854. *Liberator,* Sept. 22, 1854.

—— Letter to Enoch Price, My Old Master. *Liberator,* Dec. 14, 1849.

—— Letter to Mr. Garrison. *Liberator,* Sept. 23, 1859.

—— My Southern Home: or, The South and Its People. 253 pp. Boston, 1880.

—— Narrative of William W. Brown, a Fugitive Slave. xi, 110 pp. Boston, 1847. LOC

——— Same, revised. 144 pp. Boston, 1848. ColU
——— Same, revised. 168 pp. London, 1849.
——— The Negro in the American Rebellion. His Heroism
and His Fidelity. 380 pp. Boston, 1867. NYPL
——— The Rising Son; or, The Antecedents and Advance-
ment of the Colored Race. 555 pp. Boston, 1874.
——— St. Domingo: Its Revolutions and Its Patriots. A
Lecture, Delivered before the Metropolitan Athenaeum,
London, May 16, and at St. Thomas' Church, Philadelphia,
December 20, 1854. 38 pp. Boston, 1855. NYHS
——— Speech at the Annual Meeting of the Massachusetts
Anti-Slavery Society. *Liberator,* Feb. 8, 1856.
——— Three Years in Europe: or, Places I Have Seen and
People I Have Met. . . . With a Memoir of the Author, by
William Farmer. xxxii, 312 pp. London, 1852.
——— To the Public. *Liberator,* July 12, 1850.
——— Visit of a Fugitive Slave to the Grave of Wilberforce.
Autographs for Freedom, II, 70-76 (1854).
BROWN, WILLIAM WELLS, Compiler. The Anti-Slavery Harp:
a Collection of Songs for Anti-Slavery Meetings. 47 pp.
Boston, 1848. NYPL
DOUGLASS, FREDERICK. Abolition Fanaticism in New York.
Speech by a Runaway Slave from Baltimore, at an Abolition
Meeting in New York, Held May 11, 1847. 8 pp. Baltimore,
1847. LOC
——— Address . . . Delivered . . . Apr. 16, 1883. On the
Twenty-First Anniversary of Emancipation in the District of
Columbia. 16 pp. Washington, 1883. NYPL
——— Address . . . Delivered at the Erection of the Wing
Monument, at Mexico, Oswego Co., N. Y., September 11th,
1855. 20 pp. Syracuse, 1855. NYPL
——— Address Delivered . . . at the Third Annual Fair of
the Tennessee Colored Agricultural and Mechanical Associa-
tion on Thursday, September 18, 1873, at Nashville, Tennes-
see. 19 pp. Washington, 1873.
——— Address . . . Delivered in the Metropolitan A. M. E.
Church, Washington, D. C., Tuesday, January 9th, 1894, on
the Lessons of the Hour. In Which He Discusses the
Various Aspects of the So-Called, but Mis-Called, Negro
Problem. . . . 36 pp. Baltimore, 1894. LOC

—— Address on Wendell Phillips. In George Lowell Austin, *Life and Times of Wendell Phillips,* 1884, pp. 413-425.

—— Addresses of the Hon. W. D. Kelley, Miss Anna E. Dickinson, and Mr. Frederick Douglass, at a Mass Meeting, Held at National Hall, Philadelphia, July 6, 1863, for the Promotion of Colored Enlistments. 8 pp. N. p., n. d. ColU

—— The Anti-Slavery Movement. A Lecture . . . before the Rochester Ladies' Anti-Slavery Society. 44 pp. Rochester, 1855.

—— Bibles for the Slaves. *Liberty Bell,* 1848, pp. 121-127.

—— Claims of the Negro Ethnologically Considered. An Address, before the Literary Societies of Western Reserve College . . . July 12, 1854. 37 pp. Rochester, 1854. NYHS

—— The Color Line. *North American Review,* CXXXII, 567-577 (June, 1881).

—— The Condition of the Freedmen. *Harper's Weekly,* XXVII, 782-783 (Dec. 8, 1883).

—— The Constitution of the United States: Is It Pro-Slavery, or Anti-Slavery? 16 pp. Halifax, n. d. [1860?]. LOC

—— Correspondence between the Rev. Samuel H. Cox, D.D., of Brooklyn, L. I., and Frederick Douglass, a Fugitive Slave. 16 pp. New York, 1846. NYHS

—— Eulogy of the Late Hon. Wm. Jay. . . . Delivered on the Invitation of the Colored Citizens of New York City, in Shiloh Presbyterian Church, New York, May 12, 1859. 32 pp. Rochester, 1859.

—— Extract from a Speech Made at New York, May, 1853. *Autographs for Freedom,* II, 251-255 (1854).

—— Extracts from a Speech Delivered in London. *Liberator,* July 13, 1846.

—— The Folly of Our Opponents. *Liberty Bell,* 1845, pp. 166-173.

—— Frederick Douglass in Behalf of George Latimer. *Liberator,* Nov. 18, 1842.

—— The Future of the Colored Race. *North American Review,* CXLII, 437-440 (May, 1886).

—— The Heroic Slave; a Thrilling Narrative of the Adventures of Madison Washington, in Pursuit of Liberty.

31 pp. N. p., 1853. (Originally published in *Autographs for Freedom*, I, 174-239, 1853.)

——— Introduction to John Wallace Hutchinson, *Story of the Hutchinsons*, 1896, pp. xv-xviii.

——— John Brown. An Address . . . at the Fourteenth Anniversary of Storer College, Harper's Ferry, West Virginia, May 30, 1881. 28 pp. Dover, New Hampshire, 1881.

——— Lecture at the Dedication of the Douglass Institute, Baltimore. *Liberator*, Oct. 13, 1865.

——— Lecture on Haiti. . . . 57 pp. Chicago, 1893. LOC

——— Lectures on American Slavery. . . . Delivered at Corinthian Hall, Rochester, N. Y. 32 pp. Buffalo, 1851.

——— Letter. *New York Tribune*, May 14, 1846. NYPL

——— Letter I. *Liberator*, Sept. 26, 1845.

——— Letter II. *Liberator*, Oct. 10, 1845.

——— Letter III. *Liberator*, Oct. 24, 1845.

——— Letter IV. *Liberator*, Nov. 26, 1845.

——— Letter V. *Liberator*, Jan. 30, 1846.

——— Life and Times of Frederick Douglass, Written by Himself. With an Introduction by George L. Ruffin. xx, 518 pp. Hartford, 1881.

——— Same, enlarged. 752 pp. Boston, 1892.

——— Men of Color, to Arms! Broadside. Rochester, 1863. NYPL

——— Milton Clarke—Liberty Party—George Bradburn. *Liberator*, Nov. 1, 1844.

——— My Bondage and My Freedom. With an Introduction by Dr. James McCune Smith. 464 pp. New York, 1855.

——— Narrative of the Life of Frederick Douglass, an American Slave. Written by Himself. xvi, 125 pp. Boston, 1845.

——— The Negro Exodus from the Gulf States. *Journal of Social Science*, XI, 1-21 (May, 1880).

——— Oration, Delivered in Corinthian Hall, Rochester . . . July 5, 1852. . . . 39 pp. Rochester, 1852.

——— Oration of Frederick Douglass. In *Inaugural Ceremonies of the Freedmen's Memorial Monument to Abraham Lincoln, Washington City, April 14, 1876*, St. Louis, 1876, pp. 16-26.

—— Reminiscences. *Cosmopolitan,* VII, 376-382 (Aug., 1889).

—— Speech Delivered in Belfast, Ireland. *Liberator,* Feb. 6, 1846.

—— Speech Delivered in Glasgow. *Liberator,* May 29, 1846.

—— Speech on the Death of William Lloyd Garrison, at the Garrison Memorial Meeting in the 15th Street Presbyterian Church, Monday, June 2, 1879. 8 pp. N. p., n. d. [Washington, 1879?].

—— Three Addresses on Relations Subsisting between the White and Colored People of the United States. 68 pp. Washington, 1886. NYPL

—— Third Decade of the American Anti-Slavery Society. *Liberator,* Jan. 29, 1864.

—— To My Old Master. Letter to Thomas Auld. *Liberator,* Dec. 22, 1848.

—— Two Speeches . . . One on West India Emancipation, Delivered at Canandaigua, Aug. 4th, and the Other on the Dred Scott Decision, Delivered in New York on the Occasion of the Anniversary of the American Abolition Society, May, 1857. 46 pp. Rochester, n. d. [1857?].

—— U. S. Grant and the Colored People. 8 pp. Washington, 1872.

—— What the Black Man Wants. In *The Equality of All Men before the Law, Claimed and Defended; in Speeches by Hon. William D. Kelley, Wendell Phillips, and Frederick Douglass, and Letters from Elizur Wright and Wm. Heighton,* Boston, 1865, pp. 36-39.

—— What Shall We Do with Four Million Slaves, if They are Emancipated? In William Wells Brown, *The Black Man,* 1863, pp. 184-187.

—— Why Is the Negro Lynched? 38 pp. Bridgewater, 1895. LOC

DOUGLASS, FREDERICK, Editor. Douglass' Monthly. Rochester. Vol. III, Nos. 8, 11, Vol. IV, Nos. 1, 3, 6, Jan., Apr., June, Aug., Nov., 1861. NYHS

—— Frederick Douglass' Paper. Rochester. June 26, 1851 (Vol. IV, No. 27)-Dec. 18, 1851 (Vol. IV, No. 52); Dec. 24, 1852 (Vol. VI, No. 1)-Dec. 16, 1853 (Vol. VI, No. 52); Dec. 23, 1853 (Vol. VII, No. 1)-Dec. 15, 1854 (Vol. VII,

No. 52); Jan. 11, 1856 (Vol. IX, No. 4)-Dec. 5, 1856 (Vol. IX, No. 51). [Incomplete.] Library of Mr. Arthur B. Spingarn, New York, N. Y.

—— The North Star. Rochester. Dec. 3, 1847 (Vol. I, No. 1)-Dec. 29, 1848 (Vol. II, No. 1). CorU

REMOND, CHARLES LENOX. Letter. *Pennsylvania Freeman*, Nov. 14, 1839. NYPL

—— Letter. *Liberator*, Apr. 18, 1845.

—— Letter, from Buffalo. *Liberator*, Sept. 22, 1843.

—— Letter, from Edinburgh. *Liberator*, Oct. 30, 1840.

—— Letter, from Manchester, England. *Liberator*, Sept. 25, 1840.

—— Letter, from New-Castle-on-Tyne. *Liberator*, May 21, 1841.

—— Letter to the Rev. C. B. Ray. *Liberator*, Oct. 16, 1840.

—— Letter to William Lloyd Garrison. *Liberator*, Mar. 11, 1842.

—— New Age of Anti-Slavery. *Liberty Bell*, 1845, pp. 187-191.

—— Remarks before the Massachusetts House of Representatives. *Liberator*, Feb. 25, 1841.

—— Speech before the Hibernian Anti-Slavery Society, Held in Abbey Hall, Dublin. *Liberator*, Nov. 19, 1841.

—— Speech . . . Delivered May 30, 1854 . . . before the New England Anti-Slavery Society. *Liberator*, June 23, 1854.

—— Speech Delivered at the 25th Meeting of the American Anti-Slavery Society in New York City, on Wednesday, May 13, 1858. *Liberator*, May 21, 1858.

WARD, SAMUEL RINGGOLD. The Autobiography of a Fugitive Negro: His Anti-Slavery Labours in the United States, Canada, and England. 412 pp. London, 1855.

—— Speech on the Fugitive Slave Bill. *Liberator*, Apr. 5, 1850.

V. WRITINGS OF THE RACIAL LEADERS, 1840-1865

A. Writers Interested Mainly in Historical and Sociological Studies

ALLEN, WILLIAM G. The American Prejudice against Color: an Authentic Narrative, Showing How Easily the Nation Got into an Uproar. 107 pp. London, 1853.

—— Placido. *Autographs for Freedom*, I, 177-182 (1853).

—— Wheatley, Banneker, and Horton; with Selections from the Poetical Works of Wheatley and Horton, and the Letter of Washington to Wheatley, and of Jefferson to Banneker. 48 pp. Boston, 1849. YU

ANONYMOUS. Objects and Regulations of the Institute for Colored Youth, with a List of the Officers and Students, and the Annual Report of the Board of Managers, for the Year 1859. 27 pp. Philadelphia, 1859.

CAMPBELL, ROBERT. A Pilgrimage to My Motherland. An Account of a Journey among the Egbas and Yorubas of Central Africa, in 1859-60. 145 pp. New York and Philadelphia, 1861.

CLARK, M. M. Tract on Slavery, by . . . a Coloured Man Now on a Visit to England from the United States of America. 23 pp. Bradford, 1847.

CLARK, PETER H. The Black Brigade of Cincinnati. 30 pp. Cincinnati, 1864. NYHS

"COLORED AMERICAN." The Late Contemplated Insurrection in Charleston, S. C., with the Execution of Thirty-Six of the Patriots. 12 pp. New York, 1850.

CRAFT, WILLIAM and ELLEN. Letters, from England. *Liberator*, Jan. 16, 1863.

DELANY, MARTIN ROBISON. The Attraction of Plants. *Anglo-African*, I, 17-20 (Jan., 1859).

—— Blake; or, The Huts of America: a Tale of the Mississippi Valley, the Southern United States, and Cuba. *Anglo-African*, I, 20-29, 37-43, 69-79, 104-114, 129-140, 160-172, 193-203 (Jan.-July, 1859).

—— The Condition, Elevation, Emigration, and Destiny of the Colored People of the United States, Politically Considered. 215 pp. Philadelphia, 1852.

—— Eulogy on the Life and Character of the Rev. Fayette Davis. 15 pp. N. p. [Pittsburgh?], 1847. NYHS

—— The International Policy of the World towards the African Race. In Frank A. Rollin, *Life and Public Services of Martin R. Delany*, 1883, pp. 313-327.

—— Letter to Garrison. *Liberator*, May 21, 1852.

—— Official Report of the Niger Valley Exploring Party. 75 pp. New York, 1861.

—— Origin and Objects of Ancient Freemasonry; Its Introduction into the United States, and Legitimacy among Colored Men. 40 pp. Pittsburgh, 1853.

—— Political Destiny of the Colored Race on the American Continent. . . . A Speech Delivered at Cleveland in 1854. In Frank A. Rollin, *Life and Public Services of Martin R. Delany*, 1883, pp. 327-367.

—— Principia of Ethnology. The Origin of Races and Color, with an Archaeological Compendium of Ethiopian and Egyptian Civilization, from Years of Careful Examination and Enquiry. Second Edition. 109 pp. Philadelphia, 1880.

—— Reflections on the War. In Frank A. Rollin, *Life and Public Services of Martin R. Delany*, 1883, pp. 309-313.

FORTEN, CHARLOTTE L. Letters, from St. Helena's Island, Beaufort, S. C. *Liberator*, Dec. 12, 19, 1862.

GLASGOW, J. EWING. The Harper's Ferry Insurrection: Being an Account of the late Outbreak in Virginia, and of the Trial and Execution of Capt. John Brown, Its Hero. Second Edition. 47 pp. Edinburgh, 1860.

GLOUCESTER, S. H. A Discourse Delivered on the Occasion of the Death of James Forten, Sr. . . . April 17, 1842. 36 pp. Philadelphia, 1843.

MEACHUM, JOHN B. An Address to All the Colored Citizens of the United States. 62 pp. Philadelphia, 1846.

MITCHELL, W. M. The Underground Railroad. xi, 172 pp. London, 1860.

NELL, WILLIAM COOPER. The Colored Patriots of the American Revolution, with Sketches of Several Distinguished Colored Persons: to Which Is Added a Brief Survey of the Condition and Prospects of Colored Americans. . . . With an Introduction by Harriet Beecher Stowe. 396 pp. Boston, 1855.

—— Extracts from a Speech Delivered at an Emancipation Day Celebration in Boston on January 1, 1863. *Liberator*, Jan. 16, 1863.

—— Farewell to the Liberator. *Liberator*, Dec. 29, 1865.

—— Letter. *Liberator*, Feb. 24, 1860.

—— Progress of Justice and Equality. *Liberator*, Feb. 11, 1848.

—— Services of Colored Americans in the Wars of 1776 and 1812. 24 pp. Boston, 1851.

—— Same augmented, with an Introduction by Wendell Phillips. 40 pp. Boston, 1852.

—— Speech on the Crispus Attucks Commemoration. *Liberator*, Mar. 28, 1862.

PAUL, THOMAS. Speech of Thomas Paul, a Colored Student of Dartmouth College. *Liberator*, Feb. 19, 1841.

PRINCE, NANCY. Letter to William Lloyd Garrison. *Liberator*, Sept. 17, 1841.

PUTNAM, LEWIS H. A Review of the Cause and Tendency of the Issues between the Two Sections of the Country, with a Plan to Consolidate the Views of the People of the United States in Favor of Emigration to Liberia, as the Initiative to the Efforts to Transform the Present System of Labor in the Southern States into a Free Agricultural Tenantry, by the Respective Legislatures, with the Support of Congress to Make It a National Measure. 29 pp. Albany, 1859.

—— The Review of the Revolutionary Elements of the Rebellion, and of the Aspect of Reconstruction; with a Plan to Restore Harmony between the Two Races in the Southern States. 29 pp. Brooklyn, 1868.

REASON, CHARLES L. Caste Schools. *Liberator*, Jan. 4, 1850.

—— The Colored People's Industrial College. *Autographs for Freedom*, II, 11-15 (1854).

SMITH, JAMES MCCUNE. Abolition of Slavery and the Slave Trade in the French and British Colonies. *Colored American*, June 9, 1838. NYHS

—— An Address to the People of the United States. In *Proceedings of the Colored National Convention Held in Philadelphia, October 16th, 17th and 18th, 1855,* Salem, New Jersey, 1855, pp. 30-33.

—— Civilization: Its Dependence on Physical Circumstances. *Anglo-African*, I, 5-17 (Jan., 1859).

—— Extracts from James M'Cune Smith's Journal. *Colored American*, 1837, *passim.* NYHS

—— Freedom—Liberty. *Autographs for Freedom*, II, 241 (1854).

—— Freedom and Slavery for Africans. *Liberator*, Feb. 16 and 23, 1844. (Reprinted from the New York *Tribune*.)

—— Introduction to Frederick Douglass, *My Bondage and My Freedom*, 1855, pp. xvii-xxxi.

—— John Murray (of Glasgow). *Autographs for Freedom*, I, 46-50 (1853).

—— A lecture on the Haytien Revolutions, with a Sketch of the Character of Toussaint L'Ouverture. 28 pp. New York, 1841. NYPL

—— Sketch of the Life and Labors of Rev. Henry Highland Garnet. In Henry Highland Garnet, *A Memorial Discourse*, 1865, pp. 1-68. NYPL

"A Southerner." Sketches of the Higher Classes of the Colored Society in Philadelphia. 116 pp. Philadelphia, 1841.

B. Writings of the Church Leaders

Catto, William T. A Semi-Centenary Discourse, Delivered in the First African Presbyterian Church, Philadelphia, on the Fourth Sabbath of May, 1857: with a History of the Church from Its First Organization. 111 pp. Philadelphia, 1857.

Crummell, Alexander. Africa and America: Addresses and Discourses. vii, 466 pp. Springfield, Mass., 1891.

—— The Black Woman of the South, Her Neglects and Her Needs. 16 pp. N. p., n. d.

—— Charitable Institutions in Colored Churches. . . . Paper Read before the Ministers' Meeting of Colored Churches, Dec. 5, 1892. 8 pp. N. p., n. d.

—— Civilization the Primal Need of the Race. Occasional Papers, No. 3, of the American Negro Academy. 19 pp. Washington, 1897.

—— A Defense of the Negro Race in America, from the Assaults and Charges of Rev. J. L. Tucker, D. D., of Jackson, Miss., in His Paper before the "Church Congress" of 1882, on "The Relations of the Church to the Colored Race." Prepared and Published at the Request of the Colored Clergy of the Protestant Episcopal Church. 36 pp. Washington, 1883.

—— The Duty of a Rising Christian State to Contribute to the World's Well-Being and Civilization, and the Means by Which It May Perform the Same. The Annual Oration before the Common Council and the Citizens of Monrovia,

Liberia, July 26, 1855: Being the Day of National Independence. 31 pp. London, 1856.

────── The English Language in Liberia. The Annual Address before the Citizens of Maryland County, Cape Palmas, Liberia, July 26, 1860. Being the Day of National Independence. 32 pp. New York, 1861.

────── The Eulogy on Henry Highland Garnet, D.D. . . . Delivered . . . May 4, 1882. 29 pp. Washington, 1882.

────── The Future of Africa: Being Addresses, Sermons, etc., etc., Delivered in the Republic of Liberia. 372 pp. New York, 1862.

────── God's Dealing with Nations and Peoples, and the Lessons It Teaches. A Sermon Preached in the Methodist Church, Monrovia, at the Anniversary of the Liberian Missionary Society, January 21, 1867. *African Repository,* XLIV, 257-263 (Sept., 1867). ColU

────── The Greatness of Christ, and Other Sermons. 352 pp. New York, 1882.

────── The Man: the Hero: the Christian! A Eulogy on the Life and Character of Thomas Clarkson: Delivered in the City of New York, December, 1846. 44 pp. New York, 1847.

────── Obligation of the American Black Men for the Redemption of Africa. . . . To Colored Students, Undergraduates, at Xenia, Lincoln, Howard, and Other Colleges in the United States of America, on Matters Pertaining to the Conversion of Africa. *African Repository,* XLVIII, 55-61, 162-168, 234-238 (Feb., June, Aug., 1872). ColU

────── The Race Problem in America. 19 pp. Washington, 1889.

────── The Relations and Duties of Free Colored Men in America to Africa. A Letter to Charles B. Dunbar, M. D., Esq., of New York City. 54 pp. Hartford, 1861.

────── The Responsibility of the First Fathers of a Country for Its Future Life and Character. The Address Delivered to the Young Men of Monrovia, Liberia, West Africa, 1st December, 1863. *African Repository,* XL, 257-267, 289-296 (Sept., Oct., 1864). ColU

────── The Shades and the Lights of a Fifty Years' Ministry. Jubilate. A Sermon. . . St. Luke's Church, Washington, D. C., December 9, 1894. 31 pp. N. p., n. d. NYHS

———— The Social Principle among a People, and Its Bearing on Their Progress and Development. A Discourse, Delivered on Thanksgiving Day, Nov. 25, 1875, in Saint Mary's Chapel, Washington, D. C. 23 pp. N. p., n. d. NYHS

———— The Solution of Problems. The Duty and Destiny of Man. The Annual Sermon at the Commencement of Wilberforce University, June 16, 1895. 16 pp. Philadelphia, n. d.

DOUGLASS, WILLIAM. Annals of the First African Church, in the United States of America, Now Styled the African Episcopal Church of St. Thomas, Philadelphia. 172 pp. Philadelphia, 1862.

———— Sermons Preached in the African Protestant Episcopal Church of St. Thomas, Philadelphia. 251 pp. Philadelphia, 1854.

GARNET, HENRY HIGHLAND. An Address—to the Slaves of the United States. Rejected by the National Convention, 1843. In Walker's *Appeal*, ed. Henry Highland Garnet, 1848, pp. 89-96. NYHS

———— Defense of the African Civilization Society. *Liberator*, Dec. 27, 1860.

———— Letter. *Liberator*, Dec. 8, 1843.

———— Letter to His Wife, from Liverpool, Sept. 13, 1861. *Douglass' Monthly*, IV, 557 (Nov., 1861). NYHS

———— A Memorial Discourse . . . Delivered in the Hall of the House of Representatives, Washington, D. C., on Sabbath, February 12, 1865. With an Introduction by James McCune Smith. 91 pp. Philadelphia, 1865.

———— The Past and the Present Condition, and the Destiny of the Colored Race; a Discourse Delivered at the Fifteenth Anniversary of the Female Benevolent Society of Troy, N. Y., Feb. 14, 1848. 29 pp. Troy, 1848.

———— Speech of H. H. Garnet, a Colored Young Man, and a Member of the Oneida Institute, at the Late Anniversary of the A. A. S. S. *Liberator*, May 22, 1840.

GARNET, HENRY HIGHLAND, Editor. Walker's *Appeal*. 96 pp. New York, 1848. NYHS

HOLLY, JAMES THEODORE. A Vindication of the Capacity of the Negro Race for Self-Government, and Civilized Progress, as Demonstrated by Historical Events of the Haitian Revolution. . . . 48 pp. New Haven, 1857.

LOGUEN, JERMAIN W. Letter. *Liberator,* May 5, 1854.
—— Letter from His Tennessee Mistress, and Loguen's Reply. *Liberator,* Apr. 27, 1860.
PENNINGTON, JAMES W. C. Covenants Involving Moral Wrong Are Not Obligatory upon Man: a Sermon Delivered in the Fifth Congregational Church, Hartford, on Thanksgiving Day, Nov. 17th, 1842. 12 pp. Hartford, 1842. LOC
—— The Fugitive Blacksmith; or, Events in the History of James W. C. Pennington, Pastor of a Presbyterian Church, New York, Formerly a Slave in the State of Maryland, United States. 84 pp. London, 1849.
—— The Great Conflict Requires Great Faith. *Anglo-African,* I, 343-345 (Oct., 1859).
—— Introduction to Ann Plato, *Essays,* Hartford, 1841, pp. xvii-xx.
—— A Review of Slavery and the Slave Trade. *Anglo-African,* I, 93-96, 123-126, 155-159 (Mar.-May, 1859).
—— The Self-Redeeming Powers of the Colored Races of the World. *Anglo-African,* I, 314-320 (Oct., 1859).
—— A Text Book of the Origin and History, &c., &c., of the Colored People. 96 pp. Hartford, 1841.
—— A Two Years' Absence; or, A Farewell Sermon Preached in the Fifth Congregational Church, Nov. 2, 1845. 31 pp. Hartford, 1845.
ROGERS, E. P. An Extract of the Opening Sermon, Delivered . . . before the Presbyterian and Congregational Convention, Assembled at Philadelphia, Aug. 28, 1857. In *Minutes of the Second Presbyterian and Congregational Convention,* New York, 1858, pp. 15-19.
RUSH, CHRISTOPHER. Short Account of the Rise and Progress of the African Methodist Episcopal Church in America. Written . . . with the Aid of George Collins. 106 pp. New York, 1843.

C. Magazines

HAMILTON, THOMAS, Editor. The Anglo-African. New York. Vol. I, Nos. 1-12, Jan.-Dec., 1859.
—— Same. Vol. II, Nos. 1, 2, 3, Jan.-Mar., 1860. YU
HOGARTH, GEORGE, Editor. The African Methodist Episcopal Church Magazine. Brooklyn. Issued quarterly. Vol. I, Nos. 1-5, Sept., 1841-Dec., 1842. YU

VI. Biography, Poetry, and Miscellaneous Writings,
1840-1865

A. Biography

Aaron. The Light and Truth of Slavery. Aaron's History.
48 pp. Worcester, Mass., n. d. [1845?].

Anonymous. Aunt Sally; or, The Cross the Way of Freedom. A Narrative of the Slave-life and Purchase of the
Mother of Rev. Isaac Williams, of Detroit, Michigan. 216
pp. Cincinnati, 1858.

———— Glorying in Tribulation; a Brief Memoir of Hannah
Carson, for Thirteen Years Deprived of the Use of All Her
Limbs. 56 pp. Philadelphia, 1864.

———— The Rev. J. W. Loguen, as a Slave and as a Freeman;
a Narrative of Real Life. 444 pp. Syracuse, 1859.

———— Narrative of Sojourner Truth, Northern Slave, Emancipated from Bodily Servitude by the State of New York,
in 1828. 144 pp. Boston, 1850.

———— Same, with an Introduction by Harriet Beecher Stowe.
iv, 144 pp. New York, 1855.

———— Twelve Years a Slave; Narrative of Solomon Northrup, a Citizen of New York, Kidnapped in Washington City
in 1841, and Rescued in 1853, from a Cotton Plantation near
the Red River in Louisiana. 336 pp. Auburn, 1853.

Asher, Jeremiah. An Autobiography, with Details of a Visit
to England, and Some Account of the Meeting Street Baptist
Church, Providence, R. I., and of the Shiloh Baptist Church,
Philadelphia, Pa. 227 pp. Philadelphia, 1862.

Bibb, Henry. Narrative of the Life and Adventures of Henry
Bibb, an American Slave, Written by Himself. With an Introduction by Lucius C. Matlock. 207 pp. New York, 1849.

Black, Leonard. The Life and Sufferings of Leonard Black,
a Fugitive from Slavery. Written by Himself. 48 pp. New
Bedford, 1847.

Brent, Linda. Incidents in the Life of a Slave Girl. Written
by Herself. Edited by L. Maria Child. 306 pp. Boston, 1861.

Brown, Henry Box. Narrative of Henry Box Brown, Who
Escaped from Slavery, Enclosed in a Box Three Feet Long
and Two Feet Wide; Written from a Statement of Facts
Made by Himself. 90 pp. Boston, 1849.

———— Narrative of the Life of Henry Box Brown, Written by Himself. First English Edition. viii, 61 pp. Manchester, 1851.

BROWN, JOHN. Slave Life in Georgia: a Narrative of the Life, Sufferings, and Escape of John Brown, a Fugitive Slave, Now in England. Edited by L. A. Chamerovzow, Secretary of the British and Foreign Anti-Slavery Society. 250 pp. London, 1855.

BROWN, JOSEPHINE. Biography of an American Bondman, by His Daughter. 104 pp. Boston, 1856.

CAMPBELL, ISRAEL. Bond and Free: or, The Yearnings for Freedom, from My Green Brier Home. Being the Story of My Life in Bondage and My Life in Freedom. 320 pp. Philadelphia, 1861.

CLARKE, LEWIS. Narrative of the Sufferings of Lewis Clarke, during a Captivity of More than Twenty-Five Years among the Algerines of Kentucky. Dictated by Himself. 108 pp. Boston, 1845.

CLARKE, LEWIS and MILTON. Narratives of the Sufferings of Lewis and Milton Clarke, Sons of a Soldier of the Revolution, during a Captivity of More than Twenty Years among the Slave-Holders of Kentucky, One of the So Called Christian States of North America; Dictated by Themselves. 144 pp. Boston, 1846.

CRAFT, WILLIAM. Running a Thousand Miles for Freedom; or, The Escape of William and Ellen Craft from Slavery. 111 pp. London, 1860.

CURRY, JAMES. Narrative of James Curry, a Fugitive Slave. Liberator, Jan. 10, 1840.

DAVIS, NOAH. A Narrative of the Life of Noah Davis. Written by Himself at the Age of Fifty-Four. Printed Solely for the Author's Benefit. 82 pp. Baltimore, n. d. [1859?].

*DREW, BENJAMIN. The Refugee: or, The Narratives of Fugitive Slaves in Canada. Related by Themselves. 387 pp. Boston, 1856.

GREEN, A. R. The Life of the Rev. Dandridge F. Davis, of the African M. E. Church, with an Account of His Conversion and Ministerial Labors, from August, 1834, till March, 1847. Also a Brief Sketch of the Life of the Rev. David Canyon, of the A. M. E. C. and His Ministerial Labors. To

Which Is Annexed the Funeral Discourse Delivered at the Ohio Conference, in Zanesville, on the Decease of the Rev. D. F. Davis, by the Author. Published by Order of the Ohio Conference. 130 pp. Pittsburgh, 1850.

GREEN, J. D. Narrative of the Life of J. D. Green, a Runaway Slave, from Kentucky, Containing an Account of His Three Escapes, in 1839, 1846, and 1848. 43 pp. Huddersfield, 1864.

GREEN, WILLIAM. Narrative of Events in the Life of William Green, Formerly a Slave. Written by Himself. 23 pp. Springfield, Mass., 1853.

*GRIFFITHS, MATTIE. Autobiography of a Female Slave. 401 pp. New York, 1857.

*HAMMOND, JABEZ D., Editor. Life and Opinions of Julius Melbourn; with Sketches of the Lives and Characters of Thomas Jefferson, John Quincy Adams, John Randolph, and Several Other Eminent American Statesmen. 239 pp. Syracuse, 1847.

——— Same. Second Edition, with Additional Notes. xii, 258 pp. Syracuse, 1851.

*HAWKINS, WILLIAM G. Lunsford Lane: or, Another Helper from North Carolina. 305 pp. Boston, 1863.

HAYDEN, WILLIAM. Narrative of William Hayden. 156 pp. Cincinnati, 1846.

HENSON, JOSIAH. The Life of Josiah Henson, Formerly a Slave, Now an Inhabitant of Canada, as Narrated by Himself. 76 pp. Boston, 1849.

——— Truth Stranger than Fiction: Father Henson's Story of His Own Life; with an Introduction by Mrs. H. B. Stowe. 212 pp. Boston and Cleveland, 1858.

——— "Uncle Tom's Story of His Life." An Autobiography of Josiah Henson (Mrs. Harriet Beecher Stowe's "Uncle Tom"), from 1789-1876; with a Preface by Mrs. H. B. Stowe, and an Introductory Note by George Sturge, and S. Morley; edited by John Lobb. 224 pp. London, 1876.

JONES, THOMAS H. The Experiences of Thomas H. Jones, Who Was a Slave for Forty-Three Years. Written by a Friend as Related to Him by Brother Jones. 48 pp. Boston, 1862.

"UNCLE TOM JONES." Experiences and Personal Narrative of Uncle Tom Jones; Who Was for Forty Years a Slave. Also the Surprising Adventures of Wild Tom, of the Island Retreat, a Fugitive Negro from South Carolina. 54 pp. Boston, 1858.

LANE, LUNSFORD. The Narrative of Lunsford Lane, Formerly of Raleigh, N. C.; Embracing an Account of His Early Life, the Redemption by Purchase of Himself and Family from Slavery, and His Banishment from the Place of His Birth for the Crime of Wearing a Colored Skin. 54 pp. Boston, 1842.

*LEE, HANNAH F. S. Memoir of Pierre Toussaint, Born a Slave in St. Domingo. 124 pp. Boston, 1854.

LEE, JARENA. Religious Experience and Journal of Mrs. Jarena Lee, Giving an Account of Her Call to Preach the Gospel. Revised and Corrected from the Original Manuscript, Written by Herself. 97 pp. Philadelphia, 1849.

LEWIS, JOHN W. The Life, Labors, and Travels of Elder Charles Bowles, of the Free Will Baptist Denomination . . . Together with an Essay on the Character and Condition of the African Race. . . . 285 pp. Watertown, 1852.

OFFLEY, G. W. A Narrative of the Life and Labors of the Rev. G. W. Offley, a Colored Man and Local Preacher. 52 pp. Hartford, 1860.

PETERSON, DANIEL H. The Looking-Glass: Being a True Report and Narrative of the Rev. Daniel H. Peterson, a Colored Clergyman; Embracing a Period of Time from the Year 1812 to 1854, and Including His Visit to Western Africa. 150 pp. New York, 1854.

*PICKARD, KATE E. R. The Kidnapped and the Ransomed, Being Personal Recollections of Peter Still and His Wife "Vina," after 40 Years of Slavery. 409 pp. Syracuse, 1856.

PRINCE, NANCY. A Narrative of the Life and Travels of Mrs. Nancy Prince. Written by Herself. 87 pp. Boston, 1850. LOC

RANDOLPH, PETER. Sketches of Slave Life; or, Illustrations of the Peculiar Institution. Second Edition, Enlarged. 82 pp. Boston, 1855.

STEWARD, AUSTIN. Twenty-Two Years a Slave, and Forty Years a Freeman; Embracing a Correspondence of Several Years, While President of Wilberforce Colony, London, Canada West. 360 pp. Rochester, 1857.

*THOMPSON, GEORGE. Narrative of the Life of Moses Gandy,

Late a Slave in the United States of America. First American Edition. 45 pp. Boston, 1844.

THOMPSON, JOHN. The Life of John Thompson, a Fugitive Slave; Containing His History of 25 Years in Bondage, and His Providential Escape. Written by Himself. 143 pp. Worcester, 1856.

WILKERSON, JAMES. Wilkerson's History of His Travels and Labors in the United States, as a Missionary . . . Since He Purchased His Freedom in New Orleans, La. 43 pp. Columbus, Ohio, 1861.

*WILLIAMSON, PETER. The Life and Curious Adventures of Peter Williamson; Who Was Carried Off from Aberdeen and Sold for a Slave . . . 106 pp. Aberdeen, 1841.

"ZAMBA." The Life and Adventures of Zamba, an African Negro King; and His Experiences of Slavery in South Carolina. Written by Himself. Corrected and Arranged 'by Peter Neilson. 258 pp. London, 1847.

B. Poetry

McSIMPSON, JOSHUA. Away to Canada. *Liberator,* Dec. 10, 1852.

PAYNE, DANIEL ALEXANDER. An Original Poem, Composed for the Soiree of the Vigilant Committee of Philadelphia. *Liberator,* May 28, 1841.

PECK, THOMAS. The Day of Jubilee. *Liberator,* Mar. 6, 1863.

REASON, CHARLES L. Freedom. In Alexander Crummell, *A Eulogy on the Life and Character of Thomas Clarkson,* 1847, pp. 36-44.

——— Hope and Confidence. *Autographs for Freedom,* II, 221-229 (1854).

ROGERS, E. P. The Repeal of the Missouri Compromise Considered. 24 pp. Newark, 1856.

VASHON, GEORGE B. A Life-Day. In Daniel Alexander Payne, *The Semi-Centenary and the Retrospection of the African Meth. Episcopal Church in the United States,* 1866, pp. 172-175.

——— Vincent Ogé. *Autographs for Freedom,* II, 44-60 (1854).

WATKINS, FRANCES ELLEN. Eliza Harris. *Frederick Douglass' Paper,* Dec. 25, 1853.

———— Poems on Miscellaneous Subjects. 40 pp. Boston, 1854. LOC

———— Same, with additional poems. 56 pp. Philadelphia, 1857.

WHITFIELD, JAMES M. America, and Other Poems. 85 pp. Buffalo, 1853.

———— How Long. *Autographs for Freedom,* I, 35-41 (1853).

———— Lines—Addressed to Mr. and Mrs. J. T. Holly, on the Death of Their Two Infant Daughters. *Frederick Douglass' Paper,* Feb. 29, 1856.

———— Self-Reliance, Delusive Hope, and Ode for the Fourth of July. *Liberator,* Nov. 18, 1853.

C. Miscellaneous

CAMPBELL, TUNIS G. Hotel Keepers', Head Waiters', and Housekeepers' Guide. 189 pp. Boston, 1848. Library of Mr. Arthur B. Spingarn, New York, N. Y.

PLATO, ANN. Essays; Including Biographies and Miscellaneous Pieces in Prose and Poetry. With an Introduction by the Rev. James W. C. Pennington. 122 pp. Hartford, 1841.

WATKINS, FRANCES ELLEN. The Two Offers. *Anglo-African,* I, 288-291, 311-313 (Sept., Oct., 1859).

WEBB, FRANK J. The Garies and Their Friends. 392 pp. London, 1857.

VII. BIOGRAPHY, HISTORY, SOCIOLOGICAL TREATISES, ORATORY, AND THEOLOGICAL WRITINGS, 1865-1900

A. Biography

ALBERT, OCTAVIA V. ROGERS. The House of Bondage, or, Charlotte Brooks and Other Slaves. . . . 161 pp. New York, 1890.

ANONYMOUS. Narrative of Sojourner Truth, a Bondswoman of Olden Time. . . . With a History of Her Labors and Correspondence Drawn from Her Book of Life. 320 pp. Boston, 1875.

———— Same, enlarged. 320, 32 pp. Battle Creek, Mich., 1884.

*Bradford, Sarah Elizabeth Hopkins. Harriet, the Moses of Her People. 149 pp. New York, 1886.

—— Same, enlarged. 171 pp. New York, 1901.

—— Scenes in the Life of Harriet Tubman. 132 pp. Auburn, 1869.

Bruce, H. C. The New Man. Twenty-Nine Years a Slave. Twenty-Nine Years a Free Man. 172 pp. York, Pa., 1895.

Chesnutt, Charles Waddell. Frederick Douglass. 141 pp. Boston, 1899.

Flipper, Henry Ossian. The Colored Cadet at West Point: Autobiography of Lieut. Henry Ossian Flipper, U. S. A., First Graduate of Color from the U. S. Military Academy. 322 pp. New York, 1878.

Foote, Julia A. J. A Brand Plucked from the Fire; an Autobiographical Sketch. 124 pp. Cleveland, 1886.

Grimké, Archibald Henry. The Life of Charles Sumner, the Scholar in Politics. 415 pp. New York, 1892.

—— William Lloyd Garrison, the Abolitionist. 405 pp. New York, 1891.

Jennings, Paul. A Colored Man's Reminiscences of James Madison. 21 pp. Brooklyn, 1865.

Keckley, Elizabeth. Behind the Scenes; or, Thirty Years a Slave, and Four Years in the White House. 371 pp. New York, 1868.

Langston, John Mercer. From the Virginia Plantation to the National Capitol; or, The First and Only Negro Representative in Congress from the Old Dominion—John Mercer Langston. 534 pp. Hartford, 1894.

Majors, Monroe Alphus. Noted Negro Women: Their Triumphs and Activities. 365 pp. Chicago, n. d. [1893?].

Mars, James. The Life of James Mars, a Slave, Born and Sold in Connecticut. 36 pp. Hartford, 1866.

Mason, Isaac. Life of Isaac Mason, as a Slave. 74 pp. Worcester, Mass., 1893.

Payne, Daniel Alexander. Recollections of Seventy Years. 335 pp. Nashville, Tenn., 1888.

*Randolph, Edwin Archer. The Life of John Jasper, Pastor of the Sixth Mt. Zion Baptist Church, Richmond, Va., from His Birth to the Present Time; with His Theory on the Rotation of the Sun. 167 pp. Richmond, 1884.

RANDOLPH, PETER. From Slave Cabin to the Pulpit; the Auto-biography of the Rev. Peter Randolph . . . 220 pp. Boston, 1893.

"ROLLIN, FRANK A." (Pseudonym of Frances E. Rollin Whip-per.) Life and Public Services of Martin R. Delany. 367 pp. Boston, 1883.

SIMMONS, WILLIAM J. Men of Mark: Eminent, Progressive and Rising. 1141 pp. Cleveland, 1887.

STILL, JAMES. Early Recollections and Life. 274 pp. Phila-delphia, 1877.

STRAKER, DAVID AUGUSTUS. Reflections on the Life and Times of Toussaint L'Ouverture, the Negro Haytien. 48 pp. Co-lumbia, S. C., 1886. LOC

STROYER, JACOB. My Life in the South. 100 pp. Salem, Mass., 1898.

———— Sketches of My Life in the South. 51 pp. Salem, Mass., 1879.

———— Same, enlarged. 83 pp. Salem, Mass., 1889. LOC

TROTTER, JAMES M. Music and Some Highly Musical People. 352, 152 pp. Boston, 1878.

WASHINGTON, BOOKER TALIAFERRO. Frederick Douglass. xv, 365 pp. Philadelphia and London, 1907.

———— My Larger Education, Being Chapters from My Ex-perience. viii, 313 pp. New York, 1911.

———— The Story of My Life and Work. 423 pp. Toronto, Napierville, Ill., and Atlanta, 1900.

———— Same, enlarged. 455 pp. Toronto and Chicago, 1901.

———— Up from Slavery. An Autobiography. viii, 330 pp. New York, 1901. (Published originally in *Outlook*, Nov. 3, 1900-Feb. 23, 1901.)

———— Working with the Hands; Being a Sequel to "Up from Slavery," Covering the Author's Experiences in Industrial Training at Tuskegee. 246 pp. New York, 1904.

WILLIAMS, JAMES. The Life and Adventures of James Wil-liams, a Fugitive Slave; with a Full Description of the Underground Railroad. 48 pp. Sacramento, 1873.

———— Same, enlarged. 130 pp. Philadelphia, 1893.

B. History

Du Bois, William E. Burghardt. The Suppression of the African Slave Trade to the United States of America, 1638-1870. xi, 335 pp. New York, 1896.

Fleetwood, Christian A. The Negro as a Soldier. . . . 19 pp. Washington, 1895.

Hayden, Lewis. Masonry among Colored Men in Massachusetts. 51 pp. Boston, 1871.

Johnson, Edward Augustus. History of Negro Soldiers in the Spanish-American War and Other Items of Interest. 147 pp. Raleigh, 1899.

—— A School History of the Negro Race in America, from 1619 to 1890; with a Short Introduction as to the Origin of the Race; also a Short Sketch of Liberia. 200 pp. Raleigh, 1891.

—— Same, revised. 188 pp. Raleigh, 1894.

Mossell, Charles W. Toussaint L'Ouverture, the Hero of Saint Domingo; Soldier, Statesman, Martyr; or, Hayti's Struggle, Triumph, Independence, and Achievements. 485 pp. Lockport, N. Y., 1896.

Penn, I. Garland. The Afro-American Press, and Its Editors. 565 pp. Springfield, Mass., 1891.

Perry, Rufus Lewis. The Cushite; or, The Children of Ham (the Negro Race), as Seen by the Ancient Historians and Poets; a Paper Read before the Brooklyn Literary Union, with an Introduction by T. McCants Stewart. 31 pp. Brooklyn, 1887.

—— The Cushite; or, The Descendants of Ham as Found in the Sacred Scriptures and in the Writings of Ancient Historians and Poets from Noah to the Christian Era. 175 pp. Springfield, Mass., 1893.

Steward, Theophilus Gould. How the Black St. Domingo Legion Saved the Patriot Army in the Siege of Savannah, 1779. Occasional Papers, No. 5, of the American Negro Academy. 15 pp. Washington, 1899.

Still, William. The Underground Rail Road. A Record of Facts, Authentic Narratives, Letters, etc., Narrating the Hardships, Hair-Breadth Escapes and Death Struggles of the Slaves in Their Efforts for Freedom, as Related by Themselves, and Others, or Witnessed by the Author; Together with Sketches of Some of the Largest Stockholders, and Most Liberal Aiders and Advisers of the Road. 780 pp. Philadelphia, 1872.

STRAKER, DAVID AUGUSTUS. A Trip to the Windward Islands; or, Then and Now. 110 pp. Detroit, 1896.

WALLACE, JOHN. Carpetbag Rule in Florida; the Inside Workings of the Reconstruction of Civil Government in Florida after the Close of the Civil War. 444 pp. Jacksonville, Fla., 1888.

WASHINGTON, BOOKER TALIAFERRO. The Story of the Negro; the Rise of the Race from Slavery. 2 vols. New York, 1909.

WILLIAMS, GEORGE WASHINGTON. History of the Negro Race in America, from 1619 to 1880. 2 vols. New York, 1883.

——— A History of the Negro Troops in the War of the Rebellion—1861-1865. Preceded by a Review of the Military Services of Negroes in Ancient and Modern Times. xvi, 353 pp. New York, 1888.

WILSON, JOSEPH THOMAS. Black Phalanx; a History of the Negro Soldiers of the United States in the Wars of 1776-1812, 1861-65. 528 pp. Hartford, 1888.

——— Emancipation. Its Course and Progress from 1102 to 1875. 24 pp. Hampton, Va., 1881. LOC

——— Emancipation: Its Course and Progress, from 1481 B. C. to A. D. 1875. 242 pp. Hampton, Va., 1882.

C. Sociological Treatises

BRUCE, JOHN E. Concentration of Energy; Bruce Grit Uses Plain Language in Emphasizing the Power of Organization. 12 pp. New York, n. d. [1899?].

CHESNUTT, CHARLES WADDELL. A Defamer of His Race. Critic, XXXVIII, 350-352 (Apr., 1901).

——— The Disfranchisement of the Negro. In The Negro Problem, 1903, pp. 77-125.

——— A Plea for the American Negro. Critic, XXXVI, 160-163 (Feb., 1900).

COOK, CHARLES C. A Comparative Study of the Negro Problem. Occasional Papers, No. 4, of the American Negro Academy. 11 pp. Washington, 1899.

CROGMAN, WILLIAM HENRY. Talks for the Times. 330 pp. Cincinnati, 1896.

CURD, WILLIAM H. An Apology for the American People; a Reason and an Apology for American Slavery; a Duty. 62 pp. Chicago, 1879.

DU BOIS, WILLIAM E. BURGHARDT. The Conservation of Races. Occasional Papers, No. 2, of the American Negro Academy. 15 pp. Washington, 1897.

—— A Negro Schoolmaster in the New South. *Atlantic Monthly*, LXXXIII, 99-104 (Jan., 1899).

—— The Philadelphia Negro, a Social Study. Publications of the University of Pennsylvania: Series in Political Economy and Public Law. xx, 520 pp. Philadelphia, 1899.

—— Strivings of the Negro People. *Atlantic Monthly*, LXXX, 194-198 (Aug., 1897).

DU BOIS, WILLIAM E. BURGHARDT, Editor. Mortality among Negroes in Cities. 51 pp. Atlanta, 1896.

—— Social and Physical Condition of Negroes in Cities. 72, 14 pp. Atlanta, 1897.

—— Some Efforts of American Negroes for Their Own Social Betterment. 66 pp. Atlanta, 1898.

DUNBAR, PAUL LAURENCE. Negro Life in Washington. *Harper's Weekly*, XLIV, 32 (Jan. 6, 1900).

—— Representative American Negroes. In *The Negro Problem*, 1903, pp. 187-211.

DURHAM, JOHN STEPHENS. To Teach the Negro History; a Suggestion. 48 pp. Philadelphia, 1897.

FORTUNE, T. THOMAS. Black and White: Land, Labor, and Politics in the South. vi, 310 pp. New York, 1884.

—— The Negro in Politics. 61 pp. New York, 1885.

—— The Negro's Place in American Life at the Present Day. In *The Negro Problem*, 1903, pp. 213-234.

—— The Race Problem—The Negro Will Solve It. *Belford's Magazine*, V, 489-495 (Sept., 1890).

GAINES, WESLEY JOHN. The Negro and the White Man. 218 pp. Philadelphia, 1897.

GREENER, RICHARD T. The Emigration of Colored Citizens from the Southern States. *Journal of Social Science*, XI, 22-35 (May, 1880).

GRIMKÉ, FRANCIS JAMES. The Lynching of Negroes in the South. 81 pp. Washington, n. d. [1899?].

——— The Negro; His Rights and Wrongs, the Forces for and against Him. 100 pp. Washington, 1898.

HAYDEN, LEWIS. A Letter from Lewis Hayden, of Boston, Massachusetts, to Hon. Judge Simms, of Savannah, Georgia. 25 pp. Boston, 1874.

LOVE, JOHN K. The Disfranchisement of the Negro. Occasional Papers, No. 6, of the American Negro Academy. 27 pp. Washington, 1899.

MILLER, KELLEY. A Review of Hoffman's Race Traits and Tendencies of the American Negro. Occasional Papers, No. 1, of the American Negro Academy. 36 pp. Washington, 1897.

PRICE, JOSEPH C. Education and the Race Problem. *National Education Association Proceedings, 1890*, pp. 267-285.

RILEY, JEROME R. The Philosophy of Negro Suffrage. 142 pp. Washington, 1897.

STEWART, T. McCANTS. Liberia, the Americo-African Republic; Being Some Impressions of the Climate, Resources, and People, Resulting from Personal Observations and Experiences in West Africa. 107 pp. New York, 1886.

STRAKER, DAVID AUGUSTUS. The New South Investigated. 230 pp. Detroit, 1888.

TANNER, BENJAMIN TUCKER. The Color of Solomon—What? . . . Introduction by William S. Scarborough. 93 pp. Philadelphia, 1895.

——— The Descent of the Negro. Reply to Rev. Drs. J. H. Vincent, J. M. Freeman, and J. L. Hurbut. 23 pp. N. p., n. d. [Philadelphia, 1898?].

——— The Negro's Origin: and Is the Negro Cursed? 39 pp. Philadelphia, 1869.

TURNER, HENRY McNEAL. Negro Emigration to Africa. *Independent*, LI, 2430-2432 (Sept. 7, 1899).

TURNER, HENRY McNEAL, Compiler. The Black Man's Doom. The Two Barbarous and Cruel Decisions of the United States Supreme Court, Declaring the Civil Rights Act Unconstitutional and Disrobing the Colored Race of All Civil Protection. . . . Also the Powerful Speeches of Hon. Frederick Douglass and Col. Robert G. Ingersoll, Jurist and Famous Orator.

Also a Review by Bishop Turner. Also the Monstrous Decision of the Same Conclave, Issued May 18, 1896. 90 pp. Philadelphia, 1896.

WASHINGTON, BOOKER TALIAFERRO. The Awakening of the Negro. *Atlantic Monthly*, LXXVIII, 322-328 (Sept., 1896).

———— The Case of the Negro. *Atlantic Monthly*, LXXXIV, 577-587 (Nov., 1899).

———— Education of the Negro. 44 pp. Albany, 1900.

———— The Future of the American Negro. x, 3, 244 pp. New York, 1899.

———— Industrial Education for the Negro. In *The Negro Problem*, 1903, pp. 7-31.

———— The Man Farthest Down; a Record of Observation and Study in Europe. In Collaboration with Robert E. Park. 390 pp. Garden City, 1913.

———— Negro Education Not a Failure. 13 pp. Tuskegee, n. d. [1904?]. NYPL

———— The Negro in Business. 379 pp. Boston and Chicago, 1907.

———— An Open Letter upon Lynching in the South. 8 pp. Tuskegee, 1901. NYPL

———— The Successful Training of the Negro. 14 pp. New York, 1903. (Reprinted from *World's Work*, VI, 3731-3751 [Aug., 1903].)

D. Oratory

ARNETT, BENJAMIN WILLIAM. Biennial Oration before the Second B. M. C. of the Grand United Order of Odd Fellows. 30 pp. Dayton, Ohio, 1884.

———— The Black Laws; Speech of B. W. Arnett in the Ohio House of Representatives, March 10, 1886. 40 pp. N. p., n. d.

BRUCE, BLANCHE KELSO. An Address, Delivered in the United States Senate, March 3, 1876. *Congressional Record . . .* Forty-Fourth Congress, 1876, IV, 1444-1445.

———— Speech on the Mississippi Election, Delivered in the United States Senate, March 31, 1876. *Congressional Record . . .* Forty-Fourth Congress, First Session, 1876, IV, 2101-2104.

BRUCE, JOHN E. The Blot on the Escutcheon; an Address

Delivered before the Afro-American League ... Washington, D. C., April 4th, 1890. 18 pp. Washington, 1890.

CAIN, RICHARD H. Speech on Civil Rights, Delivered before the United States House of Representatives, January 10, 1874. *Congressional Record,* Forty-Third Congress, First Session, 1874, II, 565-567.

CLARK, SAMUEL W. The Negro Mason in Equity: a Public Address, Authorized by the M. W. Grand Lodge of Free and Accepted Masons for the State of Ohio and Its Jurisdiction, for the Purpose of Placing before the World the Historical Facts upon Which the Negro Mason in America Bases His Claim to Legitimacy and Consequent Rights. 69 pp. N. p., 1886.

ELLIOT, ROBERT BROWN. Oration: Delivered ... April 16, 1872, at the Celebration of the Tenth Anniversary of Emancipation in the District of Columbia. 16 pp. Washington, 1872.

———— Speech Delivered in the United States House of Representatives, January 6, 1874. *Congressional Record ...* Forty-Third Congress, First Session, 1874, II, 407-410.

———— Sumner Memorial Meeting: Oration Delivered in Faneuil Hall, April 14, 1874, under the Auspices of the Colored Citizens of Boston, with the Address of Edward G. Walker, President of the Meeting, and a Sketch of the Proceedings. 32 pp. Boston, 1874.

GREENER, RICHARD T. Charles Sumner. 41 pp. Charleston, S. C., 1874. NYPL

LANGSTON, JOHN MERCER. Freedom and Citizenship. Selected Lectures and Addresses. 286 pp. Washington, 1883.

———— Speech before the Twenty-Second Anniversary of the American Anti-Slavery Society Celebrated May 9, 1855, at the Metropolitan Theater, New York City. In John Mercer Langston, *From the Virginia Plantation to the National Capitol,* 1894, pp. 151-155.

———— Speech Delivered in the United States House of Representatives, January 16, 1891. *Congressional Record ...* Fifty-First Congress, Second Session, 1891, XXII, 1479-1482.

LYNCH, JOHN R. Speech on the Civil Rights Bill, Delivered in the United States House of Representatives, February 3,

1875. *Congressional Record* . . . Forty-Third Congress, Second Session, 1875, III, 943-947.

MENARD, JOHN WILLIS. Speech Delivered in the United States House of Representatives, February 27, 1869. *Congressional Globe,* Fortieth Congress, Third Session, 1869, pp. 1684-1685.

MILLER, KELLY. Address to the Graduating Class of the College Department, Howard University, June 1, 1898. 12 pp. N. p., n. d.

PRICE, JOSEPH C. The Race Problem Stated. In Carter G. Woodson, *Negro Orators and Their Orations,* 1925, pp. 488-501.

RAINEY, JOSEPH H. Speech on Education, Delivered in the United States House of Representatives, February 3, 1872. *Appendix to the Congressional Globe,* Forty-Second Congress, Second Session, 1872, pp. 15-17.

——— Speech on the Enforcement of the Fourteenth Amendment, Delivered in the United States House of Representatives, April 1, 1871. *Congressional Globe,* Forty-Second Congress, First Session, 1871, pp. 393-395.

RANSIER, A. J. Speech Delivered at Charleston, S. C., March 9, 1871. In Carter G. Woodson, *Negro Orators and Their Orations,* 1925, pp. 411-417.

RAPIER, JAMES T. Speech on Civil Rights, Delivered in the United States House of Representatives, June 9, 1874. *Congressional Record* . . . Forty-Third Congress, Second Session, 1874, II, 4782-4786.

REVELS, HIRAM. Speech Delivered in the United States Senate, March 16, 1870. *Congressional Globe,* Forty-First Congress, Second Session, 1870, pp. 1986-1988.

STEWART, T. McCANTS. The Afro-American in Politics; an Address Delivered . . . October 27th, 1891. 14 pp. Brooklyn, 1891.

STRAKER, DAVID AUGUSTUS. Citizenship, Its Right and Duties—Woman Suffrage; a Lecture Delivered . . . at Hillsdale, Washington, D. C., April 13 and 14, 1874. 20 pp. Washington, 1874. NYPL

WASHINGTON, BOOKER TALIAFERRO. An Address on Abraham Lincoln, Delivered before the Republican Club of New York City on the Night of February Twelfth, 1909. 12 pp. N. p., n. d.

—— Address Prepared . . . for Delivery at a Dinner Given by the Members of the Union League Club on February 12, 1899, in Commemoration of the Birth of Abraham Lincoln. 5, 16 pp. N. p., n. d.

—— Black-belt Diamonds; Gems from the Speeches, Addresses, and Talks to Students of Booker T. Washington. Selected by Victoria E. Matthews; Introduction by T. T. Fortune. xii, 115 pp. New York, 1898.

—— Character Building; Being Addresses Delivered on Sunday Evenings to the Students of Tuskegee Institute. 297 pp. New York, 1902.

—— The Cotton States Exposition Address. Delivered September 17, 1895. In Booker T. Washington, *Up from Slavery*, 1901, pp. 218-225.

—— The Educational and Industrial Emancipation of the Negro. . . . An Address before the Brooklyn Institute of Arts and Sciences, Brooklyn, N. Y., Feb. 22, 1903. 16 pp. Tuskegee, 1903.

—— Harvard Alumni Dinner Address—June 24, 1896. In Booker T. Washington, *The Story of My Life and Work*, 1900, pp. 210-212.

—— Putting the Most into Life. 35 pp. New York, 1906.

—— The Robert Gould Shaw Monument Address, Delivered May 31, 1897. In Booker T. Washington, *The Story of My Life and Work*, 1900, pp. 236-242.

WASHINGTON, BOOKER TALIAFERRO, and WILLIAM E. BURGHARDT DU BOIS. The Negro in the South, His Economic Progress in Relation to His Moral and Religious Development, Being the Levi Bull Lectures for the year 1907. 222 pp. Philadelphia, 1907.

WILLIAMS, GEORGE WASHINGTON. The American Negro, from 1776 to 1876, Delivered July 4, 1876, at Avondale, Ohio. 38 pp. Cincinnati, 1876. NYPL

—— The Negro as a Political Problem. Oration. 40 pp. Boston, 1884. NYPL

E. Theological Writings

ANDERSON, MATTHEW. Presbyterianism; Its Relation to the Negro. Illustrated by the Berean Presbyterian Church, Philadelphia, with a Sketch of the Church and Autobiography of the Author. 263 pp. Philadelphia, n. d. [1897?].

ARNETT, BENJAMIN WILLIAM, Editor. Proceedings of the Semi-Centenary Celebration of the African Methodist Episcopal Church of Cincinnati. Held in Allen Temple, February 8th, 9th, and 10th, 1874. 136 pp. N. p., n. d.

BERRY, HARRISON. The Foundation of Atheism Examined, with an Answer to the Question, "Why Don't God Kill the Devil?" 18 pp. Atlanta, 1882.

BRAWLEY, E. M., Editor. The Negro Baptist Pulpit; a Collection of Sermons and Papers, on Baptist Doctrine and Missionary and Educational Work, by Colored Baptist Ministers. 300 pp. Philadelphia, n. d. [1890?].

COPPIN, LEVI JENKINS. The Relation of Baptized Children to the Church. 106 pp. Philadelphia, 1890.

DE COSTA, B. F. Three Score and Ten. The Story of St. Philip's Church, New York City. 57 pp. New York, 1889.

EMBRY, JAMES C. Our Father's House, and Family, Past, Present, and Future. 95 pp. Philadelphia, 1893.

GAINES, WESLEY J. African Methodism in the South; or, Twenty-Five Years of Freedom. xi, 305 pp. Atlanta, 1890.

GORDON, CHARLES B. W. Select Sermons. 420 pp. Petersburg, Va., 1889.

GRIMKÉ, FRANCIS JAMES. The Afro-American Pulpit in Relation to Race Elevation. 15 pp. Washington, 1893.

HAGOOD, L. M. The Colored Man in the Methodist Episcopal Church. 327 pp. Cincinnati, 1890.

HANDY, JAMES A. Scraps of African Methodist Episcopal History. xiv, 420 pp. Philadelphia, n. d.

HOLSEY, LUCIUS HENRY. Autobiography, Sermons, Addresses, and Essays. 288 pp. Atlanta, 1898.

HOOD, JAMES WALKER. The Negro in the Christian Pulpit; or, The Two Characters and Two Destinies, as Delivered in Twenty-One Practical Sermons. 363 pp. Raleigh, 1884.

—— One Hundred Years of the African Methodist Episcopal Zion Church; or, The Centennial of African Methodism. xiii, 625 pp. New York, 1895.

—— The Plan of the Apocalypse. 192 pp. York, Pa., 1900.

JASPER, JOHN. The Sun Do Move! The Celebrated Theory of the Sun's Rotation around the Earth, as Preached by Rev.

John Jasper, of Richmond, Va. With a Memoir of His Life. 15 pp. New York, 1882.

JONES, ROBERT. Fifty Years of the Lombard Street Central Presbyterian Church. 170 pp. Philadelphia, 1894.

JONES, SINGLETON T. Sermons and Addresses. . . . xxx, 302 pp. York, Pa., 1892.

LOVE, E. K. History of the First African Baptist Church, from Its Organization, January 20th, 1788, to July 1st, 1888. . . . 360 pp. Savannah, 1888.

MOORE, JOHN JAMISON, Compiler. History of the A. M. E. Zion Church, in America. Founded in 1796, in the City of New York. 392 pp. York, Pa., 1884.

MORGAN, JOSEPH H. History of the New Jersey Conference of the A. M. E. Church, from 1872-1887, and of the Several Churches as Far as Possible, from Date of Organization; with Biographical Sketches of Members of the Conference. 254 pp. Camden, 1887.

PALMER, JOHN M. Was Richard Allen Great? A Sermon Delivered . . . February 20, 1898. 9 pp. Philadelphia, 1898.

PAYNE, DANIEL ALEXANDER. History of the African Methodist Episcopal Church. 499 pp. Nashville, Tenn., 1891.

—— The Semi-Centenary and the Retrospection of the African Meth. Episcopal Church in the United States of America. 189 pp. Baltimore, 1866.

—— Sermons Delivered . . . before the General Conference of the A. M. E. Church, Indianapolis, Ind., May, 1888. 64 pp. Nashville, Tenn., 1888.

PEGUES, ALBERT WITHERSPOON. Our Baptist Ministers and Schools. 622, 18 pp. Springfield, Mass., 1892.

PHILLIPS, C. H. The History of the Colored Methodist Episcopal Church in America. Comprising Its Organization, Subsequent Development, and Present Status. 247 pp. Jackson, Tenn., 1898.

SIMMS, JAMES M. The First Colored Baptist Church in North America. Constituted at Savannah, Georgia, January 20, A. D. 1788. With Biographical Sketches of the Pastors. 264 pp. Philadelphia, 1888.

SMALL, JOHN B. The Human Heart Illustrated by Nine Figures of the Heart, Representing the Different Stages of Life, and Two Death-Bed Scenes: the Wicked and the

Righteous. 258 pp. York, Pa., 1898.

STEVENSON, J. W. How to Get and Keep Churches Out of Debt, and Also a Lecture on the Secret of Success in the Art of Making Money. xxi, 283 pp. Albany, 1886.

STEWARD, THEOPHILUS GOULD. The End of the World; or, Clearing the Way for the Fullness of the Gentiles. . . . With an Exposition of Psalm 68: 31. 182 pp. Philadelphia, 1888.

———— Genesis Re-read; or, The Latest Conclusions of Physical Science, Viewed in Their Relation to the Mosaic Record. . . . To Which Is Annexed an Important Chapter on the Direct Evidences of Christianity, by Bishop J. P. Campbell, D.D., LL.D. vi, 252 pp. Philadelphia, 1882.

TANNER, BENJAMIN TUCKER. An Apology for African Methodism. 468 pp. Baltimore, 1867.

———— Hints to Ministers. Especially Those of the African Methodist Episcopal Church. 96 pp. Wilberforce, Ohio, n. d. [1901?].

———— Joel, the Son of Pethnel. 141 pp. Philadelphia, n. d.

———— An Outline of Our History and Our Government for African Methodist Churchmen Ministerial and Lay. In Catechetical Form. . . . 206 pp. Philadelphia, 1884.

WAYMAN, ALEXANDER W. Cyclopaedia of African Methodism. 190 pp. Baltimore, 1882.

———— My Recollections of African M. E. Ministers, or, Forty Years' Experience in the African Methodist Episcopal Church. xxi, 250 pp. Philadelphia, 1881.

VIII. FICTION, POETRY, AND MISCELLANEOUS WRITINGS, 1865-1900

A. Fiction

BLACKSON, LORENZO D. The Rise and Progress of the Kingdoms of Light and Darkness; or, The Reigns of Kings Alpha and Abadon. 288 pp. Philadelphia, 1867.

CHESNUTT, CHARLES WADDELL. Baxter's Procrustes. *Atlantic Monthly*, XCII, 823-830 (June, 1904).

———— The Colonel's Dream. viii, 294 pp. New York, 1905.

———— The Conjure Woman. 229 pp. Boston and New York, 1899.

—— Dave's Neckliss. *Atlantic Monthly*, LXIV, 500-508 (Oct., 1889).

—— The House behind the Cedars. 294 pp. Boston, 1900.

—— The March of Progress. *Century*, LXI, 422-428 (Jan., 1901).

—— The Marrow of Tradition. vi, 329 pp. Boston and New York, 1901.

—— The Sway-backed House. *Outlook*, LXVI, 588-593 (Nov. 3, 1900).

—— The Wife of His Youth, and Other Stories of the Color Line. 323 pp. Boston and New York, 1899.

DUNBAR, ALICE (Alice Dunbar Nelson). The Goodness of St. Rocque, and Other Stories. 224 pp. New York, 1899.

DUNBAR, PAUL LAURENCE. The Fanatics. 312 pp. New York, 1901.

—— Folks from Dixie. . . . With Illustrations by E. W. Kemble. 263 pp. New York, 1898.

—— The Heart of Happy Hollow. 309 pp. New York, 1904.

—— In Old Plantation Days. 307 pp. New York, 1903.

—— The Love of Landry. 200 pp. New York, 1900.

—— The Sport of the Gods. 255 pp. New York, 1902. (Originally published in *Lippincott's Magazine*, LXVII, 515-594 [May, 1901].)

—— The Strength of Gideon, and Other Stories. 362 pp. New York, 1900.

—— The Uncalled. 255 pp. New York, 1898. (Originally published in *Lippincott's Magazine*, LXIV, 579-669 [May, 1898].)

HARPER, FRANCES E. W. Iola Leroy; or, Shadows Uplifted. 282 pp. Philadelphia, 1893.

HOPKINS, PAULINE E. Contending Forces, a Romance Illustrative of Negro Life North and South. 402 pp. Boston, 1900.

MOORE, ALICE RUTH (Alice Dunbar Nelson). Violets, and Other Tales. 176 pp. N. p., n. d. [New Orleans, 1895].

"SANDA" (Walter H. Stowers). Appointed. An American Novel. 371 pp. Detroit, 1894.

B. Poetry

BELL, JAMES MADISON. An Anniversary Poem Entitled The Progress of Liberty . . . Delivered at the Celebration of the 3rd Anniversary of President Lincoln's Emancipation Proclamation. 28 pp. San Francisco, 1866.

———— A Poem Entitled The Day and the War, Delivered January 1, 1864, at Platt's Hill. At the Celebration of the First Anniversary of President Lincoln's Emancipation Proclamation. 27 pp. San Francisco, 1864.

———— A Poem Entitled The Triumph of Liberty. Delivered April 7, 1870, on the Occasion of the Grand Celebration of the Final Ratification of the Fifteenth Amendment to the Constitution of the United States. 32 pp. Detroit, 1870.

———— The Poetical Works of James Madison Bell. 208 pp. Lansing, Mich., 1901.

BIBB, ELOISE A. Poems. 107 pp. Boston, 1895.

"HATTIE BROWN." Catoninetales; a Domestic Epic. 100 pp. London, 1891.

CLARK, B. The Past, Present, and Future, in Prose and Poetry. 168 pp. Toronto, 1867. NYPL

COTTER, JOSEPH SEAMON. Links of Friendship. 64 pp. Louisville, 1898.

DUNBAR, PAUL LAURENCE. Candle-Lightin' Time. . . . Illustrated with Photographs by the Hampton Institute Camera Club and Decorations by Margaret Armstrong. 127 pp. New York, 1901.

———— Chris'mus Is a' Comin' and Other Poems. 48 pp. New York, 1907.

———— The Complete Poems of Paul Laurence Dunbar. With the Introduction to "Lyrics of Lowly Life" by W. D. Howells. xxxii, 289 pp. New York, 1913.

———— Howdy, Honey, Howdy. . . . Illustrated with Photographs by Leigh Richmond Miner. Decorations by Will Jenkins. 126 pp. Toronto, 1905.

———— Joggin' Erlong. . . . Illustrated with Photographs by Leigh Richmond Miner and Decorations by John Rae. 119 pp. New York, 1906.

———— Li'l' Gal. . . . Illustrated with Photographs by Leigh Richmond Miner, of the Hampton Institute Camera Club.

Decorations by Margaret Armstrong. 123 pp. New York, 1904.

—— Lyrics of the Hearthside. x, 227 pp. New York, 1899.

—— Lyrics of Love and Laughter. xi, 180 pp. New York, 1903.

—— Lyrics of Lowly Life. . . . With an Introduction by W. D. Howells. xx, 208 pp. New York, 1896.

—— Lyrics of Sunshine and Shadow. 109 pp. New York, 1905.

—— Majors and Minors. 148 pp. Toledo, Ohio, 1895.

—— Oak and Ivy. 62 pp. Dayton, Ohio, 1893.

—— Poems of Cabin and Field . . . Illustrated with Photographs by the Hampton Institute Camera Club and Decorations by Alice Morse. 125 pp. New York, 1899.

—— Speakin' o' Christmas,—and Other Christmas and Special Poems. . . . With Numerous Illustrations. 96 pp. New York, 1914.

—— When Malindy Sings. . . . Illustrated with Photographs by the Hampton Institute Camera Club. Decorations by Margaret Armstrong. 144 pp. New York, 1903.

FORDHAM, MARY WESTON. Magnolia Leaves: Poems . . . with Introductory [sic] by Booker T. Washington. 114 pp. Tuskegee, 1897.

FORTEN, CHARLOTTE L. The Angel's Visit. In William Wells Brown, The Rising Son, 1874, p. 475.

FORTEN, ROBERT B. Rome. In Daniel Alexander Payne, Recollections of Seventy Years, 1888, p. 52.

FORTUNE, T. THOMAS. Dreams of Life; Miscellaneous Poems. 192 pp. New York, 1905.

HARPER, FRANCES E. W. Moses: a Story of the Nile. Second Edition. 48 pp. Philadelphia, 1869.

—— Same, enlarged. 58 pp. Philadelphia, 1889.

—— Poems. 48 pp. Philadelphia, 1871.

—— Poems. 87 pp. Philadelphia, 1900.

—— Sketches of Southern Life. 24 pp. Philadelphia, 1872.

—— Same, enlarged. 48 pp. Philadelphia, 1896.

MENARD, J. WILLIS. Lays in Summer Lands. vii, 84 pp. Washington, 1879.

PAYNE, DANIEL ALEXANDER. The Mournful Lute, or, The

Preceptor's Farewell. In Daniel Alexander Payne, *Recollections of Seventy Years,* 1888, pp. 29-34.

RHODES, JACOB. The Nation's Loss. A Poem on the Life and Death of the Hon. Abraham Lincoln. 18 pp. Newark, 1866. LOC

TANNER, BENJAMIN TUCKER. In Memoriam, Dedicated to the Late Prof. O. V. Catto. 4 pp. N. p., n. d.

WALDEN, ISLAY. Walden's Miscellaneous Poems. Second Edition. 96 pp. Washington, 1873. NYHS

—— Walden's Sacred Poems. With a Sketch of His Life. 23 pp. New Brunswick, 1877. NYHS

WHITMAN, ALBERY A. An Idyl of the South. An Epic in Two Parts. 126 pp. New York, 1901.

—— Not a Man, and Yet a Man. 254 pp. Springfield, Ohio, 1877.

—— The Rape of Florida. 95 pp. St. Louis, 1884.

—— Twasinta's Seminoles; or, The Rape of Florida. 97 pp. St. Louis, 1885.

—— Same. (Containing also *Not a Man, and Yet a Man* and *Drifted Leaves,* a group of lyrics.) 96 pp. St. Louis, 1890.

C. Miscellaneous

ARNEAUX, J. A., Editor. Shakespeare's Historical Tragedy of Richard III. Adapted for Amateurs, and the Drawing Room. 59 pp. New York, n. d. [1886?].

COFFIN, ALFRED O. A Land without Chimneys; or, The Byways of Mexico. 352 pp. Cincinnati, 1898.

—— Origin of the Mound Builders; a Thesis. 35 pp. Cincinnati, 1889.

COFFIN, ALFRED O., and N. COLEMAN. A List of the Native Plants That Are Found in the Vicinity of Marshall, Texas. 50 pp. Marshall, Texas, 1895.

DUNBAR, PAUL LAURENCE. Uncle Eph's Christmas; a One Act Musical Sketch; Music by W. M. Cook. 11 pp. N. p., 1900. LOC

LATIMER, L. H. Incandescent Electric Lighting; a Practical Description of the Edison System. 140 pp. New York, 1890.

SAMPSON, J. P. The Disappointed Bride: or, Love at First
Sight. A Drama in Three Acts. 20 pp. Hampton, Va.,
1883.

SCARBOROUGH, WILLIAM SAUNDERS. The Birds of Aristophanes, a Theory of Interpretation. A Paper Read before
the American Philological Association . . . July 13, 1886.
36 pp. Boston, 1886. ColU

―――― The Cincinnati Law Library Association; an Address
Delivered . . . June 12, 1875. 66 pp. Cincinnati, 1875. LOC

―――― First Lessons in Greek; Adapted to the Greek Grammars of Goodwin and Hadley, and Designed as an Introduction to Xenophon's Anabasis and Similar Greek. ix, 147
pp. New York and Chicago, 1881. LOC

―――― Negro Folklore and Dialect.. *Arena*, XVII, 186-192
(Jan., 1897).

STRAKER, DAVID AUGUSTUS. Circuit Court and Commissioner's
Guide. Law and Practice, State of Michigan. 168 pp. Detroit, 1897. LOC

―――― Compendium of Practice. xi, 255 pp. Detroit, 1899.
LOC

―――― Legal Treatise on Larceny of Dogs, Delivered . . . before the Detroit College of Law, February 22, 1892. 29 pp.
Detroit, 1893. LOC

INDEX